Some Experiences of a Barrister's Life

Also from Westphalia Press
westphaliapress.org

The Idea of the Digital University
Criminology Confronts Cultural Change
Eight Decades in Syria
Avant-Garde Politician
Socrates: An Oration
Strategies for Online Education
Conflicts in Health Policy
Material History and Ritual Objects
Jiu-Jitsu Combat Tricks
Opportunity and Horatio Alger
Careers in the Face of Challenge
Bookplates of the Kings
Collecting American Presidential Autographs
Misunderstood Children
Original Cables from the Pearl Harbor Attack
Social Satire and the Modern Novel
The Amenities of Book Collecting
Trademark Power
A Definitive Commentary on Bookplates
James Martineau and Rebuilding Theology
Royalty in All Ages

The Middle East: New Order or Disorder?
The Man Who Killed President Garfield
Chinese Nights Entertainments: Stories from Old China
Understanding Art
Homeopathy
The Signpost of Learning
Collecting Old Books
The Boy Chums Cruising in Florida Waters
The Thomas Starr King Dispute
Salt Water Game Fishing
Lariats and Lassos
Mr. Garfield of Ohio
The Wisdom of Thomas Starr King
The French Foreign Legion
War in Syria
Naturism Comes to the United States
Water Resources: Iniatives and Agendas
Designing, Adapting, Strategizing in Online Education
Feeding the Global South
The Design of Life: Development from a Human Perspective

Some Experiences of a Barrister's Life

Curious and Famous Trials

---

by Serjeant Ballantine

WESTPHALIA PRESS
An Imprint of Policy Studies Organization

Some Experiences of a Barrister's Life:
Curious and Famous Trials

Westphalia Press
An imprint of Policy Studies Organization

1527 New Hampshire Ave., NW
Washington, D.C. 20036
info@ipsonet.org

ISBN-13: 978-1-63391-603-6
ISBN-10: 1-63391-603-0

Cover design by Jeffrey Barnes:
jbarnesbook.design

Daniel Gutierrez-Sandoval, Executive Director
PSO and Westphalia Press

Updated material and comments on this edition can
be found at the Westphalia Press website:
www.westphaliapress.org

A BARRISTER'S LIFE

Mr. Tom Dinwiddy.

LONDON: PRINTED BY
SPOTTISWOODE AND CO., NEW-STREET SQUARE
AND PARLIAMENT STREET

SOME EXPERIENCES

OF

A BARRISTER'S LIFE

BY

MR SERJEANT BALLANTINE

A NEW AND REVISED EDITION
(BEING THE SIXTH)

LONDON
RICHARD BENTLEY & SON, NEW BURLINGTON STREET
Publishers in Ordinary to Her Majesty the Queen
1882

PREFACE

TO

THE NEW EDITION.

THE ENCOURAGEMENT afforded to me by the reception of the early editions of my *Experiences* induces me to offer them in a more convenient and cheaper form.

I have added some few further observations in the shape of postscripts to some of the chapters, and have also been enabled, through the kindness of several correspondents, to correct errors into which I had been led through imperfect memory; and to these kind friends I take this opportunity of tendering my thanks. I may say without ostentatious humility how conscious I am of the many defects that existed in the arrangement of the work, and how grateful for the considerate manner in which they have been treated.

Should this volume obtain circulation in a more extended sphere, I can wish it no better reception than that accorded to the editions which have preceded it, and which has been to me the source of heartfelt satisfaction.

WM. B.

October 24, 1882.

PREFATORY NOTE.

I HAVE FELT AT A LOSS to know in what manner I ought to introduce the following pages to the reader, and should have been inclined to launch them without a word of preface, but that it might be thought that I formed an exaggerated estimate of their intrinsic worth, which certainly is not the case.

What I have striven to do, and trust I have succeeded in doing, has been to adhere strictly to facts in the incidents related; and the conclusions expressed are the honest results of such experience as a long professional life, not unmixed with other associations, has enabled me to form.

If my lighter sketches should amuse a leisure hour, my object will have been attained; and if any suggestions upon graver topics should furnish hints leading to any more useful end, I shall be amply rewarded.

It may be permitted to me to add that, whilst writing in no presumptuous spirit, I have not hesitated, upon some subjects, to express my opinions with perfect frankness and candour.

WM. BALLANTINE.

THE TEMPLE:
March 1882.

NOTE TO THE THIRD EDITION.

I MAY BE PERMITTED to say a few words by way of apology for some errors that have been very kindly pointed out to me. I fear that they have generally arisen from my trusting too implicitly to my memory. The edition now appearing has progressed too far to enable me to correct the whole of them, but there is one that I wish at once to set right, namely, my statement that Baron Bolland was the only judge appointed by Lord Lyndhurst (vol. i. p. 148).

At a future time I will explain the origin of the blunder.

WM. BALLANTINE.

UNION CLUB:
April 13, 1882.

CONTENTS.

CHAPTER I.

AUTOBIOGRAPHY.

CHAPTER II.

LONDON DURING MY PUPILAGE.

CHAPTER III.

COMMENCEMENT OF PROFESSIONAL LIFE.

CHAPTER IV.

MY EARLY PERFORMANCES.

CHAPTER V.

CHOICE OF CIRCUIT.

CHAPTER VI.

THE THAMES POLICE COURT.

CHAPTER VII.

THE TRIAL OF COURVOISIER.

CHAPTER VIII.

THE CENTRAL CRIMINAL COURT.

CHAPTER IX.

FRIENDS.

CHAPTER X.

SUIT IN THE HOUSE OF LORDS.

CHAPTER XVI.

CAMPBELL'S IRRITABILITY.

CHAPTER XVII.

I BECOME A SERJEANT.

CHAPTER XVIII.

THE GARRICK CLUB.

CHAPTER XIX.

INEQUALITY OF SENTENCES.

CHAPTER XX.

MURDER OF MR. DRUMMOND.

CHAPTER XXI.

TRIAL OF BARBER AND FLETCHER.

CHAPTER XXII.

CAMPDEN HOUSE FIRE.

CHAPTER XXIII.

EVANS'S.

CHAPTER XXIV.

ILLUSTRIOUS VISITORS.

CHAPTER XXV.

LORD LYTTON.

CHAPTER XXVI.

CURIOUS TRIAL FOR MURDER.

CHAPTER XXVII.

PELLIZZIONI TRIALS.

CHAPTER XXVIII.

MAGISTRATES AND POLICE.

CHAPTER XXIX.

ELECTION COMMITTEES.

CHAPTER XXX.

ELECTION COMMITTEES CONTINUED.

CHAPTER XXXI.

THE UNION CLUB.

CHAPTER XXXII.

MADAME RACHEL.

CHAPTER XXXIII.

CURIOUS TRIALS.

CHAPTER XXXIV.

SIR EDWIN LANDSEER.

CHAPTER XXXV.

CHIEF JUSTICES.

CHAPTER XXXVI.

DERBY WILL CASE.

CHAPTER XXXVII.

ENTRIES IN AN OLD DIARY.

CHAPTER XXXVIII.

PARLIAMENTARY PROCEEDINGS.

CHAPTER XXXIX.

VIVISECTION.

CHAPTER XL.

THE TICHBORNE BARONETCY.

CHAPTER XLI.

COMMENCEMENT OF PROCEEDINGS.

CHAPTER XLII.

INDICTMENT OF CLAIMANT.

CHAPTER XLIII.

LORD WESTBURY.

CHAPTER XLIV.

AMALGAMATION OF COMMON LAW AND EQUITY.

CHAPTER XLV.

PROCEEDINGS AGAINST THE GAEKWAR OF BARODA.

CHAPTER XLVI.

ARRIVAL AT BARODA.

CHAPTER XLVII.

COMMENCEMENT OF TRIAL.

CHAPTER XLVIII.

CONCLUSION OF TRIAL.

CHAPTER XLIX.

RETURN TO ENGLAND.

CHAPTER L.

CHANGES IN THE LAW.

CHAPTER LI.

OBJECTIONABLE CUSTOMS.

CHAPTER LII.

THE LAST CHAPTER.

SOME EXPERIENCES

OF

A BARRISTER'S LIFE.

CHAPTER I.

AUTOBIOGRAPHY.

HOWLAND STREET, Tottenham Court Road, was, as I have heard, the place of my birth. My first memories, however, are of a farmhouse—I have none of how I got there. I remember a large yard, and plenty of straw to roll about in; the pigs and the poultry were my earliest friends, freedom and fresh air my happiness. It was at Warboys, a small village in Huntingdonshire. The property belonged to my mother, who was a native of Somersham of the same county.

These happy days were terminated by a long journey. Stuffed inside a coach, I was sick and miserable, and was scolded for being troublesome. I remember perfectly being deposited in a dull dreary home, which I now know was No. 1 Serjeants' Inn, Fleet Street, and have a distinct impression how sour the bread tasted. It is strange that so trivial a circumstance should remain upon the memory when many much more important ones are obliterated, and it is only on that account that I have thought it worth recording.

From this period my mind is a blank, until I was sent to a school at Fulham, kept by two maiden ladies of the name of Batsford. I have no recollection of what I learnt, or how I was taught; but the Sundays passed there have remained graven on my mind—Marched, two and two, to the parish church, clad in our best clothes, and encased in a sort of moral strait-waistcoat; cramped up in a narrow pew, prayer-book in hand, listening to what we could not understand, we strove, often ineffectually, to keep awake, knowing that if we yielded to drowsiness we forfeited our share of the pudding—sole pleasure of the day.

Oh! how I envied the swallows, as they flitted across the windows in joyous sport, revelling in the blessings given them by God, and forbidden to us upon the day sanctified by Him. I do not remember how long I remained under the charge of these ladies, of whom I still retain kindly recollections.

My father had originally been in the army, but at the period of my birth had been recently called to the bar. He carried on his profession, as well as resided, in Serjeants' Inn, Fleet Street. My mother, at the time of her marriage, was a young lady of wealth and position in Huntingdonshire. The house in which we dwelt was the reverse of lively, and I fancy that my father's fortunes were not at that time prosperous. My mother was a most excellent and pious woman, and carried out with conscientious rigour the views of Sunday which had prevailed at our school. I was taken regularly to the Temple Church, and never will the memory of the hours passed within those solemn walls be effaced from my mind. Under the influence of the Rev. Mr. Rowlett, a most worthy but not enlivening clergyman, I too frequently yielded to the sleepy god, and for doing so received present punishment and was promised a terrific future.

A worthy old nurse, of the Baptist persuasion, who would not willingly have hurt a fly, helped to fill my soul with terrors; and at the top of our dreary house, in a lonely bedroom, the memory of my offences and the anticipation of their penalty drove me nearly frantic.

Unheard and unpitied, I many a time cried myself to sleep. The relation also of any horrible crime used to produce a most painful effect upon me in my lonely moments, and I particularly remember hearing talked about the murder of a Mrs. Donathy, an old lady living in James Street, Bedford Row. It caused a great sensation at the time, and it is wonderful, after a long lapse of years, how vivid my recollection of it is. The thought of it was present to me at night, and every noise conjured up a murderer to my imagination. Such memories remain—perhaps, also, their consequences.

The Temple Gardens relieved the monotony of our domicile, but even there I felt that the lynx eyes of the gardener were watching my every movement.

I cannot say what period of my life was thus occupied, but I remember one magical and delightful event. I was taken to see a pantomime. How wonderful it was, and how beautiful! I have never forgotten it. I even now remember a scene in which, in a snowstorm, Baron Munchausen fastened his horse to the steeple of a church, mistaking it for a gate, and the next morning, the snow having melted, there was the steed dancing upon air. Great was my ecstasy when the Baron, taking aim with his gun, separated the reins from the steeple, and the horse came tumbling down. And there was another welcome treat in my existence, when I went on a brief visit to one of my father's sisters. She lived at Wimbledon, and was married to the Rev. Joshua Ruddock, who prepared a few lads for the University.

With what pleasure I recall my aunt's loving hospitality, the delight of roaming on the Common and over the Danish Camp, the little present of books long looked forward to, which terminated my happy sojourn.

Once my brother and myself were taken to the seaside—Broadstairs, afterwards a favourite resort of Charles Dickens. The mode by which this pleasant watering-place was then reached was by two steam-packets. I remember their names—the 'Engineer' and 'Majestic.' They had nearly superseded the old Margate hoys, which, however, like the stage-coaches with the railways in a future generation, were then maintaining a hopeless contest with their formidable rivals. I believe that these were the first steamers upon the Thames,[1] and were allowed to die a natural death at a mature age, after a prosperous career. Their successors, although not extinct, have to a great extent yielded to the convenience and speed of conveyance by rail, and now, of the many thousands who in the course of a year visit the Isle of Thanet, only a small proportion select this very agreeable mode of reaching it.

On the morning following our arrival at Broadstairs, which had not been until late on the preceding evening, for the first time the broad expanse of the ocean disclosed itself to my astonished senses. I can but inadequately describe the sensation it occasioned. It must have been calm, with a summer haze hanging lazily over its surface, whilst to my unaccustomed eyes distant vessels seemed suspended from the sky. Once only, since that time, have I experienced the same feeling of wonderment and awe, and that was when, many years after, the view of a long range of snowy mountains burst upon my vision. On such occasions as these something seems added to our nature, exalting and purifying it. The sands, too, were a

[1] They were certainly the first that ran to Margate.

source of intense enjoyment. But most of my readers have had this illustrated by means more vivid than words, in the happy faces of the urchins playing upon the beach. Many pleasant hours have I since passed in the same locality: but what can ever replace the joyousness that knows no remorse for the past or fear for the future!

A contrast came only too soon: the blackest and most odious period of my existence arrived—I was sent to St. Paul's School. The house was then standing where it does now in the churchyard; but, shortly after I entered, the school was removed to Aldersgate Street whilst the present building was being erected.

I was a day scholar.[1] There were four masters, all clergymen. Dr. Sleath was at the head. Of him I knew nothing except by sight, never having reached the classes over which he presided. He was a man of portly presence, a good scholar, I believe, and much respected. Bean, Edwards, and Durham were the three other instructors, and, however different these were in many respects, they possessed one common attribute. They were all tyrants—cruel, cold-blooded, unsympathetic tyrants. Armed with a cane, and surrounded by a halo of terror, they sat at their respective desks. Under Durham the smaller boys trembled; Edwards took the next in age. Each flogged continuously. The former, a somewhat obese personage, with a face as if cut out of a suet-pudding, was solemn in the performance of this, his favourite occupation. The Rev. Mr. Edwards, on the contrary, though a cadaverous-looking object, was quite funny over the tortures he inflicted. Trois Echelles and Petit André, the executioners of Louis XI., so admirably described by Walter Scott in his novel of 'Quentin Durward,' treated their victims after a similar fashion. One of the

[1] Some boys boarded with the masters.

favourite modes of inflicting pain adopted by these tyrants was, when the boys came in on a winter's morning, shivering and gloveless, to strike them violently with the cane over the tips of their fingers. I nearly learnt at that school the passion of hatred, and should probably have done so but that my mind was too fully occupied by terror. Bean was a short, podgy, pompous man, with insignificant features. His mode of correction was different in form, and I can see him now, with flushed, angry face, lashing some little culprit over back and shoulders until his own arm gave way under the exertion. Amongst the amusements of this gentleman, one was to throw a book —generally Entick's Dictionary, if I remember rightly— at the head of any boy who indulged in a yawn, and, if he succeeded in his aim and produced a reasonable contusion, he was in good humour for the rest of the day. I have met them all three since my school days, and found them shallow and ignorant, no doubt with plenty of Greek and Latin in their heads, but without knowledge of human nature or power of appreciating the different dispositions of their pupils. All that was necessary for them to know was that they were capable of suffering. I have heard that of late years the school has been admirably conducted, and has turned out brilliant scholars; but I am not aware that any of my contemporaries obtained in their subsequent careers great distinction. There were, of course, the ordinary catalogue of minor nuisances in the shape of very good boys and very great bullies.

I was always badly dressed, and seldom had any money in my pocket. This was no fault of my poor mother, and I fancy, as I have before hinted, that at that time the *res angusta* pervaded our household. It is a bad thing for a boy to be sent to a school in a worse plight than his fellow-pupils; it is apt to breed meanness in himself, and invariably subjects him to tyranny from others. Of the latter I underwent my full share. I suspect I was a bit of a coward; I know I hated fighting. There was a fat brute named Thomson who used to thrash me unmercifully, but one afternoon I hurt his head with a leaden inkstand, and, although I got well caned for this little accident, I found it had a good effect on my boy persecutors.

I may mention that during the time I was attending this school my father had removed from No. 1 to No. 6 in the same Inn, and that amongst its other inhabitants were Serjeant Wilde, afterwards Lord Truro, Frederick Pollock, afterwards Chief Baron, and Mr. Jervis, a Welsh judge, father of the future Chief Justice of the Common Pleas of that name.

On my way to school I had to pass an ancient inn, called the 'Bolt in Tun.' It was situated on the south side of Fleet Street. Its sign as well as name breathed memories of the past—The Arrow into the Target. There was generally a four-horse coach standing opposite its gateway. How I lingered, gazing with admiring eyes at coachman and horses! How I envied the passengers! They were about to quit smoky London and breathe the fresh air of the fields. They had no dread of the cane descending upon frozen fingers. I knew what would be my fate; but still I looked and longed, and turned to take one look more. I could not picture unhappiness in the hearts of the passengers. I ran on to my gloomy lot, hoping not to be late; but if I were, that I should get some warmth into my trembling hands.

After I had been at St. Paul's some four or five years, my father took a house at Hampstead, and, to my great joy, I was sent to a school at Blackheath, called Ashburnham House, kept by Mr. Wigan. This gentleman was a scholar, and both kind and considerate to his pupils.

He had a brother a physician in Finsbury Square,[1] and his sons Alfred and Horace, subsequently distinguished actors, were amongst my fellow-pupils. The school was not financially a success, and broke up. I went afterwards to another private school at Hampstead, kept by worthy people named Johnson, and in the air of this most pleasant of suburban places I soon regained my spirits and looked more contentedly upon life. Here I remained for some years, having little to record until I commenced the graver studies of the law.

And I now propose to sketch, very briefly, my career up to the time when I obtained permission from the Honourable Society of the Inner Temple to gain what livelihood I could in the position of a barrister.

At the period when I was looking forward to this event, there might be seen in different parts of London an individual of somewhat eccentric appearance. He was a thin active old gentleman with powdered hair, and I believe a pigtail—certainly with knee-breeches and silk stockings. This was Mr. Platt, clerk to the celebrated Lord Chief Justice, Lord Ellenborough, and father of Thomas Platt, barrister-at-law, Queen's Counsel, and ultimately a baron of the Exchequer. This latter gentleman was a friend of my father, and kindly received me into his chambers, were I remained for some three months. He is worthy of a place in any legal records. Well educated, but with no commanding talent, with no pretence to eloquence, and starting from a comparatively humble position, by industry and perseverance and most upright and honourable conduct, he achieved the high position I

[1] I have mentioned this connection of Mr. Wigan in consequence of an utterly false account that I saw in a recent publication of the position of Mr. Alfred Wigan's parents and relatives.

have mentioned, with the respect of the public and the profession.

And yet, strange to say, he violated the obvious intentions of nature, and like Liston, the comedian, who imagined himself to have been intended for tragedy, although essentially comic in the form and expression of his features, the subject of my sketch, with a face that seemed made to create laughter, would plant upon it the most lugubrious of looks. 'Pray,' said Lord Lyndhurst to him one day, 'spare us that wife and twelve children face.' Nevertheless his appeals to common juries were very effective. The following climax, which I remember, greatly increased the damages awarded to a young lady for whom he was counsel: 'And, gentlemen, this serpent in human shape stole the virgin heart of my unfortunate client whilst she was returning from confirmation!'

The Honourable Charles Ewan Law, son of Lord Ellenborough, commenced a career at the bar about the same period as Mr. Platt, and went the same circuit, the Home, with every accompaniment to success except his own demeanour. He undoubtedly possessed ability, but it was smothered by pomposity and vulgar pride.

He signally failed at the bar, but his rank and connection obtained for him the office of Recorder of London, and he was thoroughly ashamed of the patrons who had placed him there. Although I do not consider that there is any merit in being humane, I still think it fair to say that in his administration of justice he was considerate and merciful. He was in Parliament, but never distinguished himself. I remember, after Mr. Platt became a judge, his presiding at the Central Criminal Court, Mr. Law being then in the inferior position of Recorder.

After leaving Mr. Platt's chambers, I went to those of Mr. William Henry Watson, at that time a pleader below the bar, and who afterwards became a Baron of the Exchequer. His father was a general officer, and he had himself commenced his career in the army. He was, I believe, a good case lawyer, and had a large business. He received some ten or a dozen pupils, whom he permitted to learn what they could, and, judging by myself, this was very little. He was a gentleman, and a favourite with all of us. I have little to record of the two years I passed in these chambers amongst a mass of papers, copying precedents of pleading which were a disgrace to common sense, and in gossip with my brother students, most of them as idle as myself. They were older than I was, and amongst them was a gentleman with whom I have remained ever since upon terms of intimacy. This was Mr. Joseph Brown. He was a very hard worker, and used to suffer grievously from the want of that quality in the majority of his fellow-pupils. He became a distinguished leader upon the same circuit with myself, and will go down to posterity as the admired author of the longest set of pleadings ever known. At the bar, his arguments have been most exhaustive, and never weakened by any approach to levity. Socially, his knowledge and learning render him a most delightful and improving companion, and every one who knows him respects and likes him.

John Nodes Dickenson, another pupil, was also a hard worker, and, oddly enough, like myself, had been at the school kept by the Misses Batsford. He also joined the Home circuit, and he and I were accustomed to lodge together at Maidstone. He accepted early in his career a Colonial judgeship. His brother, the eminent Queen's Counsel, has recently retired from the equity bar.

Edward Rushton, familiarly called Ned, was a pupil of a different type. Much older than any of us, he had been an active politician, and amused us with tales of election contests. We believed him to be a great orator. Perhaps he was. Cobbett had given him the name of Roaring Rushton. He became afterwards stipendiary magistrate at Liverpool, his native place.

Hamill, another pupil, obtained the post of a police magistrate of the metropolis. I must not forget, too, 'Ben Hyam,' whose real name was Marriott. His father was a magistrate, before whom a charge was made by a Turk, an itinerant vendor of rhubarb, who had been robbed of all his earnings. The case was clear enough, and the thief ordered to be committed. The Moslem was told he must appear at the next sessions. He swore by the Prophet that he could not; upon which the magistrate, legally enough, ordered him to find bail for his appearance, which of course he was unable to do, and went to prison in default. The magistrate, *ex debito justitiæ*, admitted the prisoner to the same privilege, of which he speedily availed himself. The sessions arrived, and, as might be expected, the thief did not. Ben Hyam, after the loss of his earnings and his liberty, was released. What became of him I never heard, but his reflections upon English justice could hardly have been higher than those we entertain about an Eastern cadi. Hence arose the nickname bestowed on my friend Marriott, which he retained to the day of his death, which occurred early.

I have met with an account of the above incident as having occurred in Russia, but I can vouch for the accuracy of my statement, and that it occurred in London about the year 1830.

At last the labours that led to the bar and might lead to the woolsack were over. I had eaten the requisite number of dinners. A good appetite and good digestion rendered this not difficult, and there were pleasant young fellows, full of hope and high spirits, engaged in the same occupation with myself.

The batch to be 'turned off' were summoned to the bench table. We were each presented with a glass of wine, and a speech was made to us by the treasurer, giving us good advice and wishing us prosperity in our forthcoming career; and so we were launched upon the sea, looking then so calm, but, alas! too often engulfing pitilessly the brightest ventures. Upon these occasions unpleasant truths were sometimes uttered, and on one of them a gentleman named Carden, who had to return thanks for his fellow-students, concluded by expressing his regret that none of those who had wished them success were likely to live to see it.

I propose in my next chapter to give a glimpse of London as I remember it during my pupilage, some of the scenes I witnessed, and the impressions they conveyed.

POSTSCRIPT.

I have been asked by some of my younger readers, 'What is a Margate hoy?' and I fancy the term has slipped out of our vocabulary since the days of which I have spoken. It was, as far as I know, confined to sailing vessels conveying passengers to the port of Margate, and which were the principal means by which visitors reached that watering-place.

When I wrote my sketch of St. Paul's School, I was not aware of three of my bar contemporaries having been educated there, and, although after my time, before the departure of Bean and Edwards—Sir James Hannen, the present Baron Pollock, and Dr. Pritchard, all men who confer distinction upon a school. The latter gentleman, however, has told me that the tyranny he experienced brought on a brain fever. I have also received a letter from Mr. Whitehurst, a surviving brother of the late amusing and clever correspondent of the *Daily Telegraph* newspaper, who was himself educated at St. Paul's School, more than confirming my account of the gross cruelty practised by the three tyrants I have described. It ought to be recorded, whilst referring to the school, that one of the most distinguished scholars of the age was educated there—the present Master of Baliol, and I have been told was greatly indebted to Dr. Sleath, from whom, however, he certainly did not derive those views which have rendered the name of Jowett more famous than even his eminent attainments.

CHAPTER II.

LONDON DURING MY PUPILAGE.

In giving a description of the great metropolis previously to my call, I shall confine myself as nearly as possible to the results of my own observation, and the impressions springing from it. Its surface and extent were very different from those which now present themselves to the view: bricks and mortar, marching in all directions, have eaten up many a green field and pleasant lane; and palaces now cover what were unhealthy swamps or the noisome dwellings of the poorest classes.

It is not, however, the changes only that meet the eye which have to be recorded. Science, literature, thought, have made prodigious strides, and many speculations are now openly discussed upon subjects which it would then have been thought impiety even to allude to. Steam, a sleeping giant, has been forced to work, and panting and puffing has brought people together, adding to their pleasures and enlarging their minds; and, wonder of wonders, more wonderful than any tale of magic electricity has conquered space, and seems now to be pursuing a career to which there is no apparent limit. Some crimes have assumed larger proportions, and the present has been an age of daring and gigantic fraud.

And yet in those days there existed men worthy of any period in a great nation. The battle of Waterloo was fought in the year 1815, and the greatest general since the time of Marlborough was placed by the enthusiastic voice of the nation upon a pedestal from which in that capacity he has never been displaced, although as a statesman he was unpopular, and persecuted by a thoughtless mob. Walter Scott had only recently published one of the most charming of his works, 'Guy Mannering,' which will for all ages delight young and old. Byron and Shelley had startled sober people by their wondrous poetry and reckless opinions. Great lawyers had adorned the bench, and the bold advocacy of Erskine had done much to cement the liberties of the people, whilst crimes of stupendous atrocity were not without their representatives.

The interests of medical science had created a body of men that have passed into oblivion. Like the ghouls of eastern story, they haunted grave-yards, and lived upon corpses, violating the tomb, and gaining a living by supplying the dissecting-table with its ghastly subjects. They were called resurrectionists. It occurred to a native of Edinburgh, named Burke, that an easier and more profitable method might be devised to attain the same end, and he and an accomplice named Hare established a system of assassination; lads wandering about the street were little likely to be missed, there were few to inquire for them. They might be half-starving, but still their carcases would serve the purpose of the surgeon's knife; and they must not be spoilt by external damage, and so these fiends, stealthily crawling behind them, pressed a pitch plaster over their mouths and noses, and thus suffocated them. They were then conveyed to the dissecting-rooms and sold to the anatomists, fetching a good price, as, unlike many stolen from the grave, the bodies were comely and free from corruption. There appears to have been strange carelessness on the part of the recipients; they knew that the class they were dealing with was infamous, and the appearance of the subjects ought to have created suspicion;[1] but it is fair to remember that probably those best able to form an opinion were not present at the earlier stages of the transaction. 'To burke' has become a recognised word in the English language, applicable to stopping a discussion. No one doubts that the study of anatomy, pursued through the means of dissection of dead bodies, is most useful in the interest of mankind. No one will dispute the labour, thought, and skill that have been exercised in its practice, or the enormous benefits that have been attained by it; and although there may be a sensational feeling against it, no real evil is inflicted by its exercise; and the interests both of science and humanity fully justify its use.

It is now some fifteen years ago that a man of middle height and proportionately stout, clad in one of the ordinary white smocks worn by labourers, guided by a dog and holding in one of his hands a metal saucer, might be seen slowly perambulating the streets of London. His sightless eyes, turned upwards, appealed to the compassion of the passer by. This man was Hare, the accomplice of Burke, who had been admitted as a witness against him. Subsequently to the trial he obtained employment in another name upon some lime-works. His fellow-labourers found out who he was, and threw him into one of the pits, the contents of which caused him the loss of his sight. There was a woman who was accustomed to join him at the end of the day, and apparently accompany him to wherever he lived.

I have often seen these two meet, but never noticed a smile on the face of either of them.

[1] The principal surgeon engaged in this traffic was obliged to leave Edinburgh from the feelings excited amongst the populace.

The infamy of this crime was not confined to Scotland. I remember, when a youth, I was taken to the Old Bailey to see two men tried for the murder of an Italian boy by similar means, and with the same object. It was the first time that I made my appearance in that court, and, if I remember rightly, I had a seat with the Ordinary. The names of these men were Bishop and Williams; they were both convicted and executed.

In recording the above circumstances, my mind naturally reverts to a practice which existed then as it does now, and which I believe is viewed by a great portion of the community with feelings of repulsion and horror. I need hardly say that I allude to vivisection. It is said that it promotes knowledge which is serviceable to the human race, and those who practise it defend it upon that ground. If this assertion were conclusively proved, which certainly is not the case, I should still protest against its use, and denounce it as a disgrace to a Christian land The hypothesis upon which it is defended must be that the brain, muscles, and nerves of an animal are analogous to those of a human being, and therefore will, under certain conditions, exhibit similar results. If so, vivisectionists apply to creatures formed like themselves tortures which the ingenuity of science has rendered more terrible than any invented by the savage.

There can be no doubt that some of their victims do possess thought and memory, affection and gratitude, that might shame their persecutors, but whether these qualities are developed in the same way or are dependent upon the same causes must be matter of speculation. How can the vivisectionist know that when he touches some nerve which makes the unhappy creature writhe in unspeakable agony, the same effect would be produced upon the human frame? Some slight difference may create a complete error in the conclusion arrived at, and a human patient may be treated upon an erroneous assumption that his brain is worked upon by the same influences as that of a dog. If, on the other hand, the assumption is that animals are differently formed from ourselves, it is difficult to embrace the idea that their torture can produce beneficial consequences. I believe that speculation of a kind created by vivisection is more likely to lead to blundering than to benefit, and the report which I have read of the inquiry before the Royal Commission by no means removes the impression; but as I have already said, if it were proved to demonstration that some benefit might be obtained by it, the practice is not the less abominable and unholy. I believe that the true instincts of every pure heart will throb in sympathy with this feeling. As I write, my old collie, friend and companion for the last ten years, is looking at me with his earnest brown eyes, as if thanking me for this humble protest against the torture of dumb life.[1]

Having alluded to the Duke of Wellington, I may here mention that I once met him at dinner. He was then much aged, talked gravely and with great distinctness, ate but little, drank no wine, and left early. He was a member of the Union Club when I joined it, and I have heard a story that he became a member of Crockford's, the famous gambling resort, that he might blackball his sons if they became candidates. Of course I had heard a great deal about him, after the fashion and with the accuracy usually extended to children by their early informants. I remember the touching anecdote of how he and that old Prussian warrior, Blucher, met upon the

[1] This dog when a puppy was given to me by Colonel Farquharson of Invercauld, and I could record instances of his sagacity quite equal to many attributed to reason in a human being.

field of Waterloo and mingled their tears over the bodies of the slain. The well-known and much more probable story is told of the latter that, having been entertained at a city dinner, and thoroughly enjoyed its gorgeous hospitality, he delighted his hosts by his admiration of London, concluding, however, with the startling exclamation, 'What a splendid city it would be to sack!'

The Duke afterwards gave a dinner at Apsley House to the Tower Hamlets magistrates. I remember that at the time the Duchess was ill, and the fear of her being disturbed prevented the picture gallery from being lighted up. I constantly met the Duke afterwards, and was always very graciously recognised.[1]

Streets at this period after dark blinked with the aid of oil lamps. A machine called a hackney-coach, licensed to carry six people, redolent of damp straw, driven by a still damper coachman, was the principal mode of locomotion. The driver was called a jarvey, a compliment paid to the class in consequence of one of them named Jarvis having been hanged. Omnibuses were unknown.

Those stalwart figures in blue that are now to be seen lounging gracefully by area steps, were still imbedded in the brain of Sir Robert Peel. Officers called Bow Street runners were supposed to catch thieves, with whom in their convivial hours they associated.

Watchmen—Charlies they were named—called the hours of the night, probably lest by some accident they might disturb offenders. When middle-class people went to a play, or to some little distance out of town, they performed the operation in what was called a glass coach; why so called I must leave to antiquarian research. It did not smell so much of straw as the hackney-coach, and the driver at some period or other may have washed himself.

[1] *Vide* Appendix.

It was, however, an eminently respectable vehicle, and naturally, therefore, very slow and solemn in its movements, and its employment was a great event in the family. There sprang up, however, in my comparatively early days, a dissipated-looking vehicle called a cab. It was formed of an open box placed upon two high wheels. This was for the passenger; the driver sat upon a board by the side. They were considered fast—not so much in motion as in character. However, the necessity for locomotion does away with prejudice, and I have lived to see an archbishop in a hansom cab!

The Church was represented in the main streets of London by figures that exhibited a strange appearance to my juvenile mind. These were the bishops. They then wore white wigs, surmounted by a three-cornered hat called a shovel, a long silk apron, knee-breeches, and silk stockings, for which their legs seldom seemed well suited. I have often felt grateful that Queen's Counsel in their robes are exposed to the view of only a limited circle, and the very thought of walking through a crowded thoroughfare in my full-bottomed wig throws me into a cold perspiration. In the narrow places and byways men soberly dressed in plain, and sometimes threadbare, black, then as now, brought consolation to the hovels of the poor and starving. These, a noble, self-denying race, are the working clergy, and are confined to no denomination.

London did not boast of so many theatres as it does now, and the drama scarcely presented any similar features. Drury Lane and Covent Garden were then the principal, and, possessing certain privileges, were called patent theatres. The performers were described as Her Majesty's servants. The legitimate drama, the ordinary entertainment, was varied by farces—not pieces of buffoonery, but comedies in two acts; and the pantomime at Christmas, then really justifying its name, was one of the institutions of the country. To those accustomed to the magnificent scenery, gorgeous decorations, and the semi-operatic, semi-burlesque displays now called pantomimes, the simplicity of their predecessors would be astonishing. They were played in dumb show, and a plot pervaded the whole. It was simple enough. In the beginning a benevolent fairy announced her intention of protecting certain virtuous lovers, whilst a demon was bent upon their destruction. A tyrannical father and objectionable suitor were patronised by the latter. They constantly followed the virtuous pair, who as constantly eluded their grasp, whilst they themselves met with every kind of misfortune, until they became clown and pantaloon; whilst the lovers were sprightly harlequin and columbine, still persecuted by their old enemies, until the good fairy made them happy in domains of bliss. The tricks and tumbling which characterised the performance were witnessed with shouts of laughter by the urchins who then crowded every part of the house, very different indeed from the gravity that now attends the representations. The pantomime was usually preceded by such dramas as 'Jane Shore' or 'George Barnwell,' whether with the idea of contrast or with a view of inculcating moral lessons I cannot say; but inasmuch as the gods never allowed them to be heard, whatever the purpose was, it had no chance of succeeding.

The names of Kemble, Edmund Kean, Miss O'Neil, and many others adorn the theatrical annals of those days. I have seen the two latter, but must have been too young to appreciate them. I have a vivid recollection of Charles Kemble playing the 'Inconstant,' in the comedy of that name, and every word and gesture of the actor, in his scene with the bravos, remain fresh upon my memory. Miss Foote was the heroine. How beautiful she was!

I have been frequently in the company of Charles Kemble; and I remember on one occasion dining with him at the Garrick Club. He sat immediately under a life-like picture of a scene from a drama called the 'Merry Monarch,' in which he represented Charles II. Fawcett played Captain Copp, and one of the most charming of actresses, Maria Tree, played Mary. How well also I remember Miss Love, and the ballad of 'Buy a Broom.' However, fond as I am of the subject, I must not weary my readers. Those who also like it, and there are many less amusing and instructive, will find abundant food in two pleasant volumes lately published by the veteran author and stage manager, Mr. Stirling, and a clever and very entertaining pamphlet called 'Church and Stage,' written by Henry Spicer, an old and valued friend of mine. The English Opera House stood upon the site of the present Lyceum. The only memory I have of it is seeing Miss Kelly play Meg Merrilies in a version of 'Guy Mannering.' The old Adelphi, however, a small theatre standing on the same site as the present building, deserves special mention. The first piece I remember being played there was 'Tom and Jerry.' A little unknown man, who had been given some three lines to say, contrived in doing so to create roars of laughter. His part was written up, and from that time to his death he was recognised as one of the most comic actors that ever delighted an audience. This was Robert Keeley, and it is no unjust criticism to say that he was fully equalled by his talented wife, who still lives, and, although she has retired from the stage, is as bright and lively as ever.[1] The glories of the Adelphi would fill

[1] *July* 21, 1881.—I had the pleasure yesterday, at the house of my hospitable friends, Mr. and Mrs. Levy, to meet this lady, and my description of her is by no means overcharged. She told me that she was seventy-five years old. I had a long and most pleasant talk with her. Mrs. Wigan, the widow of my old schoolfellow, the distinguished

a volume. What old patron of the drama will ever forget Yates, Jack Reeve, little Wright, Miss Honey, or that most wonderful of stage villains, O. Smith? And even out of this phalanx of talent there stood one figure, Mrs. Yates, the most perfect personator of what may be called domestic drama that ever walked the stage. I had the pleasure of knowing her in private life, where, like many other ladies then and now following the same calling, she was as much respected and admired as she was in her professional career. At the Haymarket Buckstone was in his line without a rival. But I must hurry on. There are many about whom I should like to say a loving word, but space forbids. I must not, however, forget the transpontine theatres, the Surrey and Coburg, the latter renamed after our gracious Queen. Terrific combats signalised their boards; outraged innocence, diabolical oppression, virtue rewarded, wickedness punished by means utterly impossible off the stage, drew crowds of admirers, and filled the small picture-shops with characteristic likenesses. One Italian opera house existed, but I do not fancy that it possessed attractions beyond a limited circle. Fashion reigned within its walls, and I confess that even if I could have obtained admission I should greatly have preferred a Surrey melodrama.

Whilst steam and electricity have worked their magic changes, a boon has been conferred upon suffering humanity by the application of anæsthetics.

In my early days there were great surgeons. The names of Astley Cooper and Brodie, and a crowd of others, adorned and elevated a noble profession, but they had to pursue their art inflicting great pain in alleviating disease.

actor, herself a most accomplished actress, was also present. It was delightful to see these two old ladies seemingly so happy, and receiving much attention from everybody present.

At present, happily, sense and feeling sleep whilst the knife performs its marvellous task.

Let me now take a glimpse at the surface of what I will call old London and its ways. Although there were distinguished lawyers and an imposing array of courts, justice was slow and expensive. There were no county courts, but here and there in the metropolis were dotted small debts courts, not remarkable for dignity or use; they were called Courts of Request. Debtors were incarcerated, and suffered frequently worse punishments than criminals. The Queen's Bench prison, with its misery and its shame, is a thing of the past, and the sad voice of the poor prisoner is no longer heard from the walls of the Fleet.[1] Police-courts were called offices, and the magistrates might be costermongers; Sir Richard Birnie, the chief magistrate, was, I believe, a saddler. The streets at night exhibited scenes of disorder and unchecked profligacy. The south end of Regent Street, called the Quadrant, was a covered way, and nearly every other house was devoted to open and public gambling. The same may be said of Leicester Square. There was no limitation as to the hours of closing places of entertainment, and in many of these were exhibited the coarsest description of vice. The saloons of the patent theatres could not be entered by decent women.[2] Drunkenness exhibited itself in the foulest guise, and extended to classes now generally above its influence.

Clubs were comparatively few and not accessible to the masses, and taverns, amongst which I may mention the London Coffee House, on Ludgate Hill, and the Piazza,

[1] In those days, one of the prisoners incarcerated in the Fleet used to stand behind an opening and solicit alms from the passers-by; his words were, 'Pray remember the poor debtors.'

[2] The abolition of this nuisance is due to the exertions of the late Mr. Macready.

in Covent Garden, were still used by gentlemen of position and fashion. A restaurant had never been heard of, and would probably have been denounced as savouring of Bonaparte. *À la mode* beef-shops and eating-houses of different grades, but of little pretensions, furnished the entertainment necessary to those who could not enjoy the domestic dinner. One was in Rupert Street, called Hancock's, where excellent fare was provided at a very moderate rate, and served by the neatest of waitresses; and there were two French houses, called the Sablonnière and Newton's. The former, in Leicester Square, was supposed to represent the highest order of French cookery. Ladies were not admitted into any places of this class. The small houses in by-streets, in the City especially, with sanded floors, a fire, a gridiron, and a cook at the end of the room, the broiling hot steak or chop, the appetising kidney and sausage, are almost things of the past. Supper-houses, frequented only by men, were very important features of the night, and, if they reflected truly the tastes and manners of the generation, it would not be considered refined.

I may mention Evans's, the Coal Hole, the Cider Cellars, and Offley's.[1] The suppers served were excellent, and, in addition, there was singing, the *habitués* sitting at the same table with the singers.

There were some good songs excellently sung, but there were others of a degrading and filthy character. Most of my readers will remember a scene described by Thackeray in his novel of 'The Newcomes,' referring to this subject, which is far more graphic and powerful than any I can attempt. It seems strange that in places undoubtedly frequented by gentlemen, obscenities of this

[1] In mentioning these names, I have referred to those of which I had some personal experience. There were doubtless many others.

description should have been encouraged; but it must be remembered that in those days there were many coarse features throughout society.

Vice, clothed in its most repulsive garb, stalked publicly through the streets. Pugilism, treated as a noble English institution, created an atmosphere of coarseness and slang, and even in private society toasts were given and conversation was tolerated that would now shock the least refined.

There was one song sung, or rather recited, that made a considerable impression upon my mind, called 'Sam Hall.' The name of the singer was Ross. He had been an actor at several minor theatres. The profanity of its expressions prevents my quoting the words. It was supposed to describe an interview between a condemned criminal and the Ordinary, whose well-intentioned advice is met by the felon with an account of his career, starvation, the gutter, cruelty, small theft, the corruption of a gaol, the brand upon him, robbery from a shop and the brutal sentence;—the hopelessness of his entire life was most dramatically, and I think truly, portrayed. Before quitting the supper rooms I will venture to record a painful incident that occurred in connection with one of them. I had been to a ball at Kensington, and, together with some friends, went into the Cider Cellars to sup. Amongst them was a gentleman much valued by all of us, named Darrell Stephens. Whilst we were consuming kindneys and Welsh rarebits with all the vigour of youthful appetites, he was unmercifully chaffed for confining himself to a poached egg. Poor fellow! he dropped down dead when walking in Fetter Lane the following day.

I never witnessed any prize fights; but the eloquent pen of Mr. Dowling surrounded them with a halo of glory. Spring and Langham, to my mind, appeared modern Ivanhoes, and the scene of encounter another field of Ashby-de-la-Zouch.[1] I have, however, since witnessed some of these heroes enjoying their laurels, the deities of sporting pot-houses, where, with distorted noses, and an absence of the proper complement of teeth, eyes uncomfortably bunged up, and mouths reeking with gin, they were probably recording their former triumphs. I wonder whether it is true that the paladins of old, who are supposed to have leaped so gracefully on to their gallant steeds, and performed such miracles of valour in the prize fights of those days, were, in fact, lifted upon their chargers, and, when rolled off, frequently smothered in their iron mantles.

Periodical literature, which has now reached such gigantic dimensions, was then confined within comparatively small limits: the 'Edinburgh' and the 'Quarterly' were the only reviews; 'Blackwood,' modestly calling itself a magazine, was supported by articles both grave and amusing; 'Fraser' introduced Thackeray to the public, and the 'Yellowplush Papers' have never been surpassed, even by himself; Theodore Hook rollicked in the 'New Monthly'; whilst Captain Marryat, in the pages of the 'Metropolitan,' detailed adventures and humorous scenes of sea life.

The 'Times,' conducted with wondrous ability, had become a director of public opinion, and there was scarcely a respectable household that did not secure a pennyworth of it in the course of the day, the price of which was sevenpence, precluding to many its entire purchase. Penny papers were unknown and undreamt of. In the middle classes five o'clock was an ordinary dinner hour; and six o'clock was fashionable in the rare event of a party.

[1] See Appendix. I do not include the two I have mentioned in my subsequent description.

Menus had not been heard of, and a dinner *à la Russe* had not travelled from the north. Paterfamilias presided over the food, and a perspiring carver did not dig lumps of meat from the joint and hand them with half-cold gravy to the guests. It is a great mistake of dinner-givers in modern style to have joints at all; they are invariably carved in the most sickening fashion, and, from the appearance presented by the parts that reach the guests, might belong to any animal ever created.

I have in the foregoing pages given the reader some of the memories of the past, and my reflections thereon. There are others that I may hereafter record, which belong to a somewhat later period of my life, but I think it time to say something of those matters that more particularly belong to my professional career, and I therefore propose in my next chapter to introduce my readers to its commencement.

POSTSCRIPT.

I have received a letter from a lady, who describes herself as a native of Midlothian, protesting against Burke being described as a Scotchman, and giving satisfactory reasons for supposing that her country was not disgraced by his production.

The eminent surgeon, Mr. Partridge, then consulting surgeon of King's College Hospital, and since deceased, the same gentleman who was sent to Garibaldi when wounded, is entitled to the credit of discovering and exposing this infamous trade in London.

The recent trial of the Queen against Lamson, which took place lately at the Central Criminal Court before Mr. Justice Hawkins, was preceded by a series of experiments by scientific men upon different animals, with a view of testing the effect of a particular poison. I am not aware of any other instance when, after a crime has been committed, evidence has been manufactured for the purpose of a conviction.

I cannot commend the practice. If the criminal had been a wealthy man, he would probably have employed other professors, to perform upon other animals, and thus a kind of tournament of torture would have been established, and, judging by what I have often witnessed in courts, a conflict of opinion. Fortunately for justice, the prisoner had no funds, and the facts were to my mind conclusive against him. At the same time, far too much prominence was given to the testimony thus obtained, and the trial contrasted very unfavourably with those of Palmer and Smeathurst, in which, as I have already pointed out, the true value of scientific testimony was admirably explained by the learned judges who presided at those trials.

In referring to the police magistrates, I have mentioned that, at the period of my father's appointment, there was no restriction as to the business they had previously followed. The last unprofessional person who held the office was Mr. Codd, a gentleman of position and high character, extremely conscientious in the performance of his duties, but wanting in the training necessary for their performance. I had the pleasure of his acquaintance, and passed many pleasant hours at his house in Kensington.

In reference to my observations upon the subject of dinners, I must be permitted to add a remark of my friend Mr. Archdale, copied from a most kindly article written by him upon the subject of my book.[1] 'The perspiring butler only ceases from his toil to rush about, shoving

[1] The article appeared in the *Temple Bar* magazine of June 1882.

lumps of ice into champagne glasses—an abominable custom, as wine ought only to be cooled from the outside.' With this observation I cordially concur.

It was customary for the patent theatres to bring out their respective pantomimes upon the first night of the week after Christmas Day. This was known as Boxing Night, from the practice, more universal than now, of the presents made on that day; and the heights of the galleries gave the title of gods to their occupants, and the music, by no means of a celestial character, furnished by them effectually defeated any possibility of the audience being either improved or amused by the tragedies preceding the pantomine; but a first night was a scene to be witnessed and not forgotten: the masses of heads, commencing with those of the curly joyous urchins in the boxes, and reaching row after row until the chins and noses pressed upon the rails of the galleries, presented a living collection upon which promised enjoyment fixed an unmistakable stamp. A similar scene may still be witnessed upon the first night of the gorgeous entertainment given at Old Drury at Christmas by its enterprising manager, and many of the present generation may like the entertainment better.

I ought, in my brief sketch of favourite actors, to have mentioned T. P. Cooke, who was certainly not excelled by any of his contemporaries in melodrama. Jerrold's play of 'Black-Eyed Susan' gave him an opportunity of displaying also a wonderful power of pathos.

I knew him very well in private life in my early days, a quiet, refined gentleman.

A melodrama called the 'Miller and his Men' became one of the most popular entertainments at the London theatres: it filled the character shops with supposed likenesses. Grindolf the robber, disguised as a miller and represented by Mr. Farley, fascinated children's imaginations, and the 'Chough and the Crow,' a beautiful glee composed by Bailey, introduced into the piece and sung by the robbers, has lasted as a favourite down to the present time. The frequenters of Evans's in the days of Paddy Green have often listened to it with pleasure, sung very charmingly by the lads who formed the choir of that establishment.

CHAPTER III.

COMMENCEMENT OF MY PROFESSIONAL LIFE.

I COMMENCED legal operations upon a second floor at No. 5 Inner Temple Lane—the same lane in which Dr. Johnson flourished. They were grimy old buildings then: their names even have ceased to exist, and handsome edifices fill up the space thus left. Dirt seemed at that time an attribute of the law. Now appearances are changed, and the surface is, at all events, much improved. In those days the evenings were supposed to be occupied by study, and consultations were held: now, after dark, passengers may seek in vain for the glimmer of a rushlight.

I cannot say that I burnt much midnight oil. No attorney, late from the country, ever routed me out and thrust a heavy brief into my hands—a circumstance which we have heard has so often been the origin of success to eminent lawyers. My establishment was limited. I shared with some half-dozen other aspirants to the Bench what, in Temple parlance, is called a laundress, probably from the fact of her never washing anything. I fancy that her principal employment was walking from my chambers to the pawnbroker's, and thence to the gin-shop. At the end of a short period my property, never very extensive, was reduced to little more than a pair of sheets, a teapot, and a coalscuttle, over which last it pleased Providence that she should tumble downstairs, and the injuries then sustained relieved me from her future attendance. A mischievous little urchin cleaned my boots, and was called clerk.

My means were extremely limited, and it may interest my readers to know what my professional earnings were during the first three years of my career. I was called to the bar in June, having attained the mature age of twenty-one the preceding March. Between that period and the following Christmas I made four guineas and a half; the second year I made thirty guineas, and the third seventy-five. I am afraid I must admit that I did not measure my expenditure by my income. My father had undertaken to furnish my chambers, and one of the principal articles he sent me was a horsehair arm-chair with only three legs, upon which I got so accustomed to balance myself that I scarcely felt safe on one furnished with the proper complement. He also had promised certain assistance by way of income, upon which promise I lived; but it was something like the income allowed to the Hon. Algernon Percy Deuceace by his father the Right Hon. the Earl of Crabs, recorded in the veritable History of Mr. Yellowplush. I possessed one confiding tradesman. His name was Gill, he lived close by in Essex Court, and, fortunately for me, dealt in almost every article. My transactions with him remind me of a conversation recorded between a foreign prince and his steward. The former, complaining that his horses looked thin, was informed that the corn dealer would supply them with no more oats. 'Who will trust us?' asked the prince. After deep and long consideration the steward said that he thought they still had credit with the pastry-cook. 'Feed the horses upon tarts!' said the prince.

Gill was my resource for everything, from pats of butter to blacking. At last, after long suffering, he struck, shaking his head when I told him of the clients I expected.

On the afternoon after this event I was balancing myself upon my three-legged chair in melancholy mood, and wondering whence my dinner would come, when a knock sounded at my door, and a clerk from Messrs. Allen, Gilby and Allen,[1] blessed be their names! brought me, and paid for, three half-guinea motions. With this mine of wealth in my pocket I determined to enjoy myself luxuriously, and accordingly went to Hancock's, an establishment I have already described. The glorious repast still remains imbedded in my memory—twice of saddle of mutton; I am afraid to say how many helps of jam tart. After a handsome honorarium of threepence to Mary, who had never looked coldly upon me in my worst hours of impecuniosity, I had still twenty-five shillings left.

Wretch that I was, I forgot the patient Gill, and found my way into one of those sinks of iniquity, a gambling-house, in Leicester Square, and came out possessed of thirty-five pounds!

I was a millionaire. Gill once again smiled upon me, and the penny roll and pat of butter upon my breakfast table next morning testified to his restored confidence.

When I was called to the bar the police magistrates were qualified to sit upon the sessions bench, and the county justices might preside at the police offices, which they frequently did. My father on some occasions presided at the Middlesex Sessions. The smaller class of criminals were tried before this tribunal; there was also a large amount of civil business, consisting of poor-law appeals. These involved intricate points of law, and a great deal of money was spent in ridiculous contests between parishes in relation to the support of paupers. Mr. Bodkin, who afterwards became chairman, or, as it

[1] These gentlemen were well-known solicitors in Carlisle Street, Soho Square, and almost my earliest clients.

was then called, assistant-judge of these sessions, was an extremely able advocate in this kind of case, and from his early experience possessed much practical knowledge.

Mr. Clarkson, at first his usual antagonist, contrived to blunder through them, but he and others shortly yielded to Mr. Huddleston, afterwards and now a Baron of the late Exchequer, and one whose mind was of an order peculiarly qualified to master the technicalities of this description of business. This gentleman was one of my earliest friends at the bar. He possessed qualities which made his success only a matter of time. He was fond of society, but never neglected work, and his thorough knowledge of his causes made him a most powerful and efficient advocate.

His career has been in all respects a successful one, and there are few men who are able to reflect as he can that, both in public and in private life, he has attained every object of an honourable ambition. Whilst dwelling upon the Middlesex Sessions, I must say a few words of that curious-looking figure usually seated at the corner of the barrister's bench. One who saw him for the first time might be inclined to ask, What is it? Upon minute investigation might be discovered, encased in clothes far too large for him, the gaunt figure of a very unclean-looking man.

This was Mr. Michael Prendergast—'Mike,' he was always called. Slovenly as his dress was, his mind was more so: with a greater fund of general knowledge than most people, it seemed mixed so inextricably in his brain that it was next to useless. He rarely had any but the smallest cases from the dirtiest of clients, and whilst one of them was being tried would not unfrequently sit in a state of abstraction, out of which an unhappy clerk had to wake him. He possessed, however, much power at times, and great independence. I remember a little scene which will illustrate his habits not incorrectly. A case of his had been called on. He was late, and it was half over before he arrived in court—his clerk in an agony, the chairman grumbling. Of this, however, he took no notice whatever. 'Frederick' (to his clerk), 'where's my brief?' Loud whisper from Frederick, 'I gave it you at breakfast: feel in your pockets.' A search commenced, and having first pulled out of his trousers' pocket a half-round of butter toast, from the depths of it was extracted the single greasy sheet that constituted his instructions.

He was elected by the Court of Common Council to the small debts court in the City. How he managed the business there I have no means of knowing, but I am certain that he did so in the strictest spirit of justice.

The habits of the metropolis, which I have briefly sketched in the last chapter, furnished a class of business that occupied a considerable portion of time. Although, as I have already mentioned, gambling-houses of every degree were publicly open in many of the West End streets and squares, and although at this period they were not interfered with by the police or other authorities, they were illegal, and liable to indictment, and there was a nest of scoundrels who lived upon them. The great field for their operations was the Middlesex Sessions, and the Grand Jury their hunting-ground. Indictments were prepared, and true bills having been obtained, warrants were applied for, and granted as a matter of course. Armed with these, communications were opened with the keepers of the houses, some of whom, being wealthy, did not relish the prospect of twenty-four hours in prison before they would be admitted to bail, which was the first screw put on, and so these pillagers of the public had to submit to be pillaged themselves, and large sums of money were thus obtained. If these proceedings had been confined to the proprietors of such establishments, people would be inclined to say, Let the thieves pick each other's pockets; but the trade was too profitable to be limited, and many instances occurred in which perfectly innocent people were made the victims of extortion by these harpies. Mr. Serjeant Adams, when he became chairman, put his foot upon their operations, by preventing warrants from issuing except under certain restrictions.

One of the worthies, who was a large proprietor of gambling-houses, became the lessee of the Adelphi Theatre, and Charles Phillipps used to relate an anecdote of his once meeting him and being offered a box, which he declined, thinking that some time or other he might be asked in return to defend the generous donor for nothing, and if Mr. Phillipps ever committed an irregularity, it certainly was not of that description. He asked him, however, how he was getting on. 'Capitally,' said the gentleman; 'Providence seems to watch over all my undertakings.'

There was one great field-day held at the Middlesex Sessions, from which every member of the bar had the chance of picking up a guinea or two. This was the day appointed for hearing applications for music and dancing licences. Unless some complaint was made by the police, those that had previously existed were granted, as a matter of course; but about the new ones there was generally a contest, certain of the justices taking the opportunity of ventilating what they called their ideas. A certain section of these gentlemen, none of them of position or note, opposed the grant to any of the applicants. A homily upon morals, the profanity of music, the indecency of dancing, and the length of ladies' dresses, formed the staple of their orations. Broad views upon what may fairly be deemed an important social question could not be expected from the speakers, and certainly never made their appearance. As far as I have been able to judge, assuming the perfect honesty of their worships, they betrayed simply a narrow-minded, unreasoning bigotry. One thing may be said of them, that, although their speeches rendered the tribunal ridiculous, they produced no other effect, as the result had been usually secured by a previous canvass. It seems to be time when these matters should be made subject to police regulation: it is manifestly most unjust that the interests of individuals, and the comforts and amusements of the people, should be regulated by the crotchets of a clique or the favouritism of a majority.

There existed another source of profit to the bar in connection with the magistracy. This arose from applications to local benches for the grant of spirit licences. Those not in the secret will scarcely believe what a licence was worth; and if there was not a considerable amount of jobbery about their disposition, all I can say is that the justices must have been an uncommonly pure body of men. Brewers and builders were the real proprietors of many of the houses applied for—I need hardly say in the names of nominees. I should think that in some cases their value would exceed 3,000*l.* to 4,000*l.* The justices had been to view the premises, elaborate plans were prepared, learned arguments upon the state of the neighbourhood and the necessity for further accommodation were advanced. On the other hand, the publicans already licensed rushed in a body to oppose the grant: there was no traffic, there was no custom, they and their families were starving. It was amusing to look at the rosy countenances of the starving publicans.

The justices, seated round a table in solemn conclave, listened patiently to all that was said. Spectacles upon respectable noses assisted in the examination of the plans; the rhetoric of counsel was listened to with kindly attention. The chairman states that it is an important question, and has been so ably argued on both sides that they would like to consider it in private. The room is cleared, every one knows how it is to go, except, perhaps, a confiding client who may have hope from the eloquent address of his advocate. This, however, was a rare phenomenon. The justices return, and announce the decision. I wonder, as Cicero did of the augurs of his day, that they did not burst out laughing in each other's faces.

I need not say that there were many distinguished names amongst the Middlesex magistracy, but the possessors of them rarely, if ever, expressed their views at the great 'October meet,'[1] or were to be found at the different local licensing meetings.[2]

POSTSCRIPT.

At the period when Mr. Serjeant Adams was elected as chairman, there was no salary attached to the office, and he and another member of Serjeants' Inn, Mr. Serjeant Andrews, were candidates for it. The former

[1] The sessions for the grant and renewal of licences takes place in this month.

[2] In the chapter in which I have endeavoured to sketch the state of the streets of London in the days of my pupilage, I have given them a character for coarseness, and indecency, from which it may be inferred that there is now a great improvement. I regret to say that this is far from being the case. Scenes are now nightly enacted in some of the principal thoroughfares of this metropolis that in a future age will scarcely be credited. The coarseness, impurity, and vulgarity of London appear to be massed within these localities.

gentleman was elected, and made an excellent chairman, but soon discovered that the office was one to sustain the dignity of which a salary was required, and by indefatigable exertions succeeded in obtaining it; but as this was supplied by the Crown, the office subsequently lapsed into its patronage.

CHAPTER IV.

MY EARLY PERFORMANCES.

It was at the sessions, of which in my last chapter I have given a brief account, that I made my first forensic display. The occasion was not an important one, nor productive of much profit.

I was instructed by a gentleman named Conquest to apply for the renewal of his licence, for a theatre called the Garrick, situated in Leman Street, Whitechapel. This place of amusement was within my father's district, who was then a magistrate of the Thames police, and it was probably from this circumstance that so much confidence was reposed in me. I rose, but could see nothing; the court seemed to turn round, and the floor to be sinking. I cannot tell what I asked, but it was graciously granted by the bench.

For this performance I received half a guinea, the sweetest that ever found its way into my pocket. Mr. Conquest, in addition to being the proprietor of this theatre, was a favourite low comedian, and very popular with the denizens of the East. Another great favourite was Mr. Gomersal, who, however, became better known at Astley's Amphitheatre by his impersonation of Napoleon Bonaparte in the drama of the 'Battle of Waterloo.' An additional attraction at the Garrick Theatre was the wife of the proprietor, a very pleasing and pretty actress, and celebrated as a ballet mistress, in which capacity she prepared many successful artistes for the stage. Mr Conquest migrated to the City Road, and for many years managed the Eagle Saloon and Theatre with credit and success. A son of his subsequently conducted it. He also was, and is, an actor, and now, I believe, delights the audiences of the Surrey Theatre.

My diffidence had somewhat abated, when I was entrusted with a brief by a rather shady attorney of the Jewish persuasion; and being at that time without experience, I yielded implicitly to his instructions. A young gentleman of the same faith was called as a witness. My client suggested a question. Blindly I put it, and was met by a direct negative. 'What a lie!' ejaculated my client, and dictated another question: the same result followed, and a similar ejaculation. By his further instruction I put a third, the answer to which completely knocked us over. My client threw himself back: 'Well,' said he, 'he is a liar, he always was a liar, and always will be a liar.' 'Why,' remarked I, 'you seem to know all about him.' 'Of course I do,' was the reply, 'he is my own son!'

Nothing struck me in my early days as more odd than the number of different surnames in which the same family of Jews seem to delight. One son of Mr. Saul Yates, of St. Mary Axe, was Mr. Sidney, another Mr. Daniel, whilst a third rejoiced in the appellation of Jacobs. I forget by what names my client and his hopeful progeny were known.

A gentleman of the name of Const presided as chairman of the sessions when I joined them. He was a friend of my father, and I received from him all the encouragement he could give me. Messrs. Charles Phillipps and William Clarkson, to both of whom I shall have again to refer, did the principal criminal business, and looked with no friendly glances upon new-comers. Their greediness for fees was an opprobrium to the court. Wrangles constantly occurred, in which all sense of shame seemed to be abandoned. The latter of the gentlemen I have named was under great obligations to my father, but from neither of them did I ever receive an act of kindness, or, until I had forced my own way, barely of courtesy.

I may here mention a circumstance in which I was the innocent cause of a sad catastrophe that happened to two of my clients. These were west-country farmers, who had been convicted of cruelty to animals, and had appealed from the conviction to the sessions. The question raised was as to the mode of conveying calves to market. Upon the day when the case should have been heard, I obtained a postponement to suit my convenience, and it came on the following week, when my clients were completely exonerated and the conviction was quashed.

They were returning home the same afternoon by the Great Western Railway, when a boiler burst. A mass of iron was projected into the air and fell upon the carriage in which they were seated, alighting between the two and killing them both.

Although the state of the streets was greatly improved by the institution of the new police, the gambling establishments still flourished. Leicester Square, the Quadrant, Bennett Street, Bury Street, and Duke Street were full of them. No concealment was affected. They were open to all comers, who were at some of them ushered in by powdered footmen. I learnt a great deal of the proceedings of these establishments from cases in which I was engaged at different times for and against the proprietors, and I believe that in most of these hells the chances of gain were assisted by flagrant trickery. At some of the principal—those, for instance, in Bennett Street—the decorations of the rooms were very elegant. Perfect quiet and decorum were observed by the players, who were generally of the better class.

The principal game played was hazard, of which there were two kinds: French hazard, in which the players staked against the bank, and English, or chicken hazard, in which they played against each other, with a settled profit to the proprietors. I fancy this mode of gambling was not so much exposed to fraud.

I do not think that rouge et noir was played anywhere. Roulette, which afforded abundant means of chicanery, was to be found at all the lower description of houses, and a game which seems now to be extinct, called 'une, deux et cinque.' This was played in a sort of basin lined with velvet, and a ball about the size of a cricket ball, with colours, red, black, and blue, as far as I can remember, stamped upon it. I cannot recollect how the game was played, but I was told that it was a fruitful means of cheating. With one example of the mode of procedure at roulette, through the medium of an accomplice, I became acquainted professionally. Most of my readers have seen a roulette table, and are aware that there are upon it thirty-six numbers, separated from each other by small divisions, and that the players stake upon different numbers. I need not recapitulate the way in which unwary people were inveigled into these places. A class of gentry called 'bonnets' were actively engaged in this employment; but when it was thought that a good thing was on, the proprietor would say out loud, 'We may as well be quiet: put up the bars.' The intended victim supposed this to mean that other people should be shut out, but the accomplice took it as a direction to manipulate the table by raising, which was done by machinery, an almost imperceptible obstruction before any number which would have secured to the player a large stake. I was informed that most of the tables were so constructed as to render this a very easy process. The profits made must have been enormous.

The places, however, at which gambling was to be witnessed in all its magnitude, were the different race-courses. There might be seen a range of booths, extending from the grand stand to the end of the course, in all of which play in its various forms, and at prices adapted to all classes, openly flourished.

I have read that during the gold fever there was not sufficient accommodation for the influx of diggers within Melbourne, and that a quantity of tents was erected outside the city. This was known as the canvas town. The same term might have been applied to the booths I have described, whilst greed of gold was the distinctive emblem of both.

It was at one of these establishments that a personage was pointed out to me who afterwards became famous. He was a handsome-looking man, with strongly marked Jewish features, and altogether not unprepossessing. This was Mr. Goodman, or Goody Levi, as he was usually called, twelve years afterwards the hero of the Running Rein fraud. It may be remembered that he substituted a four-year old horse called Maccabæus for Running Rein, and won the Derby with it. The fraud was discovered, and, upon a trial in the Court of Exchequer before Baron Alderson, fully exposed; that learned judge, who was not wont to conceal his opinions, observing that if gentlemen would condescend to race with blackguards they must expect to be cheated.

I noticed several well-known characters who were patronising Mr. Goodman's, men who, when I was young, were well known upon town. They were all engaged in play: Count d'Orsay, the dandy of the age, Lord Cantelupe, the Earl of Chesterfield, and many others whom I have now forgotten, and upon whom I then looked with wonder and admiration.

The altar, however, at which the greatest sacrifices were made, and which reared its head above all rivals of a similar class, was that of which Mr. Crockford was the proprietor, and which went by his name. This was no mean refuge for every-day gamblers; it was constituted as a club, and confined to members. It presented an imposing front on the upper part of the west side of St. James's Street. It is now, with little external alteration, the Devonshire Club. Personally I knew nothing of it, but heard romances of play related as having occurred within its precincts, of enormous sums changing hands, and of much sorrow and desolation invading many a family. Tales almost fabulous were related of its splendour, the luxuries that accompanied it, and of course of its orgies. I have always, however, heard that no suspicion of actual unfair play was entertained. The proprietor was himself a very large speculator upon the turf, and a story was told in connection with his death which, even if not true, shows the opinion that was entertained of the play fraternity of that day. It was said that he was very largely interested in a certain race, and that others following his lead had backed a particular horse that was considered likely to win. It is well known in the sporting world that if the maker of any bets dies before the event betted upon is determined, the wagers are off. Mr. Crockford had been very ill, and much anxiety was felt by the parties interested in the event. The horse won; but before the race the great speculator had passed into another sphere. Those around him are said to have kept this secret, and, having learnt by means of carrier pigeons the result of the race, had supported his dead body in front of one of the windows in St. James's Street, so that it might be seen by the people returning from the course. This may be a fable founded upon the character of the persons concerned. It was generally believed, or at all events was generally asserted.

I heard from one of my disreputable acquaintances another curious story in connection with the gambling sets, and about the truth of this I entertain very little doubt. Names were given to me, and circumstances related that strongly confirmed it: one or two of the persons are still living. There were letter carriers employed by the Post Office who, being in the pay of certain professional betting men, regularly furnished them with information obtained from the letters of well-known turfites, which they were in the habit of opening. In those days envelopes were rarely used, and letters written upon a sheet of paper were folded and sealed; by means of a kind of hook the sides were extracted, and the contents could be deciphered with tolerable accuracy.

He told me of one instance, giving me all the names of the parties engaged. A person of very high position was the owner of a horse, which he had entered for a handicap race, and contrived by previous public trials of its speed to convey an inferior notion of the animal's powers, with a view to secure its being lightly weighted. This he communicated to people in his confidence, so that it might be backed at long odds; but the same knowledge having been previously obtained through the medium of the postman, the market had been used up, and his device, which was successful, turned to the profit of other more skilful but not greater rogues.

A man of middle age and middle height, clad in top boots and buckskin breeches, might on most Mondays and

Thursdays be seen wending his way down Piccadilly. His goal was Tattersall's. This was Jem Bland, one of the greatest operators upon the turf. He could neither read nor write; he was ready, however, to make any number of bets, no matter of what amount. He could enter no memoranda, and no one entered any for him. But he had a most surprising memory, and upon returning to his house he dictated the list of his bets, with unfailing accuracy, to a lady connected with his establishment.

She also read all the letters addressed to him, and thus obtained a considerable amount of private information of turf doings. This, he discovered, she was in the habit of imparting to some of her favourite acquaintances. He was fully equal to the occasion. A great race was about to be run—I think The Colonel and Zinganee were the competitors. He conveyed to his fair friend a batch of false reports, the circulation of which enabled him to make a very good book, and after that he changed his amanuensis.

In one of the most foul haunts of the metropolis there used to congregate many men of exalted rank, and (with the exception, of course, of the clergy) of all professions, with them mixed evil-looking keepers of low gaming, and, probably, of other houses, betting men, prize fighters, and bullies. After the saloons of the patent theatres had disgorged their contents, those who had not met with friends found their way to this den. Unlimited drink pervaded the establishment. It was known as the Piccadilly Saloon, and occupied part of the site of the present Criterion Theatre. I had not the means, and I hope not the taste, to join in the orgies that went on; but I have upon two or three occasions visited the place, and have a lively recollection of the scenes enacted. No play, it is true, went on overtly; but there were harpies on the look out for the unwary, whom they inveigled to neighbouring slums, and there drugged, robbed, and perchance murdered them.

I could name many of those who, I believe, nightly frequented this Pandemonium, but it would serve no useful purpose. There were, however, two, both public characters, whom I saw upon the few occasions I was there, and who particularly attracted my notice. One was Sam Chifney, the well-known jockey of George IV.; the other was a police magistrate, who presided at a court in the north-west district, and who, I was told, frequently left the saloon only in time to administer justice to the drunken and profligate who came within his jurisdiction.

One night, or rather the early morning, later in date than the period to which I have hitherto been referring, a group of six men were congregated at one of the tables. I was not present, and it is from the relation of a spectator that I have gathered the following particulars. With one of the party I had a slight acquaintance, having met him at the Cider Cellars and Evans's. He was a gentlemanlike, unpresuming, and inoffensive young man. This was a person of the name of Mirfin. His position was that of a linendraper, or assistant to one, in Tottenham Court Road. He and a man named Elliott, whom I understood to be a retired Indian officer, got into a squabble. Mirfin had been drinking, and scarcely knew what he was about. Suddenly the party rose and left the room. It seems that they obtained pistols, and the whole six, occupying two hackney coaches, drove to Wimbledon Common, and there a sad combination of farce and tragedy was performed. Poor Mirfin was put up and fired at by Elliott, an expert shot. Probably Mirfin himself had never handled anything more dangerous than a yard measure. The first shot went through his hat. He was plucky enough, however, for again he stood up to be fired at, and Elliott succeeded in murdering him.

The affair, from the brutality and ridicule that accompanied it, the circumstances that led to it, and the place in which the quarrel occurred, gave a finishing stroke to an institution already tottering; and the assassins who, through the false shame of men of honour, were able to pursue a system of terrorism, are now infamies of a past generation in this country. In a neighbouring one the practice fortunately appears to be verging on the confines of burlesque.

POSTSCRIPT.

I have received several letters upon the subjects contained in this chapter, and am much obliged to the writers, who furnish me with what are, I have no doubt, some accurate details. They do not, however, alter the inferences I have drawn, nor would they, I think, enhance any interest that may attach to my account.

CHAPTER V.

CHOICE OF CIRCUIT.

In former chapters I have brought my readers to the period when it was necessary to choose my course of proceeding in the legal struggle I was about to commence, and my interests as well as my finances pointed to the metropolitan and adjacent districts. Accordingly, I joined the Middlesex Sessions, of which tribunal I have already given some description, being introduced by a gentleman named Alley, a leader of the bar. Subsequently I joined the Central Criminal Court, and almost as a consequence fixed upon the Home Circuit, which consisted of Hertfordshire, Essex, Sussex, Kent, and Surrey. In choosing a circuit, a barrister, with certain exceptions, is bound by his first choice, and it ought to be made with grave deliberation. When I was called there were no railways. We were not allowed to use public conveyances or live at hotels. The leaders generally travelled, accompanied by their clerks, in their own carriages, the juniors two or three together, in dilapidated post-chaises. It was customary for the judges to enter the town before the bar, and, as it is called, open the commission, after which they adjourned to church, affording a grand opportunity to the sheriff's chaplain, usually a very young man, to enforce upon them their duties as citizens and judges. During this ceremony the carriages came rattling in, lodgings were engaged, the juniors, two or three of them, sometimes more, occupying one sitting-room. The attorneys were to be seen hurrying with the briefs destined for their fortunate recipients, witnesses lounged about the bars of the public-houses, and the juniors wandered up and down the street wondering what they should do with themselves and whether a good time was coming.

The next morning (the commission was usually opened on a Monday) the real business of the assizes began. A flourish of trumpets, not necessarily in harmony, announced that His Majesty's judges would take their seats in half an hour, another flourish that they had done so: one in the Crown Court, the other in the Civil. The former court is the great object of attraction. A real judge is a sight to see; he is clad in scarlet; the High Sheriff, in a mysterious costume, sits beside him; solemnity is given to the scene by the presence of a parson. It is said that even the criminal is elated by a sense of the dignity of his position, so different from being tried by Squire Jones in his blue coat and drab trousers. I suspect, however, that the fact that the judge will not take into consideration his being a notorious poacher is in reality the cause of his satisfaction. His lordship, in charging the grand jury, probably congratulates them upon something, and remits them to perform the not very arduous duties of indorsing their own previous committals, that tribunal being principally composed of the magistrates of the county. The trials are then proceeded with, and disposed of with impartiality and decorum.

The criminal courts of the assizes give the junior members of the bar an opportunity of ventilating their powers, and they almost invariably receive assistance and encouragement from the judges. The feeling thus early engendered produces through a subsequent professional career the kindly intercourse that exists between bench and bar, in no respect derogating from the dignity of the former, or the independence of the latter.

I remember the great French advocate, M. Berryer, remarking upon this trait of the profession in our country with some surprise, but with warm admiration.

In the meanwhile the business in the Civil Court has commenced. There is a kind of interlude of undefended causes. The court is densely crowded by barristers, who, during the charge to the grand jury, are excluded from the Crown Court, lest they should hear what the judge says, and take a hint from it. Of course if there is anything useful to know, the solicitors, who are not excluded, repeat it. This is an old-fashioned absurdity, which ought to be abolished.

A cause is called on. The acceptance to a bill of exchange not contested has to be proved. A voice is heard from the middle of the crowd enunciating with difficulty, 'May it please your lordship——' 'Pray speak out,' says the judge. The counsel almost collapses, but, struggling and panting, at last succeeds in giving the necessary proof, and so a number of cases are disposed of, and the real business of the Civil Court commences. The leaders have taken their seats, exchanged bows with the judges, nodded to each other, and the stereotyped dialogue ensues between the judge and leader, 'On what day, Mr. ——, will it be convenient to take special juries?' 'The bar is at your lordship's disposal.' 'What do you say to Thursday?' 'It will suit admirably.' 'Thursday be it then. Mr. Sheriff, let the special juries be summoned for Thursday next.' And now horses are off, and the day is exhausted upon the trial of usually trifling causes. The adjournment at last arrives. The former opponents walk to their lodgings, chatting gaily together;

and the juniors rejoice that the time has come when all meet at a dinner, where good humour and thorough cordiality between the highest and the lowest in the professional scale usually reign. I will not run the risk of wearying my readers with any long description of the mess, but I think that I may mention, to the credit of its members, that no personal jokes prevailed, and though laughter was often excited at the expense of one or other of the members, it was thoroughly good-humoured. Officers were elected. An Attorney- and Solicitor-General brought offenders to justice. One offence was, going special to another circuit. It was one of gravity, and an exemplary fine was imposed. Getting married was passed over with a simple admonition, upon the ground that it carried its own punishment with it. There was a poet laureate, and sometimes the verses composed were amusing, and, if personal, without bitterness. Mr. Arnould, afterwards a judge in India, filled at one time this office with much credit. He was an accomplished poet as well as lawyer.

One of the means of extracting fun was making the criminal address the mess in aggravation of his offence. And I must here mention a gentleman who will not appear in any of my strictly legal recollections, but whose memory will always be regarded by members of the profession, especially those on the Home Circuit, with respect and affection.

John Locke, member for Southwark, now no more, was the very soul of the circuit table: his speeches elicited roars of laughter. I have often endeavoured to explain to myself in what particular attribute his humour consisted, but it was as little to be defined as it was impossible to resist. I have only met one instance of a somewhat parallel character. This was in another valued friend, now also passed away, the late Mr. Sothern. In 'Lord Dundreary' he created, by means especially his own, the most uncontrollable laughter, and the same mystery, as in the case of John Locke, enveloped the cause.

The apparently utter confusion of mind, the striving vainly to get hold of the threads of a subject, the look of vacancy attending the failure, and the solemn attempt to resume the struggle, were features common to both. I recall these gentlemen as having furnished many of the most amusing hours of my life, and join with all their friends in mourning over their departure.

One other institution I must not omit to mention—the dinner given by the judges to the bar, at which young and old were kindly received. A custom, now extinct, then existed of each guest giving the judge's servants two shillings. This gave rise to the entertainment being profanely called a two-shilling ordinary. As trumpets initiated the assizes, so they celebrated their termination. The rickety post-chaises were again called into requisition, and in another town the judges underwent the same trumpeting, and with their last blast each town was left to slumber in its pristine dulness.

When I joined the circuit Mr. Serjeant Spankie and Mr. Serjeant Andrews were in a partial lead. The former had held high office in India. I scarcely remember him. The latter was possessed of a very solemn appearance.

There were two members who both gave great promise, and were looked upon as the future leaders: one was Mr. Turton, who closed his career in this country by accepting an appointment in Calcutta; the other, a Mr. Broderic, who succumbed prematurely to ill-health.[1]

[1] I have no personal recollection of either of these gentlemen, but my father, who remembered them both, has described the former to me as possessing all the qualities of an accomplished advocate, and the latter as a most acute and learned lawyer.

These events left a splendid opening for Mr. Thesiger, who ultimately shared the lead with Mr. Platt. As is known, the former passed through the offices of Solicitor- and Attorney-General, and ultimately became Chancellor during Lord Derby's administration. He received this post whilst conducting the prosecution of the British Bank directors, in which I was associated with him, and I may say that I never heard a finer effort than his opening of the lengthy aud complicated facts of that cause. He was very painstaking and industrious. His appearance was greatly in his favour—tall, with well-marked and handsome features; his manner was slightly artificial, and his jokes, of which he was fond, were somewhat laboured. He had been when a boy in the navy, and was, I have heard, in one of Nelson's engagements. When called to the bar he joined the Surrey Sessions, where he soon was deservedly held in high favour, and selected the Home for his circuit. I do not think he was very popular when he became a leader. He was accused of favouritism in giving references, and was surrounded by a clique who received them.[1] As an advocate he was successful with special juries, but Platt beat him before common ones. He was eminently correct in his demeanour, and set an excellent example to the bar by his regular attendance at the Temple Church. When Chancellor he refused Serjeant Parry and myself, both of us in good business, patents of precedents, upon the ground that he had fully made up his mind never to confer that rank upon a serjeant. He afterwards very properly, but very inconsistently, conferred it upon Serjeant Simon and Serjeant Sargood. A great scandal was created by his appointing a near connection of his

[1] The selection of junior members of the bar to arbitrate becomes very invidious when a leader selects only his own personal friends.

own Master in Lunacy. This office was intended for lawyers of standing and experience, and the gentleman in question was only nominally a barrister, and held a clerkship in some public office, and, although possessing very high qualifications, certainly did not come within the intention of the statute creating the office. Mr. Disraeli, shocked at what had the appearance of a job, declined to defend it in the House of Commons. The gentleman selected instantly sent in his resignation, and Lord Chelmsford then appointed Samuel Warren, himself little better than a lunatic, although a clever one.

Warren was, at the time, in the House of Commons, and pronounced a sort of funeral oration upon himself when leaving it, which was listened to with more patience and apparent satisfaction than any of his former speeches. When Mr. Disraeli reformed the Conservative Government, he left out Lord Chelmsford, and appointed Lord Cairns to fill the office of Chancellor. One of this nobleman's acts was to raise Alfred Thesiger, a son of Lord Chelmsford, to the post of Lord Justice. The appointment was considered premature; but every one who knew Mr. Thesiger felt that his legal knowledge and indefatigable industry warranted the selection, whilst his unvarying courtesy and real kindness of heart disarmed unkind comments, and his early death caused universal regret in the profession and to all who knew him. I cannot forbear offering a personal tribute to his memory. He has been with me and against me in several cases; most pleasantly we got on together, and the friendliness which I believe existed between us was by no means diminished by his promotion. I know of no one for whom I felt a more sincere regard.

During the period that I was what was humorously called reading at Watson's, my parents were still at Hampstead, and I became acquainted with a family who, from their connections and associations, were, as well as in themselves, extremely interesting. They consisted of grandmother, daughter, and grandson. The eldest of the three was Mrs. Denman, widow of the eminent physician; the second lady was her daughter, also a widow. Her husband was the celebrated Sir Richard Croft. It is well known that the young and popular Princess Charlotte died whilst under his care. Much bitterness existed at that time against her father, and calumnies extended most unjustly to his physicians. Sir Richard was very sensitive, and his mind gave way under the pain inflicted. Sir Thomas Croft, their son, who had been in the Guards and fought at Waterloo, was frequently of the party, and it was through my acquaintanceship with them that I first knew Sir Thomas Denman, the son of Mrs. Denman, Lady Croft's brother, and uncle of Sir Thomas. He was then Attorney-General, and came frequently to see his relatives, and through the length and breadth of the land a more truly affectionate and happy family never existed.

It is impossible for memory to dwell upon a more noble figure than that of the mother of the future Lord Chief Justice. Her features were strongly marked, and greatly resembled his when he had arrived at a later period of his life. They lived upon Heath Mount, where I was frequently received by them. Mrs. Denman was very fond of whist, and would play three or four rubbers without apparent fatigue.[1] The party consisted of the three I have already mentioned and myself. I think I remember Miss Joanna Baillie on one occasion joining the tea-table. They were all most kind to me, and, independent of the boon they conferred by making me known to the future

[1] At this period long whist was always played, and I imagine that old-fashioned people thought there was profanity in the change now universally adopted, but which then, like smoking, was supposed to indicate a fast and reckless life.

Chief Justice, I shall always feel that their society was one of the most agreeable incidents of my life.

As I only profess to give my own experiences, and leave history to deal with general events, I have but little to record relating to Lord Denman's career. Every one has heard of the noble stand he made in defence of Queen Caroline, and it speaks well for William IV., upon whom during the trial he made a bitter attack, that it was by his appointment that he became Lord Chief Justice. Whilst he filled that office, my practice was confined principally to the criminal courts, and consequently, except upon the occasions when he presided at those tribunals, I had no opportunity of observing him. His manner was uniformly gracious and kindly, and his demeanour dignified. Cruelty, or oppression of any kind, would elicit from him occasional bursts of indignation, but in his administration of criminal justice he never forgot the natural frailty of human nature.

One personal incident, having an important bearing upon my career, I may be permitted to mention. I had been just four years at the bar, and neither my prospects nor finances were flourishing. The spring assizes were going on at Maidstone, when one of the boatmen attached to the Thames Police called on me, in great distress. His mother was in grievous trouble. She had committed some small offence, and was to be tried before Lord Denman. At the poor fellow's entreaty, I defended her, and she was acquitted. At the judges' dinner, afterwards, Lord Denman, shaking hands with me, said, 'You did that case very well, but it was the witnesses to character got the woman off.' He alluded also to the meetings at his mother's of which I have made mention. On the summer assizes following he was also the judge, and I applied to him for a revising barristership. There was only one vacancy, which he gave to a Mr. Kennedy. I happened, in somewhat disconsolate mood, to go into the court as it was rising, and caught his eye. As I heard afterwards, after seeing me, he sent for Montague Chambers, who held a revising appointment, and asked him if his position upon circuit was not such that he might dispense with it. That gentleman at once placed it at Lord Denman's disposal, and he sent it to me. The remuneration was not large, but at that time it was vitally serviceable. I held the appointment for four years, when the number was diminished, and those last appointed were excluded. My colleague upon this occasion was Mr. Shee, afterwards a judge of the Queen's Bench.

I am sure the members of my profession will excuse me for saying a few words on Chambers, and I believe all will join me in the tribute, that this opportunity gives me of paying, to one who not only served me on that occasion, but with whom I have always remained on terms of friendship. Originally in the Guards, he doffed the scarlet at the call of duty and affection, became an assiduous worker, a successful advocate, and leader of the Home Circuit, and no man ever attained position who, by strict honour, fairness, and integrity, deserved it better. I am glad to say that, although he has retired from the profession, I still meet him at a club to which we both belong; and whilst he has not reaped the highest honours, he is always contented and in good spirits, and not altogether unwilling to furnish his numerous friends with some of the anecdotes of his career.

POSTSCRIPT.

Mr. Serjeant Andrews was the gentleman I have mentioned in a former chapter as being the opponent of Mr. Serjeant Adams for the office of Chairman of the Middlesex Sessions.

CHAPTER VI.

THE THAMES POLICE COURT.

At the time I was called to the bar my father was a magistrate, and was residing at the official residence of the Thames Police, then situated at Wapping, on the river bank, opposite to what was called Execution Dock, where, but shortly before, it was the custom to hang pirates in chains. He had for a colleague an old sea captain of the name of Richbell. It was thought, in those days, that the experiences of navigating a ship on the sea would be a good preparation for administering the law in connection with the river. At this office there was a staff of police under the control of the magistrate, and the river was patrolled by this force. I was accustomed to accompany them day and night. They saved my limited resources the expense of cabs; and many is the chase I have joined in of suspicious wherries, and sometimes a scamper, not unattended with danger, upon shore, when the officers were in the performance of their duties. I believe them to have been an admirable body of men, joining discipline with much of the knowledge possessed by the old Bow-Street runners; and it was to one of these men that I was indebted for the brief that, as I have already mentioned, brought me to the attention of Lord Denman.

A Mr. Broderip became colleague with my father upon the decease of Captain Richbell. A barrister, a good lawyer, and refined gentleman, he was a fellow of the

Zoological Society, and took great delight in the inmates of the Gardens. I cannot refrain from mentioning an anecdote that occurred many years after, when he had been transplanted to the Marylebone Police Court. I was then in some criminal practice, and appeared before him for a client who was suggested to be the father of an infant, and about which there was an inquiry. Mr. Broderip very patiently heard the evidence, and, notwithstanding my endeavours, determined the case against my client. Afterwards, calling me to him, he was pleased to say, 'You made a very good speech, and I was inclined to decide in your favour, but you know I am a bit of a naturalist, and while you were speaking I was comparing the child with your client, and there could be no mistake, the likeness was most striking.' 'Why, good heavens!' said I, 'my client was not in court. The person you saw was the attorney's clerk.' And such truly was the case.

My father afterwards took a house in Cadogan Place, where he died. I remember the late Charles Mathews canvassing him for his vote for the appointment of district surveyor at Bow. He obtained it, and also the place. Fancy one of the brightest of mortals amongst the chimney-pots of Bow! He did not long remain in this uncongenial sphere; and I remember shortly after, in company with a large party, consisting of Adolphus and others, old and fast friends of his father, seeing him make his first appearance at the Olympic Theatre in the farce of 'Old and Young Stagers,' inaugurating the brilliant career which, to the sorrow of all acquainted with him, has recently terminated.

Mr. Const, who, as I have already mentioned, presided at the Middlesex Sessions when I joined them, occupied a house at the eastern corner of Clarges Street, in Piccadilly. He kept an open table for his intimate friends who were in the habit of notifying their intention to dine—within a certain number and up to a given hour of the day. My father was one of the privileged—and I was frequently received at these parties, where I met very pleasant people—amongst others, William Dunn, 'Billy Dunn'—treasurer of Drury Lane Theatre—and sometimes departed, after a hospitable dinner, with tickets in my pocket for Old Drury, no small boon to a pocket that did not contain much cash.

Sir Frederick Roe was also a constant and very welcome visitor. I believe that he succeeded Sir Robert Baker as chief magistrate at Bow Street. He was a tall, handsome, gentlemanly man, who had the reputation of having enjoyed life in many phases. He succeeded to a large fortune, and retired from the bench. I remember my father congratulating him upon his accession to wealth. 'Ah!' said he, with a deep sigh, 'it has come too late.'

A very different style of magistrate was Mr. Laing, whom I also frequently met. I never saw him without thinking of a shrivelled crab apple. In the story of 'Oliver Twist' Charles Dickens caricatured him under the name of Fang.

A reverend gentleman complained of him to the Home Office. I fancy he had exhibited some irritability of temper in a case before him, and the authorities were not sorry to follow the lead of a popular author, and dismissed him. His accuser was shortly afterwards convicted of stealing a silver spoon at a charity dinner at which he presided.

Mr. Laing, notwithstanding an unfortunate temper, was a thoroughly honourable gentleman, a good lawyer, and accomplished scholar, very precise in his dress, but, as I have said, very sour-looking. Every day of his life he might be seen at the same hour wending his way to the Athenæum Club, where he always dined.

I do not think that glibness and self-confidence exhibited early in court are a good augury for ultimate success. No one, until he has measured himself with others, has a right to form a high opinion of himself. It is true that after a young barrister has ejaculated with difficulty a few incoherent words, he sits down with a parched throat, and a sort of sickening feeling that he will never succeed; but the most successful of advocates have experienced these sensations, and to this day I believe that many rise to conduct cases of importance with some of their old emotions. In a former chapter I have described my sensations when first I was called upon to address the court, and it was long before I could do so with any amount of confidence.

Although in the legal scale criminal courts and criminal trials do not hold the first places, they are of far more importance in the eyes of the general public than those tribunals and elaborate investigations by which the greatest reputations and highest rewards are obtained, and the Crown courts ought to be presided over by men who can command and enforce respect. Such certainly was not the rule when, in natural connection with the Middlesex Sessions, I first joined the bar at the Central Criminal Court; and there can be no doubt that the mode in which business was conducted in that tribunal made it a term of opprobrium to be called an Old Bailey barrister. Except in very grave cases, the business was presided over by judges appointed by the City. A canvass amongst a parcel of by no means the highest class of tradesmen, who were quite incompetent to form a judgment, obtained for candidates the places of Common Serjeant and Commissioner the Recorder being appointed by the Court of

Aldermen. The sittings of the court commenced at nine o'clock in the morning, and continued until nine at night. There were relays of judges. Two luxurious dinners were provided, one at three o'clock, the other at five. The Ordinary of Newgate dined at both. The scenes in the evening may be imagined, the actors in them having generally dined at the first dinner. There was much genial hospitality exercised towards the bar, and the junior members were given frequent opportunities of meeting the judges and other people of position; but one cannot but look back with a feeling of disgust to the mode in which eating and drinking, transporting and hanging, were shuffled together.

The City judges rushing from the table to take their seats upon the bench, the leading counsel scurrying after them, the jokes of the table scarcely out of their lips, and the amount of wine drunk, not rendered less apparent from having been drunk quickly—this is now all changed. The early dinners and evening sittings have been interred with other barbarisms, and the hours are the same as in the civil courts. At the period I am speaking of, Mr. Cotton was the Ordinary—not easily to be forgotten, somewhat tall, very portly. His rubicund visage betokened the enjoyment of the good things of this life. He was most punctual in his attendance at both dinners, and never affronted the company by abstinence at either. He possessed a sort of dry humour, and I fancy was popular in the City. I had no opportunity of learning whether he performed the very different offices connected with his appointment with the same success that he did his prandial ones. One of the jokes recorded of him has often been repeated. It was part of his duty to say grace, including in it a prayer for the principal officials. 'Why,' he was asked, 'do you not name the under-sheriffs?' 'I only pray for *great* sinners,' was his reply.

The Honourable Charles Ewan Law, whom I have already mentioned, was the Recorder: dignified in manner before dinner always, and merciful, pompous, and disagreeable, he possessed ability quite equal to the necessities of his office. I remember an amusing incident connected with him. On one occasion, *after dinner*, he overturned his tray of coffee, which was resting upon the bench. He said not a word. The same jury sat the next morning. He had some coffee brought in—quite an unusual thing at that hour. Somehow it went over, to the great discomfiture of the Clerk of Arraigns, who sat underneath. Turning to the jury, he said: 'Gentlemen, I have constantly begged that the desk should be made broader. I met with the same accident on another occasion.' Mirehouse, the Common Serjeant, always called Taffy, was a hot-headed Welshman, good-humoured and kindly enough. He turned the court into a low-comedy theatre. Arabin, the Commissioner, a shrewd, quaint little man, enunciated absurdities with most perfect innocence.

'I assure you, gentlemen,' he said one day to a jury, speaking of the inhabitants of Uxbridge, 'they will steal the very teeth out of your mouth as you walk through the streets. *I know it from experience.*' It ought to be mentioned, to the credit of the Corporation, that it had upon a former occasion elected Mr. Denman as Common Serjeant,[1] and the most pleasant years I passed in the court were during the time that the Honourable James Stuart Wortley was Recorder. This gentleman was an excellent judge, and extremely popular with everybody.[2]

[1] This was before my time.

[2] He afterwards became Solicitor-General, and was succeeded by Mr. Gurney.

On a morning in October 1834 I was entertained at breakfast in the Regent's Park. A tall, gaunt old gentleman was my host. Afterwards I was taken down in a most respectable family coach to the Sessions House, Clerkenwell Green, and there introduced to my future companions at the bar. Mr. Alley, as I have before mentioned, one of its oldest members, performed this kindly office. He had had formerly a large business in the criminal courts, sharing it mainly with Mr. Adolphus; but both these gentlemen were now succumbing to the inroads of younger men, Charles Phillipps and Clarkson, with Bodkin bringing up the rear, getting the cream of the business. Peter Alley was an Irishman; he had the reputation of being a good criminal lawyer, and although his manners were rough, his feelings were those of a gentleman. He was most hospitable and kind. I have already mentioned a well-known tavern called the London Coffee House. It still exists, but its character is changed. Then it was frequented by merchants and City men of position, and during the sittings of the Central Court Alley used to dine there often, and invited from time to time members of the bar, to whom the dinner was both an object and a compliment. I was many a time his guest. He and Adolphus had numerous quarrels, one of which led to the oft-recorded duel on the Calais Sands. I have heard a story in connection with it which is rather amusing. I imagine that neither of them wanted to fight; but after one of these disputes, Adolphus sent a letter of the most insulting character to Alley's house. He might have addressed it to his chambers. By accident, of course, Peter left the letter on the table, where Mrs. Alley found it, and, naturally, also read it. Alley blamed his carelessness bitterly; but his wife, having true Hibernian blood in her veins, holding the missive in her hands, exclaimed,

'Peter, much as I love you, I would sooner see you brought home on a stretcher than submit to such an insult.' The two fought, and one, I forget which, shot off a part of the other's ear. They were both very proud of the exploit, and, with a few growls, remained afterwards tolerable friends. Let me say a few words of Adolphus. He was nearly a great man, and but for an unfortunate temper would probably have risen to the highest honours of the profession. He was a lucid and impressive speaker, and possessed a singularly logical mind. A fair judgment may be formed of his powers by reading a speech he made upon the Cato Street conspiracy case, in which he greatly distinguished himself.

He was called to the bar at a comparatively late stage of life, and, although occasionally engaged in civil causes, remained almost to the day of his death a practitioner in the criminal courts. During some portion of the period when he was in practice, Tenterden, a morose judge, who was supposed to be much under the influence of Sir James Scarlett, was Chief Justice of the Queen's Bench.

Sir James upon one occasion, how provoked I do not know, said, 'Mr. Adolphus, we are not at the Old Bailey.' 'No,' was the response, 'for there the judge presides and not the counsel.'[1] When I first knew Adolphus he had attained an advanced age, and it was sad to witness the wreck he had become; sad to think of a life so wasted, of great abilities so cast away. There was little generosity shown him by those who were at this time doing the principal business; and pigmies to him in intellect were enabled, through his unhappy irritability, to drive him almost to madness.[2] Whilst referring to his temper, I am

[1] Since writing the above, I have met the anecdote differently worded in Campbell's *Lives of the Chief Justices*.

[2] These observations do not include Mr. Bodkin.

pleased to record that to his juniors and his inferiors it was never exhibited. To them he was unvaryingly considerate and kind; and I must also mention that he had been for years a sufferer from a painful disease, which he bore with the greatest patience and magnanimity. He lived in Gower Street, where he gave frequent parties, which were very popular, mainly through the accomplishments of his daughter and daughter-in-law, the wife of his only son, John Leycester Adolphus, afterwards a county court judge. He himself was a thorough-going Tory, and wrote a history of George III. through Tory glasses, and when he died, an affectionate father and sincere friend passed away.

Mr. Charles Phillipps was a curious compound of intellectual strength and weakness. He possessed undoubted genius, and power of speech amounting at times to eloquence, but was deficient in moral courage and self-reliance. He was an Irishman by birth, and his face and figure were greatly in his favour—tall, with well-formed and expressive features, and a musical voice. He had commenced his career on the Munster Circuit, where he produced a great impression upon juries more impulsive than those he had to address in England. Several specimens are given of his style by a gentleman who has written some very amusing articles in a magazine which until lately was called the 'Dublin University.' He was still young when he came over to this country, and, somewhat inflated by the praises he had obtained, imagined himself to possess all the attributes, instead of only the more superficial ones, of a great orator. Wanting in discretion when before a tribunal of which he had no experience, he laid himself open to a merciless attack at the hands of Brougham in one of the first cases in which he appeared in the Court of Queen's Bench. He collapsed under the punishment, and rarely appeared afterwards in any of the civil courts. A romantic incident occurred at the commencement of his residence in this country, in the shape of a love-affair with a very beautiful girl, whom he subsequently married, and a duel with an unsuccessful rival.

When I commenced my career he was signally the prisoners' counsel at the Old Bailey, the Middlesex Sessions, and also upon the Oxford Circuit. In this capacity he was certainly at that time unrivalled. He had great readiness, a power of repartee, earnestness when it was required; and whatever deficiency he may have shown in his earlier career, he had acquired a very sound judgment. He was never dull, and the juries liked him. I remember upon one occasion, in the robing-room, when poor Adolphus, in a state of irritation and when his business had nearly all fallen into the hands of Phillipps, said to that gentleman: 'You remind me of three B's—Blarney, Bully, and Bluster;' 'Ah!' said Phillipps, 'you never complained of my B's until they began to suck your honey.'

I may here mention an incident that occured in connection with the trial in which Brougham and Phillipps were opposed, and which I believe to be perfectly true. A friend of the latter gentleman, of the name of MacDowell, was a reporter upon the staff of the 'Times' newspaper, and it fell to his lot to report his friend's speech. The reply of Brougham came within the province of another gentleman. MacDowell wished his associate to leave out some of the more stinging passages, but he would not be persuaded to swerve from his duty. MacDowell contrived, however, to soften their effect by omitting the parts in Phillipps's speech to which they referred, and, this being discovered, he lost his position on the 'Times.'

My father, from whom I heard the story, knew the poor fellow, who never afterwards rallied, and died, I fear, in great poverty. Phillipps himself kissed the rod that had chastised him and became a constant associate of Lord Brougham, who made him Commissioner of Bankruptcy at Liverpool, an office for which he was singularly unfitted. Subsequently he was appointed to be one of the judges of the old Insolvent Court, which required a good knowledge of figures, about which he knew nothing; and his colleague, who knew little more, was a gentleman notoriously more insolvent than most of the suitors who sought relief at his hands.

POSTSCRIPT.

My friend Mr. Archdale, in alluding to the first appearance of Charles Matthews, mentions the following incident in the article to which I have already alluded: 'Poor Liston had to deliver a poetical and pathetic address upon the occasion, but the moment he appeared roars of laughter from every part of the house greeted him, and although the tears were streaming down his cheeks as he delivered the lines, they had no effect upon his audience.'

Liston, with whom I had a slight acquaintance, was essentially a melancholy man. He seemed to have been created to afford amusement to the masses by the exhaustion of all power of retaining amusement for himself. He was also very sensitive, and I believe he never would allow his children to witness his acting, which he considered to be in violation of the intentions of Providence and a desecration of the great attributes of his nature.

CHAPTER VII.

THE TRIAL OF COURVOISIER.

SHORTLY before Mr. Phillipps left the bar his name became associated with the Courvoisier trial, which for many reasons interested me, and some of the circumstances of which may, I think, equally interest my readers.

On May 6, 1840, Lord William Russell was found murdered at his house, No. 14 Park Lane. London was in a state of excitement. The age of the nobleman, his great historic name, and position in society, all combined to aggravate the horror naturally excited by such an event. The circumstances clearly pointed to domestic treachery; and Courvoisier, his confidential valet, was apprehended, and, on June 18 following, was put upon his trial, charged with the murder. The occasion might, from the appearance the Old Bailey presented, have been thought one of the most festive character. The court was crowded with ladies dressed up to the eyes, and furnished with lorgnettes, fans, and bouquets; the sheriffs and under-sheriffs, excited and perspiring, were rushing here and here, offering them what they deemed to be delicate attentions. A royal duke honoured the exhibition with his presence, and, upon the occasion of a witness giving a particular answer to a question from counsel, showed his approval by an ejaculation of 'Hear, hear!'

Sir Nicholas Tindal, the presiding judge, was so

hemmed in by the extensive draperies of the surrounding ladies that he had scarcely room to move, and looked disgusted at the indecency of the spectacle; and I may here say that the scenes still occasionally presented upon celebrated trials at the Old Bailey do little credit to the officials who encourage them. Mr. Baron Parke, to whom I shall hereafter allude, was associated with the Chief Justice upon the trial. Mr. Adolphus led for the prosecution, and in opening it made allusions, scarcely in good taste, to the fact of the accused being a foreigner, giving Mr. Phillipps, who defended him, an opportunity for a display of eloquent protest. The trial lasted for three days; and the proceedings upon the two first were scarcely conclusive enough to have secured the conviction. Upon the third day, when I came into the robing-room in the morning, I found Mr. Phillipps there, evidently very much agitated. I learnt afterwards that some new evidence of an important character had come to the knowledge of the prosecution and been communicated to him.

A considerable quantity of plate had disappeared from Lord William's house, and it was discovered that immediately after the murder it had been deposited by Courvoisier with some people in the neighbourhood of Leicester Square. This circumstance had been disclosed on the previous evening. Courvoisier, to whom it was made known, requested an interview with his counsel, which was very properly accorded, and upon this occasion he admitted the correctness of the statement as to the discovery.

He did not, as was generally supposed and asserted at the time, avow that he had committed the murder, although doubtless what he did own was very stringent evidence of the fact; and the communication was certainly made, not for the purpose of admitting his guilt, but merely to prepare his counsel to deal with the evidence.

The course pursued by Mr. Phillipps showed the inherent weakness of his character. It was peculiarly a situation for self-reliance and sound judgment. He was bound to continue the defence; although no doubt his mode of conducting it could not but be materially affected by the new circumstances. Mr. Phillipps, however, adopted a line that was wholly inexcusable. He sought an interview with Mr. Baron Parke—who, it must be remembered, although not the presiding judge, was assisting at the trial—communicated to him the confession of his client, and asked his advice. This conduct placed the judge in a most painful position, and was grievously unjust to the accused. It is probable that if Baron Parke had not been taken by surprise, he would have declined to express any opinion. I happen, however, to know that, having learnt that the prisoner did not intend to relieve his counsel from the defence, the learned baron said that of course he must go on with it. And, if he gave any advice at all, this was the only advice he could give, and ought to have been patent to the inquirer ; and certainly no censure can be too severe upon the conduct of Phillipps, who, when assailed for his management of the case, violated the confidence that his interview with Baron Parke demanded, and endeavoured to excuse himself by saying he had acted under that learned judge's advice.

I heard Phillipps's speech : it was extremely eloquent. He made the most of some indiscretions in his opponent's opening, but he was overweighted by the facts ; and certainly, since I have been at the bar, juries have not shown themselves apt to be carried away by flowers of rhetoric. Many of those used by him in this speech were not only in bad taste, whatever might have been the circumstances, but upon this occasion they were utterly unjustifiable. I have refreshed my memory of some of them, from a most useful and admirably arranged work of a Mr. Irving, called 'Annals of our Time,' and from his work I extract the following specimens: 'Supposing him to be guilty of the murder, which is known to Almighty God alone;' 'I hope for the sake of his eternal soul that he is innocent.' Such expressions from the mouth of an advocate possessing the knowledge that Phillipps did at the time he used them, were not only offensive to good taste, but scarcely escaped conveying a positive falsehood.

It is of the essence of advocacy that counsel should under no circumstances convey his own belief, or use expressions calculated to do so; and the only excuse that I can find for Phillipps is from the knowledge that he always composed his important speeches before he delivered them, and that up to the morning of the last day he believed that Courvoisier was innocent. But whilst this may redeem him from the imputation of conveying a falsehood, it does not excuse the language in which he indulged.

There is not, I think, any ground for saying that he endeavoured to fix guilt, by unworthy means, upon a servant girl. It may be said that in every case where it is acknowledged that an offence has been committed, the defence of the client must be founded upon the assumption that some one else is guilty; but, excepting those expressions to which I have alluded, and which do not point to any one in particular, I cannot recall anything that went beyond the bounds of legitimate advocacy; and I am sure that, whatever his faults of taste and judgment, he would not have been capable of so grave a crime.

He felt very bitterly the comments made upon him

by the press. I think they went beyond what his conduct deserved, but, as I have been obliged to admit, he certainly laid himself open to very grave censure. I suppose few counsel have defended more accused persons than myself, and I must allow that innocence was not the characteristic feature of the majority of my clients; but I cannot remember any case in which I received an unqualified admission of guilt. The utmost that approached to it was a mild suggestion that if the evidence was too strong for me to obtain an acquittal, it was hoped that I would save my client from transportation.

I think that it may not be unserviceable at the existing time to make a few observations upon this subject. I am greatly struck by many of the features that now present themselves in connection with crime. I think they are very formidable, more so than ever I remember them, and, unless they are checked, point to an appalling future. There seems to me to be more abstract brutality amongst the criminal classes, and more recklessness of human life, and certainly the contingencies to which the police are subjected whilst executing their functions are extremely frightful. The question, therefore, must come to the front, whether our present punishments are the most efficacious that can be applied.

When transportation was in force, it created much dread in the minds of the criminals. There was a mystery attendant upon it, and a sense of final separation from every home tie. It operated also most strongly upon their friends and accomplices, thus creating, what is most to be desired, an efficient example to others. Now their friends know where they are, and in the miserable holes in which they themselves grovel, in cold, starvation, and wretchedness, they are apt almost to envy the food and warmth of a prison. There is also another point to be considered, if I am right in the view that I have formed. There are classes of criminals that can never be reformed whilst they are allowed to remain in this country, and yet their offences may not justify imprisonment for life. Practically a gaol educates them for graver ones. These include thieves from their birth, but who carry on their trade without resorting to violence. In another country they might find an opening for redemption; in this, none. There may be political grounds which make it impossible to revert to the system of transportation. With these I am not capable of dealing; but my experience may be trusted for knowing that, next to death, it inflicted the greatest terror, and to those capable and desirous of repentance, the only chance of reformation.

The crimes, however, that are now creating a feeling allied to terror in the public mind are those which subject our fellow-creatures to death or cruel injury, and the question requires very grave consideration and a freedom from morbid sentimentality. The punishment of death is still continued, and is thought to be sufficient to intimidate brutal offenders; and of one thing I have no doubt, that there is no example of a criminal, under a capital sentence, who would not with joy exchange the penalty for any other form of punishment known to our law. Why, if it be inflicted and is supposed to be thus efficacious in any case, should it be applied to a result and not to the intention? Why should a villain, armed with a revolver, maim a man for life whilst in the performance of his duty and escape the gallows? I think that the police ought to be told that they shall be furnished at least with every protection possible. There were many conscientious and kindly hearted people who objected to the lash being used; but surely if a deliberate war is waged by crime, and carried on by reckless violence and brutality against society, the most efficacious means ought to be used to defeat it. I am quite aware that any punishment that shocks the bulk of thinking and observant people could not be established; but humanitarianism may be carried too far, and we have arrived at a crisis when order must assert itself in language which will produce a deterrent effect upon criminals.

Whilst upon the subject of scoundrels and their doings, it will not be amiss to mention two who, amongst a crowd of smaller ones, flourished about the time of the Courvoisier trial. The cut-throats and garotters who at different periods have infested the metropolis were not greater pests than the proprietors of two newspapers called the 'Age' and the 'Satirist.' The weapons with which they effected their robberies were slander and threats. They hunted out the secrets of families, and lived upon the fears of those to whom they appertained, and for some time these miscreants drove a thriving trade. Their names were, I believe, Westmacott and Barnard Gregory. I witnessed the former in the dress circle of Covent Garden Theatre howling under the horsewhip of Mr. Charles Kemble, whose daughter he had foully slandered, and I had the satisfaction of convicting the latter at the Old Bailey.

A volume might be filled with a record of their villanies, and of the desolation that followed upon their trial. Let us hope that, like the murders committed by professional duellists, they are the filthy emanations of a bygone age, and are buried in the infamy generated by their existence.

POSTSCRIPT.

Although in the above and following pages I have not assumed to myself the position of a dictator to those who have means or knowledge far greater than mine, I, nevertheless, have possessed opportunities of witnessing under many phases the operation of crimes and the application of punishments; and if suggestions of mine can be of any service, it would gratify me to feel that my career has not been without some value to my fellow-creatures. I do not believe in the preventive effect of long imprisonments. I do believe that mentally and physically they demoralise its victims, whilst after a time the labour ceases to be a punishment, and warmth and food are recognised as the only happiness of life.

When released they may still have mind enough left to become the instructors of youth in the quarters already corrupt enough to which they return. I have glanced at the reasons why I strongly advocate a system of transportation. I am confident that it is a most deterrent punishment, and I cannot help thinking that in some of our African colonies it might be carried out. It is said that the unhealthiness of the climate makes it in many cases a death sentence; but surely, when our soldiers and sailors are sent there, and when lawyers accept positions embodying every risk, the climate is good enough for our malefactors. It may not be generally known that when transportation was first in use it was not part of the penal code, but in cases of death sentences the choice was offered to the criminals.

There is at the present moment in a part of the United Kingdom an organisation of the foulest crimes, and so long as any punishment is inflicted that keeps the perpetrator within the reach of his friends, its dread possesses but small effect. Let the conviction under the summary processes which are now proposed be followed by a removal from the country for ever, whether with additional punishment or not. Unless I have greatly misjudged the effect of transportation, and my knowledge of human nature has gone far astray, there will be introduced a means of checking crime that at present does not exist either in England or Ireland.

CHAPTER VIII.

THE CENTRAL CRIMINAL COURT.

William Clarkson enjoyed a large business at the Central Criminal Court. He was not without ability of a certain kind, which was greatly assisted by his connection by marriage with a respectable firm of solicitors. Loud-voiced and swaggering, with one undeviating form of cross-examination, whatever might be the position or character of the witness, and that the very reverse of gentle or refined, he did much to maintain the opprobrium attaching to those who practised at the court. He was by no means considerate to his juniors, but succumbed at once to those capable of resistance. My recollection does not furnish me with any circumstances in his career, professionally or privately, that I can record to his advantage.

William Henry Bodkin was a man of a different type, and, in my opinion, if his education had been equal to his natural ability, he would have attained a very high position. He was acute and clear-headed, and, as I have already mentioned, he was very successful in the civil business of the Middlesex Sessions. He was a pleasant companion and extremely popular, and there were many, including myself, who received from him substantial marks of kindness.

When Mr. Phillipps obtained the appointment which I have recorded in the last chapter, I acquired a considerable accession of business, which, however, greatly diminished upon the advent of Mr. Charles Wilkins, a man who had already attained a high position at sessions in the North of England. He was at once patronised by the solicitors practising in the court, and the qualities he possessed were calculated to create early impressions in his favour. An imposing person and a deep sonorous voice controlled the audience. He was a fluent speaker, and arranged the matter he had to deal with very clearly. His experiences in many walks of life[1] must have furnished him with extensive knowledge of human nature; his mind, however, was incapable of grasping the niceties of law, and he possessed no readiness in dealing with any matter suddenly started. A successful repartee threw him upon his back, and ridicule drove him frantic. He greatly diminished my business when first he came, but I fancy after a time I discovered his weak points, and I do not think he maintained the reputation he had gained when he first joined the sessions. He afterwards changed the scene of his labours by taking the coif, and in a certain class of civil business again, for a certain time, obtained considerable success. Whilst practising at the Central Criminal Court he defended a solicitor, named Barber, in a very celebrated trial, of which I propose hereafter to give some account.

Subsequently to his departure I shared the lead with Mr. Parry, a man of great knowledge, power, and ability, until both of us quitted the field and followed Mr. Wilkins's example by taking the degree of the coif. We were often subsequently brought in special to the Central Criminal Court, and probably even upon this stage did not lose much by our promotion.

[1] There were many stories told of the vicissitudes of his life which I have no means of verifying. He was at one time certainly in the medical profession, and at another an actor in the provinces.

Before concluding my recollections of the Court, I ought to mention two firms of solicitors who divided between them much of the defence business. Mr. Harmer, an alderman of the City of London, was at the head of one of them, and carried on business in Hatton Garden. His appearance indicated good living and good nature; he was gifted with great shrewdness, and possessed amongst the classes whose natural destination was the Old Bailey, an immense reputation, and a most profound confidence was reposed in him by a large body of clients, none of whom had reason to regret their trust. He was rejected as Lord Mayor upon the ground of certain opinions, now to be found in many respectable journals, that were ventilated in the 'Dispatch' newspaper, of which he was proprietor. He realised a good fortune, and built a villa on the banks of the Thames, which he christened Ingress Abbey, but which his friends called Newgate, where he entertained with great hospitality.

The other firm to which I allude was that of Messrs. Lewis and Lewis of Ely Place, the senior partner of whom, of small stature and quiet manner, with features characteristic of shrewdness and a kindly nature, might often have been seen unpretendingly making his way to the barristers' table. His movements were watched with anxiety and hope as he quietly walked about and slipped a brief into the hands of a pleased recipient. His firm possessed a large business, which he principally had built up by means in all respects honourable to himself. There were two other solicitors of high standing and character who did a large business, Mr. Humphreys and Mr. Wontner, but they more usually appeared on the part of the prosecutions.

What was called the Rope-walk was represented by a

set of agents clean neither in character nor person, and I fear that the guinea eagerly sought by counsel in his early days told a sad tale of misery and self-denial endured by those who, as too often is the case, had to suffer for the sins of their relatives.

During my experience I have rarely known a thoroughly innocent person convicted, although there are certain charges scarcely sustained by strict evidence, but which carry with them a moral conclusion, and in which juries are apt to reject law and yield to prejudice; but little evil arises from such results, and substantial justice is obtained.

I must, however, except one class of cases in which I have seen very grave errors committed by juries, and I fear that many innocent people have suffered. I allude to charges preferred by women against the opposite sex. Juries in many of these instances seem to bid adieu to common sense. The tears of a good-looking girl efface arguments of counsel and the suggestions of reason. However absurd and incredible the story told may be, a fainting fit at an appropriate time removes from their minds all its improbabilities. I have often wished that such charges might be disposed of by a jury of matrons. In cases that might fairly be the subject of an action before a civil tribunal the juries take up a high moral tone, and think themselves justified in inflicting the punishment awarded to one of the highest of crimes. I could reccrd many instances in which, I believe, there has been a lamentably wrong conclusion arrived at against the person charged. In one case that I was engaged in, and in which the jury would scarcely listen to me, they were persuaded by the earnest exhortations of the judge to acquit the prisoner, but they appended to their finding the hope that his lordship would see that he was severely punished.

I remember a fashionable perruquier being tried many years ago at the Central Criminal Court for an outrage upon a young person in his employment. I cannot give the details of the story, which carried to my mind falsehood upon the face of it, but being plausibly told by a weeping complainant of prepossessing appearance, the hearts of the jury were moved, and their common sense was washed out. He was convicted and sentenced to a long term of transportation, which was, however, subsequently remitted.

A good story, for the truth of which I should, however, be sorry to vouch, is told, that the wife of the Governor of New South Wales, happening to be in England, implored the Home Secretary to carry out the sentence, as there was not a decent hairdresser in the colony.

It is well known that the Old Bailey, rechristened the Central Criminal Court when its jurisdiction was enlarged, was of civic origin, and still retains its original character. The aldermen, although they act by deputy, are judges, the Lord Mayor being the nominal head. The sheriffs represented by the under-sheriffs appertain to it; and these latter perform their more painful functions through the medium of the executioner. The citizens of London and their representatives have, in the days when the liberties of the people were threatened, made many a gallant stand, and done good service, and for this deserve the gratitude of posterity; but now the Lord Mayor, his state coach, the aldermen, the men in armour, the sword-bearer, and the City marshal are tawdry and useless monuments of a past age. The magisterial functions are discharged by paid clerks, of whom the aldermen are merely the mouthpieces, and might just as well be represented by their chains and robes. The mode by which officers called upon to perform high judicial duties are elected is a scandal to the age. The great merchants shrink from all connection with the corporation; and the definition of a good chief magistrate is one who has been most profuse in his hospitalities.

I should be very ungrateful if, in recording my opinion of the aldermen in their public capacity, I were not to acknowledge the number of most estimable, kindly, and excellent men who have at all times belonged to their body, and, during the early period of my practice at the Central Criminal Court, I and other members of the bar had to thank them for very liberal and unpretentious hospitality. My comments apply solely to their position in relation to the administration of justice, which I regard as mischievous and absurd.

There was one alderman of whom I have a very distinct recollection: this was Sir Peter Laurie. He was a great friend of my father: he was a shrewd and far-seeing Scotchman, quaint and conceited, but with plenty of sound good sense and an honourable character. I mention him, however, not so much on his own account as to introduce to my readers one of the most original rogues of the time, and the mode in which, upon one occasion, Sir Peter dealt with him. Joseph Adie was his name, and amongst other modes of raising money he hit upon one of circulating letters to numerous people, professing that he had obtained knowledge which would be most beneficial to them, and by these means for a time he drove a thriving trade.

He was brought up before Sir Peter, who, finding that he had committed no punishable offence, was obliged to discharge him; but in doing so the worthy alderman said, by way of reprimand: 'Now, Joseph, if any one wants to know your character refer him to me.' Adie, in all his future letters, headed them 'referred, by permission, to Sir Peter Laurie.' Ultimately Mr. Adie fell a victim to a suit by the post-office authorities for the price of stamps he had omitted to pay, and in default was sent to gaol. Whether he has since flowered in some other shape I know not; if so, probably he has also thought it convenient to appear in some other name.

As a wayfarer passed in the neighbourhood of the Mansion House about the period I have been more particularly recording, he might frequently have seen two neatly dressed personages, somewhat past middle age. They bore a great likeness to one another, although one affected juvenility in a brown wig, the other wearing his own perfectly white hair. Each presented a rosy-faced countenance, and a mild benevolence appeared to beam upon it; they might have been the brothers Cheeryble. They were the brothers Forester, the celebrated city officers; their hands were never profaned by touching vulgar thieves, and those whom they did touch usually terminated a career of great crime upon the gallows.

Notwithstanding their occupations, they were really as kindly as they looked. In many a heart-rending scene they had, as far as their duty would allow them, given solace to the afflicted. And their evidence in court was always truthful and unexaggerated. I have had many a gossip with both of them, and heard some painful episodes of criminal life, which I may some time hereafter record in these volumes. I have confined myself as nearly as possible to personal experiences.

The institution of the new police probably superseded their employment. Their cheery faces are no more seen, probably no longer exist. I have no doubt, if living, they are provided for by the generosity of the corporation, never wanting towards those who have served them conscientiously.

It is only right, whilst mentioning the celebrities connected with the Old Bailey, that I should allude to one other personage. Rarely met with upon festive occasions, he was, nevertheless, accustomed to present himself after dinner on the last day of the sessions. He was a decently dressed, quiet-looking man. Upon his appearance he was presented with a glass of wine. This he drank to the health of his patrons, and expressed with becoming modesty his gratitude for past favours, and his hopes for favours to come. He was Mr. Calcraft, the hangman.[1]

POSTSCRIPT.

In referring to the higher officials of the corporation, no slur can be cast upon their thorough uprightness, but it is obvious that in the great metropolitan court they are simply ornamental, and that in the minor courts the business is substantially performed by subordinate officers without responsibility, and whose names are not even known to the public; and although the selection of a recorder has upon many occasions been creditable to the Court of Aldermen, it is no less the result of a canvass, which cannot be commended, and the selection of other persons called upon to perform important judicial functions by a large body of small tradespeople. The scenes attending the canvass, and the mode in which the result is usually attained, must be highly reprobated.

[1] This occurred in a past generation.

CHAPTER IX.

FRIENDS.

Amongst the friendships I formed and greatly valued during the early period of my career at the bar was that of Charles Edward Jerningham, nephew, I believe, of the Earl of Stafford. We sat together briefless at the Central Criminal Court; we shared a room over a butcher's shop during the assizes at Maidstone; and sighed in unison for the trumpets that announced the dinner hour to be approaching. He was a charming companion and an accomplished scholar. In consequence of his health failing he quitted the profession and went abroad, and I never saw him again, although I occasionally heard from him. I have, however, had the pleasure of meeting his son, Hubert, a gentleman who has distinguished himself in diplomacy and literature.[1] Huddleston and Jerningham were in those days my most intimate companions at the bar.

I was, however, fortunate in possessing some very pleasant acquaintances out of the profession, and amongst them was a gentleman well known in London society—Mr. Dubois. He lived in Sloane Street, where he exercised a liberal and ungrudging hospitality to a large circle of friends, chiefly connected with literature and art. Amongst them were the brothers Smith, authors of the 'Rejected Addresses,' of whom, however, I have no very

[1] He has now added M.P. to his distinctions.

precise recollection; and Barham, the charming author of that wonderful collection of drolleries, 'The Ingoldsby Legends.' This gentleman I also had the pleasure of meeting elsewhere, and his quiet, refined humour has often been a source of great delight to me. Theodore Hook—bright, improvident, reckless genius—was a constant visitor, and with him a little rosy-faced individual, his tried friend and worshipper, Mr. Hill. This latter was a mystery. No one knew when he came into the world, and it used to be said that if really he had been born after a legitimate fashion, the records of his birth had been lost in the fire of London. Mr. Dubois, in addition to being a recognised patron of literature, performed judicial functions in a small debts court, in a street leading out of Holborn, called the Court of Requests, but his duties never seemed to give him anxiety or to affect his cordial good temper. His house formed a fair example of the hospitality of a former generation. The dinner hour, as far as I remember, was half-past five, when the guests met substantial fare and a hearty welcome, the pleasure derived from which was greatly enhanced by the cordiality and kindness of Mrs. Dubois and her pretty and accomplished daughter. But the hour when fun reigned supreme approached nearer to midnight. Then it was that I have heard Theodore Hook, who seemed to brighten for the occasion, sing some of his most amusing songs. They were supposed to be extemporary, but his friend Hill might be detected furnishing a cue.

Poor Theodore, although upon these occasions brilliant, was a sad wreck when seen at other times. He had lived hard, which meant something in those days, and had seriously damaged his constitution. As is well known, he once filled the post of Treasurer of the Colony of the Mauritius, and his carelessness had resulted in a serious deficiency in the funds over which he had control, no imputation, however, beyond carelessness resting upon his character. His answer when asked how he came to leave the island has been often told. 'It was,' he said, 'through a complaint of the chest.' He was sued by the Government for the amount deficient, and thrown into the Queen's Bench prison; a step which would not have been taken but that they were forced into it by the Opposition, who were furious at the attacks made upon Queen Caroline in the 'John Bull' newspaper, which he edited. My friend Dubois as Duberly, and Hill as Hull, will be recognised in his amusing novel of 'Gilbert Gurney'; and I am inclined to think that the description in that work of the scene at the Old Bailey and of the deaf judge will fully bear comparison with the great trial of 'Bardell *v.* Pickwick,' immortalised by Dickens.

I also remember Poole, the author of 'Paul Pry,' a character suggested to him, umbrella and all, by Mr. Hill. It used to be the pride of this latter gentleman to learn everything about his neighbours. He could inform his associates which of their friends had a party, and what they had for dinner. He used to look down the areas and watch the confectioner's man; in fact, he acted the *rôle* of a busybody for the amusement of his friends, but was too much liked ever to have been a mischievous one.

It was about the time of these convivial meetings that I became a member of the Clarence Club, called by its detractors the Clearance, from the fact of its having been founded upon the Literary Union, dissolved to get rid of some objectionable members. There were many agreeable people belonging to it. Amongst others, a prominent member was Mr. Dilke, founder of the 'Athenæum' journal, father of the first baronet, who also was a member, and grandfather of the present statesman. Those who knew this gentleman well spoke of him as possessing an intellect of great capacity and power. His son, an old friend of mine, was a very agreeable companion. He was most useful in the management of the very difficult details connected with the Exhibition of 1851, and his services were much appreciated by the late Prince Consort, himself no mean judge of the capacity of those with whom he had dealings, and in recognition of them a baronetcy was conferred upon him by her Majesty.

Tom Campbell, the author of 'The Pleasures of Hope,' did not present a romantic figure; and his carelessness about dress rendered his appearance much less agreeable than his poetry. The late Lord Justice James was also a member. I was not personally acquainted with him. I fancy that he always exhibited those marks of ability which, when he was promoted to the Bench, rendered him one of its greatest ornaments.

Another gentleman, a member of the club, and with whom I had the pleasure of being on terms of intimacy, was the late Frank Stone, an artist who possessed a great charm. There are few pictures, to my thinking, more pleasant to look at than those that came from his brush. His health was not good, and he died whilst in the full vigour of his mind. I need not mention how honourably and successfully his son Marcus Stone has followed in his father's steps.

As I am professing to write experiences of my own life, I cannot forbear mentioning two members of the club who were intimate associates and friends of mine. Their names are not inscribed upon the tablets of fame, but they are worthy to be remembered. Captain Barberie was one of them, an Englishman by parentage, but, being either born in India or taken there very early, he presented a complexion nearly Eastern. He had only one leg, his other having been amputated at the thigh-joint. He had served in India, and his limb was shattered at one of the sieges which the British had been obliged to raise, and it showed wonderful vitality, that, with the wounded leg dangling to his body, he bore the fearful trial of a retreat before it could be amputated. His face had the mark upon it of a fearful cut which he received from a native whom he had discovered embezzling stores; it also bore the marks of a severe attack of small-pox which he had suffered from in India. I have not drawn a very inviting picture of his personal appearance; he was, nevertheless, pleasant to look upon, and much beloved by his many friends. His daily companion and associate was a Major Henderson, also an Indian officer, who was wounded at the same siege. His wound was upon the head, and had been received whilst storming the fortress where his friend had his leg shattered. He was taken up apparently dead, but it turned out that the bullet had carried his handkerchief, which he wore under his regimental cap, into the wound, and with the handkerchief the bullet came out. He was trepanned, and although at times suffering great pain, lived for many years after.

One day Barberie was missing from the club; and when on the next day he did not turn up, I went to Duke Street where he lived, and, opening the door of his chambers, saw him stretched upon a sofa. 'Do not come in,' he said to me. 'I have got the small-pox.' Of course I asked whether I could assist him. He said that Henderson was doing all that he required. Daily inquiries were made after him by his friends, and, to the satisfaction of all, we heard that the crisis was passed, and he was in a sound, healthy sleep. Ten minutes after, he was dead. A tray of crockery had been dropped in the court-yard and startled him from his sleep. His mind wandered for a moment, and then passed into eternity.

Although naturally very clever, he was a perfect child in the world's ways, and a designing woman having obtained great influence over him, his friends feared he would marry her. He was not upon good terms with his relatives, and had made a will bequeathing everything to her. One afternoon, shortly before his death, Henderson, myself, and he were at the club, and we were laughing at him for his infatuation; he got very much annoyed, left the club, and, as we heard afterwards, went off to the dwelling of this person, and, being quite unexpected at that hour, he found her in company which fully justified our opinions. He came home, destroyed the will, and never left the house afterwards. His illness prevented his making another disposition of his property, and his relatives got all he left behind him. He received a pension of *50l.* per annum for the loss of his leg, and he had an amusing mode of appraising everything according to that value. He would describe, for example, a sum of *25l.* as half a leg, and in this way divided it into fractions with great accuracy.

Barberie wrote a very vivid account of his calamity in 'Bentley's Miscellany,' headed 'How I Lost my Leg.' He was only thirty-five years old when he died, after undergoing more misfortunes than most people are subject to in the longest life, and succumbed at last to the combined action of a disease he had previously suffered from and the carelessness of a stupid servant. Major Henderson survived his friend for some years; but the affairs of the club not having been prosperous it was dissolved, the members were scattered, and amongst others I lost sight of this gentleman.

I had the pleasure of the acquaintance of Mr. Bransby

Cooper, the nephew of the eminent surgeon, Sir Astley Cooper. He was himself in the same profession; but early in his career had the misfortune to fail in an operation, which cost the patient his life.

His mode of performing it was severely criticised by Mr. Wakley in the 'Lancet,' and, although he obtained a verdict in an action he brought against that gentleman, the damages were scarcely sufficient to clear him from blame. In another respect, through no fault of his own, he was unfortunate. His uncle retired from the profession, leaving him in the occupation of his house in Spring Gardens, and securing for him one prosperous year; but, getting sick of leisure, Sir Astley returned suddenly from abroad, and, as I have heard the story, wandered to the end of the Chain Pier at Brighton, having half a mind to terminate the misery of idleness. Instead, however, of availing himself of the ocean for that purpose, he ordered a post-chaise, and turned up in Spring Gardens as quickly as four horses could carry him, and there renewed his profession, which he carried on successfully for many years. Bransby Cooper, after this, although possessing surgical skill and excellent judgment, never obtained any hold upon the public. He used often to complain to me of a soreness and irritation in his throat, which he attributed to a laceration caused by his having swallowed a fish-bone. He died suddenly whilst at the Athenæum Club, his death being caused by a cancer in the throat. It is probable that he was aware of the fact, although he affected to ignore it.

Wakley was a man of mark in his time, and the action brought against him by Bransby Cooper gave him notoriety. He was himself plaintiff against the County Fire Office to recover the amount insured upon his house, which had been burnt down, and the office raised the defence that he had himself done it. He recovered a verdict; but I believe the damages were never paid, and he took no steps to enforce them.

He was a popular speaker, and was returned to Parliament for a metropolitan borough. Some one, alluding to a speech he had made, remarked to Sheil, the Irish orator, 'that he would never set the Thames on fire.' 'No,' said Sheil, 'unless he had first insured it.' He became coroner for Middlesex, and in that capacity held an inquest upon a body presumably that of Mr. John Sadleir, member for Sligo, an Under Lord of the Treasury, and the perpetrator of stupendous frauds. The corpse was found upon Hampstead Heath, and it was alleged that death had resulted from suicide. There were circumstances about the appearance and the finding that led some people to doubt whether it really was the body of Sadleir; but Mr. Wakley knew him well, and could make no mistake, and it was also identified by Mr. Edwin James, the Queen's Counsel; but, as far as I remember, these were the only witnesses to its identity.

Bransby Cooper was fond of narrating an anecdote of his uncle in connection with a murder committed at Rotherhithe by a man named Patch. The deceased had been shot; and from the position that he was in at the time, and the direction of the wound, Sir Astley, then Mr., Cooper was satisfied that the shot was fired by a left-handed man.

Patch assured his counsel that such was not the case with him; but, when called upon to plead, held up his left hand. It may be necessary to mention, for the information of some of my readers, that at that period the prisoner pleading was always told to hold up his hand. He was convicted and executed.

I may here mention another acquaintance that I

formed, of not so reputable a character as those whom I have had the pleasure of describing heretofore. This was an Italian nobleman, who came over to this country with good introductions, and whose manners and varied information were calculated to create a very favourable impression upon society. It turned out that, although his rank was unquestionable, he was one of a gang of forgers, and engaged in carrying out a conspiracy of a very remarkable and daring character. The course contemplated was to pass simultaneously, in the principal cities upon the Continent, forged letters of credit purporting to issue from Messrs. Glyn and other bankers in London. The scheme failed by a mere accident; and the circumstances connected with it were investigated and exposed with great ability by the 'Times' newspaper, against which journal, in consequence of its strictures, a person who was supposed to be an accomplice brought an action. It was tried at the Croydon summer assizes in the year 1841, and the substantial correctness of the articles was clearly established. The merchants of London subscribed for a testimonial to the paper to mark their sense of the great ability which, regardless of expense, had been exhibited by it in exposing the fraud. The proprietors dedicated the large sum of money subscribed to public purposes.

It was said that the nobleman committed suicide, but no very authentic account of the circumstance, if it really occurred, ever reached this country. I cannot help thinking that I had some hand in assisting the design of the conspirators, as I was inveigled to a party at the Grecian Tavern in the Strand, where I lost what was for me a considerable sum of money to the nobleman. I learnt afterwards the character of the people whom I met, all of whom were gentlemen by birth and swindlers by profession.

POSTSCRIPT.

I remember one extemporary verse of poor Hook's which caused a good deal of laughter, although I do not quote it as possessing much merit. There was a well-known personage about town who was a frequent visitor at Dubois's. His name was Sir Burgess Camac. He had, I believe, made a fortune in the East. One night, after Theodore had amused the company with a poetical sketch of some of the people present, but omitting Sir Burgess: 'Have you nothing to say about me?' asked that gentleman, upon which Theodore, seating himself at the piano, recited—

> This is Sir Burgess Camac,
> Whose name spells the same
> Both forwards and back,
> Which is all I can say of Sir Burgess Camac.

CHAPTER X.

SUIT IN THE HOUSE OF LORDS.

It is somewhat remarkable that the first case of much importance in which I was engaged was in the House of Lords, before a tribunal composed of the following noblemen: the Earl of Devon, chairman; Lord Lyndhurst, Lord Campbell, the Earl of Radnor, the Earl of Lonsdale, Lord Sudeley, Lord Mountford, and others. A bill had been introduced to annul the marriage of a young lady, Miss Esther Field, contracted with a person named Samuel Brown, upon the grounds of coercion and fraud on his part, accompanied by the allegation that the marriage had not been consummated. The circumstances were very extraordinary. The lady was possessed of a large fortune —£1,200 per annum in land, and £40,000 in money. She was barely eighteen years old, whilst Brown was fifty-two, of humble origin, and no apparent means. However, he prevailed upon the lady to marry him, much, I fancy, to the disgust of a young gentleman, the son of an attorney, who would very willingly have taken his place, and probably, in the event of the bill having passed, would have succeeded in doing so. There was a formidable array of counsel in support of it—Sir Fitzroy Kelly, Mr. Rolt, Sir John Bayley, Mr. Walford, and Mr. Austin. I was alone in opposition to the bill.

Sir F. Kelly opened the case with a considerable amount of colouring, which was maintained by Esther under the examination of Mr. Rolt. In my cross-examination I endeavoured to make her relate the facts in a natural manner, and to get rid of the exaggerations that had coloured her evidence in chief. Other witnesses were called, and Mr. Rolt having addressed the House in favour of the bill, the case was adjourned until the following Friday. On that day I was about to address their lordships, when the Earl of Devon interposed, and I copy from the 'Times' of August 11, 1848, the observations that he made:—

'He said that their lordships did not feel it necessary to call upon the learned counsel to address them. He had in the first instance, he was free to admit, come down to the house with a strong bias in favour of the bill for annulling the marriage; but the evidence he had heard, and the able cross-examination of the learned counsel against the bill, had created a contrary opinion in his mind. In that opinion he was supported not only by Lord Brougham, whom, in common with other learned lords, members of this House, he had consulted, but by Lord Lyndhurst, who had most carefully perused the whole of the proceedings in the Court of Chancery, and had heard the arguments and evidence which had been offered at the bar of their lordships' House, and informed him that there was not a sufficient case to sustain a bill for annulling the marriage of this young lady. From the Lord Chancellor he had also received a similar intimation.

'Such being not only his own opinion, but that of his noble and learned friends, he felt it impossible for him to move the further progress of the bill.'

The eminent physician, Dr. Locock, had been subpœnaed as a witness by the petitioner, but was not called.

At the end of the first day, Lord Lyndhurst came up

to the bar of the House, where I was standing, mentioned that he had known my father, and paid me a kind compliment upon the mode in which I had conducted the case, concluding by asking me whether I intended to call witnesses; and upon my replying that it depended upon the result of a consultation, remarked, with a significant smile, 'I do not think you will.'

It will not be out of place here to make some remarks upon cross-examination. The records of courts of justice from all time show that truth cannot in a great number of cases tried be reasonably expected. Even when witnesses are honest, and have no intention to deceive, there is a natural tendency to exaggerate the facts favourable to the cause for which they are appearing, and to ignore the opposite circumstances: and the only means known to English law by which testimony can be sifted is cross-examination. By this agent, if skilfully used, falsehood ought to be exposed, and exaggerated statements reduced to their true dimensions. An unskilful use of it, on the contrary, has a tendency to uphold rather than destroy. If the principles upon which cross-examination ought to be founded are not understood and acted upon, it is worse than useless, and it becomes an instrument against its employer. The reckless asking of a number of questions on the chance of getting at something is too often a plan adopted by unskilful advocates, and noise is mistaken for energy. Mr. Baron Alderson once remarked to a counsel of this type, 'Mr. ——, you seem to think that the art of cross-examination is to examine crossly.'

In order to attain success in this branch of advocacy, it is necessary for counsel to form in his own mind an opinion upon the facts of the case, and the character and probable motives of a witness, before asking a question. This, doubtless, requires experience; and the success of his cross-examination must depend upon the accuracy of the judgment he forms.

Great discernment is needful to distinguish material from unimportant discrepancies, and never to dwell long upon immaterial matters; but if a witness intends to commit perjury, it is rarely useful to press him upon the salient points of the case, with which he probably has made himself thoroughly acquainted, but to seek for circumstances for which he would not be likely to prepare himself.

And it ought, above all things, to be remembered by the advocate that, when he has succeeded in making a point, he should leave it alone until his turn comes to address the jury upon it. If a dishonest witness has inadvertently made an admission injurious to himself, and, by the counsel's dwelling upon it, becomes aware of the effect, he will endeavour to shuffle out of it and perhaps succeed in doing so.

The object of cross-examination is not to produce startling effects, but to elicit facts which will support the theory intended to be put forward. Sir William Follett asked the fewest questions of any counsel I ever knew; and I have heard many cross-examinations from others listened to with rapture by an admiring client, each question of which has been destruction to his case.

What is called a severe cross-examination, when applied to a truthful witness, only makes the truth stand out more clearly; and unless counsel is able to arrive in his own mind at a satisfactory opinion, it is far better to ask nothing than to flounder on with the chance of getting out something by a crowd of questions. A truthful witness usually adheres to the dry statement of facts, and avoids diverting attention by introducing irrelevant matter; and I think a remark I made to a jury upon one occasion is a sound one. It was upon a trial before Chief Justice Erle. I had put a question to a witness as to what he was doing at a particular time, this being a matter important to the inquiry. 'I was talking to a lady,' was his answer; adding, 'I will tell you who she was, if you like. You know her very well.' I made no observation at the time, but when addressing the jury said that my experience led me to the conclusion that honest witnesses endeavoured to keep themselves to the facts they came to prove, but that lying ones endeavoured to distract the attention by introducing something irrelevant; and I think this remark is worth consideration, and points out one of the tests of truth or falsehood in a person under examination.

Some judges upon the bench never shone in this branch of advocacy, and scarcely appreciate the value of it, and a refinement that now attends trials, and contrasts in many respects favourably with the coarseness of a former period, occasionally interferes with the force and persistence required in dealing with some persons in the box.

In the equity courts, the notion of cross-examination is ludicrous; it has, however, the merit of being thoroughly inoffensive.

I have heard two or three specimens of it. In these cases the witnesses had filed affidavits which the adverse counsel examined from, and made them repeat orally what they had already sworn to, as if the object of the process was to obtain from the mouth of the witness in court what had already been put upon paper in the solicitor's office.

An experienced equity judge once said to me in relation to a question I had asked, 'Really, this is a long way from the point.' 'I am aware of that, my lord,' was my answer. 'If I were to begin any nearer, the witness would discover my object.'

It is impossible to over-estimate the acuteness and argumentative powers of the judges and practitioners in the equity courts, but I am confident that they would find great assistance if the examination of witnesses were less of a sham.

Embarrassment exhibited under a searching cross-examination is not to be relied on as a proof of falsehood; the novelty of the position or constitutional nervousness may frequently occasion it.

I remember a remarkable instance of this in a trial in which I was engaged to defend a prisoner. It was a curious case. Messrs. Coutts, the bankers, were in the habit at certain periods of remitting specie to a bank at Oxford by a coach that went to that city. The money was contained in a box, and placed under the charge of the coachman. Upon a particular day, when the supposed box arrived at its destination, it was found to contain rubbish, the real one having been subtracted. It was proved that my client, who was a passenger, had got down before the end of the journey, with no apparent excuse, and did not take his seat again. Beyond this, however, there was little to sustain the charge against him. The coachman naturally was a principal witness, but became so embarrassed, and answered questions in so shuffling a manner, although with perfect truth, that both judge and jury believed that he was an accomplice in the robbery, and in this opinion I confess I shared.

My client was acquitted, but shortly afterwards was tried and convicted of another offence. I took the opportunity (I think, through the medium of the chaplain) to ask how the Oxford robbery had been effected, and learnt that the coachman had, against orders, gone into a public-house to get a glass of ale, and it was during his absence that the prisoner contrived to convey the dummy to an accomplice in front, receiving from him the genuine box, with which he decamped.

I have myself succeeded, by cross-examination, in cases where claims were made for injuries received in railway accidents, in showing that the claimant had not even been present at the time of the occurrence; and I may mention that, in a case tried this very year before the Lord Chief Justice, I assisted in exposing a very gross fraud of this nature attempted by a medical man. No witnesses were called by the company, which I represented, and upon my cross-examination, supplemented by some very important questions by the judge, the jury, upon the plaintiff's evidence alone, found a verdict for the defendants, and I believe the plaintiff had not been near the place when the accident occurred.

Cross-examination has recently become more important than ever in sifting the evidence of professional witnesses in cases where injuries have been sustained from the above class of accidents, and in which the most eminent professional men occasionally fall into grave errors, and I feel obliged to add that some in the lower walks of the profession make the manufacture of these cases a not unprofitable trade. One of these worthies admitted in a recent trial that he might have been engaged in a hundred of them.

A remark was recently made by the Lord Chief Justice, which accords most thoroughly with my experience, that perjury is greatly on the increase, and although, when detected, severe punishments may help to check it, it must be remembered that cross-examination is the only means by which it can be exposed.

I cannot forbear relating an anecdote in connection with one of the most amiable and excellent of judges, the late Lord Hatherley, when he was Vice-Chancellor. I was counsel before him, and had to cross-examine a very plausible, but certainly not truthful, witness. I did so with some severity, and I imagine that I should have been successful before a jury.

His lordship, however, was of a different opinion, and was much struck with the ingenuousness of the young man, and he evidently thought that he had been exposed to a cruel ordeal. As the witness himself was going out of the court, he was heard to whisper to a friend, 'Why, the old gent believed every word I swore.'[1]

I was very well acquainted with Mr. Rolt, the second counsel in the case with an account of which I commenced this chapter. I visited at his house, and met him frequently at the Garrick Club, and at the houses of mutual friends. He was a most distinguished member of the Chancery Bar, and became Lord Justice. He planted the seeds of a premature death by giving himself too little relaxation from intensely hard work. I have seen him come into the club of an evening looking worn and exhausted, swallow a hasty dinner, and rush off to further labour. He earned a high reputation, but paid a heavy price for it. Very different in appearance and habits was another of the counsel, Sir John Bayley, son of the eminent Baron of the Exchequer. He was jovial and kindly, and, although esteemed a good lawyer, was more known for his social than his legal eminence; mainly through his support and assistance, I became a member of the Union Club, and through his kindness also I enjoyed some of the most charming of gatherings at the grounds of Mr. Lumley, situated on the bank of the Thames, near Hammersmith Bridge. He was at that time the lessee of Her Majesty's Theatre. The site of his villa

[1] The term applied to his lordship was not of so refined a description.

is now occupied by wharves. There, in the midst of a most brilliant scene, were on these occasions assembled distinguished guests of different ranks, who were delighted to meet all that was bright and beautiful in the theatrical and operatic world. At one of these fêtes, I remember two ex-Chancellors enjoying the conversation of that most fascinating of danseuses, Mademoiselle Duvernay. No doubt, as Lord Campbell said of himself when he was met at Cremorne Gardens, they considered it their duty to study the habits of all classes of the community. The period when this occurred renders it unnecessary for me to say that they were not Lord Selborne, Lord Cairns, or Lord Hatherley.

Mr. Delafield, who had been a member of the great brewing firm of Combe, Delafield, and Company, took to the less profitable venture of the Covent Garden Opera House, and he also gave charming parties of a similar character at a pretty villa on the Fulham side of Putney Bridge. The large fortune with which he retired from the brewery was soon engulfed in the expenses of his operatic venture; and when, in after-years, I met him, as I did not unfrequently, he was living at Brussels for the sake of economy, but seemed to bear the loss of his fortune with philosophy and cheerfulness.

Sir Fitzroy Kelly and Mr. Austin were both men of mark, but I shall postpone any observations about them to a future chapter.

I trust that I shall not be thought guilty of unjustifiable vanity in recording the circumstances of the case commencing this chapter, and quoting the observations of Lord Devon. I hope also that in the comments that I have made upon the mode of dealing with witnesses it will not be considered that I arrogate to myself any superior knowledge. At the same time it is possible that a record of the experience I have obtained in a long career may not be without its use to some of my younger professional friends.

POSTSCRIPT.

In reviewing the above chapter, I cannot but feel that it is more appropriate to readers of my own profession than to the general body of the public, and, looking at it in that view, it is apparent that it is very imperfect. It passes over an element quite as important as cross-examination, namely, examination-in-chief, which I would venture to define as the art of making a witness tell his story naturally and in the manner most calculated to affect the minds of the hearers favourably; and in cases where facts are complicated and witnesses either unwilling or unintelligent, a case is not unfrequently put in peril by an inexperienced advocate having the duty cast upon him. Instructions constantly contain much matter that it is unnecessary and imprudent to introduce. I can only lay down one rule that may be of service, and which I venture to commend to my young friends at the bar. Make yourself thoroughly acquainted with the story that each witness has to tell, and without following the proofs in the brief; make him tell it in the way that if you were asking questions for your own information you would adopt, having made notes of the signal points and important dates.

For other purposes trust to your own memory, and mind skill in examination as well as cross-examination does not come from intuition; and I have frequently felt it was my duty to my client, and certainly intended no disrespect to my junior, to take a witness that in order would be appropriated to him into my own hands.

CHAPTER XI.

FAMOUS AUTHORS.

UNDER the colonnade of Covent Garden there existed a cluster of taverns: Evans's, the Gordon, New and Old Hummums, the Tavistock, the Piazza, and the Bedford. The two last had been the resort of noblemen and people of rank and distinction in society, who dined there at hours that would now be considered early, and consumed a considerable quantity of port wine. So I have heard and read. When I knew the houses themselves their glory had waned, although the Piazza still carried its head somewhat higher than its neighbours. In a large room in this tavern was held a nightly meeting called the Shakespeare Club. Its name suggests its character, and that of the majority of its members. Here it was that for the first time I met Thackeray. His appearance has often been described, and, although he was then unknown to me, it at once commanded my attention—tall above the ordinary height and proportionately broad. His face had been disfigured by a blow received in boyhood, and in repose would have been called plain. Although characterised by great solidity, it was only when he lifted his eyes that it became illumined, and the observer felt that it was one of rare intelligence. When I met him upon this occasion I was not aware that he was the author of the papers published in 'Fraser's Magazine' entitled the Yellow Plush Correspondence, which, in its anonymous form, I had read with intense amusement, nor have I found reason upon reperusal to alter my judgment. I am not, however, a great worshipper of his more elaborate works, although I do not presume to dispute the great power, thought, and knowledge that they exhibit. They present an unpleasant, and I do not think entirely correct, view of human nature. I believe it is better than he paints it. Thackeray appears almost to divide it into knaves and fools. My experience—and much of it has been gained amongst what would be deemed the outcasts of society—is that in every class there is much that is good and estimable; but even assuming his views to be correct, and that his novels are skilful and accurate analyses of human nature, the scenes they exhibit sometimes pain, and do not always amuse, me. Colonel Newcome, the very pattern of amiability, presents an unpleasant picture whilst victimised by an Asiatic swindler, whom the reader sees through from the outset. Doubtless the Colonel's resignation in adversity is very noble, and affords an excellent example, but can hardly be called a pleasant picture.

I follow the career of Becky Sharpe with mingled compassion and disgust. I cannot imagine anything more repulsive than her betrayal of her husband. And I am not sure that the virtuous indignation of Colonel Crawley is quite consistent with his character as previously described. I do not forget 'Pendennis,' and the old Major—a perfect sketch; and I am almost wonder-struck at the learning and research exhibited in 'Esmond'; but when I read a novel I want a hero who does not give me lessons, and I do not care for the anatomy of human nature, however skilfully it may be laid bare.

I am willing to admit and regret my heterodox opinions, and own myself to be whatever the great mass of

Thackeray's admirers may choose to call me; but they are my opinions, and I do not wish to make capital by borrowing those of other people.

Although not amongst his intimate friends, I met him frequently. We were members together of the Garrick Club, and I often saw him elsewhere.

I never thought him an agreeable companion. He was very egotistical, greedy of flattery, and sensitive of criticism to a ridiculous extent. He may have possessed great powers of conversation, but did not exhibit them upon the occasions when I had an opportunity of judging.

He did not hesitate to introduce his associates and the members of his club into his novels, and one of these latter, a curious compound of drollery and simplicity, named Archdeckne,[1] figures in 'Pendennis' under the name of Foker; and on one occasion I think that Albert Smith had great reason to complain of his proceedings.

This gentleman and a poor fellow now dead, Joe Robins, had been associates and friends; the latter, who originally had been in a lucrative business, quitted it for the stage and got into a very sad plight. I know that Albert Smith had been most considerate and kind to him, but had on one occasion refused to join in some subscription that had been set on foot on his behalf. Thackeray circulated throughout the club a caricature, in which the likenesses were unmistakable. Robins was represented wounded by thieves and being assisted by some good Samaritan, also portrayed, whilst Albert Smith, the Levite of the parable, was passing scornfully upon the other side. There was another member of the club who had injudiciously published some remarks about him, for which he pursued him with but little consideration or mercy. And

[1] I am told that this gentleman was by no means offended by the celebrity he obtained through figuring in Thackeray's novel.

I cannot forbear expressing my sorrow that a man so really great should have descended to most unworthy sneers at another equally great man and brother author, Sir Edward Lytton Bulwer, as he did on several occasions.

The last time I saw him was about three weeks before his death. He was sitting alone at a table at Evans's, poring over an obscure Irish journal in which some derogatory remarks about himself were published. He attributed them to an individual whom I need not name, and was intensely angry, which I confess I thought at the time was eminently absurd. His description, however, of the Irish in many of his works was not calculated to make him popular in that country. Having ventured to make these strictures, founded upon my observation and judgment of a man who has established a great mark on the literature of his age, I ought to mention a fact which was within my knowledge, that he suffered from a most painful and irritating disease, and also that among those who knew him well, and to whom he extended his confidence and friendship, he was most enthusiastically beloved.

I remember one other member of the Shakespeare Club, John Forster, the biographer of Dickens. His temper was not a very comfortable one to deal with, and I fancy was mainly instrumental in breaking the club up.

At the house of some very agreeable people named Levien, living in Woburn Place, I first had the pleasure of meeting Charles Dickens, and also his sister, a young lady of great talent and accomplishments, who unfortunately died when still quite young. Dickens had already won his spurs under the sobriquet of Boz. He and Thackeray happened to be contemporaries, otherwise there was no similarity between them, either in their writings or their character.

The works of both of them, published as they were

periodically, were eagerly looked forward to. Their styles were very different; it may be said that Thackeray invited thought and reflection, whilst Dickens, although by no means losing sight of the true delineation of human nature, showed that his main object was to amuse. How great a genius it must have been that immortalised Pickwick!

What other man could have enshrined such a mass of absurdities in the minds of the public by genuine fun and shrewd knowledge of human nature? Bardell against Pickwick is a burlesque, and yet there is nothing impossible in a deaf judge or an inflated address by counsel, and a speculative firm of attorneys may be found even during the present days of purity. My dear old friend Toole still creates roars of laughter whilst personating Serjeant Buzfuz, in a wig and gown with which I presented him for the purpose. Mr. Pickwick becomes almost a hero when he goes to prison upon principle. Many of Dickens's novels had higher ends, which they have fully attained, and some of the characters are drawn with a force of description and knowledge certainly not surpassed by any writer of any age.

Imagine yourself in the parlour of a country inn on a wet day. How the misery you are looking forward to is changed into content by the discovery of one of his novels! They amuse man, woman, and child alike, and they furnish good thoughts and kindly feelings towards their fellow-creatures. I was very much attached to Charles Dickens; there was a brightness and geniality about him that greatly fascinated his companions. His laugh was so cheery, and he seemed so thoroughly to enter into the feelings of those around him. He told a story well and never prosily; he was a capital listener, and in conversation was not in the slightest degree dictatorial.

He, like Thackeray, was very sensitive, and I remember a period when his conduct had been so misinterpreted that he suffered agonies. No man possessed more sincere friends, or deserved them better. He was the best after-dinner speaker I ever heard, and I cannot forbear recording a trifling incident that occurred the last time I met him, and shortly before his death. We were both dining at Mr. Cartwright's, in Old Burlington Street; I was sitting nearly opposite to him, and referred to a speech that he had made at the previous Royal Academy dinner in terms of praise certainly not exaggerated. He replied, 'Praise from Sir Hubert!' I and Mr. Spicer, a friend of his and mine, had put him up at the Union Club, and, to our great grief, the news of his death reached us upon the day on which he would have been elected.

A mutual friend, and one equally dear to us both, was Mr. Serjeant, afterwards Mr. Justice, Talfourd, lawyer, orator, and poet. Those who knew him will never forget his kindly, genial face, the happiness radiating from it when imparting pleasure to others, and his generous hospitality, extended in no niggard spirit.

He occupied a large house in Russell Square, and the gatherings that frequently took place in it included not only those who had obtained eminence in their profession, but the young who were striving to do so. Science and literature were represented by their most distinguished members. Painters, poets, historians, and actors mingled together and enjoyed themselves, Talfourd moving about and welcoming his miscellaneous company with cordial smiles and greeting. I remember poor Frank, his eldest son, and whose youth showed much promise (terminated, unhappily, by premature death), bending over the chair of a pretty and popular actress with looks and words of devotion, and it will be no improper breach of confidence to say that she refused his hand lest at his early age she might injure his prospects. He was an amusing writer, and initiated the modern school of burlesque, and it is no reflection upon the clever authors of the present day to say that his works would bear comparison with any of them.

Macready, always the actor, was happy to be the guest of the author of 'Ion,' one of his best parts. And there also he could converse with Sir Edward Lytton Bulwer, whose plays of 'The Lady of Lyons' and 'Richelieu' had furnished him with brilliant materials for the display of his talents. The author of 'The Hunchback' was no unworthy or unconsidered guest. Huddleston also, who had been early appreciated by his host, who never lost the opportunity of giving beginners a lifting hand, was a frequent and favoured visitor.[1]

And Albert Smith, full of life and jollity, but who had not then climbed his mountain, seemed none the less happy because he had not yet obtained fame. How many others I might mention, and, alas! how many, with Talfourd himself, have left the earthly stage! I need not say that it was not only in social and literary life that Talfourd distinguished himself. In the House of Commons he was much respected, and his successful efforts in carrying the Copyright Bill conferred a real boon upon his brother authors. He attained one of the objects of his ambition by a seat upon the bench, and, as is well known died suddenly whilst in the performance of his duties at Stafford assizes.

In the slight sketch I have ventured to offer to my readers I must not forget to mention the great aid he received from the loving, true, and cordial co-operation of Lady Talfourd, who, with her most charming daughters

[1] Mr. Huddleston went the same circuit as Mr. Serjeant Talfourd.

and niece, assisted with heartfelt cordiality in diffusing happiness throughout the assembly.

When at the bar, Mr. Serjeant Talfourd was counsel, in conjunction with Campbell and Thesiger, for Lord Melbourne in the action brought against him by Mr. Norton for criminal conversation. In his Diary, lately published, Lord Campbell does not mention the names of either of these gentlemen. Serjeant Talfourd was, as I know, retained at the express desire of Mrs. Norton, and he always entertained an undoubting conviction of her innocence. I was greatly interested in the case, not only from its public character, but from the fact of being acquainted with both Mr. and Mrs. Norton, the former being a brother magistrate of my father. I had myself met the lady upon one or two occasions. She was probably one of the most beautiful women of her age, and extremely clever and accomplished. There is no doubt that a great intimacy existed between her and Lord Melbourne, but he was quite old enough to be her father, and was possessed of great power of conversation, and I see no need whatever to assume impropriety, and certainly none was proved by credible testimony. I have recently read through the evidence very carefully, and if I had been counsel for the defendant, I should not have entertained any doubt of a successful result; indeed, I cannot understand how her husband could have been so ill-advised as to bring the action. Notwithstanding the ability of Sir William Follett, the jury gave a verdict for the defendant without the slightest hesitation. The case was tried in the Court of Common Pleas, before Sir Nicholas Tindal, a most painstaking judge. Mrs. Norton herself felt very acutely the indignity she had been subjected to, but society entirely absolved her—a conclusion that I have heard was fully indorsed by her Majesty whose opinion must have been a source of great comfort and satisfaction to her in after-life.

However innocent Lord Melbourne may have been, Sir John Campbell was not justified in stating 'that his client solemnly and upon his honour declared his innocence.' Most clients would do the same if they could find counsel who would lend themselves to repeating the assertion. Sir John was at this time the leader of the bar, and this extremely unprofessional proceeding was not a good example to his juniors. He certainly told the jury in the same breath that they ought not to be influenced by it. But Sir John was not a man to waste his words.[1]

In the course of my subsequent career I was frequently engaged in cases before Mr. Norton. He was an extremely pleasant, gentlemanly man, and a good magistrate.

POSTSCRIPT.

I have been subject to some but not unkind criticisms for my description of Thackeray. They were genuine, and certainly not conceived in an unkindly spirit. It is with pleasure I mention a conversation I had since my volume appeared with Sir Henry Thompson, the eminent surgeon, who told me that he had seen very much of him, and had never met a man more kind-hearted, more ready to listen to a tale of sorrow or want, or possessing more extended benevolence.

[1] The following are the words of the Attorney-General, copied from the report of the trial in the *Times* newspaper, dated June 23, 1836: 'I think it right, in the name of Lord Melbourne, to declare, as he has instructed me to do in the most clear, emphatic, and solemn manner that he never had any criminal intercourse with Mrs. Norton, nor had he done anything in the slightest degree to abuse the confidence of Mr. Norton. The jury were not to be swayed by this declaration.'

CHAPTER XII.

LORD LYNDHURST.

LORD LYNDHURST, when I saw him upon the occasion I have related in a former chapter, was of advanced age, but possessed a singularly noble and prepossessing appearance. The intellect stamped upon his features was accompanied by an expression of kindliness, his voice was musical, his manner refined and courteous.

His Life has been written by Lord Campbell, and fully justified what he himself said when he heard that it was contemplated, that the prospect added another pang to death.[1] Although born at Massachusetts, it was whilst it was a loyal colony, and he was consequently a British citizen. His father, an artist, painted several pictures that obtained great reputation, amongst others one now in the National Gallery, the subject being the Death of Lord Chatham. I am not aware whether it is considered a great work by connoisseurs. I do not myself like the treatment of the subject. According to all his contemporaries, Lord Lyndhurst, whilst at the bar, was a most brilliant and successful advocate. His powers were tested in a case in which, with Sir Charles Wetherall, he was

[1] I quote the following passage from a criticism upon Lord Campbell's Lives of Lyndhurst and Brougham that appeared in the *Times* newspaper of April 3, 1869: 'All through the Lives we see Lord Campbell running a literary muck, striking right and left with so sublime an impartiality that scarcely a man he jostles in the crowd of public characters he threads escapes unharmed.'

retained for the defence of a certain Dr. Watson, charged with high treason. Upon reading the evidence, it is difficult to avoid wondering that, instead of indicting him for the capital offence, the officers of the Crown had not proceeded against him for sedition. Lord Lyndhurst was at that time Mr. Serjeant Copley, and it fell to his lot to sum up the facts in favour of the accused, a duty which he performed with admirable skill and judgment. I do not myself think that even with inferior advocacy the conviction would have been warranted, although, in such cases, much depends upon the prepossessions of the jury, and it was doubtless from this knowledge that Mr. Serjeant Copley wound up his address with an elaborate but most eloquent and powerful appeal to them, entreating them to dismiss all prejudice from their minds, and be governed solely by a fair construction of the evidence. Lord Castlereagh, the most influential member of the Government, was upon the bench during the trial, and was greatly struck by the ability displayed by the counsel, and through his lordship's influence a seat in Parliament was obtained for him, and subsequently he was made Solicitor-General. The Government under which he accepted the post was a Tory one, and Mr. Serjeant Copley had always professed strong Liberal opinions. He had not, however, taken any part in politics, nor did he betray any confidence or trust. And whatever may have been the views of the party he joined, his performance of the duties of his office was consistent with the liberal sentiments that he had previously expressed.

My earliest recollection of him was when he was holding the office of Chief Baron of the Exchequer, and it was in that capacity that he pronounced judgment in the celebrated case of Small *v.* Attwood. This case involved many complicated facts, and the question was as to the falsity or truth of certain representations in relation to the qualities of a mine; and although his decision was reversed in the House of Lords, it was admitted at the time to be a model of clearness, and I believe now that the conclusion he arrived at is considered to be sound law.

He did not hold the place of common law judge for long, but during that time gave satisfaction to the public and the bar, to which latter he was kind and considerate. The tendency of his mind was always to the side of mercy. He aided and encouraged an inexperienced advocate, and was careful that a client should not suffer through any deficiencies of counsel. It is told of him that when he became Chancellor, and upon one occasion was describing the principles upon which he selected a judge, he said, 'I look out for a gentleman, and if he knows a little law so much the better.' Sir William Bolland, who, I believe, was the first one he made, certainly fulfilled the former condition. With Lord Lyndhurst's subsequent career history has dealt, and with it I had no acquaintance, except occasionally having listened to some of his brilliant displays in the House of Lords when in opposition to a Liberal ministry.

Sir Charles Wetherall, although engaged against the Government in the case of Dr. Watson, was one of the last specimens of a thorough Tory of the oldest school. He was a very learned man, and much respected for his conscientious adherence to opinions that were getting much out of fashion; but whilst strait-laced in his principles, his ideas of dress were much the reverse; in fact, he was one of the greatest slovens that ever walked, and it was a wonder when he did walk how his clothes and his body contrived to keep together. He was Recorder of Bristol, where his High Church and State views had not rendered him particularly popular, and a story is told that during the Bristol riots he made his escape from the fury of the mob in the disguise of a clean shirt and a pair of braces.

Reverting to the case before the House of Lords, I ought not to pass over without a few words the name of Charles Austin. He was a distinguished lawyer and scholar, but latterly confined himself to parliamentary business, in which he attained immense success, and realised a large fortune. He did not add to the character of the profession by accepting numerous cases which he well knew he could not attend to. Doubtless they were delivered by solicitors who were aware of the risk they ran, and preferred taking it to the chance of his being retained against them. I cannot, however, think the practice was honourable or one that could be justified on any grounds whatever. Mr. Austin himself retired early from the profession, and, marrying the accomplished step-daughter of Charles Dance, the author of many comediettas, in the performance of which Madame Vestris, Liston, Mathews, Mrs. Orger, and others delighted the public, retired into Norfolk, his native county, took to rural pursuits, and became Chairman of Quarter Sessions, in which capacity he gave great dissatisfaction to the county gentry by not properly appreciating the enormity of poaching.

With Sir Fitzroy Kelly I early formed an acquaintance, and was upon intimate terms with him down to his death. He was a skilled lawyer, and most industrious, and, although not a brilliant speaker, earnest, forcible, and logical, and in cases involving technicalities and complicated details I never knew any one his superior; nothing ever disconcerted him or turned him from his point.

One of the best instances I can recall of his advocacy was when he was counsel for the London Docks in an information laid against that company by the Crown. I was with Sir A. Cockburn, then Attorney-General, for the prosecution. Nothing could be heavier than the subject, or more masterly than the way with which Kelly dealt with it. He was listened to by Court and jury with rapt attention, and the reply of the Attorney-General showed how much he felt the overwhelming power of his opponent. There was another case in which I remember him, and in which a defendant had great reason to be grateful for his advocacy.

This was a charge against a city merchant of wealth and position, named Zulueta, who was tried at the Old Bailey for trafficking in slaves, the only instance I fancy in which such an offence has been charged against an English citizen. The facts proved against him were very formidable, and the view taken by Mr. Justice Maule, the judge who tried him, was unfavourable. The jury debated for a considerable time, but ultimately returned a verdict of not guilty.

Kelly was very ambitious, and his election for Ipswich was on one occasion followed by a petition which was attended by a painful incident. I knew something of the circumstances. There had been a great deal of bribery, and a person named Pilgrim had been the principal agent of Kelly's party. He had been got out of the way, of which fact Kelly must have been aware. Charles Phillipps had undertaken to conduct the case for him, but, tempted by a fee elsewhere, had deserted it and left him to manage it himself; whilst doing this he was most improperly asked by a member of the committee if he knew anything about Pilgrim, and he answered that he did not. If his counsel had been asked such a question, he could, with truth, have answered in a similar manner. Kelly ought to have declined to answer at all, but of course the inference then would have been conclusive against him. But no sophistry can justify what he did. It is well known that Sir Walter Scott constantly denied that he was the author of 'Waverley,' justifying himself by saying that when impertinent questions were put to him he had a moral right to do so; but in all these cases it is the motive that colours the act. There is, however, no doubt that the question put upon this occasion was perfectly unjustifiable. Sir Fitzroy was subsequently much persecuted by a Mr. Wason, who had been his opponent upon the above occasion, but who failed in his efforts to do him any substantial injury.

Sir Fitzroy became Chief Baron upon the resignation of Sir Frederick Pollock. He was a most painstaking and conscientious judge, but latterly became tedious, and doubtlessly interfered with the progress of business. He died at an advanced age, and up to a few days before his death, when I saw him, was in full possession of his faculties, and exhibited the greatest cheerfulness.

Kelly presided at the Central Criminal Court upon the trial of a woman named Margaret Waters, charged with murder. The case was known as the baby-farming case, and the accused was found guilty. I prosecuted upon the part of the Crown, and although the details were very shocking, and the conviction perfectly proper, I should have been glad if the jury had given a more favourable verdict, and I did what I could to obtain a commutation of the sentence of death; but Sir Fitzroy, although he had been a strenuous advocate for abolishing the punishment of death, would not interfere on this occasion, and the woman was executed.

There is no doubt, however, that a severe example was required, as the system pursued was horrible in the extreme.

Sir Fitzroy Kelly's appearance was very striking: he had a finely chiselled face and regular features, with an intelligent forehead and lively bright eyes; his manner was somewhat artificial, and his demeanour, always courteous, was of the old school. He was very hospitable, and also went out a great deal into society, where his pleasant manners and varied information made him always welcome; by his death I lost a most kind and valued friend.

I ought, I think, before concluding this sketch, to mention a trial in which he was engaged whilst at the bar, and which entailed upon him, I think unjustly, a good deal of ridicule. This was the case of Tawell, a Quaker of eminent outward respectability, who, to maintain it, had poisoned a woman with whom he was connected, under circumstances of singular atrocity.[1]

The poison indicated was prussic acid, and Sir Fitzroy accepted the suggestion of Dr. Letheby, the scientific chemist, that the odour discovered from the stomach of the deceased might have been caused by her eating apple-pips. The folly of the suggestion was due to Dr. Letheby, but I cannot approve of the judgment of the counsel in accepting it. I shall have something to say hereafter of the opinions in such matters of professional witnesses; for the present I will only observe that, whilst listened to with respect, they ought to be adopted with great caution.

After I had been called some few years to the bar, I was engaged in a case of some importance, but of no interest to the public, and I only refer to it for the purpose of introducing the name of Mr. Justice James

[1] Since these volumes were published I have been informed that Tawell, although professing to be a Quaker, had never been received into the body.

Alan Park, who presided upon that occasion, for the last time before his death. He is not unworthy of being remembered as a lawyer of the old school, with prejudices of the oldest. I am not sure whether he wore a pig-tail; he ought to have if he did not. He was singularly like his Majesty George the Third, a fact of which he was proud. He was called 'St. James's Park,' to distinguish him from the judge of the same name, who was called 'Green Park.' He was well versed in the more abstruse branches of the profession, and was generally respected by the public and the bar. In his latter days he had acquired a habit of thinking aloud, which led on one occasion to a rather amusing incident. Whilst trying an old woman upon a charge of stealing faggots, he unconsciously ejaculated, 'Why, one faggot is as like another faggot as one egg is like another egg.' The counsel defending the case heard the observation, and repeated it to the jury. 'Stop,' said Sir James—'stop; it is an intervention of Providence. This was the very thought that passed through my mind. Gentlemen' (addressing the jury), 'acquit the prisoner.'

I cannot resist telling a story, although it does not say much for the decorum of the old Midland Circuit, or of the eminent lawyers who practised upon it in those days. Serjeants were then an institution, and the old Midland boasted of many most learned and eminent ones: Goulburn, Clark, Vaughan, Adams, Hayes, are no mean names, and were all of this rank; but those were times when even serjeants were not always distinguished for sobriety, and it so happened that upon one particular evening much conviviality had been indulged in, the merry party being congregated at an hotel where the judge, Sir James Alan Park, was staying. One of the body had escaped early, and was supposed to have gone to bed, contrary to all circuit rules; it was determined to seek him, and the whole party, with as much steadiness as they could preserve, entered what they supposed to be his bed-room, and jerked the clothes off the bed of its sleeping occupant. Imagine their horror when they were confronted with the venerable countenance of the judge.

Their disappearance was quickly made, and grave deliberations were entered into as to what was to be done, and it was determined that Serjeant Goulburn, a great favourite and friend of his lordship, should explain and apologise. Accordingly, next morning, with no small trepidation, he proceeded to do so, stating whom it was intended to have awakened. 'No, no,' said Sir James, shaking his head, 'brother Goulburn, it was no mistake, for I heard my brother Adams say, "Let us unearth the old fox."'

Many other tales are told of the merry days of a circuit that nevertheless produced some of the brightest ornaments of our profession, and upon whose records are inscribed names that will never perish—those of Copley and Denman.

POSTSCRIPT.

Tawell, whose execution for murder I have referred to in this chapter, although professedly a Quaker, was not a member of the Society of Friends. He was always distrusted by that body, having been mixed up with transactions of a disreputable character upon former occasions.

CHAPTER XIII.

MR. BARON PARKE.

THE learned judge who obtained the sobriquet of Green Park, to distinguish him from Mr. Justice James Alan Park, was one of the Barons of the Exchequer, and in my opinion no man ever held a place upon the bench with greater honour to himself and benefit to the public. Undoubtedly he had his defects, but in the higher attributes of his office he has never been surpassed.

Much of his character was reflected upon his countenance, which exhibited great power and intelligence. Upon the bench his deportment was grave without being in the slightest degree pompous. He paid the most profound attention to the proceedings, never exhibited signs of impatience, was courteous to every one alike, and would now and then go out of his way to say a kindly word of encouragement to a beginner. He was admitted to be a learned and accomplished lawyer, although accused of yielding his mind too much to the subtleties of the profession. He loved the law, and probably, like lovers of more material things, could see no fault in the object of his love. His tendency to uphold technical views gave rise to a very clever squib by the late Mr. Justice Hayes, in which the spirit of the baron is supposed to arrive in Hades, where, instead of receiving the applause that he expected from admiring ghosts, he is mobbed by several of them, who had been obliged to quit their earthly tenements before he had settled a point really immaterial to their respective claims.

When late one day at a party, he told a lady of my acquaintance that he could not tear himself away from a beautiful demurrer. His fondness for fresh air will long be remembered by those engaged in some of the trials over which he presided. On the coldest day in the early spring he insisted upon every window of the court being open, and the jury, each member with a different coloured handkerchief over his head, a shivering sheriff, and despairing Ordinary presented a sufficiently comical scene to those not too frozen to be amused by it. He was occasionally in the habit of sitting until late in the evening, which I am obliged to say I cannot altogether excuse, as very few of those engaged in a cause had equal powers of endurance with himself. He suffered fearfully from gout, but this never affected his temper or impaired his faculties. Upon his retirement from the bench he was created a life peer, but objections being taken to the power of the Crown to establish such an office, he received a peerage in the usual way, and was called up to the House of Lords under the title of Baron Wensleydale, and here he assisted most usefully upon the hearing of appeals. He might be seen of an afternoon wending his way to the House upon a roan cob, as grave and respectable in its deportment as its rider. He did not survive his promotion very long, and, leaving no male issue, the title became extinct.

Baron Parke presided in two cases on the Home Circuit in which I was engaged to defend the prisoners. They were both charges of murder; one was tried at Chelmsford, and the other at Lewes. I look back to them with considerable interest. They were the first in which I was counsel and where the life of a client was involved;

and I think that the circumstances of both of them were such as to render them worth relating.

In the first case, a young woman of somewhat prepossessing appearance was charged with poisoning her husband. They were people in a humble class of life, and it was suggested that she had committed the act to obtain possession of money from a burial fund, and also that she was on terms of improper intimacy with a young man in the neighbourhood.

The solicitor instructing me was vehement in expressing belief in his client's innocence. I was of a different opinion. He, acting upon his belief, desired that certain witnesses should be called. I, governed by my convictions, absolutely refused to do so, offering at the same time to return my brief. This, however, was refused, and I was left to exercise my own responsibility. The above question frequently arises, and some counsel have considered themselves bound to obey the wishes of the solicitor. There is no doubt that this is the safest course for the advocate, for if he does otherwise and the result is adverse, he is likely to be much blamed, and the solicitor also is exposed to disagreeable comments; but I hold, and have always acted upon the opinion, that the client retains counsel's judgment, which he has no right to yield to the wishes or opinions of any one else. He is bound, if required, to return his brief, but if he acts against his own convictions he sacrifices, I think, his duty as an advocate. When the case came on, another incident occurred in which again I was called upon to exercise my view against the wishes of the solicitor. He desired that I should challenge one of the jurymen, but, not giving what I thought were valid grounds, I refused to do so, thinking then, and I have no reason since for considering otherwise, that using this privilege produces an unfavourable effect, and that it ought never to be exercised except upon very substantial grounds.

I do not propose to go through the details of the trial. It is sufficient to say that a minute quantity of arsenic was discovered in the body of the deceased, which in the defence I accounted for by the suggestion that poison had been used carelessly for the destruction of rats. Mr. Baron Parke summed up not unfavourably to the prisoner, dwelling pointedly upon the small quantity of arsenic found in the body, and the jury without much hesitation acquitted her, and, oddly enough, the juryman, whom it was suggested I should challenge, showed himself strongly in her favour throughout the trial. Dr. Taylor, the professor of chemistry, and an experienced witness, had proved the presence of arsenic, and, as I imagine, to the great disappointment of my solicitor, who desired a severe cross-examination, I did not ask him a single question. He was sitting on the bench and near the judge, who, after he had summed up and before the verdict was pronounced, remarked to him that he was surprised at the small amount of arsenic found; upon which Taylor said that if he had been asked the question he should have proved that it indicated, under the circumstances detailed in evidence, that a very large quantity had been taken.

The professor had learnt never to volunteer evidence, and the counsel for the prosecution had omitted to put the necessary question. Mr. Baron Parke, having learnt the circumstance by accidental means, did not feel warranted in using the information, and I had my first lesson in the art of 'silent cross-examination.'

Some years after, at the Central Criminal Court, I was engaged in an unimportant trial, the prosecutrix of which was a comely middle-aged woman. The officer in the case told me that she was my old Chelmsford client. She had married her former lover, and they were keeping a public-house in the east end of London, under other names, and bore highly respectable characters.

On the outskirts of the town of Hastings, at the time of the occurrences I am about to relate—a time that my readers may guess when I tell them the railway had not extended beyond Tunbridge—there lived in a detached residence an elderly couple of respectable position. Their establishment consisted of two maid-servants and a housekeeper, who had for many years been a valued and trusted servant. A man whom we will call Smith—his real name has escaped my memory—had been footman, but had left some weeks before. It was upon a certain Sunday at this date that, according to their usual custom, the master and mistress and the two maid-servants had gone to morning church, leaving the house in charge of the housekeeper. Upon their return, shortly before one o'clock, they found the old lady weltering in her blood, barbarously murdered. Plunder had evidently been the object, as many articles were missing, and the poor creature had probably met her fate endeavouring to protect the property of her employers.

A reward was offered for the discovery of the murderer, and in the result Smith was apprehended and ultimately tried at the Lewes assizes before Mr. Baron Parke, and I was retained for and defended him.

It appeared that upon the Saturday afternoon preceding the murder he had been met in London by an acquaintance, to whom he had applied for the loan of some small sum of money. He told this person that he was going to return to Hastings, and at about half-past eleven o'clock on the Sunday morning he passed through a turnpike gate upon the outskirts of the town, and near to the house where the crime was afterwards committed. He was well known to the turnpike man, who proved this fact, and no doubt was thrown upon the accuracy of these witnesses. The subsequent evidence, if true, was conclusive of his guilt, and yet partly through error and mismanagement by the police, and partly through falsehood and exaggeration introduced by the witnesses in hopes of the reward, it crumbled to pieces, and I obtained an acquittal with the entire concurrence of the judge, although neither he nor I had the slightest doubt of the prisoner's guilt.

The first witness called was a cobbler, of a religious turn of mind. He swore that he was taking home a pair of boots to a customer, and being ashamed to be seen pursuing carnal avocations on the Lord's day he had gone through some fields behind the house where the murder took place, and saw the prisoner entering by the back way. Under cross-examination he speedily came to grief. No one in court could doubt that his evidence was utterly false. He could not tell who his customer was, and as for the boots they were perfectly mythical, and he was obliged to admit that he had been very diligent in his inquiries about the reward.

The stolen property was found under a hedge, concealed in a pocket-handkerchief, which I have no doubt whatever belonged to the prisoner, and one of the maid-servants swore that she had seen him using it when formerly he had been her fellow-servant, but, by way of making her evidence more conclusive, pointed to a hole which she declared she noticed at that time. A washer-woman from London was called also to speak to it. She had washed it after he had left the service, and she swore positively that there was no hole in it when in her possession. Footsteps, identified by the police as the prisoner's, were said to have been discovered near the place where the property was found, but the gravest doubt was thrown upon this evidence by a riding-master, who declared that after the articles must have been deposited where they were found, and before the discovery, there had been a storm which, to use his own expression, would have washed out the hoof-marks of a horse; in truth, the whole of the evidence was tainted by the existence of a promised reward.

The discrepancies which were patent, and the undoubted falsehood told by the cobbler, were sufficient, in themselves, to wreck the case; but another portion of the evidence produced failed in so singular a manner, that anything like a conviction was rendered impossible.

The prosecution undertook to prove that the prisoner was at a village between Tunbridge and Hastings called Robertsbridge on the night before the murder. This proof was obviously superfluous, as the evidence of the turnpike man was undisputed, and brought the prisoner conclusively upon the spot of the murder. But this endeavour gave rise to the most dramatic scene I ever witnessed in a court of justice. The postman of Robertsbridge swore positively to having met him, and, noticing that he was looking tired, invited him to come to a public-house and take a glass of ale; that he did so, and remained for some half-hour talking to him and three other persons, who corroborated this statement. None of them had the slightest doubt of his identity. Nor were they shaken by cross-examination. They not only recognised his person, but, having heard him speak before the magistrate, stated that they remembered the tone of his voice. At my request a person was placed in the dock beside him. The postman was desired to look at the two then standing together. He trembled, turned ghastly pale, and I thought he would have fainted. The excitement in court was intense, and a pin might have been heard to drop. The likeness between the two men was marvellous; the postman looked and looked again; at last he gasped out, 'I do not know which is the man.' And, in fact, he had been mistaken; it was incontrovertibly shown that the man I produced was the person whom the postman had met. He had come down by the same train as the prisoner, and was on the way to Hastings at the time he was met at Robertsbridge. He had not appeared at the preliminary proceedings, not wishing, for family reasons, that his journey to and from London should be known. Thinking, however, that his silence might endanger the life of a fellow-creature, he had communicated with the prisoner's solicitor. Either the police knew of his existence, in which case the Robertsbridge witnesses ought never to have been produced, or they must have been guilty of gross negligence if they did not.

I have since endeavoured to find out what had become of the accused man after his acquittal. I heard that for a short time he had been guard to a coach, but could learn nothing of his subsequent career. The learned Baron had summed up the case with his usual clearness and impartiality. The jury did not debate for five minutes, and to illustrate a habit of the learned judge, to which I have already alluded, when they were pronouncing the verdict of 'not guilty' a neighbouring clock was tolling the hour of midnight.

POSTSCRIPT.

The juries in both the cases recorded in the above chapter exhibited the most untiring attention, and this is a characteristic of this tribunal in cases involving serious issues, whether criminal or civil. There seems at the present time a disposition to undervalue it in legal proceedings, and a distinction is drawn between criminal and civil cases; but if they are useful and necessary, as seems to be admitted in the latter, I cannot see why they should be dispensed with in the former: in both, their function is to deal with facts. The result, no doubt, must greatly depend upon the judge, whose duty it is to preside and, by his technical knowledge and experience, bring the facts clearly before the jury; and I do not think that this tribunal is always to be blamed for what may sometimes be deemed an absurd and inconsistent conclusion.

CHAPTER XIV.

IMPRESSIONS OF SWITZERLAND AND HOMBURG.

MY readers will have discovered by this time, if I had not already told them, that whilst I pledge myself to the substantial accuracy of the facts I relate, I possess but little method in stating them. I rarely give dates, and make no attempt at chronological order; all I seek is to reproduce impressions that were made upon me at the time of the occurrences to which they refer, and my opinions and thoughts upon them for whatever they may be worth, and thus, in defiance of all order, I travel from grave to trivial, and from matters of business to those merely of pleasure.

My last chapter might have been extracted from the 'Newgate Calendar.' I will now ask my readers to image a certain long vacation, and, quitting the region of crime, to accompany me upon a very unpretending excursion to what I have always thought the most beautiful of lands. My passport has been obtained, and I have without a sign of regret bidden adieu for the present to forensic costume, and am attired for foreign travel. Switzerland is my goal, and there I expect to meet my old friend Albert Smith; it is the year after he has taken possession of Mont Blanc, and has laid the foundation of fortune which, up to this time, had been coy to no unworthy courtship. For he was a man of genius, and, if inferior to Thackeray and Dickens, he was by no means wanting in the descriptive powers of the latter author. He possessed much sense of humour, and was capable of writing a story that maintained a strong interest throughout with the reader. As a companion he was full of fun, and bubbled over with high spirits. He had passed some years of his early life in Paris in the study of medicine, and could record many an amusing scene of the Quartier Latin. He spoke French fluently, and the good-looking, fair-haired young Englishman must have been a favoured partner at the dances, when grisettes, now a departed class, after the honest labour of the day, indulged in much joyousness without coarseness or crime.

One of his early productions was a novel called 'Mr. Ledbury's Tour.' It was extremely entertaining from the beginning to the end; the first volume contains some powerful writing; it also gives the account of an incident which happened when I was in his company. We were returning from some place of amusement, and were walking on the banks of the Seine close to the Pont-Neuf, when we were startled by a splash. We saw a body in the stream about the centre under the bridge—only for a moment, and then the dark waters closed over it. On the following day the lifeless body of a good-looking young man, apparently English, was stretched out upon the slab of the Morgue. His dress betokened that he was of the better class. I never learned any of the facts connected with the catastrophe, and do not know whether the account of the gambling-house scene introduced into 'Mr. Ledbury's Tour' has been founded upon any knowledge subsequently obtained of this unfortunate man's history.

I had engaged to meet my friend at Geneva, but will commence my tour at that well-known refuge for travellers, the Trois Rois at Basle. Fancy that I am standing in its spacious hall, awaiting the decision of a grave official as to whether I shall be allowed to enter farther within its precincts. I am at last invited to climb a number of stairs, fit preparation for mountain travel, and am assigned a few feet of uncarpeted floor with a tiny bed, but sheets very tempting in their whiteness. I hear a rushing noise, and looking out of the little window of my room I see for the first time the broad expanse of the Rhine hastening upon its downward voyage to the ocean.

It was long before I could tear myself from the view of the mighty river. It was an autumn evening, and a moon nearly at its full was silvering the waters as they careered along, whilst small lights began to show themselves from the gabled buildings on the opposite side, and, when I cast my eyes up the stream, the hills but dimly seen furnished the imagination with a glorious promise of beauty and grandeur.

I descend into the well-known *salon*. The *table d'hôte* is over, and the tables are laid out for tea; everything looks fresh. Honey, the prominent feature of the tea-table, tempts to a beverage of which the innocence is in keeping with the purity of the scene.

There is a balcony outside running the entire length of the room ; it is here that Anthony Trollope has fixed the locality of one of his charming love-scenes. And where could be found a better ? The warm soft feeling of an early autumn evening, the moon upon the waters, the music of the stream—all these, perchance, as new sensations as the words of a first love whispered in their presence.

Let us now go to the front of the hotel, where in those days was witnessed a sight that will never be seen there again—a large open space filled with carriages of every description, and coachmen in every guise, the tinkling of bells, and now and again the loud cracking of whips, which secure a space for travelling-carriages to dash up to the door, where an obsequious porter receives the inmates. The conveyances waiting around have deposited their freights, and their drivers are looking out for the chance of a party returning to the localities to which they respectively belong.

Now all is changed. The railway disgorges its hundreds at fixed times. The only vehicles to be seen are the unromantic omnibuses, and a miscellaneous crowd hustle their way into the hotel, their object apparently being to visit the greatest number of places in the shortest possible period; the most earnest inquiries generally being about the time that the next train will start.

The Rhine still pursues its downward course from the mountains. The Trois Rois stands where it did, the same official disposes of the human mass, but instead of the groups that one remembers dwelling with newly awakened sensations of pleasure at a beautiful and novel scene, and viewing with interest the curiosities of the country which ornament the saloons, there appears to have sprung up a feeling of indifference. 'Move on, move on,' seems to be the cry. The crack of the postilion's whip and the jingling bells of the horses are no longer heard; they have been superseded by the scream of the steam engine, and the traveller, hot and almost suffocated by the closeness of the railway carriage, passes in a semi-comatose state through the most lovely and glorious of Nature's works. From Basle I went to Zurich, sharing a carriage with two travellers whom I accidentally met. A charming drive it was; it is now accomplished by train. And upon this journey it was that for the first time a range of snow-clad mountains presented themselves to my wondering eyes, a sight, indeed, that surpassed everything that my imagination had pictured. From Zurich I hastened on to Geneva, where, at one of the hotels in the town—the palaces since built did not then exist—I met my friend Albert Smith and his brother Arthur, and with them innocently amused myself by catching small fish and admiring the exquisite scenery of the lake. After a day or two I accompanied them to Chamouni, where I profited by the celebrity that they had acquired. It is sad to think that none of us will ever hear again the story told by Albert of his ascent of the great mountain. His pleasant voice and manner and really graphic description of the incidents gave it a great charm, and his introduction, under the title of 'Galignani's Messenger,' of a topical song, was a great success. The prettily ornamented room at the Egyptian Hall was nightly filled, and the amusement afforded was of a kind that offered no impediment to the presence of the most strait-laced of moralists.

In returning from Geneva I passed over the Jura, one of the most lovely ranges of mountains in Switzerland, now lost to the traveller in consequence of the railway. From the banquette of the diligence each turn of the road presented a new scene of beauty to its occupier. Having reached Dijon, at which place we stopped, the journey home was shortly accomplished. I cannot imagine that the impression made by this my first visit to Switzerland will ever be effaced.

A very different place, dependent more upon art than natural beauty, although by no means deficient in the latter quality, was Homburg. Sparkling it was and brilliant when I first knew it, which was a long time ago. Its beauties and its naughtinesses have been often described.

How joyous was the scene it presented in the early morning, and who would guess that any of the gaily dressed throng crowding round the springs were invalids in search of health! Everything was there that could enliven. The crisp air, through which vibrated the lively strains of music, gave freshness to the charms of the scene. What a place for a gossip, or for a flirtation! Dangerous, I admit, for under such influences words may be spoken not easily, if repented, to be recalled. Those seats with honeysuckles and jasmine twining around the trellis-work have, I will venture to say, been the scene of many a vow breathed, and many a soft response. Then the parade, shaded on each side by trees, was crowded with company exchanging friendly salutes as they sauntered from one spring to the other. The visitors on the occasion I am now thinking of were principally English, most of them well known in the world of fame and fashion. I could mention the names of many ladies, but it would be invidious to select among so much that was beautiful in the fair sex any particular example.

Amongst the men one figure might every morning be seen striding manfully along, battling gallantly with an old enemy, the gout, recognising with a kindly nod and smile those whom he knew—and they were many, for with one of the known characteristics of his family he never forgot a face. This was the Duke of Cambridge, who annually sought these springs, and was always an object of interest to his fellow-countrymen. Another visitor, seen also frequently leaning upon a gentleman's arm and pacing slowly up and down, was the Grand Duke of Mecklenburg Strelitz, the blind prince, his great calamity making him the object of compassion, whilst the courage with which he bore it obtained for him feelings of admiration and respect. It was my great privilege to join some small parties in which he entertained many affectionate friends, and in the course of which he displayed qualities proving that his grievous calamity had in no respect impaired his power of feeling as well of imparting intellectual enjoyment. It was during this visit to Homburg that I had the honour of being introduced to his Royal Highness the Prince of Wales, from whom since that time I have met with many instances of kindly feeling. In the evening, after the cafés and hotels had, in some instances, furnished reasonably good dinners, a different scene was presented in another locality. On a terrace outside the conversation rooms were numerous tables, seated at which the visitors were enjoying coffee, ices, and no small quantity of beer. They were composed of all ranks, ladies of the highest, in costumes of exquisite taste, mingling with the peasantry from the surrounding country, decked in their village finery; and mixing amongst the crowd was to be met the flashily dressed tradesman from Frankfort, and the unlucky gambler who had just lost his last napoleon. A fine band played a succession of popular airs, and thus the evening afforded a fund of amusement to those content to enjoy the natural beauties of the place and the means of enhancing them so liberally supplied by the proprietor of the gambling establishment. There were occasional operas, at which Patti delighted the visitors, and the drives in the surrounding woods afforded both health and pleasure in the daytime to those who preferred to seek them to the fascinations presented in the gorgeous saloons of the establishment. It was in these that the naughtinesses prevailed. I wish I was able to speak of them with becoming reprobation, but prefer to leave this office to others better qualified to do so.

No doubt all the evil passions which are supposed to

emanate from a certain place were present at the gambling tables, but there was such an air of decorum that they were concealed from an ordinary observer. A serious lady of my acquaintance called it a feast of Satan; but the attendants upon the banquet were so decently clad, and conducted themselves so quietly, and looked altogether so very respectable, that it was difficult to take them for that gentleman's satellites. Still, the word of the moralist went forth: Homburg was purified and gambling driven into holes and corners where there is no supervision to prevent the worst of frauds, or else it has a decent coat put on and is called speculation.

I wonder whether Monsieur Blanc in his splendid palaces, with his *refaits* and zeros, has broken more hearts and disseminated more ruin than that scrupulously washed and dressed gentleman whom on a Sunday you may see walking so decorously to church, who occupies two dirty rooms in Throgmorton Street, and is a shareholder in that mighty gambling house the Stock Exchange.

Before bidding adieu to Homburg it is only right to say that everything was conducted with perfect fairness. No imputation to the contrary has ever been suggested. Every one knew or might have known the chances secured to the tables. No one could fail to see around him, in the amusements and luxuries provided by the proprietor for the visitors, proof of the enormous profits he must be realising; and, independently of the advantages incident to the tables, the most important of which was the limit that players were restricted to, and which almost without an exception could beat the capitalist, whilst the funds of the bank defeated the smaller speculators—it really was a machine working uninfluenced by passion or feeling against those who were operated upon intensely by both.

Most of the *habitués* practised a system, but I never

yet knew of a case in which it succeeded for any length of time, although I have heard and known of large sums won by strokes of luck where the player has succeeded without any pretence to science or calculation. Around the table, and wandering listlessly about the rooms, might be seen shabbily dressed individuals, apparently without an object on earth: they are ruined gamblers—the passion still strong upon them, the means of gratifying it departed. You might sometimes see one of these individuals move stealthily up to an apparent novice, and suggest to him that for a few florins he could teach him an invaluable mode of play. If the novice listens to him he will explain the mere accident which prevented his own success. Perhaps he obtains what would get him one decent meal, but with flushed face he creeps to the roulette table, puts the piece upon his favourite number, with a haggard smile upon his face sees it swept off by the croupier, and steals back penniless and starving, to continue his hopeless wanderings.

An observer might also notice certain ladies who, whatever might be their character, are quiet and unobtrusive. When first seen they shine with much jewellery: this from day to day diminishes, and finally the whole has disappeared.

I do not fail to remember that Mr. Goldsmidt, the obliging banker, in High Street, had always some diamonds that he could sell you, 'a very great bargain.'

The countenances of the visitors departing from Homburg are graver than they were when starting to reach it. It is to be hoped that enough remains in their pockets to secure a meal at the Hôtel de Russie at Frankfort, which, if anything can do it, will restore their cheerfulness. Stories are told of the hotel keepers at Homburg having some specific by which they find out when their customers are ruined, and furnish them with means to take their unlucky carcases to some other locality, where they may dispose of them as they please.

Upon one occasion I must own to having been guilty of a very unjustifiable ruse to get possession of a seat at the rouge-et-noir table. It was occupied by a lady well known at the springs: she was of the highest respectability, and although she could not resist the temptation of play, she indulged in it upon thoroughly economic principles, making three or four crown pieces last for a considerable time. She was not young, she was not beautiful, and was very jealous of her husband, which was a fact pretty notorious. Well, there, upon one occasion, she was sitting staking a crown about every half-hour, and, having five crowns left, she had evidently capital enough upon this system to last the entire day. I looked around; no vacancy seemed likely to be made by other players, and so it occurred to me, moved, as we say in the criminal courts, by the instigation of the devil, to say to a friend, loud enough for her to hear, 'I wonder who that pretty girl is that Charlie —— is flirting with on the parade,' naming her spouse. The legs of her chair grated upon the ground as it was drawn rapidly back; the five crowns were swept together and deposited in her reticule, and hastily and anxiously the lady departed. I trust I may be forgiven, and I am glad to say that I heard of no domestic calamity.

One other little incident I cannot forbear relating. There was a well-known frequenter of the rooms—I will furnish her with a fancy name. Mrs. Delamere was an elderly female, with a countenance that did not attract, and who certainly could not be charged with using any meretricious ornament. She took her seat daily at the roulette table: with much diving into a bag she would produce her capital, six or seven florins being apparently its limit. She secured a chair early, and kept it resolutely against all comers, watching the chances of the table. The incident I am about to relate will show what she considered them to be. One day there entered the rooms a lady of a type very different from that of the ordinary frequenters. She was clad in a sober dark dress, almost quaker-like in its neatness. A bonnet that at once established the respectability of its wearer surmounted a middle-aged and not unpleasing countenance. The stranger seemed fascinated by the tables; she approached them, walked round them, peeped over the players' heads, and after an evident inward struggle placed a napoleon upon a number immediately in front of Mrs. Delamere. Round went the wheel, and to that number thirty-five napoleons were pushed by the croupier. These Mrs. Delamere immediately clutched. The lady to whom they belonged mildly expostulated, saying they were hers. 'Yours!' yelled Mrs. D., looking her victim sternly in the face. 'Don't try that game with me—this is not the first time you have attempted it.' The lady shrank back abashed, and Mrs. Delamere thus became an instrument in the hands of Providence to check, at its very outset, a tendency to the debasing vice of gambling in a fellow-creature.

Homburg is still charming, and still attracts. The springs are, as formerly, crowded in the morning, and on my last visit I recognised many old faces. The band still played; the same mixed crowd was to be seen in the evening; and it certainly had this advantage, to those who studied economy but were unable to resist temptation, that it was much cheaper than in former days.

At Monaco there still exists an establishment in which in one of the most lovely spots in the world, rouge-et-noir and roulette are played with every circumstance of outward decorum. It is said that the prince of the country derives his principal revenue from the proprietors. Lately a movement has been got up by certain English sojourners to procure their expulsion. A friend of mine, who possesses a very beautiful villa in the neighbourhood, was solicited the other day by another resident to sign a memorial for this purpose, but as he considered that those who did not like it might keep away, and that it was pure impertinence to interfere with the arrangements of a foreign place, he absolutely declined. His friend exhausted every argument upon the score of morals without avail, and, making a last effort, he pointed out how much it would increase the value of their property. I should be very sorry to treat with disrespect the conscientious scruples of any class, and, if pressure comes from the natives of a country to abolish an institution, it ought to be treated with consideration; but really the opinions of foreigners who might find plenty of improprieties in their own country to reform, are, in my humble judgment, worthy not only of no attention, but are generally the outcomings of self-interest, and signal examples of impertinence and conceit.

CHAPTER XV.

LORD CAMPBELL.

In the year 1850 Lord Denman, stricken by illness, retired from the bench. If not so profound a lawyer as some of those who had filled the office of Lord Chief Justice in former years, he possessed the highest qualities of a great judge, and the necessity for his retirement occasioned general regret, and a more complete contrast can scarcely be imagined than that presented between him and his successor, Lord Campbell. The high-minded feeling and heartfelt courtesy of the one was replaced by a superficial veneer of forced politeness, that concealed the natural bad taste and peevish temper of the other.

I have indicated in former pages the importance I attach to the demeanour of a judge when upon the bench. He has no excuse for discourtesy, he naturally commands the respect and consideration of all present. Fractiousness and impatience seriously impair his usefulness. They produce nervousness in counsel of inexperience, who ought to be encouraged, if not out of kindness to themselves, for the sake of those to whom it is the duty of the judge to see, to the best of his power, that justice is done. Lord Campbell was a learned and skilled lawyer, but his manner was harsh and irritable. He had no compassion for weakness. He crushed where he ought to have striven to raise. It is of no value for a sufferer to be told, even if it be the fact, that under an offensive demeanour there exist a kind heart and amiable disposition; such knowledge affords no comfort to a young barrister who has been snubbed before his first client and the entire court. Lord Campbell ought to have had mercy, for he was by no means himself insensible to applause, and sometimes sought it by not very dignified means. His Life, unlike the Lives of those whose history he has written, has been delivered to posterity by himself, and he escaped the death-pang that others, not without reason, apprehended from his undertaking their biography.

He undoubtedly was a consistent partisan, and his views were enlarged and liberal upon the great political subjects with which he had to deal; at the same time it must be admitted that the services he performed met with sufficiently substantial rewards, and his Diaries show that he pursued his material interests with skill and unflagging perseverance. He obtained a peerage for his wife as a consideration for remaining Attorney-General at a time when his resignation of that office would have been of serious inconvenience to the Ministry; and when, in 1841, the Government to which he was attached was tottering, he created a scandal by securing to himself the appointment of Irish Lord Chancellor and a peerage. His services in that capacity lasted about a fortnight—a fact that the long-headed Scotchman must have foreseen. When the vacancy occurred in the Chief Justiceship, it was only proper that he should obtain a post which not only his services but his great legal attainments fully entitled him to. And of his subsequent appointment as Chancellor there is no reason to complain. I do not know whether he was popular with the equity bar, or what judgment was formed of his ability in that branch of the law, but he certainly possessed the merit of unwearying industry, and exhibited upon all occasions a conscientious endeavour to make himself master of his subject.

His Lives of the Chancellors and Chief Justices are pleasant and readable books, and exhibit his love for work, although he by no means disdained to avail himself of the labours of others, which I do not remember that he ever acknowledged. I heard Charles Phillipps tell a story of having been talking to Lord Brougham at the House of Lords, when he pointed out to him an elderly female in a poke bonnet standing at the bar. 'Do you see,' said he to Phillipps, 'the old lady standing there? She is Miss Strickland. She is waiting to reproach Campbell with his literary larcenies. He will escape by the back way.' It appears, however, from an extract that I insert from his Diary, that he was not successful in doing so. The following is his account of, I presume, the occurrence related by Phillipps:—

'My exploit in the House of Lords last night was introducing myself to Miss Strickland, authoress of the "Lives of the Queens of England," who has been writing a violent letter against me in the newspapers. After I had conversed with her for half an hour, she exclaimed, "Well, Lord Campbell, I do declare you are the most amiable man I ever met with." I thought Lord Brougham would have died with envy when I told him the result of my interview; and Ellenborough, who was sitting by, rubbed his hands in admiration. Brougham had thrown me a note across the table saying, "Do you know that your friend Miss Strickland is come to hear you?"'

I suspect that, if it had been possible to have heard Lord Brougham's account of the interview, if indeed he witnessed it, more amusement would have been afforded to the reader than that transmitted to posterity by the most amiable man Miss Strickland ever knew.

Whilst he was at the bar, I had not many opportunities of hearing Campbell. He was, beyond doubt, a very skilful advocate. His manner was dry and not pleasing, but he commanded attention, possessed great power and force, and was, I should think, with rare exceptions, thoroughly judicious. In strictly legal arguments few men at the bar surpassed him, although Kelly was equally earnest and as well versed in legal subtleties; Follett, with certainly equal attainments, possessed a more fascinating voice and manner.

I have already given some account of the case of Norton *v.* Lord Melbourne, of the result of which Lord Campbell was very proud; but he has succeeded in many cases of far greater difficulty, though not of such public interest.

There was another case in which he was engaged, which also attracted a great deal of attention, and it so happened that my old master, the General, as Watson was always called, was engaged in it. The day before it came on I was dining with him, and the following morning I accompanied him to the Court of Queen's Bench, where it was tried before Lord Denman. It was an action brought by a Lord de Ros against a gentleman named Cumming for defamation, and Watson was with Thesiger and Alexander for the defence. It arose out of play transactions at different clubs, and it was alleged that Lord de Ros had been habitually guilty of cheating. The court was crowded to the ceiling, and I remember Lord Lyndhurst, amongst many other gentlemen, being upon the bench, taking apparently a great interest in the trial.

The story was a very strange one. Lord de Ros was a man of high family, I believe Senior Baron, and was not only a popular man, but wealthy and liberal in the ordinary transactions of every-day life, and a member of several of the best clubs in London and elsewhere. There was no doubt that, long before the matter was brought to an issue, whispers had circulated imputing to his lordship unfair practices. He had received a well-meant although anonymous communication advising him to desist from play, and a paragraph charging him broadly with cheating had appeared in a newspaper. Ultimately certain gentlemen, amongst whom was Mr. Cumming, undertook the responsibility of the charge, upon which the action was brought against the latter gentleman by Lord de Ros for slander. The transactions attributed were alleged to have occurred at a club at Brighton, the Travellers' in Pall Mall, and more markedly at a proprietary club that was then in existence, and kept by a gentleman named Graham, from whom it took its name, and of which many distinguished men, including Lord de Ros, were members.

His lordship was an excellent whist player, and considered quite a match for the finest of the day. Nevertheless, it was asserted that he resorted to an elaborate trick to obtain an unfair advantage. I will endeavour to explain its nature, but it is difficult to do so clearly. It consisted in a reversal of the cut, that is to say, that after the cards had been cut to the dealer he would contrive, by an act of legerdemain, to replace the last card, which ought of course to have gone amongst the other cards, into its original position at the bottom of the pack. It is obvious that for the purpose of rendering this trick of benefit to the dealer he must have acquired a knowledge of what the card so replaced was. And it was said that for this purpose Lord de Ros contrived to mark certain court cards in such a manner as to be able to distinguish them and secure the presence of one of them at the bottom of the pack when he presented it to his adversary to be cut.

It is really incredible that any sane man should have conducted his proceedings with such recklessness as he did, and one cannot help thinking of the saying, 'Quem Deus vult perdere prius dementat.'

The witnesses examined against him had noticed that when about to deal he endeavoured to distract attention by coughing, an infirmity that did not trouble him at other times, and one of them, Sir William Ingelby, declared that he did not remember an instance of his dealing without turning up a king or an ace; the cards with which he played were afterwards examined and found to be marked, apparently with the thumb nail. Colonel Anson, George Payne, and Lord Henry Bentinck were amongst the witnesses deposing to having noticed Lord de Ros in his mode of dealing.

These gentlemen were amongst the finest players of the day, and he must have known that they were looking on whilst he was transposing the cards, which adds to his extraordinary folly, if it does not almost prove him to have been insane.

Sir John Campbell, who with Sir William Follett and Mr. Wightman appeared for Lord de Ros, made a long, energetic, and powerful speech, showing his capacity in a hopeless case. I cannot, however, think that a suggestion he made of conspiracy upon the part of the gentlemen called could be either prudent or justifiable, as it was clear that they had all come forward most unwillingly. After an anxious and thoroughly impartial charge by the Lord Chief Justice, the jury, without hesitation, found the only possible verdict, for the defendant.

The trick was not a new one, and was known by the name of *sauter la coupe*, and Sir William Ingelby excited much laughter by undertaking with a pack of cards to show the mode in which it was performed, and, fortunately for his reputation, he made a very clumsy exhibition of it. Sir John Campbell also caused a good deal of fun by inadvertently describing it as *couper la saute.* An anecdote was related in connection with this case of a young member of the club who had noticed Lord de Ros performing this trick, asking an older member what he ought to do. 'Bet upon him,' was the advice given, of course in a joke.

An endeavour was made to show that Lord de Ros had some physical infirmity connected with the muscles of the hand, which would have prevented his manipulating the cards in the manner described, and for this purpose the eminent surgeon, Mr. Lawrence, was called, but did not succeed in substantiating this view. Mr. Lawrence was a skilful surgeon, and also a literary man of great attainment. He wrote a work in early life which was said to be anti-Christian, and he lost position with the public in consequence of it. The views enunciated in it are now to be found in the common literature of the day, but in those times freethought, or rather the expression of it, met with scant favour. I frequently met Mr. Lawrence during the latter days of his life, in professional matters. He laid himself open to be a witness in cases of railway accidents, but although his appearance was greatly in his favour, and his knowledge deep and varied, he was too hasty in forming an opinion, and too dogmatic in asserting it. I always thought it dangerous to call him, and preferred his being on the opposite side.

Of Sir William Follett, who was counsel both in this and the Melbourne trial, I knew personally but very little. From what I did know I should say no man ever lived more thoroughly unaffected or with a kinder heart, and of the greatness of his attainments all were agreed. Once only, when junior to Sir Frederick Pollock, I was opposed to him. In the absence of my leader a somewhat complicated verdict was returned, and Sir William, seeing my difficulty, helped me out of it. He had never spoken to me before, or I to him. His early death was a great source of sorrow to his private friends, and a very grave one to his country.

Mr. Wightman afterwards became one of the judges of the Court of Queen's Bench, and a very efficient and useful one. He had a certain amount of dry humour, an instance of which I remember upon a trial at the Maidstone assizes. A very excellent and learned friend of mine, not however famed for his brevity, had been for some considerable time enforcing his arguments before a Kentish jury. Mr. Justice Wightman, interposing, said, 'Mr.——, you have stated that before,' and then, pausing for a moment, added, 'but you may have forgotten it, it was a very long time ago.' I have been before this judge very often, and have a very pleasant recollection of his courtesy and good humour, and his shrewdness was very formidable to a guilty client.

I only remember being present at one other case which Sir John Campbell, then Attorney-General, conducted. This was an indictment at the Central Criminal Court against a solicitor named Williams upon a charge of forging a will. Campbell was for the defence, and I followed his conduct of the case with great interest and attention, and certainly it was a fine specimen of powerful advocacy, and, against the view I had formed, it was successful. The prosecution gave rise to much subsequent litigation in our courts, which, however, as I believe, ended in the establishment of the will.

CHAPTER XVI.

CAMPBELL'S IRRITABILITY.

I HAVE not hesitated to express my opinion of Lord Campbell's demeanour upon the Bench; but his great knowledge and unwearying industry rendered him an extremely powerful common law judge. There is no doubt that a very learned man in his position may feel weariness at the occasional prolixity of counsel, but it is not less his duty to restrain the exhibition of it where the advocate is genuinely endeavouring to convey his views. The impatience occasionally exhibited by Lord Campbell took a form at times that was positively grotesque. I remember upon one occasion, during the speech of a very able counsel, now a judge, that after having shown many signs of irritability, his lordship could no longer keep his seat, but, getting up, marched up and down the bench, casting at intervals the most furious glances at the imperturbable counsel, and at last, folding his arms across his face, leant as if in absolute despair against the wall, presenting a not inconsiderable amount of back surface to the audience. A very clever caricature was drawn of him by a barrister, representing his half-dozen phases of disgust, and terminating with his dorsal exhibition.

In 1856 he presided at the Central Criminal Court upon the trial of William Palmer, upon a charge of murder. This case was peculiarly one of cold-blooded crime. Palmer was by profession a surgeon, by practice an assassin, and he was tried for poisoning a person named John Parsons Cook.

Sir Alexander Cockburn conducted the prosecution, admittedly in the very highest style of excellence. Palmer was defended by Mr. Serjeant Shee, a man of power and eloquence, and very earnest and conscientious. He was induced, and I am sure with sincere conviction, to express a personal belief that the accused was innocent, meaning, however, merely that he was not guilty of committing the crime by the agency suggested. Lord Campbell did not check or reprove him, probably having Lord Melbourne's case in his recollection, and not wishing to be reminded of it. The prosecution based their theory mainly upon the death having been caused by strychnine; which was founded upon descriptions given by different witnesses of the appearances the deceased exhibited before his death.

There were, however, circumstances that weakened this theory, and certainly antimony had also been employed. Professor Taylor was very confident upon the subject, and attributed the death solely to the former poison; and if the case had been allowed to drift into chemical refinements, serious difficulties might have arisen. Sir Benjamin Brodie would give no opinion as to the actual poison used, but declared without hesitation that he had never known a natural death attended with the appearances described. The strong good sense of Lord Campbell brushed away the merely scientific question; showed that it was not material to discover by what poison the deed had been effected; dwelt with overwhelming force upon the facts, to which, as he explained, the medical evidence was merely subsidiary, and only used for the purpose of demonstrating that the appearances presented were consistent with the means suggested. I have no doubt that Palmer was a practised poisoner, and that he had hoped to evade justice by mingling the poisons and deceiving the scientific witnesses. If this was his aim, Lord Campbell signally defeated it.

He was convicted without much hesitation, and received his doom with perfect calmness. He was a sporting man, and when the verdict was returned, wrote upon a slip of paper which he handed to his attorney, 'The riding did it,' alluding to Cockburn's speech.

Mr. Serjeant Shee had an impossible task. He was an old companion of mine upon circuit, and when Lord Denman appointed me a revising barrister I was associated with him as a colleague. He was subsequently made a judge of the Queen's Bench, the first Roman Catholic of late years appointed to that post in England, but did not survive his honours very long. He was highly esteemed and respected, especially by his brethren at the bar.

The reputation of Lord Campbell for politeness was amusingly illustrated by a remark made by the crier of the court to a friend at the commencement of this case. His lordship had said with great suavity of manner, 'Let the prisoner be accommodated with a chair.' 'He means to hang him,' said the crier.

History, it is said, repeats itself, and crime is no unimportant part of history, and will be found much the same, although in various disguises, in different generations. The motives actuating its commission, and the character of the criminal, can be clearly traced and recognised, but the modes by which the deed is accomplished vary with the period. Thus there is a close analogy between Palmer and a murderer named Thurtell, who was convicted some half-century ago. Both were called gentlemen: Thurtell, because he kept a gig; Palmer, because he kept an apothecary's shop. Both were turfmen and gamblers. In both instances the victim was a particular friend and intimate associate of the murderer; and in both, the object of the crime was to get rid of debts incurred at play or by betting. Thurtell's crime represented the coarseness of the age; Palmer's, its improved intelligence. Had the former lived in Palmer's time, instead of first shooting and then battering out the brains of Weare, he would have invited his friend to supper, and put strychnine or antimony into the apple-sauce accompanying the roast pork of which that supper consisted, and with which Thurtell and his accomplices regaled themselves after the murder.

I dare say few of this generation recollect anything about the circumstances of the case to which I have referred.

Thurtell had lost money to Weare, and got an accomplice named Probert to ask him to a cottage belonging to that person down in Hertfordshire, and he himself undertook to drive him. In a lane near their destination, Thurtell drew a pistol and shot Weare in the head; the wound not being fatal, he finished his work with the barrel of the pistol. The body was conveyed to Probert's cottage and deposited under a sofa, whilst a party, consisting of the owner of the cottage, Thurtell, a man named Hunt, and Probert's wife, had supper. The body was afterwards deposited in a pond, where it was subsequently found through the information of accomplices.

Probert and Hunt turned king's evidence. The former was subsequently hanged for what in any other person would have been treated as borrowing a horse, but the jury were only too glad to make him pay the penalty of his former crime. Hunt was transported, and I have heard was killed by the crew upon his outward voyage.

I remember two causes in which I was engaged before Lord Campbell: they were both founded upon railway accidents, and in both of them, through no fault of the judge, there was a miscarriage of justice; and although not of any great public interest, they illustrate some of the phases that present themselves, in actions of this kind, where the verdict depends not upon a question of fact, but upon the character of an admitted injury and the amount of compensation to be awarded. If such injury is outwardly apparent and none is said to exist internally, the task is not difficult, but almost in every case some occult evil is said to have occurred, sometimes without any foundation, and nearly always exaggerated, and a jury are obliged to rely upon the truthfulness of a claimant and the accuracy and sound judgment of professional men. It is somewhat unfortunate that many undoubtedly able medical men have made this class of cases a specialty, and some of these gentlemen are almost invariably selected as witnesses, and I fear quite unwittingly act too often with a spirit of partisanship.

A gentleman named Glover was the plaintiff in the first of the two cases to which I have called attention. He had been, I believe, member for Reading, and, although no external injury was apparent, it was stated that he had received a serious spinal shock, and that the result might be fatal. His appearance, however, in the witness-box did not support this idea, and his manner prejudiced his case exceedingly. It was finikin and coxcombical, and many, of whom I confess myself to have been amongst the number, thought that he was not candid in giving his evidence; and the statements of the doctors, which gave a very grave aspect to the alleged symptoms, had in consequence less weight than they deserved. Lord Campbell took an unfavourable view, and evidently thought that there was gross exaggeration. The jury, coinciding in this opinion, returned a verdict quite inadequate to the injuries if truly represented. Within three months the unfortunate gentleman, a comparatively young man, died, and it could not be doubted that his premature death resulted from the effects of the injuries he had undergone, and which had been correctly indicated by the medical men.

I have, in a former chapter, whilst considering the mode of treating witnesses, cautioned an observer against being too much biassed by appearances, not necessarily indicative of a desire to deceive, but resulting from the natural infirmities of the human mind which become developed by the nervousness of an unaccustomed position, and I have seen a thoroughly honest witness show himself from this cause in a very unfavourable light.

In the other case, tried, I believe, before the same judge, the plaintiff was brought into court apparently in a moribund state. He seemed scarcely able to articulate, and his limbs were without power or sensibility. According to the doctors, and I do not impugn their truth as to the fact, his powers of sensation had been tested by a needle, which had been inserted in his arm without his exhibiting any sign of feeling; in fact, he created general sympathy, and obtained a very large verdict amounting to many thousands. It was thought useless to move for a new trial. Within a week after the time had elapsed for doing so the plaintiff was recognised climbing Snowdon in full activity and strength, and within the twelvemonth was presented with an heir, who, thanks to his father having been so nearly killed, was likely to have something to inherit.

The manufacturing of injuries has become a regular trade amongst a low class of practitioners—men who, although utterly ignorant of the elements of their profession, have had no difficulty in learning what are the usual symptoms of a grave shock. The patient is sometimes a rogue, and deliberately misrepresents his feelings. Sometimes the nervousness that follows a railway collision leads him readily to embrace ideas suggested by questions put to him by his attendant. The doctor has probably made a bargain by which he will secure to himself a percentage upon the damages awarded by the jury, which amount, the action being against a railway company, is certain to be paid.

There is a specimen of this kind of medical man well known in our courts. When last I saw him he would not swear that he had not been the doctor in more than one hundred cases arising from railway accidents, and he certainly could not have been selected for his knowledge, as he was unable to tell the normal temperature of the human body. It is not likely that a majority of general practitioners have legitimately had half a dozen of such accidents under their care.

Lord Campbell tried the case of the British Bank Directors, charged with the falsification of accounts and of various misrepresentations with a view to defraud the public; and although greatly assisted by the opening of of Sir Frederick Thesiger, to which I have already alluded, this does not detract from the ability with which he mastered and dealt with its complicated details. His summing-up seemed to me to be conclusive of the guilt of all the defendants, although he recommended the jury to acquit one of them. They, however, were unable to realise any distinction between the different parties, and convicted them all; but whilst inflicting different terms of imprisonment upon the others, Lord Campbell did not punish the defendant in whose favour he had summed up. Speaking of this incident in his Diary, he says, 'I let one of them off with a nominal fine because he was improperly convicted.'

This was a very high-handed proceeding, and was severely commented upon, and motives not of a creditable character were suggested. I do not know whether there was, or not, any foundation for them, and therefore forbear to repeat them. The jury had throughout exhibited great intelligence, for which, before the verdict, they were highly complimented by the judge. I confess that it struck me that if the gentleman in question was entitled to be let off, the punishment of his companions could scarcely be deemed consistent with equal justice.

I shall have again to refer to Lord Campbell in his position of head of Serjeants' Inn. The last time I saw him was on the afternoon of the day preceding his death. He was then Chancellor, and had, I believe, been presiding in the Court of Chancery. He was walking sturdily towards his own residence, in apparently perfect health and vigour, and, although he had attained an advanced age, the news of his death occasioned universal astonishment. I had not heard that he had exhibited any failure of power or diminution of intellect in the performance of his onerous duties, and certainly to the last he exhibited his untiring industry.

He was, to my great satisfaction, succeeded by Sir Richard Bethell, from whom I had already received many marks of kindness, and it was by his direction (he being Attorney-General) that I had been appointed one of the counsel to conduct the prosecution of the British Bank Directors; and it was from him also that I afterwards obtained what I venture to think was a bare act of justice —a patent of precedence.

POSTSCRIPT.

I heard the following amusing anecdote in connection with an action against a railway, and, although the facts were not within my knowledge, I have no doubt of their truth. A stockbroker of the Jewish persuasion, equally famous for his wealth and benevolence, assisted a member of the same persuasion with the funds necessary to carry on an action. This personage was carried into court, a melancholy object, unable to walk, and destined to be a cripple to the end of his days. He obtained very large damages. Not very long afterwards he walked into his benefactor's office, apparently in excellent health and spirits, to employ him in investing the damages.

The very eminent surgeon Mr. Erichsen has published a work upon railway accidents, detailing the symptoms that may be expected to be exhibited in them. This I believe to be, amongst that class of practitioners whom I have described, a kind of *Vade mecum*, and probably comprises their entire law library.

CHAPTER XVII.

I BECOME A SERJEANT.

As this chapter will, I fear, to ordinary readers be very dull, I have postponed it beyond many of the incidents that I have already related; but as it refers to one of the most important events in my career, I must entreat their consideration and patience. I became a serjeant. The term is one that with the general public is surrounded with a sort of mysterious haze. Every one knows what a sergeant is in the body militant; and a sergeant of police is viewed by the masses with mingled feelings of terror and respect. We all know that the one is dressed in red, the other in blue. But what is a serjeant-at-law? that is the question. Once, after I had attained this rank, I was counsel before a court-martial at Aldershot, and most hospitably invited to dinner at the mess—I think it was of the Welsh Fusiliers. When I presented myself and announced my name and title to the orderly, he informed me, with a scornful air, that it was an officers' mess. As a matter of fact, we are only inferior in rank to a knight; and formerly the position was a most important one, all the great judicial offices being filled from its ranks, and many a distinguished name is recorded in its annals. The Queen's ancient serjeant, the head of the body, was the foremost man at the bar. It was not until the reign of Elizabeth that Queen's Counsel were heard of; that arbitrary lady created the first in the person of Francis Bacon.

These possess, however, no distinctive rank in society, but simply precedence in court. The serjeants were, and still are, joined in the commission with the judges going circuit, which, until a comparatively recent date, was not the case with Queen's Counsel. Formerly they had exclusive audience in the Court of Common Pleas; this is now abolished, and no fault can reasonably be found with doing away with a restriction injurious to clients and scarcely just to the rest of the bar. Upon the abolition of this privilege, the existing members of the court were placed upon a level with the Queen's Counsel in court by the grant of a patent of precedence.

I have already alluded to what I considered a great grievance that I was subjected to by the refusal of Lord Chelmsford to grant me this rank. It had, subsequently to the opening of the court, been granted to members of our body, and it could not be asserted that my business was not such as justified my application. Lord Campbell also passed me over, as he did Mr. Serjeant Parry, who had an equal claim, although he gave it to Mr. Serjeant Hayes, by which gentleman he sent a message that my claim should be considered on a future occasion. His death intervened, and I obtained the dignity from Lord Westbury, but not before the delay had been a considerable source of inconvenience to me, if not of injury.

I do not propose giving any elaborate account of the institution. My friend Serjeant Pulling has done so in a very able article in the 'Edinburgh Review.'[1] There was, however, one distinction between their rank and that of Queen's Counsel that ought to be mentioned—the latter could not hold a brief against the Crown without a licence; the coif was essentially a popular institution, and no such

[1] The date of this extremely able and interesting article is November 1877.

restriction existed. It is true that the permission may be obtained, and the value set by her Majesty upon her counsel being, I believe, 1*l.* 5*s.* 6*d.*, he can for that price obtain permission to serve the enemies of the State. This facility did not always exist, and I believe that the difficulty occasioned the employment of Mr. Serjeant Copley in the defence of Dr. Watson, the circumstances attending which I have already related. I cannot help thinking that it is a great pity that the order should have been practically abolished, which however is the case, although legally it still exists. The result has arisen from the discountenance shown to it by later chancellors, their inconsistency with regard to patents, and ultimately by the necessity for judges taking the rank which formerly they were obliged to do being abolished.

I became serjeant in 1856, having been recommended by Sir John Jervis and created by Lord Cranworth, and I was duly elected to the Inn attached to the society.

The Lord Chief Justice (then Lord Campbell) presided, and the business of the Inn was conducted by a treasurer, a post filled at that time by Mr. Serjeant Manning, Queen's ancient serjeant. In the biography, recently published, Lord Campbell has recorded his opinion of his brethren upon the bench and of the serjeants. He had dined there only twice, but does not allow any want of self-confidence to interfere with the candour of his views. His words are: 'My brethren of the bench are a most respectable set. I believe them to be superior to their predecessors who filled their places fifty years ago.'

It would occupy too much space to describe the different most learned and able judges who formed the subject of this commendation, but by some process of self-exaltation Lord Campbell upon more occasions than this has apparently assumed that the puisnés were a kind of inferior beings to himself. Amongst the names that occur to me are those of Mr. Justice Coleridge and Mr. Justice Erle, afterwards Chief Justice of the Court of Common Pleas, both judges in the court over which Lord Campbell presided, and Mr. Justice Maule. The first-named, a most justly distinguished judge, had retired before I had obtained much civil business, and I can only therefore speak of his conduct of this branch of the profession from hearsay, but I have always understood that he was a very learned lawyer, and had great confidence reposed in him by the profession and the public. I can, however, speak of him as having been counsel before him in many criminal trials, and I have no hesitation in saying that no judge ever presided with greater dignity, patience, and courtesy; and if Lord Campbell had taken an example from him, he would certainly have given more satisfaction, both as a judge and a gentleman. I may here venture to record a very trifling circumstance which exhibited, as I then thought and still think, great kindness of heart. In my early days I managed my voice very badly, and was accustomed to strain it too much, and having a case before him at the Kingston assizes, Mr. Justice Coleridge sent me down a note conveying a hint to me to avoid doing so, couched in very kind words.[1]

Of Mr. Justice Erle I shall speak hereafter, having seen more of him than of many of the other judges. I have had, however, many opportunities of forming an opinion of Mr. Justice Maule. I was very well acquainted with him, for in addition to practising before him we were members of the same club, the Union. He was one of Lord Campbell's respectable set, and certainly did not

[1] The last time I saw this learned judge was upon the Tichborne trial, when he had the satisfaction of seeing his son filling the office of Solicitor-General.

extend to the Lord Chief Justice even the modicum of praise accorded by that learned judge to himself. He entertained and constantly expressed for him the greatest contempt, and there is no doubt that Mr. Justice Maule did possess a much higher and nobler class of intellect. I used very often to dine with him, and was amazed at the variety of his knowledge, his acute grasp, and great reasoning powers. I have heard Sir John Jervis, who was chief of the court in which Maule sat, express quite as warm an opinion as I have done about his intellect. He was admitted to be a first-rate lawyer, and had been senior wrangler and senior medallist at Cambridge.

His manner was cynical, but he possessed a kind and humane disposition. He abhorred cruelty, and punished it with severity; but wherever he could find excuses in the natural failings of the human mind, he always treated them with mercy. His jokes upon the bench were sometimes wanting in dignity, which laid him open to unfavourable comment. On one occasion a savage onslaught had been made upon him by Albany Fonblanque, the editor of the 'Examiner.' When told of it by some kind friend, he merely said, 'Well, I can't understand it, I never did him a favour.' Many good sayings are recorded of him, but they are more adapted to professional than general readers. He suffered dreadfully from asthma, and resigned his appointment after a paroxysm from which he suffered whilst sitting in the House of Lords.

The serjeants escaped the negative praise accorded to the judges. They were deemed by Lord Campbell to be entitled to something more positive, and his description of them is short and pithy. 'The serjeants,' says he, 'are a very degenerate race.' At the time this good-natured and charitable description was written I had not become a member of the body, but I should have been very happy to have shared their company. They were generally well-educated gentlemen, with an average of ability equal to any of the same number of members of the bar; and, amongst them, there were those entitled upon many grounds to claim professional distinction. Mr. Serjeant Manning, the treasurer, was a very learned and distinguished lawyer, well versed in black-letter writings, and his opinions upon such subjects were esteemed of great value. I can thoroughly well understand the contempt that Lord Campbell entertained for him, as he never knew how to turn his knowledge into profit. I cannot, however, but smile at the recollection of this gentleman. He was old himself when I joined the Inn, and ably represented its antiquity. He was very strict in making us eat and drink after the manner of our ancestors; any relaxation gave him serious disturbance, and I am afraid that my want of reverence caused him no small amount of heart-burning; but after all, his foibles were innocent enough, and might have been recorded by a kindly pen. Another degenerate was Mr. Serjeant Storks. To be sure, he was a gentleman and a wit. He was a good lawyer also, and led the Norfolk Circuit. It was no disgrace to him that a more powerful man, Sir Fitzroy Kelly, was too much for his calibre. When I first knew him, his powers were somewhat impaired by age. He was a great admirer of men whom he called the giants. Lord Ellenborough was his idol. Of Lord Campbell he used to say that he had got on as much by trickery as by real merit, and that he was the greatest jobber that had ever flourished at the bar. As one instance of his accomplishment in this capacity, Storks used to relate, that in his reports Campbell, for the first time, published the names of the attorneys in the various cases, which he found led to useful introductions. If degenerate himself, Serjeant Storks had the good fortune to be father of General Storks, the well-known and distinguished officer. Mr. Serjeant Hayes came within his lordship's list. He also possessed the qualities that probably entitled him to the description at Lord Campbell's hands, for he was a thorough gentleman, an accomplished lawyer, and a kind friend, but never succeeded in making a large income. As long as he remained amongst the degenerates, he was the soul of the table. He was a leader upon the Midland Circuit, at the mess of which his conversational powers added greatly to the enjoyment of the members, and his kindness of disposition endeared him to every one.

Lord Campbell himself, pitying his degeneracy, raised him to the ranks of respectability, in which atmosphere, however, he did not long survive.[1]

Mr. Serjeant Shee, another gentleman coming within Lord Campbell's category, was a Roman Catholic. He led with great power and success the Maidstone sessions, and, subsequently taking the coif, obtained a considerable lead upon the Home Circuit. He was a very able speaker, but somewhat heavy. He was certainly a scholar and a high-minded gentleman, but not having met with great success was entitled to the sneers of Lord Campbell. He too became a judge, but did not enjoy his promotion for any great length of time. He was greatly liked at Serjeants' Inn, and would have been respected in any association where gentlemen and lawyers met. He it was who defended Palmer in the case of which already I have given some account.

One more degenerate, Mr. Serjeant Pigott, became eminent as a Baron of the Exchequer. He was a contemporary of Baron Huddleston, both of them being

[1] He was created a Judge of the Queen's Bench and died suddenly at the Court.

called upon the same day, and both of them leaders of the Oxford Circuit. He was much liked, and, if not a powerful man, was a thoroughly conscientious judge.

Upon Mr. Serjeant Manning's retirement, Mr. Serjeant Gazelee became treasurer of the Inn. This gentleman was the son of a judge. His father has been delivered to posterity as having presided at the famous trial of Bardell *v.* Pickwick. I just remember him, and certainly he was deaf. I believe him to have been a learned lawyer. His son was a man of good ability, and had the advantage of a college education and first-rate introductions. He was not troubled with much diffidence, nor did he extend extravagant praise to his fellow-creatures; but as far as I know he never behaved with unkindness, and I have heard of many generous and disinterested acts that he has performed. He was succeeded, I believe not immediately, by Mr. Serjeant Tozer in the office of treasurer.

In the year 1872, upon his resignation, I was elected in his place. I found that for some time past the expenditure had been excessive, and that many gross abuses had gradually crept in. I dismissed most of the servants, and made many alterations. I found that better entertainment could be supplied at a cheaper rate, and I remember with much satisfaction the cordial way in which I was supported by the judges and my brother serjeants. Our little dinners in the hall, formerly a chapel, on the windows of which were emblazoned the arms of many old and distinguished members of the Inn, and upon whose walls hung the pictures of eminent lawyers, were marked by good temper and friendly feeling. I was elected annually until the year 1875, when I accepted a retainer to go to India, and sent in my resignation, and my friend Mr. Serjeant Simon was elected in my place; but upon my return that gentleman resigned, and, being reinstated, I remained treasurer until the abolition of the Inn; and now, although its duties are abolished, and its convivialities are no more, the order still exists, and, if I have no other word inscribed on the roll of fame, I shall be recorded as the last treasurer of one of the most ancient, and at one time the most honoured, of the institutions of Great Britain. As the order was virtually abolished, it was determined to sell the property of the Inn, which was accordingly done, and the last meeting was held on April 27, 1877, when the resolution recorded below was come to.

Present—Lord Chief Justice Cockburn; Lord Chief Justice Coleridge; Lord Chief Baron Kelly; Mr. Baron Bramwell; Mr. Justice Brett; Sir Montague Smith; Mr. Justice Mellor; Mr. Justice Lush; Mr. Justice Denman; Mr. Justice Grove; Mr. Baron Pollock; Mr. Baron Huddleston; Mr. Justice Lindley; Serjeant Parry; Serjeant Simon; Serjeant Wells; Serjeant Petersdorff; Serjeant Pulling.

It was proposed by the Lord Chief Justice, and seconded by the Lord Chief Baron, and carried unanimously, 'That the cordial thanks of this meeting, on behalf of all the members of the society, be given to Mr. Serjeant Ballantine for his long and valuable services as the Treasurer of Serjeants' Inn, and that he be requested to select from the property of the society such a piece of plate as he may think proper as a substantial memento of the good feeling towards him of the members of the society.'

It would be very ungenerous on my part if I did not acknowledge my obligations to Mr. Serjeant Pulling, whose industry and research had much to do with the successful arrangements that were made, and who also received a piece of plate. Three of my brethren have passed away, Serjeant Parry, Serjeant O'Brien, and Serjeant Sargood, all men of ability. The first attained great distinction, Serjeant O'Brien not as much as his talents deserved, and Serjeant Sargood was one of the ablest of the advocates in parliamentary business; and, although my meetings with the remainder are now, I am sorry to say, but rare, my feelings of respect and affection for them are undiminished.

When I joined Serjeants' Inn I was compelled to leave the Inner Temple, into which society I have since been received back, and also am generously permitted to enjoy the hospitality of the bench table as an honorary member.

POSTSCRIPT.

The instructions received by Mr. Serjeant Shee in Palmer's case were very positive that no strychnine had been used, and, notwithstanding the strong evidence of the scientific witnesses, I cannot help believing that this was the case: there is no doubt that symptoms were detailed consistent with death from that particular poison, but they were related by ignorant people, who probably had their minds more or less imbued by the questions put to them. Brodie positively refused to indorse that view, although he had no doubt that the deceased had been poisoned. I have already expressed my opinion of Lord Campbell's direction in that case, and of the essential importance pointed out by him of not allowing charges of this character to drift into mere medical and scientific questions.

I have omitted to mention Mr. Serjeant George Atkinson, who for a short time presided as treasurer—an amiable and thoroughly conscientious man, but with ideas upon the subjects of old institutions which were certainly not consistent with some of the ideas that prevailed in the inn. He retired after a time and went out to Bombay. I endeavoured to see him during the short time I stayed there, but was not successful. He was a most amiable gentleman, and good but pedantic lawyer.

CHAPTER XVIII.

THE GARRICK CLUB.

AGAIN in defiance of chronology, I am about to go back many years and describe another institution. I could wish that an abler pen than mine would perform the task: nevertheless, it is a labour of love. My theme is the old Garrick Club, then occupying a small, unpretending-looking house in King Street, Covent Garden. There was, however, no resort in London that could boast of attracting so much of brilliancy and wit.

Named after Garrick, it was naturally sought by actors, poets, artists, and novelists; and members of the graver professions were only too glad to relieve the labours of the day by the society of all that was distinguished in literature and art. Although I joined it early in my career, I was not an original member, and missed those convivial meetings that I have heard described, in which Theodore Hook, Barham, and the brothers Smith[1] shone and sparkled with so brilliant a light; and when the memory dwells upon 'Gilbert Gurney,' the 'Ingoldsby Legends,' and 'Rejected Addresses,' I can imagine at times, when their authors met in the social smoking-room, there must have been an absolute surfeit of fun. Of Theodore Hook I am well able to judge, having, as I have already related, frequently met him. I also knew Barham. He used to dine with a

[1] Authors of the 'Rejected Addresses.'

friend of mine named Walsh, delighting the guests with his refined humour. The Smiths I never have had the pleasure of meeting. But I must not gibbet myself as a 'laudator temporis acti,' for, although a new generation had sprung up when I joined the club, it was by no means an undistinguished one. Dickens and Thackeray had made their marks, and they were broad and lasting ones. But of these writers I have already recorded my impressions.

Stanfield and David Roberts were noble representatives of art. The former, the great painter of ocean beauty and grandeur, was not often at the club, and I can scarcely recall his appearance. But David was there constantly, when his kindly, good-humoured face, reminding one of a country farmer upon market day, would often expand itself at our pleasant gatherings. I do not think that a greater favourite existed in the club. Charles Kemble was frequently there, but, alas! no one could have recognised in his appearance the gentleman-like swagger with which once upon a time he portrayed 'The Inconstant,' or the mixture of fun, dignity, and embarrassment he had been wont to convey in 'The Merry Monarch.' If any of my readers would like to obtain an idea of this charming actor during his best days, there is an excellent picture of him in a scene with Fawcett and Maria Tree, in which he portrays Charles II. It hangs upon the walls of the club: he was then the embodiment of life, but the light of those days had departed, he had become very deaf, and, like many people suffering from that infirmity, used every endeavour to make himself hear. This was impossible, but others were fully informed of his thoughts; and as these were occasionally far from complimentary to the hearer, his presence latterly in the club was looked upon with some apprehension.

Charles Kean was a most worthy representative of the drama. He, it is well known, was the son of one of the greatest and most original actors that ever lived. He was highly educated, and his tastes and feelings were refined. He set an example of most careful and laborious study, and, whether in a particular piece he attained success or not, he never spared time or pains to deserve it. There were some parts in which he was very successful. I think that his best effort was in 'Louis XI.,' a play translated from the French. If he were alive, however, I would not venture to say that he excelled in melodrama, and certainly did not in Shakespeare. In the 'Corsican Brothers' he was admirable, and in a translation of Carré's 'Faust,' in which he played Mephistopheles, I never saw any better performance.

Upon its first night he deviated from the strict propriety that ordinarily characterised everything he did by offering to bet two to one in bishops; but it being suggested that this would indicate a superfluity of such articles in his dominions, he excised it from his part. He was the most sensitive man I ever knew in my life. A great feud existed between him and Albert Smith. The original cause I forget, but he had offended Albert, who put into some penny paper that a patient audience had endured the infliction of Charles Kean in 'Hamlet' in the expectation of seeing the Keeleys in the after-piece. One night I and a member named Arabin, the son of Mr. Serjeant Arabin, were talking with Albert Smith in the coffee-room. At the opposite side stood Charles Kean, scowling. Presently Albert departed. In about three strides Charles Kean reached us. 'Richard,' he said, in the most tragic of voices, 'I never thought that you, my old school-fellow, would have consorted with that viper.' Poor good-natured Dick had heard nothing of the quarrel.

On another occasion it is related that he addressed an old orange woman at his theatre whom he had discovered applauding Ryder,[1] who had been playing in the same piece with himself, in something of these terms, 'Ungrateful wretch! thou who hast eaten of my bread and enjoyed the hospitality of my roof, how couldest thou applaud that man?' But, after all, these were but foibles, and he was in all substantial respects a credit to his profession.

I have already spoken of that little round object with a bald head and fresh-coloured face, and somewhat serious expression of countenance, no longer almost a supernumerary, but now the very funniest of comedians, not trusting to grins and distortions, but thoroughly artistic in his comedy, Robert Keeley. There are many now upon the stage of equal ability, but none with the same characteristics. There are some, but they are still alive, whose names I ought next to record, but as I am down amongst the dead men, and my living friends will feel no jealousy about precedence, let me mention poor Leigh Murray. What a promising actor he was, and how much courted! It was unlucky for his future fame that he was so. He followed pleasure, and sacrificed life. Albert and Arthur Smith—how sad to be obliged to class them in the death-category! Their addresses had not been rejected, but their enjoyment of their success was only too short. Albert married the eldest daughter of Keeley, and she very soon followed him to the grave. There were plenty of lawyers, some still alive, but many of them have passed away.

Ought I to say more than I have already done of

[1] This gentleman was a member of Charles Kean's company at the Princess's, and is still a well-known actor.

Serjeant Talfourd—as genial in the club as in his own house, and qualified as member in every capacity that formed a claim for entering it? Another serjeant was there also; he was not great, nor did he possess literary powers, but he was connected with the editor of 'Bell's Life,' who was, I believe, his brother. His name was Dowling, and he was once, when a junior, in a cause with Gurney as his leader. A witness had been called and told to go down. 'Allow me to ask a question,' said Dowling. 'Certainly,' said Gurney, who would have snapped his head off if he had not been allied to a newspaper. He asked one single question. In the next Sunday paper a paragraph in the following words appeared: 'Here Mr. Dowling rose and, with a most impressive tone and manner, asked the witness where he lived.' Yet another let me mention of those who are no more—kindly, genial, good-natured Morgan John O'Connell. He was contented with his illustrious name, being nephew of the Liberator, and did not seek to add to its laurels; but everywhere he was a favourite. We witnessed together a most appalling incident; it will never pass from my memory. We were seated one night at the club, when the whole sky became lighted up, and it was apparent that a large fire was raging. We started off in search of it, and found that it had broken out upon some warehouses situated upon the south-east side of London Bridge. They had contained an immense quantity of oil, which escaped in a state of ignition and spread itself over the surface of the river, presenting to the eyes of a beholder a sea of flame. Some unhappy creatures in a boat approaching too near were sucked into the fiery gulf. We heard one horrible shriek as if coming from a single voice, we witnessed arms struggling in unspeakable agony, and then the pitiless element closed over them for ever. No picture of pandemonium has ever equalled the horror of this frightful reality. It haunted me for weeks.

From a sad scene, where could my thoughts more pleasantly wander than to Shirley Brooks and my friend and brother Serjeant Parry, who was one of the most popular of the lawyers belonging to the club; and, although not a member, I have often met Douglas Jerrold there, the very bitterest of satirists and most epigrammatic of authors. Of Albert Smith I have already spoken. And let me end my obituary—how sad to think how long it is!—with one celebrity, by no means the least valued or appreciated. He was almost an institution in himself, and pity it is that he was only mortal: it was Mr. Hamblet. He called himself the steward of the club, but this was only the modesty of a great man. He was its dictator, and reigned supreme. The sense of his position sat in placid dignity upon his countenance, as he moved about extending an occasional recognition to a favourite member. Sometimes, if he discovered any breach of the rules, a single frown upon his face made the culprit shrink abashed. For many years he ruled, and there were no rebels to his authority; but at last he also yielded to the decrees of fate, and his like will ne'er be seen again.

It seemed only proper that, after he had passed away, the old house should not long survive, and now the members of the Garrick occupy a handsome edifice in a street named after it. Some of its rooms are very good, the drawing-room and the smoking-room particularly so: in the former, the fine pictures of its excellent collection are very advantageously seen; and in the latter, there are upon the walls paintings presented by Stanfield and Roberts, and some interesting ones by an artist of the name, I believe, of Haig. I doubt, however, whether the club is so cosy as it was; although there are still members in it whom I knew in early days, and who will, I trust, long keep out of my former list.

The stage could not be better or more honourably represented than by the veteran Walter Lacey, a sterling actor, always ready to do his very utmost to please, both in public and private; excellent in some parts, and far above mediocrity in all he has attempted. I have known him well throughout the greater part of his career. Then there is my old friend Palgrave Simpson, accomplished as a writer, and almost unrivalled as an amateur actor. But what business have I to call him old? He is as young as ever, and would have been without a rival were it not for Tom Holmes, to whom every accomplishment seemed to come by nature. History gives him many years of life, his appearance and talents much fewer. His last performance was in an amateur pantomime, where he delighted an immense audience, including royalty, by a wonderfully active and witty performance of pantaloon.

Of course in recording old reminiscences it would be impossible to forget Frank Fladgate, now, I believe, the father of the club, and who, for all the years it has existed, and through all its changing scenes, has never made an enemy. No one of the present day is so conversant with the records of the stage and the lives of the greatest actors; and it is a real treat to listen to his pleasant talk, and note his adoration of his beloved Shakespeare.

One other of my oldest friends I must mention, and then adieu to the old Garrick. Not only in this club did I know Isadore Brasseur, but we were brother members of the Clarence, and we frequently met amongst mutual friends. He had been a professor at King's College, and in that capacity became known to the Prince of Wales, who has ever since exhibited towards him the most cordial affection. We do not now often see him amongst us; but there are no lack of English friends who are glad to seek 'Le Chevalier Brasseur' in his pleasant Paris home.

And now *vale valete.* It would be an agreeable task to refer to other living members distinguished in literature, in art, in the drama, in the army, and in my own profession; but the catalogue would be too long, and so I have confined myself to a word or two about those only whom, dead or living, I have known and valued in the early days of the old club-house, and the estimation in which it is now held could not be better testified than that it boasts amongst its members His Royal Highness the Prince of Wales.

POSTSCRIPT.

Dick Arabin was a great favourite both at the Garrick and the Union Club, indeed in all places to which he resorted. He was the son of the quaint old gentleman who presided at the Central Criminal Court, and whom I have described in the sketch of that tribunal. The premature death of Charles Kean was attributable to the incessant labour he devoted to his profession, his anxiety to provide for relatives whose support he generously undertook inducing him to overtax a not very strong frame.

CHAPTER XIX.

INEQUALITY OF SENTENCES.

A REFLECTION that forces itself upon the mind of every one who has observed the machinery of our courts is how very much the fate of men and causes must depend upon the temper and disposition of those who preside; there is such an enormous amount of discretion vested in judges, which might be limited, although it could not be abolished. I do not believe that a code could be so formed as to meet the multifarious requirements of our complicated state of existence: but I do think that in certain matters grave scandals are created by the apparent inequality of decisions, and I think it would look better in the eyes of the public and be much more satisfactory for the judge if a certain sentence always followed the same verdict, and mitigating circumstances were left for the executive to deal with. This subject is a very large one, and it is not upon any assumption that I am capable of dealing with it that I have made the allusion I have done; but it has arisen from thinking how very different in every mental feature was Sir Frederick Pollock, who became Chief Baron of the Exchequer after the death of Lord Abinger, from his contemporary, Lord Campbell. I remember the former, from the earliest period of my life, as Mr. Frederick Pollock. He lived opposite to our house in Serjeants' Inn. His elder brother David practised in the old Insolvent Court in Portugal Street, where my father also endeavoured to obtain business. Pollock was at one time member for Huntingdon, and Somersham, my mother's birthplace, being in the same county, as he rose in the profession he was a man of mark in the eyes of my family. It also so happened that in very early days I possessed a client and friend, Frank Betham, who entrusted him with his business, and occasionally gave me the junior briefs of which I have already recorded one instance. When franks were in use I was proud to obtain Pollock's signature. I have watched him in and out of office, and no one had more vicissitudes. A banker of Huntingdon named Veasey was his intimate friend. This gentleman occupied a house that once belonged to my mother in that town, and he also belonged to the Union Club, where I often heard him repeat the praises of Sir Frederick, who received the appointment of Chief Baron whilst conducting a case at the Central Court of which hereafter I have given an account, and I hope that I shall not detract from his dignity by saying that he did not conceal his delight. I look back to him with much affectionate regard, which may possibly bias my opinion; but I am not afraid to assert that no stain ever found its way upon his escutcheon, and no charge of jobbery ever followed his well-deserved success. He was in fact an upright and honourable gentleman. His attainments were of a very high order. He took the first honours at Cambridge, and almost down to his death took delight in the most abstruse problems in mathematics. He belonged to a race of lawyers to whom the latest hours of night and the earliest in the morning presented no impediment to study, and almost to the last he was fond of putting upon his letters the very early hour at which they were written. I am not quite sure that I must not attribute to him some small share of personal vanity, as he was accustomed to sit upon the bench nursing a very handsome leg and foot, and looking at it with great complacency. One of his numerous daughters was married to Mr., afterwards Baron, Martin, and the active, energetic, and powerful mind of this gentleman possessed great weight with his father-in-law, and gave rise to some comments which certainly, as far as intentions went, were not deserved.

There is always great difficulty in avoiding criticism, however honest may be the endeavour, when a successful advocate practises before a near connection. It has been my lot to be engaged before him in many cases. He possessed firmness and decision, and, though sometimes hasty, he was never harsh or discourteous. I do not think a young counsel ever had to complain of injustice being done to him, and he thoroughly appreciated merit. Although solemn in his manner, both upon the bench and in society, I have heard him make the best after-dinner speech that I ever listened to, except from the lips of Dickens. Amongst the *causes célèbres* that were tried before him was that of the Mannings, for a very brutal murder in Bermondsey. It excited much attention at the time, Mrs. Manning having been maid to a lady of distinguished rank, and having subsequently followed a career that made her somewhat generally known. I defended her unsuccessfully, as she was hanged; and, although she was my client, I suspect she was the power that really originated the deed of blood.

I was once counsel in the Court of Exchequer in a curious and interesting case. It was an action brought by executors against a life insurance company to recover the amount of a sum insured upon the life of a person who, it was alleged, was accidentally drowned. It appeared that shortly after the insurance had been effected he went down to Brighton, and stated to the people at the house where he put up that he was going out to bathe, and his clothes were found upon the beach, but he himself did not return. His relatives claimed the amount of the insurance money. The company disputed the claim. Some little time after the disappearance, a body, in a partial state of decomposition, was cast on shore on one of the Channel islands. The parties interested did not feel the least difficulty in identifying the body as that of their lost relative, but, on the other hand, there were no natural means by which it could have got from Brighton to the coast where it was found. Several witnesses were called upon this point, and I remember making the Chief Baron laugh by a very indifferent joke. A doctor had been examined, and some little delay occurred. My lord got impatient, and said somewhat pettishly, 'Who is your next witness, brother?' 'Well, my lord,' I answered, 'having called the doctor, the next in order will be the undertaker.'

The jury were ultimately discharged, and the claim was never renewed. Of its fraudulent nature there is not the smallest doubt. It was shown that in all cases of drowning at Brighton the body was cast back if the immersion had taken place near the shore, and the currents made it simply impossible that it could reach the spot where the body identified was cast. Sir Frederick had a very retentive memory for faces, and on one occasion that he was trying a case a little attorney named Cyrus Jay was a witness. This gentleman, one &c., was not known in the higher professional walks, and I fancy entered the witness-box with some trepidation. The chief, however, as was his habit, and is the habit of all experienced judges, scanned Cyrus very attentively, and, having heard his name, said, 'Are you any relation of my old friend the

Rev. Mr. Jay, of Bath ?' 'I am his son,' said the witness. In subsequently telling this anecdote, Cyrus added, 'After that I felt I could swear anything I liked.' In the case I am about to record I think that Sir Frederick Pollock laid down the law wrongly ; in the way, however, he directed the jury the verdict returned was the only one open for them to give ; but the history of it, for many reasons that I shall mention, is worth recording. It was an action against the Great Eastern Railway Company by a gentleman who undoubtedly had been seriously injured in an accident upon that line, and which had been occasioned by the fracture of the tire of one of the wheels of the engine.

Now whether such a fracture could have been prevented by reasonable care is a question of great difficulty, and can only be determined by the evidence of engineers. These gentlemen have undergone an apprenticeship before committees of the House of Commons, and have learnt to give plausible reasons for all the propositions they advance, and, as counsel can rarely shake their evidence, he had better leave them alone, trusting to the same number of witnesses he is instructed to call on the other side. It is then that Greek meets Greek. Engineers have more power, for the above reason, when in a witness-box, than other professional witnesses. The inside also of a bar of iron is more of a *terra incognita* than even the inside of a human body; at all events there are fewer people who know anything about it; but medical men who do not make a trade of being witnesses are frequently much embarrassed when called upon to give reasons for their opinions. They are accustomed to rule supreme in the sick chamber, and their judgment there is not disputed. Very likely they are right in their evidence, but are not the less embarrassed. I doubt much whether a parson who had preached the soundest of doctrine would be able to uphold it in the teeth of a rigorous cross-examination. I have been engaged in many cases involving mechanical and medical questions. In the former I have trusted to members of the same profession; in the latter, generally to myself. In the case in question no fault was to be found with the wheel that had given way, but two most eminent engineers, amongst the very highest in their profession, declared that they had seen the corresponding wheel, which had not been removed from a siding upon the railway where it had been taken to after the accident, and that they had examined it with great care, and had discovered in it a fissure into which they could easily have placed the blade of a knife. One of them said he had actually done so. As the company did not anticipate any evidence about this particular wheel, counsel were not prepared with engineers upon the other side, who might have treated the fissure as totally immaterial, and the Lord Chief Baron, as I think improperly, held that its existence was evidence of negligence. Perhaps it was, but surely not negligence affecting the accident. However, the jury found, as they were bound to do upon the ruling, a substantial verdict for the plaintiff, who had lost a leg.

Another person injured in the same accident brought an action against the company in the Court of Common Pleas, but in the interval the wheel alleged to be defective was exhumed and examined, and upon the trial it was produced, and it showed incontestably that there was not upon it either speck or blemish. An endeavour was made to discredit the fact that it was the same wheel, the engineers who had obtained the verdict in the Court of Exchequer reasserting and repeating their evidence. Thus it became a matter of fact and not of science, and Lord Chief Justice Cockburn, before whom the case was tried, so left it to the jury, and they, with scarcely a moment's hesitation, found for the defendants.

Whilst upon this subject, I may mention a case in which I was counsel for the same company, tried at Croydon before Chief Baron Kelly, and in which the tire of a wheel had given way, and much of the engineering talent of the country was called upon one side or the other. After a very long trial the company obtained a verdict. But the case is interesting principally from the evidence that was given in relation to the smelting of the iron previous to formation into bars, showing how an almost imperceptible grain of any foreign substance getting into the molten mass would create the nucleus of extensive injury, which, if not upon the surface, would be undiscoverable by any tests; consequently that the accidents that happened to the tires usually occurred with perfectly new wheels, the old ones having had their capacities thoroughly tested.

Sir Frederick Pollock was very fond of the Home Circuit, and I have frequently had the opportunity of enjoying his great social qualities at Farnham Castle, the residence of the late Dr. Sumner, then Bishop of Winchester. It was a real relaxation to go from Guildford to this very beautiful spot, where the prelate extended to the bar the most liberal hospitality. His parties were rendered more agreeable by the guests from Aldershot, and young and old, red coats and black, met with the most cheery welcome, greatly enhanced by the accomplishments and courtesy of the ladies of the family.

The bishop was very fond of his garden, and with him, and enjoying his simple thoughts and polished conversation, and sharing, as I did, his love for birds and flowers, I have passed many an hour that in a circuit town would have hung heavily enough. I have already mentioned

David Pollock. He went out to Bombay as chief justice, and there died. Another brother, as is well known, was a most distinguished general, and received the thanks of his country for the services he performed. Sir Frederick retired from the Bench, receiving the honour of a baronetcy, and making way for Sir Fitzroy Kelly. He was a consistent Tory, and passed through the different changes that the party underwent, and when at last he came to the front I fancy there were very few in the profession that grudged him his good fortune.

It is not a bad story that is told of him when upon the Northern Circuit. A gentleman named Alexander had a large leading practice, and it was noticed that Mr. Pollock, as he then was, always made complimentary allusions to him. Some one asked him how he could possibly do so. 'Why,' said he, 'do you not perceive that if I did not keep Alexander in business, I should have that fellow Cresswell against me in every case?'

When the Guildford assizes, the last place of the summer circuit, ended, I seldom lost much time in hastening abroad, and my steps seemed naturally to turn to Boulogne-sur-Mer. I was very fond of the place. It is now a good deal changed. The abolition of imprisonment for debt has enabled most of the unwilling sojourners to return to their native shores, and thus it has lost the gayest and most careless of its residents. At the time I am now recalling, most of them belonged to a little club, held in Rue de l'Ecu. Taken generally, their original social rank was good, and their manners were easy and gentlemanlike. We played whist at franc points, and I need not say that no credit was asked for or given. One or other of the members would disappear for a time. It was understood that he was putting up at the 'English hotel,' by which name the debtors' prison was designated.

If any of us were fortunate enough to have a run of luck, and win some five pounds or so, the club was deserted by the whist-players during the week following, whilst the lucky winner might be seen, probably for the only time that season, enjoying his dinner and Lafitte at one of the best *tables d'hôte.* One of the characters I remember was an Irish major, a thorough good specimen of his country. He was a tolerably regular frequenter of the whist-table, and played an excellent rubber. He had a son, an officer of high distinction, in the Indian army. Very precise was the major in his demeanour, and careful in his play. From the few words that occasionally escaped his lips, and from what was heard of him from other quarters, it was clear that he had moved in the higher circles, and had at one time been possessed of large means; but he never either boasted or complained. We learned that after a short illness he had died in a solitary lodging, and also a sad tale of the poverty that surrounded him. The circumstances which existed in India at that period prevented his son from knowing anything of his position. When his desk was opened, a number of memoranda were found, showing that, however polished his associates may have been, they did not possess much honesty; and there were signatures of some well-known persons to I O U's who might, if they had paid a tenth of what they owed him, have enabled him to live and die in comfort.

Should the above lines meet the eyes of his son, I trust he will not feel that I have improperly drawn aside a curtain that ought to have been kept closed, but it has been done in no unkindly spirit.

Amongst the figures that were not gay or thoughtless, I well remember Alderman Kennedy, who was one of those convicted upon the British Bank trial, and upon whose face and in whose weary footstep the observer would discover hopeless despondency. Vanity had been his ruin. He had by most honourable means realised a large fortune in India, and he believed that he was equal to cope with the intrigue and trickery of the rascals of this metropolis. By his connection with the British Bank he sacrificed fortune and character.

I knew him very well before his fall, a weak, pompous, kindly hearted man. He could not see any element in nature, superior to himself. Oh, how wearily he trod those stones! I sought to renew my acquaintance with him, but he rejected all my overtures. Poor fellow, sinned against, but having in truth no fraud in his own thoughts, he died in a foreign place, and the epitaph upon his tomb ought to have been—Victim of self-conceit.

Charles Dickens was very fond of Boulogne, and, on the occasion that I particularly remember him in the place, he occupied a villa upon the Calais road. Albert and Arthur Smith were also frequent visitors. They used to catch little fish in the harbour, as in former days they did in the lake of Geneva. And I also met an old acquaintance of mine, an eminent physician, Dr. Elliotson. He carried on his profession in Conduit Street, Regent Street, and had formerly enjoyed a very large practice; but he became a convert to mesmerism, which he fancied could be made a valuable agent in the treatment of disease. Unless a reformer can crush, he must be crushed, and Elliotson being an enthusiast and not an impostor, the holy war of etiquette was waged by his profession against him and ruined his business.

Upon one occasion this gentleman, Charles Dickens, and myself started together in the packet from Boulogne, for Folkestone. Neither of my comrades was a good sailor, and they knew it themselves. The illustrious author armed himself with a box of homœopathic globules; and the doctor, whose figure was rotund, having a theory that by tightening the stomach the internal movements which caused the sickness might be prevented, waddled down to the boat with his body almost divided by a strap. The weather was stormy, and neither remedy proved of any avail.

I frequently met Dr. Elliotson in society. He was a man of very varied attainments, and a great favourite. Amongst the houses at which he was a constant visitor was that of a lady, Mrs. Milner Gibson, who at one time gathered around her a large circle, comprising most of those famous in literature, art, and the professions; and here also every foreigner possessing a grievance and an unhappy country was always made heartily welcome.

Dr. Elliotson was also a much valued guest at Mr. Justice Crowder's, where I used to meet him. This judge I remember with great feelings of pleasure, joined to regret at his comparatively early death.

He had been on the Western Circuit with Cockburn, and, being his senior in the House of Commons, might have contested with him the honour of the Solicitor-Generalship; but he preferred the safer and easier position of a seat on the Bench, which he filled with general respect and approval.

POSTSCRIPT.

If I obeyed the voice of some of my critics, I might without much difficulty add the dates to the matters I have related, and it is with no disrespect to their opinions that I still omit to do so. If the accuracy of any of the facts had been challenged, the 'Anno Domini' might be necessary, but I cannot help thinking that what is intended as a gossiping sketch, and claiming no controversial importance, would be rather impaired than improved by such a formality.

CHAPTER XX.

MURDER OF MR. DRUMMOND.

IN the commencement of the year 1843, as a gentleman named Drummond was walking down Parliament Street, he was fatally wounded by a pistol-shot, fired by a man of the name of MacNaghten, a Scotchman. It was clear that he was mistaken by him for Sir Robert Peel, whom it was his intention to have killed. As Mr. Drummond was a man generally respected, and of the most inoffensive habits, it was not unnatural that a storm of indignation should arise against the perpetrator of the act, whilst the patience exhibited by his victim during the few days that he survived the attack added to the general sympathy of the public.

MacNaghten was placed upon his trial for murder in the following February, Sir Nicholas Conyngham Tindal, Chief Justice of the Common Pleas, presiding. I have had occasion to refer to this judge, although not at any length, when giving an account of the Courvoisier trial. He was certainly not a man of startling characteristics, but upon the bench presented a singularly calm and equable appearance. I never saw him yield to irritability or exhibit impatience. I should say in fact that he was made for the position that he filled, and sound law and substantial justice were sure, as far as human power could prevail, to be administered under his presidency.

It required a judge of this calibre to control the violent feelings of indignation launched not unnaturally against the accused. Sir William Follett conducted the prosecution, and the late Lord Chief Justice, then Mr. Cockburn, was retained for the defence.

The facts were easily proved, and the only question that was in issue was whether the prisoner at the time of the commission of the crime was of sound mind, and the onus of showing the contrary practically devolved upon the prisoner's counsel.[1] MacNaghten had been treated as a lunatic, and he appears to have imagined that Sir Robert Peel was bent upon his destruction, which he intended to prevent by the assassination. There was no ground whatever for even the belief that Sir Robert Peel knew him.

In a case not altogether analogous, but bearing some similarity to it, Erskine had made a most masterly and argumentative speech, dealing with the different phases of insanity, and Cockburn in his defence of MacNaghten had the advantage of that great advocate's views and treatment of the subject. This, however, did not detract from the merit of one of the most masterly arguments ever heard at the English bar. Several witnesses were called, and the facts that I have briefly stated were fully proved. Before the evidence was concluded, the Chief Justice appealed to Sir William Follett, who admitted that he must submit to a verdict acquitting the prisoner upon the ground of insanity, and this verdict was accordingly pronounced. A storm of indignation followed it. Mad or not, the prisoner ought to have been hanged. Such was no uncommon expression, and a general denunciation of mad doctors, and some not very complimentary remarks upon lawyers, might not unfrequently be heard. This outcry resulted in a very singular proceeding on the

[1] This is not so theoretically, as the indictment in terms declares the accused to be of sound mind and understanding.

part of the House of Lords, which had no precedent, and fortunately has never been repeated. The judges were summoned by their lordships to express their opinions upon the law applicable to insanity in criminal cases. It seems to me surprising that they did not point out that such a proceeding was extra-judicial, and that their opinions could only properly be given upon certain facts arising before them in their judicial capacity, and that what was asked of them was to make a law in anticipation of facts that might hereafter arise. The same proceeding also might be adopted in relation to any subject, civil or criminal. However, the judges went and sat in solemn conclave, but as might be expected, being called upon to found abstract opinions with no facts to go upon, they have not greatly assisted the administration of justice.[1]

The important points propounded by the judges seem to be as follows:—

'The only ground upon which an alleged lunatic is entitled to an acquittal is *that he did not know the difference between right and wrong in the act that he committed.*' If they had proceeded to say upon what principles this question was to be determined, some benefit might have arisen from their opinions.

The judges further say, 'that although a person may in a particular matter act under an insane delusion, and act in consequence thereof, he is equally liable with a person of sane mind.' I presume this to mean that unless it be shown that the delusion destroyed his knowledge of the difference between right and wrong, which is to be discovered and proved independently of the admitted delusion, he must be considered of sane mind. If these dicta are to be received as law, then a totally different principle governs civil and criminal cases, and a person

[1] Mr. Justice Maule pointed out this difficulty.

incapable of making a will or executing a deed may, nevertheless, be liable to be executed for the commission of what in a sane person would be a crime. However startling this proposition is, it cannot be controverted, and it appears to me that the subject is one worthy of further consideration and much more careful analysis than has ever been applied to it. In the observations that I have already made, and in those that follow, I do not pretend to lay down any proposition or dictate any solution of the difficulty, but merely wish to suggest certain matters that in the course of my practice have presented themselves, with a view of attracting the attention of men better-informed and more experienced upon the subject.

That insanity exists to a most deplorable extent is testified by the numerous establishments, both public and private, for the care of lunatics, and the question of how far mental derangement, admitted to exist upon a particular point, affects the conduct of an individual beyond the scope of that point, is a subject worthy of the research both of medical men and lawyers. Doctors have introduced the term 'uncontrollable impulse,' and an excuse has been sought under this term for violent bursts of passion arising from natural causes; but may not such symptoms be also the result of insanity? Have we not numerous instances in which under such influences the victims have destroyed themselves? It is not difficult to presume that they knew they were doing wrong; and, indeed, the cunning that in many cases attends their acts indicates that they did; but assuming one of the qualities of the sane human mind to be self-restraint, and supposing this barrier has been removed by insanity, ought the sufferer to be held criminally liable for his acts, although evidence existed that he was conscious of the difference between right and wrong?

When Ravaillac assassinated Henry IV. of France, he believed that in doing so he was commending himself to God, and as many enthusiasts at all times and in all countries have acted under such impressions, it would be a dangerous doctrine to declare that because the sense of right and wrong had disappeared, a criminal should be deemed irresponsible; and yet, on the other hand, an utter lunatic may possess a sense of right and wrong in many actions of his life. The case is well known of a madman who was cross-examined by Erskine ineffectually for some time. At last the counsel obtained the clue, and in answer to a question he put the witness said, 'I am the Christ.' Upon a subsequent occasion, when again cross-examined, he carefully avoided the admission that had defeated him upon the former occasion. He was admittedly a lunatic, but certainly if he had been charged with a crime it might fairly have been contended that he knew the difference between right and wrong.

As I have said already, a civil act is destroyed by proof that the person performing it was at the time subject to mental delusion upon one subject, although in every other perfectly reasonable. The only principle upon which this rule can be founded is that the mind is one and entire, and if diseased it is impossible, whatever may be the external signs, to say to what extent, and in what direction, the disease extends. If this be good reasoning, surely it is equally applicable to the mind of a person charged with a crime. I cannot think that, where an insane delusion is clearly proved, although numerous facts may be brought forward to show that the lunatic distinguished, up to the time of the offence, the difference between right and wrong, that he ought to be consigned to the gallows. The gout that has taken possession of a man's toe suddenly leaps to his heart.

When a man believes himself to be the Saviour, how is it possible for human skill to tell what thought or opinion is likely to control any act of his life? The law must yield to the dispensations of Providence, however much prejudice and passion may seek to sway its administration.

I was witness of the result of the outcry that Drummond's assassination occasioned in a case tried before Baron Alderson at the Central Criminal Court. That very learned judge summed up strongly for an acquittal upon the ground of insanity. The jury, however, took the matter into their own hands and convicted the prisoner. The judge made urgent recommendations to the Home Secretary, but, nevertheless, the man was executed. It will not, I think, be uninteresting to record here one or two cases involving these questions, and in which I have at different periods of my career been engaged as counsel. One of them was of a very distressing character.

A lady of the name of Ramsbottom, the wife of an eminent physician, herself of middle age and generally respected, was suspected of pilfering from a draper's shop in Baker Street, Portman Square. She was watched, followed, and her person was searched, and several small articles were found concealed in different parts of her dress. She was given into custody, went through the painful ordeal of an inquiry at the Marylebone Police Court, and was committed for trial at the Middlesex sessions. At the period when this occurred, Mr Serjeant Adams was the presiding judge. He was thoroughly impartial and knew all the law necessary for his position, but it was not very well packed in the receptacle of his brain, and the particles constantly came out at wrong times and places. The case, however, could hardly have been confused, the facts were perfectly clear, the whole of the lady's life, as far as its history was known, was not only free from reproach, but thoroughly rational. The only point that could be relied upon for the defence was that the articles stolen were so trivial that no sane object could exist for intentional theft, and the only suggestion that could be made in her favour was that she was not responsible for her actions, being compelled by an uncontrollable impulse, or, to use a technical term, that she was the victim of kleptomania, not a very popular defence before a jury of tradesmen. However, after having been locked up for some hours, they were ultimately discharged without giving a verdict, a result arising probably more from compassion for the lady's husband than any doubt about the facts.

I thought at the time that if, instead of laying a trap for her, the proprietor of the shop had conveyed a hint either to herself or to the doctor, it would have been the kinder course, and subsequent circumstances showed that in reality her conduct was attributable to insane influences, although certainly she knew thoroughly well that she was acting wrongly.

She died very shortly after the ordeal she had undergone, broken down in health and spirit with the shame and disgrace, and I was consulted, after her death had taken place, by Dr. Ramsbottom under the following circumstances. Every drawer and cupboard in the house was found to be full of new goods, which she must have been in the habit of abstracting during many years, and I believe that in every instance they were contained in their original wrappers. Mrs. Ramsbottom was a religious woman, and I cannot doubt that every Sunday she listened with respect and veneration to the lessons taught in church, and fully realised the commandment of 'Thou shalt not steal.' And it is clear that she by the acts she committed incurred danger and obtained no advantage. I advised Dr. Ramsbottom not to make the discovery public, and the articles found were distributed amongst different charitable institutions.

Can any one doubt that insanity irresistibly controlled her conduct?

Many instances are upon record in which this extraordinary mania is alleged to have developed itself. And one case is known where an attendant always accompanied a lady of high rank when she went out shopping and paid for the articles she stole. Supposing in any of these instances the parties had committed a crime of a different description, would it be just to hold them responsible? The question is not unimportant, as such acts, if clearly proved, would, as the law now stands, invalidate a will.

Certainly the most remarkable and interesting case connected with mental derangement, in which I acted as counsel, was in connection with the will of a lady named Thwaites. She died at an advanced age, leaving a very large fortune, which she bequeathed to different persons with whom she had associated during her lifetime, and none of whom were her relatives; and her next of kin disputed the will upon the ground that she was insane at the time of making it.

She had inherited the fortune in early life, unexpectedly, upon the death of her husband, and had administered it with judgment and discretion. She was neither niggardly nor profuse. She was charitable without being reckless, and kept her accounts, which were somewhat complicated, with accuracy and in excellent order. No restraint of any kind was ever placed upon her. She played whist, and, I am told, played it fairly well. She endured pain on different occasions with great resignation,[1] and moreover there was nothing extraordinary in the disposition of her property, as she had never held much intercourse with her own relatives.

Unquestionably, however, she was guilty of some very extraordinary proceedings, and expressed some singular views. She asserted that she had been chosen by our Saviour to receive Him upon His return to earth, and that this event would therefore occur during her lifetime, and she indicated the reality of this belief by making very extensive preparations for His reception, principally in the upholstery line, and there was a great deal of absurdity exhibited in the arrangements she made. Lord Penzance, before whom the case was tried, without the intervention of a jury, held that her will was invalid. The circumstances of this case suggest reflections as to how far religious opinions, absurd and ridiculous as they may appear to others, are to be accepted as proof of insanity. The main idea, round which every thought and act rotated in her mind, was the approaching return of the Saviour to earth. This surely cannot be treated as insane. The notion that she was selected to receive Him might be the product of vanity and the misunderstanding of some of the mysterious passages that occur in portions of the Scripture, whilst the preparations she made were only the natural consequences of such a belief on the part of a person of utterly unrefined ideas; and it is to be noted that she was a woman of no education, and from her earliest youth had been the object of fulsome attentions and flattery.[2]

[1] Dr. Turner, an old friend of mine and a physician of great eminence at Brighton, gave me an account of her great patience under suffering.

[1] Sir Roundell Palmer led me upon the first trial, and his speech is well worth the perusal of those who desire to look deeply into this subject.

But a grave doubt has occurred to me as to whether the belief in question really had full and undivided possession of her mind, and whether there was not rather a pride in putting forward the claim. She sacrificed nothing of personal interest and comfort, and never appeared to undervalue the good things of this world in consequence of the great honour that was in store for her.

These speculations, however, are beside my main object in discussing the subject. For that purpose I assume that a delusion, utterly inconsistent with sanity, had taken possession of her senses, and that, therefore, she was unfit to execute any legal document. In what manner ought she to have been dealt with if she had committed what in a sane person would have been a crime? Her whole life showed that she understood the distinction between right and wrong, and if the issue left to a jury had been narrowed to that question, unless the fact that she was under a delusion upon the subject of the Saviour's returning to earth and becoming her guest could be treated as evidence that she was unable to tell right from wrong, she must have been convicted.

I have been engaged in many cases of interest since the constitution of the Probate and Divorce Court before the three judges who have severally presided, and, amongst others, the very unhappy one of Lady Mordaunt. This unfortunate lady became insane after a confinement, and continued hopelessly so from that period. This was an instance where the mind was entirely destroyed, and therefore it presented none of those difficulties which I have pointed out in other cases, and which I venture to think deserve the attention both of those who make the laws and those who administer them.

Having mentioned the Court of Probate and Divorce, this may not be an improper place to allude to its formation and the judges who have presided in it. When first constituted, Mr. Justice Cresswell, then a member of the Court of Common Pleas, was selected as its head, and it would have been difficult to make a better choice. He was a most able lawyer and a man of the world. He had been a successful leader at the bar, was an acute cross-examiner, and an utter despiser of all shams. He narrowly watched the demeanour of the witnesses who gave evidence before him, and usually formed just conclusions. I wish I could finish my sketch without a word of reproach or blame, but, in justice, I must say that his manner was too often supercilious, thus detracting from his high qualities. At the same time he was eminently just, and never carried any feeling he might have shown against either counsel or witness into the comments that he made to the jury, and his perfect impartiality will, I am sure, be admitted and remembered by every one who knew him. He tried one very remarkable probate case, in which I opposed a will propounded by a person named Smethurst, presenting features which I think are of a very singular character. This man succeeded in upholding the will, which I attribute to one of the most admirable speeches I ever heard from Dr., now Sir Robert, Phillimore, who was his counsel.

Lord Penzance, a Baron of the Exchequer, succeeded Cresswell, who died from the result of an accident. He possessed all the high judicial qualities of his predecessor, whilst his demeanour was most courteous to every one, and, if it was his duty to differ from counsel, he did so with good taste and gentlemanly bearing. He had mixed much in the world, and thus obtained that knowledge which in the Divorce Court is peculiarly required. It was a matter of sincere regret when, in consequence of ill health, he was obliged to retire from the office.

It would not become me to discuss the merits of Sir James Hannen, the present presiding judge, but I may say that I have been engaged with and against him in many cases whilst he was at the bar, and I never knew a more conscientious or painstaking advocate.

CHAPTER XXI.

TRIAL OF BARBER AND FLETCHER.

In the month of April 1844 a trial took place at the Central Criminal Court which brought to light a very elaborate and complicated system of fraud. The parties alleged to have been engaged in it were a person of the name of Fletcher, who was by profession a medical man, an attorney of the name of Barber, and three women. The forgery of wills and the personation of individuals was the basis of the different transactions. No doubt whatever exists as to Fletcher having been largely and criminally engaged in them; but Barber alleged that he had acted simply in a legal capacity without any knowledge of the character of the acts. Fletcher also from the commencement entirely exculpated him, and there was nothing to show that he derived any profit except such as he was entitled to for his professional charges. At the same time it was difficult to account for a shrewd man of business being mixed up in so many transactions as were proved against Barber without his having a suspicion of their nature. The prosecution was conducted by Sir Frederick Pollock on the part of the Bank of England. A very excellent lawyer of the name of Graves (who is recently dead), with myself, defended Fletcher, and for him the only hope could be from some technical point, which, however, all the ingenuity and legal acumen of my leader were unable to discover, and he was unhesitatingly found guilty.

Barber was defended by Wilkins, a gentleman whose qualities I have already described. The judge who tried the case was Mr. Baron Gurney, who had obtained for himself the reputation of being very harsh and severe in his administration of justice, and certainly his manner warranted the opinion. I do not remember that whilst presiding upon this trial he did anything that could invite censure; but Wilkins made a most bitter attack upon him in the course of his speech. The words he used, as far as I can remember them, were as follows: 'There exist those upon the bench who have the character of convicting judges. I do not envy their reputation in this world or their fate hereafter.' Mr. Baron Gurney was at this time an old man and in feeble health, and Sir John Bailey, who was one of the junior counsel for the prosecution and a great friend of the baron, told me that he felt the attack very much. I do not consider that the position of a barrister could justify expressions of such a character, and, although his client was acquitted on this occasion, I cannot help thinking that when he was subsequently tried on another case this attack was not forgotten. I can, however, very well remember that early in my career it was with fear and trembling that I appeared as counsel before the object of them.

Mr. Baron Gurney, when at the bar, possessed great power and cleverness in dealing with facts, a quality which also distinguished him upon the bench; but certainly he had earned the reputation of being a very pitiless judge, and his manner at times was almost brutal, and already in these pages I have more than once expressed my opinion of how grave a defect this is in those who have to administer justice.

In early life Mr. Gurney was nearly a rebel, but it will be more polite to describe him as having been a very advanced Liberal; as, however, he progressed in the profession, the vivifying light of Toryism began to affect his senses, and before he arrived at the bench high Church and State doctrines had taken firm root in his mind. He must often have lamented that when he named his children he had not been endowed with the spirit of prophecy, as certainly in that case they would have sailed under very different names than those of Russell, Hampden, and Sidney. The first of these gentlemen afterwards filled the office of Recorder of London; he possessed all his father's clearness and precision, with great gentleness of manner and kindness of heart. He did the greatest credit to the corporation who elected him, and it will be long before his loss is forgotten.

After the acquittal of Barber, both prisoners were again put upon their trial for uttering the forged will of a lady named Ann Slack. In the interval, however, between the two trials a change had taken place. Mr. Justice John Williams presided, and Sir Frederick Pollock having become Lord Chief Baron, Mr. Erle, afterwards Chief Justice of the Common Pleas, conducted the prosecution. This gentleman did not possess eloquence, and suffered from a slight impediment in his speech, but was nevertheless a very acute and able advocate. As I was still representing Fletcher, although his fate was sealed, watched the conduct of the case very carefully. Mr. Erle laboured the strong parts against Barber, and contrived almost to make it appear that he was the *fons et origo* of the whole conspiracy. Wilkins made a very indifferent defence, and Mr. Justice Williams simply followed in the most servile manner the lead of the counsel for the prosecution. Both prisoners were convicted, and sentenced to transportation for life. As regards Barber, the verdict was most unjust, for, without affirming his absolute innocence, it is impossible to say that there was not very grave doubt as to his guilt. After Barber had been sent out of the country in pursuance of his sentence and had undergone great hardships, he was pardoned, and received some compensation. I often saw him during the short period that he survived his return, his tall form gaunt and haggard, and the sufferings he had undergone stamped upon his features. He must have been an object of pity to every one possessed of human sympathy.

Johnny Williams—so every one called him, except when he was 'my lord'—had been one of the counsel for Queen Caroline, associated with Brougham and Denman. His knowledge of the Italian language was supposed to have been the reason why he was selected for that position, as he had not held any distinguished place at the bar. I fancy his business was pretty much confined to criminal cases, in the conduct of which he had the reputation of sharpness and sagacity. He was much given to strong expletives, which in the following anecdotes I must be excused for omitting.

Upon the trial of a prisoner for a capital charge, he had been induced by the urgency of an attorney, although against his own opinion, to ask a question, the answer to which convicted his client. Turning to the attorney, he said, emphasising as may be imagined every word with strong additions: 'Go home, cut your throat, and *when* you meet your client in H—— beg his pardon.' Another story told of him is that a clerk, recently married, hanged himself. Another person who afterwards entered his employment expressed a hope that Johnny would not be offended at his entering into the holy bonds of matrimony. 'Certainly not,' said he. 'Marry by all means; but *when* you hang yourself do not do so in my chambers,' which his former clerk had done. He was a capital shot, and whilst enjoying the sport upon some gentleman's preserves, and knocking over the birds right and left, the gamekeeper whispered confidentially to his comrade, 'They tell me this 'ere gent is a judge. I'll take my Bible oath he has been a poacher.'

Mr. Erle became, as is well known, puisné judge in the Court of Queen's Bench, and afterwards Lord Chief Justice of the Court of Common Pleas. He possessed a very judicial manner, thorough independence, and an earnest desire to secure justice in the cases he tried. He was, however, very obstinate, and when once he had formed an opinion it was almost impossible to get him to change it. His experience in life had given him but little knowledge of some of its by-paths. He put too much faith in outside respectability, and was almost as weak as some juries in cases where injuries were alleged to have been inflicted upon women. Upon one occasion at Guildford, when I was engaged to defend a prisoner upon a charge of this description, I ventured respectfully but strongly and earnestly to allude to this, which I considered an infirmity of his mind, and I referred to cases in which I thought injustice had been done. In summing up he commented with a good deal of emotion upon my observations, but gave me credit for sincerity. In a former chapter I have alluded to this case, which resulted in an acquittal owing to the impressive caution which, I venture to think, I caused him to introduce into his charge to the jury.

I was counsel in the last cause that he tried, and his dealing with it illustrated what I have said about his want of knowledge of the ways of the world. It was an action arising out of the sale of a horse, for which my client had given three hundred guineas. It was a magnificent-looking animal, and had been shown off by a very pretty girl before it was purchased. The horse was a screw, and the whole affair a plant. The Chief Justice was indignant at my defence. He could see nothing to justify the imputations I had made, and so he summed up. The jury, however, with very little hesitation, found in favour of my client. I met Erle leaving the court. He was greatly vexed at the verdict, and could not understand it. I told him that the parties probably were known to the jury, but I cannot help thinking that he felt his power and influence were waning. His predecessor, Sir John Jervis, would have seen through the whole fraud in a moment.

Whatever may have been his deficiencies, and although the Court of Common Pleas has been presided over by most distinguished judges, none ever sat upon the bench who left behind him a higher character for the most unswerving integrity.

He was a man of great benevolence, and I have heard many anecdotes indicative of his kindness of heart, and one example happened to come within my own knowledge. He was presiding in the Civil Court at Northampton, and was obliged to direct a jury against some poor people who had been scandalously but legally swindled. To them the result was absolute ruin. On the following morning an elderly gentleman on horseback made his appearance in the alley where the sufferers resided. This was Sir William Erle. He gave them some very good advice, and with it a sum of money that replaced them in their old position.

Having, as I have already mentioned, a slight impediment in his speech, he had contracted a habit of looking into the air instead of into the faces of his audience. The effect of this was peculiar. After his retirement from the bench he went to live in the country, where he enjoyed himself for many years, and died at an advanced age. The last time that I saw him was when I was counsel in the Petersfield Election Committee; the place was near his residence, and he came over and took his seat beside Mr. Justice Mellor, who was the judge. I need not say that he was cordially recognised by such members of the bar as were present. I took the opportunity of quoting one of his decisions in the Court of Common Pleas which was, I fancy, bad law. Very quietly he got hold of the report from which I had quoted. Of course he could not interfere, but I fancied that his look was almost agonised when Mr. Justice Mellor decided the point mainly I believe out of respect for his opinion.

Sir William Erle had been a member of the Western Circuit, and it is no unpleasing task to record the eminent men whose early professional life commenced upon it: Sir William Follett, Mr. Justice Crowder, Lord Chief Justice Cockburn, Sir Montague Smith, Sir Robert Collier, and now Lord Chief Justice Coleridge. But not less in ability, and in all those qualities which make a man loved and respected, was a gentleman whose premature death has deprived the profession of one of its greatest ornaments.

When first I met Sir John Karslake he was one of the gayest and brightest of a pleasant circle at the house of Mrs. Crealock, in Stanhope Place, Hyde Park. He speedily attained a very high position at the bar, and no rank was so exalted that he might not have fairly aspired to it. He broke down from over-conscientiousness. He was never satisfied that he had done enough for a client, and he wore himself out by labour and anxiety where an equally successful result might have been attained at a much less cost.

I have been with him in cases from which his attention never flagged, although his brain was being racked by the most horrible of agonies. No wonder he succumbed.

The last time that I was with him was in an action

brought by, I think, the Italian Government against an English firm for breach of contract in the supply of boots for the army. He was suffering fearfully, and I was very anxious to relieve him of the work, which it was quite within my power to do, but I could not prevail upon him to accept the slightest help. It must have been some, though a sad, satisfaction to his oldest friend to offer the tribute to his memory which appeared lately in a morning journal, and which those who read it will admit was by no means overcharged.[1]

POSTSCRIPT.

Since I published my former volumes I have again looked through the trial of Barber and Fletcher: it is extremely interesting, from having been one of the very few in which a reasonable doubt may not be entertained as to whether a man entirely innocent had not been convicted, and it is one also in which the power of advocacy was very signally exhibited. If the counsel had been reversed, the result would almost certainly have been different. It also shows how great is the effect of the reply of an able counsel in a case presided over by a weak judge.

Really the least favourable conclusion that ought to have been arrived at against Barber was that he had been incautious. He was a poor man, and probably did not desire to look too deeply into the proceedings of one of his best clients. But the fact, clearly proved, that he received nothing beyond his proper costs, ought to have secured his acquittal.

[1] A letter from Lord Coleridge, referring to Sir John Karslake, appeared in the *Times* newspaper of the date of October 10, 1881.

CHAPTER XXII.

CAMPDEN HOUSE FIRE.

In 1862 Campden House was a feature at Kensington. It was occupied by a Mr. and Mrs. Woolley, who received a good deal of company, and were said to be persons of wealth. The parties they gave would now be called æsthetic.

Mr. Woolley was himself a confirmed invalid, his eyesight defective, and he could scarcely move about without the assistance of a valet. In the commencement of the above year, and in the middle of the night, a fire broke out upon the premises. It spread with singular rapidity, and consumed the whole of them with their alleged valuable contents. The property was insured in different offices to the aggregate amount of 30,000*l.*, and the companies disputed the payment. They alleged that Mr. Woolley was in distressed circumstances, that the amount of property in the house was grossly exaggerated, and that he had himself set fire to it in pursuance of an elaborate system of fraud. They alleged that his apparent feebleness was simulated for the purpose of successfully carrying it out. It was clear, if he really was the invalid he appeared to be, that their theory must be abandoned; and if he were shamming, that he must have contrived to keep up the appearance for a considerable time before executing his contemplated design.

He brought an action against the Sun Insurance

Company, it being arranged that all the other claims should stand or fall by the result. It came on to be tried at the Croydon summer assizes, before Mr. Baron Bramwell. Mr. Bovill, myself, Mr. James (the present Attorney-General), and a Mr. Rosher were counsel for Mr. Woolley. Mr. Lush, the late Lord Justice (I forget who was with him), represented the company.

There were many circumstances that justified the resistance of the claims, and it was pretty clear that the result would turn upon the mode in which Mr. Woolley underwent examination. If he was playing a part, he was the very best actor that I ever saw. He was unshaken by the cross-examination, and his painful infirmities secured the sympathy of the jury, who found a verdict in his favour, which was not subsequently disturbed.

A rather amusing incident occurred in connection with the case. The fire had broken out after midnight, and a gentleman saw and reported it; but when the question arose of calling him as a witness, he protested against our doing so, as it would inform some inquisitive connections where he was on that morning, which, for some reason, he had a very strong objection to. It occurred to me that his evidence might be admitted, and I sounded Lush upon the subject, and learnt that there was a witness in his brief who had exactly a similar objection, and so we agreed that the two should pair off together, and we called neither of them; and I believe that this benevolent arrangement prevented some little inconvenience in two domestic circles.

The assizes for the Home Circuit were held every alternate year at Croydon, and for many years I was accustomed to lodge with two worthy old people, who kept a small shoemaker's shop in the High Street; very honest they were, and kindly, and professedly Christians of great strictness, but of the not uncommon denomination of those from whose creed charity is expunged. I was engaged for the prosecution at an assizes many years ago of a young German charged with murder; and for the purpose of tracing the alleged murderer it was necessary to call the celebrated singer, Madame Titiens, who had afforded him pecuniary relief after the commission of the act. I had known this lady for some years, and always entertained the greatest respect for her character as well as admiration for her talents and accomplishments. She was extremely generous, and her own country-people especially were always sure of assistance. It was this reputation that had induced the accused to apply to her. As is well known, the hotels during the assizes are very full, and I invited Madame Titiens and her niece to occupy my lodgings whilst she was waiting to be called. On the following day my old landlady gave me notice to quit, saying 'she would have no stage players in her house.' Madame Titiens had a pretty little residence in the Finchley Road, where I have often enjoyed most pleasant evenings. Amongst those whom I was in the habit of meeting was Signor Giuglini, the wonderful tenor. His career was but a short one: the climate of Russia and a habit he unfortunately contracted of taking stimulants destroyed his nervous system, and for some time he was an inmate of the asylum kept by my old friend Dr. Tuke at Turnham Green. But there was no hope of recovery. Madame Titiens frequently called upon him there and took him out for a drive. He was perfectly harmless, and not discontented with his lot, expressing himself grateful for the kindness he received from the doctor. He ultimately was sent into Italy, where he died. Many also were the pleasant parties in which I met Madame Titiens at the Star and Garter at Richmond, not then the great ugly staring barrack of a place that occupies the site where Mr. Ellis, the picture of a host, used to receive the guests. The old house was burnt down. In itself it had not much pretension, but the garden behind was a perfect picture of loveliness; the small garden-rooms, with honeysuckles, jasmine, and roses twining themselves up the sides, with a lovely sweep of lawn, on which were scattered trees that had flourished there for many a long day, affording shade as well as beauty; one magnificent spreading beech, itself a sight, and an avenue of limes forming the prettiest of walks at the bottom of the garden, with a view beyond: none fairer to be seen through the length and breadth of England. A company possessed themselves of it. To their eyes and imaginations nothing was so beautiful as bricks and mortar. The trees were in the way, and have been cleared off; in the place of flowers that seemed to flourish of their own free will, formal beds are stiffly planted. The dear old lime-walk is supplanted by a terrace without an atom of shade, and which is not improved by the perfume of the stables, over which it has been constructed. No modern improver can ever make Richmond otherwise than beautiful, but the loveliness of the Star and Garter is one of the things of the past. The very obliging manager of the hotel is not responsible for the vandalisms that have changed the fair scene that existed into its present shape, and as far as attention and good fare will satisfy the visitor he will have no reason to complain. On a Sunday at the period I speak of the garden was usually crowded. Artists and singers, whose avocations kept them in London during the week, revelled in the landscape, and amongst them I have often enjoyed it; and there were representatives of every other class, well-known figures of the literary, political, and social worlds. There was a party I well remember in connection with one of the most delightful days of many that I passed there; it consisted of Balfe the composer, and his surpassingly lovely daughter, whose career was only too short. She was twice married; once to Sir J. Crampton, who I think was our ambassador to the Court of Russia, and afterwards to a grandee of Spain, and died when quite young. Mowbray Morris was another of the group. He was manager of the 'Times' newspaper, and with him I was very intimate. I was his counsel in a case that caused him anxiety and pain, but ended successfully for him. The fourth of the group in addition to myself was Mr. Delane, the editor of the same paper, and upon the shoulders of these two men rested the entire weight of its management. No one could be in the society of the latter gentleman without feeling that he was a man of the age. There was a quiet power in his conversation, his knowledge was very varied, and a vein of agreeable *persiflage* adorned and lightened whatever he talked about. The last time I met him was at a dinner party at Dr. Quain's, the eminent physician.

At that time his mind had partially given way under the attacks of incurable disease, and it was painful to witness how occasional were the flashes of an intellect that in former days was wont to shed so bright and lasting a light. On this occasion his brougham came for him at the time it had been his custom to go to the office, and he still had the idea that he was actively engaged, although the real editorship had passed into other hands. It seems so short a time since we five were stretched upon the grass plot in full health and spirits, and now I alone of all that party am left to recall it.

Another of whom I am obliged to speak in the past,

and with whom I have passed at the Star and Garter, as well as elsewhere, many a pleasant hour, was Charles Lever, the author of 'Harry Lorrequer' and other works of fiction; a bright, well-educated, witty Irishman. His stories at table were as amusing and improbable as many that came from his pen. I believe he was a member of the Garrick Club, but I do not remember ever meeting him there. I cannot recall whether it has been at some of the pleasant gatherings in those old days that I have met George Augustus Sala. Wherever it was, I know that he added fully his share to the joyousness of the party. Every one has read his graphic sketches of different phases of London life, and amusing details of travels abroad; but not so many his very clever novel of the 'Seven Sons of Mammon,' which I think bears comparison with most of the fictions of the day.[1] Amongst others from whose society this pleasant resort derived an additional charm were Signor and Madame Arditi, with whom I was fortunate enough to form an acquaintance shortly after their arrival in this country, and I believe it was upon my invitation that they, for the first time, made its acquaintance, and, since that period, in their company I have often and much enjoyed myself. I have been glad, in concluding the brief sketch that I have ventured upon of this hotel, and after bemoaning the destruction of honeysuckles and rose-trees and the barbarous disfigurement of a favourite spot, and mourning over departed friends, to be able to refer to those who are still living, and affording pleasure to a large circle of friends, and to express a hope that they may long continue to do so.

[1] In it will be found the apprehension of his heroine, by a French detective, on the Derby racecourse, which equals, in skill and power, any sensational incident that I have ever read.

CHAPTER XXIII.

EVANS'S.

LET me now change the scene and present my readers to one of a very different description, although there are many to be found here who might have been seen on the preceding Sunday enjoying the pleasures of the Star and Garter.

It is the interior of a large hall, and the hour about midnight. The atmosphere is thickened by smoke. There are numerous tables, at which gentlemen are seated taking refreshments. The walls are covered with paintings of celebrated actors and actresses, and upon a raised platform at the further end of the room are some dozen boys singing with taste and accuracy a popular glee. Moving amongst the tables, upon legs rather shaky, a rotund figure with a rubicund face and yellow wig offers with much courtesy his snuff-box to the occupiers, hoping at the same time that they have been supplied with all they want. The hall is Evans's, Covent Garden. Since I last saw it, twenty years before, it is much changed; a handsome edifice is added to the long room of which it consisted when Colonel Newcome left it in disgust at the obscenity that went on. The owner of the snuff-box is the proprietor of the hall, and to him is due the change in its character that has taken place. It is conducted with perfect propriety, the amusements are refined, and the refreshments good and moderate. My readers will recognise Mr. Green, Paddy, as he was always called behind his back, and by those who knew him well in speaking to him. Originally he had appeared upon the stage at the Adelphi, not, I fancy, in a higher capacity than a chorus-singer; and in the days that I have previously spoken of he sang at the old rooms, not, however, any songs that were reprehensible; although I must, I am afraid, admit that he was present during the time that they were sung, and when reminded of the improprieties of those days he would shake his head gravely; but as he was a devout Catholic, I have no doubt he had obtained absolution. I used to take a great deal of pleasure in his conversation. He was possessed of a very retentive memory, and could relate, and did so pleasantly, many scenes of London life. Artists, lawyers, writers, actors, and men of fashion congregated in the hall of a night, and in a corner of what once was formerly the old room a circle of friends used to meet, and in cheerful and not unintellectual gossip spend much agreeable time. Paddy was very proud, and might not unreasonably be so, of some who joined this group.

There was also a gallery, the visitors to which were concealed by trellis-work, and to this ladies were admitted, and here they could listen to the songs and eat suppers supposed generally to be confined to the other sex. Paddy also prided himself upon these visits, and recorded with much gusto the names of distinguished guests; and it was a well-known fact in the establishment that royalty had condescended to accept a pinch of snuff from his hospitable box.[1]

Another personage, scarcely of less interest than Mr. Green himself, was always to be seen in the rooms. He also wandered from table to table, and was received with a

[1] This gallery was only occupied by visitors known to Mr. Green, and was not open to the public generally.

welcome by the *habitués*. He professed to sell cigars, but when the eye of his chief was not upon him he would pull out of his pocket a well-worn card, and express a hope that the visitor would honour his concert which was shortly about to come off; but no one ever lived who witnessed it. This was Herr von Joel, once upon a time a popular singer in refined circles.

He used to sing Swiss mountain melodies. He also whistled and imitated birds very naturally, and towards the end of an evening would give an amusing imitation of a farmyard. He sang one night; the next he did not appear, nor the next, and on the following we heard that he was dead.

Mr. Green retired from its management, and it gradually sank in character. Now the building has become the property of a club to which has been given the name of the Falstaff, it is to be hoped that some of the old associations may be revived, and from what I know of the subscribers I think that the wish may be fulfilled.

I was a favourite with Mr. Green, and one chair was always kept for me. I belonged to several clubs, but during the years I am now dwelling upon there were no meetings so convivial as these, and the faces to be seen in the room, even if the visitor was not in direct communion with them, were pleasant to behold. Thackeray was constantly there: he was not social, but people liked to be in apparent company with the great novelist. He sat apart generally, wrapt in contemplation. Charles Dickens would flit in only rarely, but always in apparently good spirits, and glad to respond to the many words of welcome he received. Albert Smith, after he had descended from Mont Blanc at the Egyptian Hall, never missed the pleasant reunion, and there were none who came amongst us more deservedly popular than he and his brother. I have met Douglas Jerrold there. To him I have before alluded. I have seen him in company with men of great ability, but I never saw any one who, for a short period, sparkled so much; but, meteor-like, he too soon sank into darkness. Shirley Brooks was often amongst us. I need say no more of him than I have already done. A very constant guest was Robertson, the creator of a style of drama which, with the assistance of Mrs. Bancroft's talent, has filled with splendid audiences a theatre which for years before had wooed in vain the patronage of the public. Poor Robertson died only too early, almost before he could witness the triumphs of his sister Mrs. Kendal, one of the most fascinating actresses of the present day.

Quaint little Buckstone would sometimes hop in, and excite amusement and fun apparently without intention. I think it was here that I was introduced to Mr. Barry, an Irish barrister, since Attorney-General, and now judge, and from whom I have since received a substantial mark of friendship. There was one amongst those I met who fills a melancholy space upon the page of history; I allude to Prince Maximilian. Paddy Green took me up to him one night whilst he was indulging in a tankard of ale, and introduced me to him very effusively, and we met on other evenings and drank beer together. He was very unaffected, although with a reserved manner. I cannot help thinking, though possibly this may result from after events, that there was upon the countenance of the future Emperor of Mexico a cloud that seemed to foretell his melancholy fate.

And there was another, not so illustrious and not known to history, whose fate was fully as sad. This was Mr. Bowlby, a man of great ability, engaged upon the staff of the 'Times' newspaper. He had suffered many troubles, about which he had consulted me, and I entertained for him a sincere friendship. One night very late we were seated together at Evans's; on the following day he was to start for China, to which place he had accepted the post of correspondent with the English army.

He was not in high spirits, and told me that it was only for the sake of those dependent upon him that he went. He sailed, as he had proposed, on the following day, and joined the army. Shortly after his arrival there was an engagement in which our troops had been victorious. My friend, with some companions, rode on in advance of the main body, and being surprised were all of them taken prisoners by the Chinese. They were subjected to frightful tortures, from which poor Bowlby died. In the far distant land a monument has been erected to his memory, and the object for which he sacrificed his life has been attained through the liberality of those he served.

It is only very recently that a well-known face is missing from the tables of those who love the society of artists, and, old as he was when he passed away from the scenes of his successes, his death caused surprise, for he had looked for so many years the same, his cheery spirits never seemed to flag, and he appeared to have defied the inevitable.

This was Planché. I knew him well and met him often. I suppose that in his long journey through life, although he met with great success, he never made an enemy; and though many of his contemporaries might be named whose literary fame is greater, very few have caused more amusement. He was, moreover, fortunate in being associated with Madame Vestris, who seemed to be created to embody upon the stage, and even to give additional charm to his refined and elegant burlesques.

There was another friend of mine who defied age, whose good temper and high spirits never flagged, who could have been an eminent architect, who was an accomplished painter, but who preferred the stage and its trials; this was Charles Mathews.

The fame of his father, and the popularity that from his earliest age he had himself obtained, secured him a reception on the first night of his appearance at the Olympic Theatre never before equalled by any actor. The promise he then gave he entirely fulfilled, and within six months of his death he drew large houses and played with vigour and spirit. I had a very agreeable meeting with him and his accomplished wife upon one of my visits to Homburg, and I remember with pleasure a dinner that I gave to them at the Hôtel de Russie, at Frankfort, and afterwards how the actor, who himself never failed when he desired it to excite fun and merriment, laughed most heartily at the tricks of a clown in a circus to which we all adjourned after an excellent repast.

I have in a former chapter mentioned meeting Macready, but I had no particular acquaintance with him. He was a conscientious manager, a scholar and a gentleman, but fractious and overbearing. Such, at least, was his reputation. I cannot say I think he was a good delineator of Shakespeare's characters. The one which, in my opinion, he played best was Prospero, in the 'Tempest.' I was present one night, the first that it was played at Covent Garden Theatre, when a young lady made her appearance in Ariel. She was wafted across the stage, and sang, with exquisite sweetness, the well-known song commencing 'Where the bee sucks.' This was received with rounds of applause, and practically raised her into the prominent feature of the play. This was Miss Priscilla Horton, then scarcely known, but who has since been continuously gathering laurels as Mrs. German Reed. I could not hope to recall to the memory of those who have witnessed the extravaganzas of Planché their effect upon the audience, or to give an idea of it to others who have not, without naming a performer who was of no small assistance to them. The most blustering he was of monarchs: his swagger conveyed a volume, and so did his voice, which he used with infinite effect and humour. The name of this gentleman was Bland, and he, like Madame Vestris, seemed to have been created for the special illustration of Planché's genius.

In the allusions I have made to members of a profession from all of whom I have met with much kindness, and amongst whom I have enjoyed so many pleasant hours, I need hardly say I have been governed solely by the memories that have presented themselves to my mind, and not with any notion of exhausting the subject; and I have not ventured to refer to those with whom I still have the pleasure of an acquaintance, lest the sincere terms I should be obliged to use might cause me to be accused of flattery.

There are public performers who do not strictly belong to the theatrical profession, and with one of these I happened in a business matter to be brought into contact. He was an acrobat, and plaintiff in an action for breach of contract. I was much struck with the amount of simple truthfulness that he displayed in giving evidence, and asked him to call upon me, which he did. I was curious to learn something of a life of so exceptional a character. He was a sinewy little fellow, and born into the world in the name of Martin, but he called himself Martini. His brother, he told me, was just dead, and he was looking out for another, not a real brother, but a professional one. His last brother was named Jones, and he had fallen from the trapeze and broken his neck. 'You see,' he said, in relating the story, 'it is very difficult to get suited, as we may not know each other's tricks.' He was quite aware, he said, of the dangers of his profession, but then the salary was large and he hoped to save enough in two or three years to retire. He ate no meat whilst under an engagement, and never took stimulants at any time. He told me of some shocking accidents, where the sufferers were only crippled, and said that they were usually occasioned by the carelessness of the people employed in the performances. Exhibitions of the sort that this poor fellow described are a scandal to a civilised country. My friend, however, was by no means despondent, and considered his branch of the profession much higher than that of gymnasts who did not risk their lives. Whatever we may think of the taste that encourages the latter class of performers, their exhibition does not, at all events, shock humanity. My client won his verdict, but whether he succeeded in finding another relative, or what became of him afterwards, I never heard. I once remember, during a pantomime at Drury Lane, a great professor of what he called gymnastic art. He wore a mask of truly satanic appearance, and three urchins, representing imps, assisted him in his performance. I saw him between the acts in the green-room. His theatrical head was lying on a table. His own real one was very gentle and mild. The boys were tumbling; one of them performed an unusually good somersault. 'God will reward you, my boy,' he said, patting him upon his head. Turning to me, he added, 'They are good children. Their mother hears them their prayers night and morning.' It was evident that there was real affection between those four, and that they felt no small pride in their monkey tricks.

I was inducted behind the scenes very early in my life, and have been told that I ran away from Miss Foote, the beautiful actress, when she wanted to kiss me. I have, however, never fully believed this story. I have since known much of the life behind the curtain and of the heart-aching that is concealed within the glare and tinsel exposed to the audience, and I believe that a very wrong estimate is formed of those who make part of the splendid pageant. The chorus-singers and ballet-girls are consigned, by the opinion of those who know little about them, to much undeserved obloquy. Of course, amongst them, as in all classes, there are those who merit this opinion, but I believe the majority are honest, hard-working girls, and that there is many a household saved from starvation by their patient industry.

Those who have known Drury Lane Theatre as I have done for many years, before and behind the curtain, will have had great pleasure in the acquaintance of Mr. Sterling, for long the stage manager. He was not only most excellent in this department, but was a thoroughly kind-hearted though strict disciplinarian. He has confirmed the opinion that I have expressed of the character of the employées. Mr. Sterling has recently published an amusing account of the actors and actresses that he has known, and is the author of several pleasant farces. I met him at dinner shortly ago at my old friend's, Sir Mordaunt Wells, and had a charming gossip about former days. He told me a little story that pleased me. It was of three young children who were fairies or angels in the pantomime last Christmas. It was on one of the bitter snowy nights, and all the vehicles were off the road. The eldest of the three was only eight years old. The two infants, each clinging to the arm of the elder child, set off to walk to Camberwell, and got there safely. How soon necessity teaches courage and self-reliance! Those who have read the Life of Grimaldi, edited by Charles Dickens, will have learnt with what agony of body on the part of the performer roars of laughter from the audience are sometimes elicited. The career of these poor fellows is seldom long.

Their great muscular exertions, and the draughts they are exposed to, soon bring on disease. The clown of one pantomime may not be seen in the next, but the motley is there, and no one asks for him who wore it last. There have, however, been some who have played for many consecutive years, and I remember a pantaloon with whom I often had a gossip, named Barnes. He was a very sober, decent fellow. Once when I was behind the scenes at Old Drury he told me, almost with tears in his eyes, that he was not to be engaged for the next Christmas. 'And to think,' said he, 'that they have turned me off, although I have played for thirty years, and engaged a mere boy.'

Before I close my theatrical recollections, I must relate an incident in which I placed a most distinguished and highly respectable friend of mine in a very embarrassing position. He was induced, by a desire to add to his knowledge and by my persuasion, to accompany me behind the scenes during the performance of a pantomime. To him the sight was a novel one, and, doubtlessly engaged in admiration of some of the mechanical effects, he was unconscious of the flight of time, which I also disregarded. Suddenly the scene was changed, and we found ourselves in a storm of carrots, cabbages, and turnips, which terminated the act, technically termed, I believe, a 'general rally.'

I will not mention my friend's name, as in the minds of some highly conscientious people the contact with a stage cabbage would cause pollution. Notwithstanding this experience, once again my friend trusted himself to my care, to drive him home from a Greenwich dinner. The whitebait, somehow, had got into my head, and, like myself, my horses were somewhat fresh. We went at a spanking pace until suddenly brought to a stand-still by the pole of my phaeton running through the back of a costermonger's cart. My friend declared that I instantly fell fast asleep, and left him to pacify a furious lady, whose back had been placed in no small jeopardy. He succeeded in doing so, and I never asked how. He always had a way with the ladies. We reached home safely. There was an omnibus that got into our way near St. Martin's Church, but this peril we also escaped, or the country might have lost a valuable servant.

Ought I to forget the first theatrical performance that I ever beheld, that tyrannical and brutal husband Punch! I did delight, and half believed in him. Now, when I notice the poor fellows whom I see wearily treading the street with the show upon their shoulders, I think of two pictures painted by a French artist, entitled 'Avant et Devant,' one representing the laughing audience in front, the other a starving wife and children behind.

CHAPTER XXIV.

ILLUSTRIOUS VISITORS.

IN the month of June, in the year of our Lord 1847—I like to make the most of a date when I possess one—I received a visit at my chambers of a very unexpected character. It was from two personages who were then amongst the most noted in London society. One of them was Prince Louis Napoleon; the other, the prince of dandies, Count D'Orsay. Of course I knew the former by sight, and with the latter I had some personal acquaintance from having met him at the house of a well-known physician, Dr. James Johnson, residing in Suffolk Place, Pall Mall, and with whose family I was upon terms of intimacy.

The object of their visit was to consult me with relation to a fraud of which Prince Louis Napoleon had been made the subject. It appeared that a bill-discounter had, under the pretence of raising money for the Prince, obtained from him two bills of exchange, amounting to 2,000*l.*, the proceeds of which he had converted to his own use.

The circumstances were explained to me, and, although there could be no doubt that the Prince had been swindled, the mode in which it had been effected did not bring the perpetrator within the operation of the criminal law; and this to the best of my ability I explained, but I could not convince the Prince, who seemed quite unable to grasp the idea that the law of this country was not regulated by the Code Napoléon. They remained with me for some time, but my arguments had no effect. He reiterated his views with scarcely a change of expression, and seemingly could not get mine into his mind. Shortly after they had left, the Count returned, and expressed himself thoroughly satisfied with the correctness and wisdom of the advice that I had given, but said that it was useless to argue with the Prince; that he was possessed with one idea upon the subject, and that nothing would remove it. He said that he himself was greatly annoyed, and with some embarrassment offered me a fee; but I declined to treat our conversation from a professional point of view. We parted upon very agreeable terms, and I met him occasionally afterwards.

It would be very presumptuous to assume that upon so short an opportunity I should be capable of forming a correct opinion of the Prince's intellect, but there can be no impropriety in expressing the view left upon my mind at the time; and this certainly was not favourable. It seemed to me that he shrouded himself with a solemn air as if he was thinking profoundly, but that really it arose from a slowness of comprehension. Whether or not the wild exploits of Boulogne and Strasburg and some other events of his subsequent career may justify this opinion, I leave it for historians to determine. He proceeded with the case, and the bill-discounter was committed for trial at the Central Criminal Court, which came on before Mr. Baron Alderson, a learned and very strong judge, and he at the conclusion of the counsel's opening address interposed and pointed out the difficulty which I had in my interview with the Prince attempted to explain. His counsel was obliged to yield to it, an acquittal took place, and a scandal was avoided.

I have described Count D'Orsay as the prince of dandies; and so he was. I never saw a man who in personal qualities surpassed him, and his dress deserved the epithet of artistic. Whether he was riding through the park, mounted upon a horse that seemed made to show off his handsome figure, and which he managed with a grace that did not in those days distinguish his countrymen, or he was in the omnibus box at the opera, arrayed, I must admit, somewhat gorgeously, he always commanded admiration.

The term dandy conveys to my mind, when associated with those of whom I have read—the Brummells and other characters of the Regency—by no means a pleasant impression. I should have expected to see something grotesquely dressed, with cynical manners and offensive demeanour.

Count D'Orsay was courteous to every one, and kindly. He put the companions of his own sex perfectly at their ease, and delighted them with his varied conversation, and I never saw any one whose manner to ladies was more pleasing and deferential; and I am not ashamed to record the fact that when, as occurred occasionally, he stopped and spoke to me in the park or elsewhere, I used to hope that some of my ordinary companions might witness me in converse with this 'glorious creature.'

It was many years after the circumstances that I have detailed that I again saw Prince Louis Napoleon, and he had then by a wonderful concurrence of events attained the object of his ambition and prophecy. He was Emperor of the French. It was upon the racecourse in the Bois de Boulogne that I then saw him when I was with a party of friends. He noticed me, and sent the Count de Morny to desire that I should be presented to him. He received me with great civility—I fancy his manner seldom reached cordiality—made no particular allusion to the circumstances of our former meeting, but desired that my friends and myself should be accommodated in what I suppose was the royal stand. He was looking very ill and worn. I never saw him afterwards.

Mr. Baron Alderson was a man worthy of more notice than I have been able to give him from any personal experience. He is one of those designated by Lord Campbell as respectable, and that he deserved that character there is no doubt; but he was in addition a splendid scholar and highly cultivated lawyer. His manner was somewhat brusque, but he was a very humane judge, and, forming an opinion from what I saw of him, almost nervous when trying capital cases. I was counsel in two murder charges before him, in both of which he leant strongly to the side of the accused. One of them was that of a young man, who was acquitted, though certainly guilty, and was afterwards practically proved to be so, being convicted of the robbery which the murderer only could have effected. Alderson's father had been a physician of great eminence at Norwich, one, indeed, of the lights of the profession. I was well acquainted with a son of the Baron's, a very agreeable, gentlemanly person; but the combined talent of the two generations has centred in a female branch.

The counsel who was selected to conduct the prosecution on the part of Prince Napoleon in my place was a gentleman named Humfrey. He was a Queen's Counsel, and leader upon the Midland Circuit. I knew but little of his forensic powers, but I was a witness to the gallant bearing he exhibited under a fearful trial, and happened to be associated with him almost up to the hour of his death. Some eighteen months previously he had been operated upon for cancer. He continued to practise, and upon the occasion I am now referring to I was his junior in a cause before Sir John Jervis in the Court of Common Pleas. Humfrey was suffering intensely, and obliged to conduct it sitting. I learnt, whether from him or not I do not remember, that his daughter was to be married on the following morning. He knew that his end was approaching, and his anxious hope was to live over this marriage.

He left court at four o'clock, and shortly afterwards was found clinging to the rails of Westminster Abbey, was conveyed home, and died during the night. I am able to mention that the marriage which he so much desired to witness took place when the year of mourning had terminated. During the progress of the trial he told the Chief Justice that he had no hope, and that he was so sorry for his clerk. Jervis told him not to trouble himself, and that he would provide for him, which he did after Humfrey's death by giving him an office in the Court of Common Pleas.

The operation to which I have referred was performed by the eminent surgeon whose name has already occurred in these pages, Mr. Lawrence, who sent a report (of course without names) to the 'Lancet.' His patient, who used to read everything upon a subject he was so painfully interested in, recognised that it referred to himself. The concluding words of the report were to this effect: 'The operation was most successful, and will, I trust, prolong life for twelve months.' Another actor in this painful episode soon followed his friend. Sir John Jervis, a man of indomitable pluck, had but a feeble constitution, and it was very painful to witness his sufferings. He was a member, as well as Maule, whom I have already mentioned, of the Union Club, and I have seen him there almost in a state of suffocation from asthma. The incident that I have related of him was by no means the only one that exhibited his kindness of heart.

I was counsel before Mr. Baron Alderson in the case of Sir John Dean Paul, the banker in the Strand. He was indicted with his partners, Messrs. Strachan and Bates, for embezzling property entrusted to them by their customers. Sir John was believed in by a large circle of confiding friends as the most devout of men, and the evidence upon the trial proved that he certainly was amongst the most fraudulent. They were all three found guilty.

My old friend Henry Allworth Merewether, who had an account with them, is credited with a good joke in connection with their failure. After it had occurred he was coming down the steps of the banking house and nearly tumbled. A friend who happened to be passing expressed a hope that he was not hurt. 'Oh no,' said he, 'I have only lost my balance.'

About the period during which I received the visit that I described at the beginning of this chapter, there might be seen on most afternoons, driving up and down in Hyde Park, an elegantly appointed barouche, and in it two ladies, both strikingly handsome: the one approaching middle age, the other was quite young. These were Lady Blessington and her niece, Miss Power. I knew neither of them, and only introduce their names as their house was the nucleus that attracted much of the brilliant society of the time, including the two personages who had honoured me with a visit, and also two others, with one of whom I became slightly acquainted, and with the other I was upon terms of some intimacy. The first of these two was Benjamin Disraeli, the other Sir Edward Lytton Bulwer.

I met the former upon two occasions, both at a comparatively recent date. The first was at a dinner party given by Lord Henry Lennox. He sat next but one to me at the dinner table, but I had no conversation with him, and indeed he was very silent. Of course I was interested in observing him, and pleased with the opportunity which I was afforded of being introduced to him. I met him once afterwards at a garden party of the Prince of Wales at Chiswick. He was with Lady Beaconsfield; but although he spoke to me I doubt very much whether he knew who I was. He left to join some one, and not returning I saw Lady Beaconsfield to her carriage. I suppose that the sympathy exhibited by all classes and of every shade of politics during the illness that terminated in his death has never been surpassed.

The etiquette existing amongst medical men was curiously illustrated upon this occasion; but I confess that whilst I should be very loth to blame an adherence to rules that have been created both for the honour of the profession and the interest of the public, it is difficult not to feel that there are contingencies which would justify a deviation from them. I have reason to know that Dr. Quain entertained but little hope of the recovery of his distinguished patient from the first, and in this instance it cannot be said that the etiquette of the medical profession in any way interfered with the most skilful treatment of so illustrious a patient.[1]

I was well acquainted with the brother of Lord Beaconsfield from a very early period. He was a member of the Clarence Club. I also used to meet Montagu Corry, who not unfrequently joined the little corner that

[1] It is well known that a question arose about meeting Lord Beaconsfield's regular medical attendant, who professed homœopathy. No one has more rigidly maintained the honour of the profession han Dr. Quain, whom I am proud to call my friend; and the course of conduct he pursued was universally approved.

I have described at Paddy Green's; and although I knew so little of Lord Beaconsfield personally, I fancied that I could gather from the terms with which he was spoken of by others the clue to that affection he had the reputation of creating in the minds of all who had the pleasure of his intimate acquaintance.

CHAPTER XXV.

LORD LYTTON.

WHEN Lord Lytton was Secretary of State for the Colonies some papers were removed from the office in which they had been deposited. This had clearly been done surreptitiously, and it turned out that the person doing it had been actuated by some idea that he could obtain from their possession a personal benefit. Lord Lytton was greatly annoyed. He thought that some reflection would be cast upon him for want of sufficient care, and he determined to prosecute the offender, who was given into custody, and after which I was consulted by his solicitors upon the subject. Lord Lytton requested that I would call upon him, which I did one morning at No. 1 Park Lane, where he then resided. I went at the time he appointed, and found him at breakfast.

I remember that he had several animals about him, amongst others a parrot, of which he appeared to be very fond. He had always gone in for artistic dress, and had shone in London another star with Count D'Orsay. If I remember correctly, he was even then somewhat deaf. I thought that he attached to the affair far more consequence than it really deserved, as it was quite absurd to suppose that any one would dream of blaming him. However, the man was sent for trial at the Central Criminal Court, and was made the subject of a State prosecution. Sir Fitzroy Kelly, then Attorney-General, conducted it with his accustomed solemnity. Serjeant Parry defended, and in a very able speech made the most of the importance that had been attached to a very trivial matter. Baron Martin summed up against the prisoner, as in law he was bound to do, but did it in a way to show that he should have been glad if the law had been otherwise, and the jury accommodated themselves to his views by acquitting him. From that time I used very frequently to meet Lord Lytton, and upon several occasions dined with him, both in Park Lane and afterwards in Grosvenor Square. He was certainly a man well worthy of record in the history of his generation.[1]

As a statesman he is the property of history. He certainly possessed the merit of being most painstaking, and I should say almost too anxious. As an orator, his style was elaborate and his speeches most carefully prepared. The unfortunate infirmity of his deafness was a bar to his being an efficient debater. Of his literary works I, in common with the rest of society, am able to form a judgment. They were very popular, and generally exhibited much care, research, and knowledge, and his novels certainly possessed what I may perhaps place too highly in the category of excellence, the power of amusing. It is difficult to imagine four writers of the period, all engaged in works of fiction, whose attributes were so entirely different as those of Thackeray, Dickens, Bulwer, and Disraeli, and the age is not to be despised in which they flourished. Of the two latter it must be remembered that other pursuits than that of literature principally occupied their minds.

[1] A critic remarks that this latter observation is superfluous. I may, admitting this to be the case, I think, be nevertheless excused for making it.

It is no small compliment to Bulwer's dramatic compositions that several of his plays still hold possession of the stage. The principal parts, both male and female, have been played by the best of our actors and actresses, and still form the ambition of novices. 'The Lady of Lyons' and 'Richelieu' are said to be stilted, but whenever they are performed by actors of intelligence they invariably command good audiences, and the play of 'Money' is always popular, especially in the 'provinces.' The best performance that I ever witnessed of 'Richelieu' was by Mr. Booth, the well-known American actor.

Lord Lytton consulted me upon another matter in which he had acted upon very bad advice, and which was a source of great annoyance to him, and I am vain enough to believe that he placed considerable confidence in my opinion. I have upon several occasions remained with him after other guests had left. He was not a good conversationalist, as he was too didactic, and appeared rather to be giving a treatise than inviting a discussion, but what he said was very instructive as well as amusing. I noticed that he dwelt with great apparent pleasure upon the supernatural, and those who have read some of his works, 'Zanoni' for instance, and 'A Strange Story,' can scarcely doubt that he was strongly impregnated with a belief in it. It is very interesting to note the number of remarkable men who have exhibited similar impressions. They are rarely, if ever, boldly avowed, and are nearly always protested against; but still the feeling creeps out, and it is also remarkable how willing the mass of people are to receive it with apparent concurrence.

I suppose that no one thinks of calling 'Guy Mannering' a supernatural novel, and yet the main interest of the story turns upon a horoscope cast by an Indian soldier, whilst Meg Merrilies, one of the most powerful of the author's characters, is clearly endowed with a spirit of prophecy, and we have never heard this most charming of works of fiction charged with improbability. I am convinced that Mr. Const, whom I have before mentioned, a lawyer and a man of pleasure, one of all others whom I should have thought least capable of fanciful ideas, was fully possessed with the notion that he had lived before. He kept a diary, recording events in the Latin language, and once he lent me two or three pages which detailed some incident in which I was interested, and there I found a scene in the description of which he stated that he recognised every feature, and the actual spoken words, although he never could have witnessed it during his present life. When I was translating this aloud, he snatched the diary from my hand.

I do not think it will be out of place whilst upon this subject to relate a story told of Sir Astley Cooper. I am not certain that it has not already been in print, but I know that I have had frequent conversations about it with his nephew.

There had been a murder, and Sir Astley was upon the scene when a man suspected of it was apprehended, and Sir Astley, being greatly interested, accompanied the officers with their prisoner to the gaol, and he and they and the accused were all in a cell, locked in together, when they noticed a little dog, which kept biting at the skirt of the prisoner's coat. This led them to examine the garment, and they found upon it traces of blood, which ultimately led to the conviction of the man. When they looked round, the dog had disappeared, although the door had never been opened. How it had got there, or how it got away, nobody could tell. When Bransby Cooper spoke of this, he always said that of course his uncle had made a mistake, and was convinced of this himself; and Bransby used to add that, no doubt, if the matter had been investigated, it would have been shown that there was a mode of accounting for it from natural causes. But I believe that neither Sir Astley nor his nephew in their own hearts discarded entirely the supernatural.

In relating these anecdotes I am only recording how men of great intellect may be affected by such circumstances. I thought at one time that the last incident applied to the case of Patch, which I have told in a former chapter; but although it may do so I am unable to substantiate it, and must leave it therefore upon no more solid foundation than my memory of its relation to myself as having occurred during some portion of Sir Astley Cooper's early career.

Lord Lytton was extremely interested in criminal investigations, and I could always obtain his attention when I related any of those in which I had myself been engaged, and in novels that he had written previous to my acquaintance with him he had used the records of crime in their construction. A leading idea in 'Pelham,' although the details were dissimilar, was suggested by the case of Thurtell, of which I have already given some particulars; and there was a trial that took place at the early part of the present century. The history of a person named Wainwright had furnished incidents very similar to those related in the novel of 'Lucretia.' In that case the man was convicted of forgery and transported, but no doubt whatever existed that he had also been a practised poisoner.[1] I have always thought that the prologue to this work was one of the most powerful pieces of writing that ever came from Lord Lytton's pen. He told me himself that the character of the banker in 'The Disowned' was suggested by Fauntleroy, and those who remember the history of this man are aware that he was a voluptuary as well as a forger. Lord Lytton describes him

[1] Before his death he confessed to having done so.

also as a craven; and I was able to relate an anecdote that showed that this appreciation of his character was correct.

At the time of the committal of Fauntleroy my father was a visiting justice at Coldbath Fields, to which prison he was sent. An old Bow Street officer—or runner, as these officials used to be designated—of the name of Vickery was the governor. A suspicion arose that some one in the gaol had been tampered with to enable the prisoner to effect his escape, and my father assisted in the investigation of the circumstances, and I learnt from him that it was clearly proved that a ladder of ropes and other conveniences for escape had by some agency been supplied to him; but, as was supposed by those engaged in the inquiry, his courage failed him, and he did not make the attempt.[1]

Although 'The Disowned' is an excellent and interesting work of fiction, the author has, I cannot help thinking, been guilty of a slight slip in one of the episodes contained in the work. A very graphic and amusing sketch is given of the arrest of the banker. He is supposed, before the crash had taken place, or anything was known about its probability, to have gone disguised to the White Horse Cellar, to have asked for a letter directed in an assumed name, and on reading it pretend that he was suddenly called abroad, and ordered a post-chaise. A police officer—why or wherefore is not stated—is seated in the room, orders another post-chaise, follows the banker, and apprehends him at Dover, exhibiting an amount of sagacity that even in those days was more than remarkable. I ventured once to draw Lord Lytton's attention to the difficulty presented to my mind, but got

[1] I have since writing the above had the incident confirmed by a correspondent, who states that preparations had been made upon the Dover road to convey this criminal to the coast.

no explanation, and he did not seem to me to be much pleased with the subject.

Once when I was enjoying a somewhat confidential talk with him at the commencement of our acquaintance, I related an episode in my own life in which he seemed to take a kindly and sympathetic interest, and he afterwards embodied it with little alteration in one of his novels called 'What will He do with It?'

Lord Lytton was very fond of whist, and he and I both belonged to the well-known Portland Club, in which were to be found many of the celebrated players of the day. He never showed the slightest disposition of a gambler. He played the game well, and without excitement or temper, and apparently his whole attention was concentrated upon it; but it was curious to see that at every interval that occurred in the rubbers he would rush off to a writing-table, and with equally concentrated attention proceed with some literary work until called again to take his place at the whist-table. There was a member of the club, a very harmless, inoffensive man, of the name of Townend, for whom Lord Lytton entertained a mortal antipathy, and would never play whilst that gentleman was in the room. He firmly believed that he brought him bad luck. I was witness to what must be termed an odd coincidence. One afternoon, when Lord Lytton was playing, and had enjoyed an uninterrupted run of luck, it suddenly turned, upon which he exclaimed, 'I am sure that Mr. Townend has come into the club.' Some three minutes after, just time enough to ascend the stairs, in walked this unlucky personage. Lord Lytton, as soon as the rubber was over, left the table and did not renew play.

The last time I saw Lord Lytton was after I had ceased to be a member of the club, but was invited to dine there by a Mr. Dommett, a very old and valued friend of mine. It was shortly before Lord Lytton's death. He was about going into Devonshire, and invited me to visit him there. I cannot remember whether he had just undergone or was about to undergo an operation with a view to ameliorate his deafness. Unhappily there was such an operation performed, resulting in an abscess, which, suppurating internally, caused his death. This event, I am certain, created great commiseration in all the circles where his unaffected courtesy, as well as other qualities, rendered him a most agreeable companion.

Amongst those who were cotemporary with Lord Lytton, and, like him, statesman, orator, and author—I am tempted to say novelist also, although such a description might be protested against—was Thomas Babington Macaulay, whose painting of his favourite hero William is just as fanciful as Walter Scott's description of Claverhouse in 'Old Mortality.' Fanciful, however, be it or not, it and other of his works have afforded to this, and will afford to generations to come, instruction and delight.

It is not, however, to criticise his works that I recall his name, but to mention that a very pleasing incident in my own life was making his acquaintance and travelling for three days in his company. He was with Mr. Ellis, an eminent lawyer and a friend of mine. We passed through some of the cities of Belgium. Every one has heard of his marvellous memory and inexhaustible fund of information; he delighted to impart it. There was no subject about which he talked that he was not eloquent and instructive upon, and I did not at all regret that during the time I was in his company I myself was constrained to preserve almost uninterrupted silence.

In recording my recollections of Lord Lytton, I have not been sorry to introduce my readers to the Portland Club. It comprised amongst its members many well-known personages, with some of whom I was upon terms of intimacy.

It was considered to be a play club, not similar to Crockford's and Graham's, as the games allowed were confined to such only as combined skill with chance, and, as I have previously mentioned, many first-rate players belonged to it. There was a dinner in the evening, which brought people together, and at which much good fellowship prevailed. The play at times was high, but a moderate game could generally be obtained by those who desired it.

When first I entered the club my attention was attracted by an active, lithesome old man engaged in a game of billiards, which, considering his age, he was playing with wonderful power and skill. This was 'the Squire' Osbaldestone. He had filled for half a century before I knew him no small space in the sporting world, and it was not difficult to discover in him the weakness that had wrecked a fine fortune. Although few surpassed him in his knowledge of horses, and no amateur in riding them, and although he was a first-rate pedestrian, cricketer, and shot, he overestimated his powers in playing, as it were, against the field, and laid the odds on himself instead of obtaining them. He bore his fate with apparent equanimity, and the lessons he had received did not seem to have in any respect lessened his opinion of himself.

A very constant player at afternoon whist was Lord Henry Bentinck. His name, as may be remembered, was introduced with those of George Anson and George Payne upon the Lord de Ros trial, and by itself would have been sufficient guarantee that no hasty or unconsidered charge had been launched against that unfortunate nobleman.

I think that Lord Henry was a man of considerable intellect, but he was extremely reserved, and, although I have met him at Lord Lytton's and elsewhere, he furnished but few opportunities for forming a judgment. He was a fine whist player, indifferent to the stakes he played, and a rigid adherent to the rules of the game, from which, as he understood them, nothing would induce him to deviate.

An excited adversary might display by a gesture what he had in his hand, but it was lost upon Lord Henry; and if cards were exposed under his very nose, his eyes might see them, but it altered not his play. I can remember well a member, who did not so much respect accuracy in play as he did the result of it, gnashing his teeth at what he deemed the idiotism and folly of his lordship. There are many alive who may guess to whom I allude; he himself is dead.[1]

I was once walking home with Lord Henry from a dinner party at Cavendish Square. He told me that Lord de Ros had received frequent warnings, but seemed blind to all of them; and from my perusal of the trial—I have heard about his lordship from other sources—I am convinced that Lord de Ros furnished an example of a mind in most respects sound and intelligent, but subject to this one uncontrollable impulse. Lord Henry considered that no one surpassed himself in skill in any game that he played, but he told me that although in the long run he had been a winner, it was to a very trifling extent—saying, I remember, that he should have made more as a journeyman glazier!

James Clay, the recognised authority upon the game of whist, was a member, and played frequently. There was an amusing rivalry between him and Lord Henry; each of them declared that the other knew nothing about the game. Mr. Clay was a great proficient in all games of skill. He was champion billiard player amongst

[1] A very friendly critic is mistaken in supposing that I join in the disapproval.

amateurs. His work upon whist was recognised as the great authority until 'Cavendish' rather supplemented it than wrote a new one. He might, however, be remembered for higher qualities than these exhibit. He was extremely well informed, capable of taking correct and forcible views upon most subjects. In the House of Commons, where he sat for the borough of Hull, he was much looked up to, and his house in Bryanston Square was the scene of many pleasant gatherings.

One of the most amusing companions I ever met with, whether in this club or out of it, was John Bushe, not a young man when first I made his acquaintance, but full of life and good spirits. He was an Irishman, and the son of the well-known Chief Justice of the Irish Court of Common Pleas, a judge whose witty sayings somewhat startled the decorum of the Bench, even in times not famous for that characteristic. His son was bright and amusing, and his little parties in the Albany were always highly appreciated. No one, probably, had seen more of life in all its phases. In the early part of it he had been engaged in one or two 'affairs of honour,' as they were called; there were few Irishmen who had not been, but no one could be less prone to quarrel than he was, or possess a more perfectly even temper. He was a good player at most games, and, as may be supposed, very popular in the club.

There is still a figure that I recall, indeed it would be very difficult to forget it—Dr. Jones, father of 'Cavendish,' and himself as good a whist player as his son the author of its rules, who also belonged to the club.

I have frequently played a rubber with another member, whose name became famous during the Crimean War—General Windham. The gallantry universally exhibited during that memorable struggle has prevented individual traits from standing prominently forth upon many of the occasions on which they were exhibited; but Windham was fortunate in the particular event which has rendered his name celebrated, and even more fortunate in the eloquent and able pen that has connected it with the storming of the Redan. For this he is indebted to William Russell, of whom I believe I may say, without prejudice to others, that he created what has become an institution—the 'military correspondent' to a newspaper. His career and his example have been ably followed, and it would be difficult to exaggerate the qualities necessary for the performance of the duties involved. It requires not only literary attainment of no mean order, but he must be a man possessing military knowledge, unflinching courage, and great powers of endurance. It was in an ardent desire to fulfil his duties that my poor friend Bowlby, as I have previously mentioned, became the victim of Chinese barbarity.

I knew Russell well in the early part of my career, and before he had made his name famous; and, although not thrown much into his society, we have met at the Garrick Club and elsewhere during the intervals of his freedom from work. He, like so many who bear honoured names, is an Irishman, and it was through some of my friends belonging to that country that I first made his acquaintance.

Kingston is an old friend of mine, and, apart from his professional merits, would, I am sure, enliven the dullest of campaigns. The reputation of Forbes and others cannot be enhanced by anything I say. I only regret that I do not possess the personal knowledge of them to enable me to add to the interest of these pages.

The Crimea—nearly thirty years have elapsed since the name became famous in English annals. The reality of the war was scarcely dreamt of by its authors, and I do not believe that any such terrible conflict was expected. I know that Lord Raglan, when he rearranged his insurances, stated with confidence that the expedition would be a merely military march.

I remember the event in connection with its social aspect, and even at this distance of time I can recall happy young faces that before the event I have seen at the Garrick Club and at Evans's, and with the owners of which I have often enjoyed myself, who soon after found their graves in a foreign land. The war made a sad clearance in many a place of amusement, but now that the pangs first experienced have become deadened by time, there is many a family reconciled to a loss that has left a noble fame behind.

One of the most amusing evenings that I ever passed in my life was with one to whom before the war I had bidden good-bye, and who, having been upon nearly every battle-field through the campaign, and become the proud possessor of the Victoria Cross, had escaped without a wound—Colonel Goodlake. How he did escape is one of those marvels difficult to be accounted for, as he stood about six feet five in his boots, and presented a corresponding breadth of person. I dined with him *tête-à-tête* at the Tower on one night shortly after his return, and listened with intense interest to his simple but not less graphic details of the different fights, and his affecting account of deaths of lads whom we had both known. I was filled with admiration for the courage and endurance of our soldiers, officers and men, and with a detestation and horror of what is called 'the glory of war.'

It is a general trait of great men in all professions that they rarely blazon their own exploits, and this applies signally to those belonging to the military profession. My old friend, Colonel Napier Sturt, himself a Crimean officer, when on guard at St. James's Palace, gave me frequent opportunities of meeting his comrades at very agreeable dinner parties, and of listening to anecdotes, serious and gay, of the campaign.

Amongst the latter I was much amused by one told me, that an attack made upon a hamper of good things from Fortnum and Mason, which had suddenly invaded their quarters, invalided more men in the regiment than the fire of the enemy.

At one of these entertainments I met Mr. Greville, whose 'Memoirs' have caused so great a stir. He talked agreeably, but said very little, and seemed somewhat bored. I have read with great interest his recollections, and certainly his life ought to have furnished him with incessant enjoyment, mixing as he did with all that was famous and intellectual in society; but if the entry he made in his diary when he attained his fortieth birthday was a true index of his feelings, the reader would be apt to exclaim, 'All is indeed vanity!'[1]

The following is the extract referred to, April 3, 1834:—

'Yesterday I was forty years old—an anniversary much too melancholy to think of. And when I think how intolerably these forty years have been wasted, how unprofitably spent, how little store laid up for the future, how few the pleasurable recollections of the past, a feeling of pain and humiliation comes across me that makes my cheeks tingle and burn as I write. It is very seldom that I indulge in moralising in this journal of mine. If anybody ever reads it, what will they care for my feelings and regrets? It is no reason, they will think, that because I have wasted my time they should waste theirs in reading the records of follies that are nothing more than the great mass of the world are every day committing. Idleness, vanity, and selfishness are our besetting sins, and we are perpetually whirled about by one or other of them. It is certainly more amusing, both to other people and to myself (when I look back to what I have written), to read the anecdotes and events of the day than all this moral stuff (by which I mean stuff as applied to me, not as being despicable in itself), but every now and then the fancy takes me, and I think I find relief by giving vent upon paper to that which I cannot say to anybody—"Cela fait partie de cette doctrine intérieure qu'il ne faut jamais communiquer" (Stendthal). I am satisfied, and I will go to other things—the foreign or domestic scraps I have picked up.'—*Greville's Journal*, vol. iii. p. 77.

CHAPTER XXVI.

CURIOUS TRIAL FOR MURDER.

I AM about to tell a story the circumstances of which would be thought improbable in a romance, and yet every word of it is true; and there are incidents which I believe to be connected with it that would add to its strangeness, but which I suppress because I do not possess the proofs requisite for their authentication.

What I shall relate will disclose a series of blunders, the danger of placing too great reliance upon scientific testimony, and the want of a tribunal capable of revising decisions alleged to have been erroneous in criminal cases.

The unfortunate victim was a lady of the name of Banks, who, at the date of my narrative, might still be entitled to be called young, and certainly was of that opinion herself. She was a member of a highly respectable family, and possessed of some 2,000*l*. entirely at her own disposal, and had some further expectancies. She was not fond of the trammels of home life, and, preferring to reside at a boarding-house, she selected the establishment of a respectable lady at Bayswater, where also resided a medical man and his wife, of the name of Smethurst, the former about fifty years old, the latter twenty years older. An intimacy sprang up between the doctor and the lodger, of which the mistress of the house did not approve, and gave Miss Banks notice to leave, which she did upon November 29 in the year 18—. The doctor also left upon December 12 following, and was married the same day to Miss Banks at Battersea Church. Oddly enough, no surprise was expressed by the doctor's wife, and her position in the affair is very difficult to be understood; it will certainly be made apparent by the course of events that she was in communication with her husband and upon apparently affectionate terms throughout the events I am about to detail. Nothing more is known with certainty of the doctor and Miss Banks until February the 4th, when they took apartments in one of the suburbs, where they remained until April the 15th, living as man and wife, and upon leaving went to another residence in the neighbourhood. It is to be remarked that from the time of their removal in February Miss Banks was apparently suffering from illness, and Dr. Julius, one of the best-known medical men in the neighbourhood, was called in to see her. It must be borne in mind, in reference to statements subsequently relied upon by the prisoner, that no suggestion was then made by him that she was pregnant, but he stated that she was suffering from a bilious attack. It would not, however, assist the general reader or help to develop the story to give any details of the symptoms then exhibited.

Suffice it to say that Dr. Julius found, to his great astonishment, that none of his remedies produced the slightest effect, and he felt confident that some agent was at work to counteract them. Naturally he was very loth to express such an opinion, and he continued to watch the case with great anxiety; and, without mentioning his suspicions to his partner, requested that gentleman to take charge of the patient for two or three days, which accordingly he did. At the end of that time he also was impressed with the same conviction, and declared his positive opinion that the lady was being placed under the influence of poison, thus fully supporting the view previously arrived at by Dr. Julius.

Towards the latter end of April, the sister of Miss Banks was for the first time communicated with, and she at once came. Her evidence does not throw any light upon the case, except that she deposed that her sister's health was generally good, and that, although she occasionally suffered from bilious attacks, they succumbed readily to simple treatment. Her appearance at this time was so alarming that, at the sister's suggestion, another medical man was sent for, and one of the most eminent physicians of the day attended, and saw her on the last day of April. No communication was made to this gentleman of the suspicions entertained, but the first words he uttered after his examination were, 'That lady is being poisoned!'

A portion of arsenic was discovered in some vomit that was analysed by the well-known chemist Professor Taylor; and this, joined to the absolute conviction of all three medical men, induced one of them to apply for a warrant, and the pseudo-husband was arrested upon it. He was, however, by an utterly unaccountable blunder, released, the magistrates accepting his statement that his absence would kill his wife, and allowing him access to his apartment without supervision. His release, however, did not prevent the fatal result, for on the following day, May 3, the unfortunate lady died in great suffering. A *post-mortem* examination was held upon her body, and both arsenic and antimony were discovered in different parts of the intestines. It was proved by the landlady of the house in which she died that the supposed husband alone waited upon her, declining upon the ground of poverty (for which there was no foundation) to employ a nurse, and that no portions of the food sent up to their rooms were ever returned. In giving an account of the illness and death of this poor lady I have avoided details of a technical character as much as possible, but I think I have said enough to make my views intelligible; and I have now to call attention to certain facts that must be taken in conjunction with the medical evidence to enable the reader to form a sound conclusion upon the case.

On Saturday, the 12th of April, preceding the death, the accused man went to a solicitor, and requested him to call at his lodgings the next day for the purpose of drawing out a will, at the same time showing him the draft of one which he said a barrister had prepared. The solicitor objected to doing so on Sunday, but, being told that the lady was ill, consented, if sent for, to come. His visitor called upon him again the next morning, and brought him to where he and Miss Banks were residing. The lawyer wished that a medical man should be present, but this was declined. The draft that he had seen before was produced; and a will was drawn up founded upon it, which left everything to the accused, and Miss Banks executed it, signing her maiden name.

It was proved at the trial that in a box belonging to the prisoner were found subsequently many forms of wills, and also a letter, which for some reason had not been forwarded, directed to his wife, and which appeared to me one of the most significant incidents in the case. The letter was dated May 2, and contained an intimation that he (the prisoner) had been prevented by circumstances from leaving for town so soon as he expected in consequence of his professional assistance being required by a patient on whom he was attending, and that, *if anything unforeseen prevented him from leaving before the* 11*th*, money should be sent to her for certain purposes, and concluded with the expression of a hope that he might find her quite well on his return, which he trusted would not long be delayed.

I have already stated that Miss Banks died upon May 3, and the supposed widower, who in the meanwhile had unrestricted access to his room, being again taken into custody, was examined before a bench of magistrates, and finally committed to take his trial for murder at the Central Criminal Court, and in due course was arraigned before the Lord Chief Baron Pollock. It so happened that upon the second day of the trial a juryman was taken ill, the jury were consequently discharged, and the case was adjourned to a subsequent sessions, when the same judge presided. I conducted the prosecution, and the facts as I have related them, but in greater detail, were proved. Mr. Serjeant Parry, with whom was Mr. Giffard, defended, and two abler men could not have been selected. Medica practitioners were called by them to prove that the appearances detailed were consistent with natural causes; and one gentleman, who had figured for the same purpose upon the Palmer trial, started a theory to support this opinion.

The Lord Chief Baron pointed out that it was not from isolated symptoms that a conclusion could be formed, but by the aggregate of all of them joined to the independent facts of the case—the same doctrine in fact as that enforced by Lord Campbell upon the trial of Palmer—and the jury, as it appeared to me at the time, and I still think, came to the right and almost inevitable conclusion of the prisoner's guilt. A great outcry, however, subsequently arose, a medical war was waged with great vigour in the newspapers, and petitions were forwarded to the Secretary of State. Two documents also were produced; one a letter to Miss Banks' sister, and another an entry by the prisoner in a diary. The fact was suppressed that copies of both were in the hands of the prisoner at the time of the trial, and that I had offered to put them in evidence if it was desired on his behalf, and the Secretary of State was probably drawn into the conclusion that they had been kept back against his wishes.

Ultimately the matter was referred to Sir Benjamin Brodie to report upon, and he obviously could only deal with it in its purely medical phase, and without the light thrown upon it by the other evidence. Of course no one on the part of the prosecution could interfere. The Home Secretary ultimately released the prisoner, who afterwards proved the will of Miss Banks and thus secured possession of her property.[1]

When the following facts are brought to the attention of the reader, this result can easily be understood.

It will be remembered that on the day before the death of Miss Banks, the accused man was given into custody, but released. Whether this could have been undei any circumstances prudent, it is abundantly clear that either everything that could throw light upon the subject ought to have been taken possession of beforehand, or some watch placed upon the supposed husband; but neither was done. He obtained access to his room, and I have very little doubt that he laid a trap, into which Dr. Taylor innocently fell. *After* the death, everything that the prisoner had allowed to remain was secured, when it was noticed that the medicines supplied by the local practitioners were nearly untouched, but there was nothing besides to excite suspicion but one bottle filled with colourless liquid. This was immediately pounced upon; it was known that arsenic had already

[1] After the pardon for the murder he was tried, convicted, and imprisoned for twelve months for bigamy.

been discovered in the body, and so Professor Taylor set to work upon a portion of the liquid with the usual test for the discovery of that poison. This is called Reinsch's test, and consists in mixing a small quantity of hydrochloric acid with the liquid to be tested, and then dropping into it a piece of copper gauze, upon which, if there be any arsenic in the mixture, it is supposed to attach itself. Accordingly this was done with a portion of the liquid in question, but, instead of the gauze attracting anything, it became itself dissolved. Another piece of gauze, and then a third, met with the same fate: at last traces of arsenic did attach themselves to a piece of the wire which had not dissolved, and when before the magistrates the Professor, without explaining the difficulty that he had encountered, simply stated that upon analysis he had discovered arsenic. The remaining portion of the contents of the bottle was preserved,[1] and, being subjected to a different test, turned out to contain no arsenic whatever, but was a bottle containing a solution of chlorate of potash, and Professor Taylor ultimately found out that the arsenic he had discovered after so many trials had actually emanated from his own copper gauze, which had been dissolved in the early experiments.

Although really the arsenic and antimony that had undoubtedly been discovered in the body rendered it immaterial whether any was contained in this particular bottle, there can be no doubt that so terrible an oversight on the part of a man of great eminence was calculated to affect public opinion, and lead it to cast discredit upon the whole of the scientific testimony produced, and I have now to relate an incident in connection with it

[1] I well remember that upon the inquest Dr. Smethurst showed great anxiety that this should be done.

which will, I think, throw some light upon the origin of this most serious mistake.

A physician now of great eminence, who was present when the vomit was analysed, and who gave evidence upon the subject of dysentery, of which he had obtained much experience in the Crimean campaign, forwarded to the solicitor who was conducting the prosecution a number of the 'Lancet,' containing a letter from the prisoner, written some seven or eight years before, upon the subject of the extraction of teeth, and in this number, and upon the opposite page to that which contained his letter, was one of a series of lectures by an eminent chemist on the detection of arsenic, in which it was stated that wherever chlorates were used Reinsch's test would invariably be defeated. It was probably perfectly known to the prisoner that this test had been usually applied by Dr. Taylor, and I have never been able to make up my mind whether there was really any poison in the bottle, or whether it was a contrivance which had been arranged for the purpose during the interval between the prisoner's first and second apprehensions, with a view to the result that occurred; but, whatever was the intention, it undoubtedly saved his life.

It is due to the memory of Dr. Taylor to state that a doubt crossing his own mind led to the discovery of the mistake which was disclosed upon the trial, and did not really affect the weight of the evidence, or apparently the minds of the jury, it being shown that it would not affect the analyses of the vomit and intestines. It may not be altogether satisfactory to mankind to mention that Dr. Taylor wrote to several of the most eminent chemists to obtain specimens of the gauze used by them in their experiments, and that it was in every instance found impregnated in the same way. The difficulty that presents itself to my thoughts is, why the presence of the chlorate was not ascertained before the test was applied.

It is a pregnant example, however, of what I have been so anxious to enforce—that the speculations of scientific men, however eminent, ought never to be made the basis of a case. They may and constantly do materially assist it. In the instances of Palmer and many others they were so far auxiliary to the other evidence that they showed it to be perfectly consistent with the natural conclusion that the facts themselves had presented to all reasoning minds.

The solicitor of the deceased was indefatigable in his exertions in the conduct of this case. His sympathies and indignation were both roused, and it occurred to him, in looking at the letter of the prisoner in the 'Lancet,' to see where it was dated from, and he found that it was dated from a street in the West End, where the prisoner was living with his wife, and practising as a doctor. His brother carried on business as a chemist in an adjacent street. They both left somewhat suddenly, after an event upon which the subsequent history throws a somewhat ghastly light.

A gentleman named G——, thirty-three years old, accompanied by his wife, a young lady possessing some attractions, came to lodge at the brother's house, and shortly afterwards was taken ill; he was attended only by the prisoner, the drugs being supplied by his brother. None of the invalid's family saw him, and some of them were refused admittance. He died, and shortly after both brothers disappeared from the neighbourhood, as also did the widow. The certificate of his death described it as resulting from disease of the kidneys. No medical man's name is attached. The application of arsenic would produce symptoms that might be mistaken for this disease,

No investigation seems to have taken place, and nothing was heard of the poor fellow's wife until between the period of the two trials of the prisoner, when the solicitor received an extraordinary communication through an equally curious channel. A lady sitting in the gallery during the first trial made some remark to a neighbour favourable to the prisoner, when that person said, 'Oh, he is guilty; he is one of a gang of poisoners.'

The lady asked what she meant, and received a statement, and also the person's name and address, which she communicated, and an officer was sent to make inquiries.

She turned out to be the widow of a sergeant and quartermaster in the army, and she furnished a long statement, which it is not necessary for me to set out *in extenso*. The important part of it was, that she was residing with her husband in a house at Brompton, that the prisoner's brother was living next door, that the prisoner was constantly there, and that a lady calling herself Mrs. G—— was living in the same house. The witness stated that, about three years before, this lady had come into her house in a highly excited state, and said that the prisoner had been trying to force her to make a will in his favour, and made further statements indicating a belief that she should be poisoned if she did.

The witness saw Mrs. G—— upon other occasions; once the servant fetched her when she was in a fit, and a doctor was also present. The patient made statements about the prisoner that showed she was in great apprehension as to the food she was taking. Mrs. G—— appeared to be about forty years of age.

On the 9th of December preceding the marriage of Dr. Smethurst with Miss Banks the same witness saw the prisoner with another lady, who, from the description, was probably the unfortunate deceased. The foregoing statement was made to Sergeant MacIntyre, a police constable, and, whether the conclusions of the witness were correct or not, there seems but little doubt that Mrs. G—— must have been the widow of the prisoner's former patient.

I think also that it will be admitted that if the circumstances I have related be substantially correct, they show that through a variety of unfortunate causes the case must be regarded as exhibiting a most lamentable result.

I have already mentioned that a strong contest went on in the press upon the result of the trial, and representations, some of which were certainly untrue, were made to the Home Secretary. The facts were of such a peculiar character that the whole of them should be taken together to enable a sound conclusion to be arrived at. It is simply impossible that this can be done without ordinary legal machinery. Every lawyer knows that in civil cases a rule for a new trial is constantly granted until light is thrown upon the facts by those opposing it. In criminal cases no power exists for such a purpose. The scheme of a Court of Appeal frightens our Legislature, but justice demands it, and I believe that it might be effected with both ease and benefit. I was well acquainted with the leading physician in the case, who was certainly one of the foremost men in his profession. He never swerved for a moment in his conviction that the unfortunate woman was poisoned; and I fancy that he agreed with Brodie and other eminent medical men; that an experienced eye witnessing a death-bed can scarcely be mistaken as to the signs presented if poison has been administered.

POSTSCRIPT.

In the first and subsequent editions the names of the principal persons described in the above remarkable case were suppressed through the caution always exercised by Mr. Bentley, but I think unnecessarily on this occasion, and I publish them in the present edition without hesitation, taking upon myself any responsibility for doing so. In recording the incidents I have abstained from stating many about which I entertain little doubt, but of which I do not possess conclusive proof.

About one part of the case, and that not the least extraordinary, I am perfectly clear that there existed a secret understanding between husband and wife. Whilst the proceedings were in progress a very intimate friend of mine, Captain Ward, who had been a distinguished officer in the Indian Service, took great interest in them, and read certain correspondence that had passed between the two. He was much struck by the similarity it bore to the communication between the Thugs, which body of assassins he had been largely instrumental in suppressing.

There probably never existed in the medical profession a man of more varied knowledge or sounder judgment than Sir Benjamin Brodie, but all that he was able to say was that the symptoms as related to him as attending the death of Miss Banks were consistent with other causes than those imputed to the prisoner, and such must be the case in most deaths by poison; but the facts which ought to create the substantial grounds for a verdict being entirely out of the province of the medical referee, his conclusions, however sound they may be from a scientific point of view, must be an unsatisfactory basis to act upon.

CHAPTER XXVII.

THE PELLIZZIONI TRIAL.

During the year 1864 a trial took place at the Central Criminal Court which presents features worthy for more reasons than one to be recorded. In the first place, the life of a perfectly innocent man was placed in jeopardy, and in the next the course pursued by the police deserves attention and calls for remark.

It appeared that upon the 26th of December in the previous year a serious disturbance had taken place in a public-house situated on Saffron Hill, Clerkenwell. This locality was at the time inhabited by the humbler class of Italians, and a squabble arose between them and some Englishmen of the neighbourhood, resulting in the death of a man named Harrington, who was mortally wounded, and in serious injury to another man of the name of Rebbeck.

In both cases the injuries inflicted were by some sharp instrument, and in all probability by the same one. An Italian named Pellizzioni was found lying upon the body of the deceased man, and was then seized by the police, who naturally inferred that he was the perpetrator of the acts. He, however, declared that he had only come in after they were committed, was endeavouring to quell the disturbance, and in the scuffle still going on was thrown upon the body of Harrington, who was not quite dead. No weapon of any kind was found near the spot. After some examinations at the police court Pellizzioni was committed for trial, and tried before Mr. Baron Martin upon the charge of wilful murder.

This learned judge had been a very successful advocate upon the Northern Circuit, where, however, he had not had any experience in the criminal courts, and, although essentially humane and kind-hearted, was hasty in forming opinions, and slow in changing them; and it was obvious that very early in the case he took a strong view against the prisoner, and, summing up in accordance with it, a verdict of guilty was pronounced. Sentence of death was passed, the judge stating in the course of it that 'he had never known more direct or conclusive evidence in any case.' It would serve no useful purpose to discuss the testimony given by the various witnesses called, and I shall dismiss the question with this remark—that it was extremely conflicting, and there must have existed upon one side or the other very gross perjury. Several policemen were called and were examined at great length. *No knife was produced or alluded to on the part of the prosecution.*[1]

The conviction of Pellizzioni produced a great sensation in the neighbourhood where he resided, and where he bore the character of a singularly inoffensive man; and those who had known him entertained a very different opinion from Mr. Baron Martin, and a shrewd suspicion, if not a certainty, existed amongst them as to who the culprit really was. Doubts were ventilated through the columns of the 'Daily Telegraph,' and the proprietors of that journal took a strong personal interest in the matter. Mr. Negretti, the well-known optician, who was also a countryman of the convict, was indefatigable in his

[1] I have been told that the knife was in court, but it certainly was not alluded to.

behalf, and ultimately the force of public opinion in the neighbourhood, and the interference of a Catholic priest, induced a man named Gregorio Mogni to confess that he was the person who had committed the crime, although, as he alleged, in self-defence.

Mogni was committed and tried at the following sessions of the Central Court upon a charge of manslaughter. It fell to the lot of Mr. Justice Byles to try the case. This learned Judge possessed great acuteness, but showed very clearly that he was influenced by the strong view previously taken by Mr. Baron Martin.

I was instructed by the friends of Pellizzioni to prosecute, and Mr. Montagu Williams, upon very slight materials, and with very great ability, defended. Mogni was convicted, nor can I see how any other result could have been arrived at. This, however, brought about a very peculiar state of things, as there were two men now lying in Newgate convicted of the same crime. In the one case the judge had declared that he had no doubt of Pellizzioni's guilt; in the other Mogni, who could not be mistaken, declared that he alone committed the crime. Fortunately for the ends of justice, whoever killed Harrington also stabbed Rebbeck, and so, to solve the difficulty, the Government put Pellizzioni through the ordeal of a trial for this latter offence, and Mr. Giffard prosecuted on their behalf, which ensured the certainty that the evidence would be fully sifted. The case occupied some time, I forget how long, and Mogni was called, and adhered to his confession. He was cross-examined very rigidly, but in the end the jury without hesitation acquitted the prisoner; and I do not entertain the slightest doubt that he was perfectly innocent, and very unpleasantly for himself, and at the risk of his neck, illustrated the old lines commencing, 'Those who in quarrels interpose.' It is, however, very seldom that a man who has engaged solely in the endeavour to prevent strife has been placed in such jeopardy, and it is worthy of consideration to what this can fairly be attributed: I believe it arose from the haste and impetuosity with which the police first adopted a conclusion, and afterwards adhered to it, although they were well aware of circumstances that strongly militated against its correctness.

It will be remembered that upon the first trial no weapon was produced or alluded to on the part of the prosecution, though it will scarcely be credited that the knife with which both injuries were inflicted had been for some time before in the hands of the police. This fact was not brought before those who conducted the prosecution, nor before the jury who tried the case, and it is difficult to find satisfactory reasons for this concealment. The knife had been found at some distance from the spot where the crime had been committed, and could not have been conveyed there by Pellizzioni. It was known throughout the neighbourhood that it was Mogni's knife, and it is difficult to believe that the police alone were ignorant of this fact.

Upon the subsequent trials it was produced, and identified by Mogni. He had, after stabbing the two men, handed it to a fellow-countryman named Cetti, who had thrown it into an out-of-the way place, where it was subsequently found.

The public-house in which the occurrence took place was evidently of a very low description, and the witnesses called upon the trial were not unlikely to be influenced by the opinion of the police. The police had the practical management of the prosecution before it came into court; and I have felt that in calling attention to its remarkable details I am performing a useful duty to society.

It must be borne in mind that very few in the position

of Pellizzioni would be likely to receive the aid of a powerful journal, or obtain the sympathy and assistance of influential friends.

Upon the original trial certain deathbed statements made by Harrington, when *in extremis*, were sworn to by a policeman, which inculpated the prisoner, and which were said to be taken down by another constable. This circumstance doubtless was instrumental in obtaining the first verdict, but through the conduct exhibited by these witnesses it was entirely discredited by the juries upon the two subsequent investigations.

A short time after the acquittal of Pellizzioni I received a visit from the Marquis D'Azeglio, the Sardinian Minister, who was instructed to convey to me the thanks of his Government for my exertions in the case. This was the means of my forming a most agreeable acquaintance. The Marquis was very popular in English society, and I met him occasionally in London, and subsequently at Homburg, where, through his introduction, I passed many pleasant hours.

I understood from him that the services rendered to Pellizzioni in this country had been very warmly appreciated in his own. I believe that the Marquis died not very long after I had the pleasure of knowing him, and if so it must have been in the prime of life.[1]

It is manifest that in all investigations in criminal matters the police must form a very material element, and the correctness of the result must greatly depend upon their truth and accuracy. It is therefore most important that those who preside upon such inquiries should understand the characteristics of the body, and know something of their organisation. I fear that without such knowledge

[1] I am very glad to hear that in this I am mistaken, and that the Marquis is alive and well.

very serious mischances, and perhaps fatal ones, are likely to arise. I have had constant opportunities of forming a judgment, and my remarks are not founded upon any prejudice against a necessary, and in many respects trustworthy, body of men; but from the conclusions that my experience has forced upon me, I am obliged to say that the evidence given by the police ought to be viewed with a considerable amount of caution.

Wherever men are associated in a common object, as in their case, an *esprit de corps* naturally arises, and this not unfrequently colours the testimony of individual members. Their duties are extremely trying and calculated frequently to cause anger and irritation, feelings which almost invariably induce those possessed by them to exaggerate if not to invent. The classes against whom they appear are usually without the position that commands consideration, and consequently statements made to their prejudice meet with the more ready belief.

The feeling of sanctity that probably once attached to an oath becomes deadened in the minds of those who are taking it every day, and an easy manner and composed demeanour are acquired by persons constantly in the witness-box. There exists a very bad habit in the force, of communicating their opinions at the outset of an inquiry, thus pledging themselves to views which it is damaging to their sagacity to retract. The Pellizzioni case furnishes an example of the evil arising from this habit. Everybody knows that 'an experienced and intelligent officer has, with his accustomed acuteness,' secured the murderer, &c.; and in this case the police did not like publishing the fact that they had committed a flagrant blunder, and so an innocent man was very nearly being executed. On the other hand, in many cases where constables have discharged their duties in a most exemplary manner, and may have been either disabled or killed, I cannot think that their services are sufficiently considered, or properly rewarded; and, as I have said in a former portion of these pages, I do not think that nearly sufficient protection is thrown around them by adequate punishments being meted out to those from whom they have been subjected to serious injuries. In the earlier days of their existence they were very unpopular, and it was only natural that the Executive should use every effort to support them, and magistrates were censured occasionally for the views they took in certain cases against members of the force. Now, however, I am sure that as efficient a control as is possible is exercised by the Commissioners, and the magistrates perform their duties without dread of the Home Secretary, formerly a feeling not wholly without justification. And as far as my observation has enabled me to form a judgment, the police preserve order in the streets with good temper and firmness.

The preceding reflections are made in no unkind or unfriendly spirit, but now especially, when judges who have never been inside a criminal court are called upon to preside in trials where the issues possibly involve the life of a human being, and where the police perhaps are material witnesses, my observations may not be altogether out of place or unworthy of consideration.

I am unable to furnish the date of the following case, in which I was engaged on the part of the defendant, a policeman; it was, however, after the trials of which I have in the last chapter given an account. In relating the circumstances I shall not express any belief as to the truth or falsehood of the charge made, but the view taken by the jury justifies me in quoting it as an illustration of some of the observations that I have presented to the reader.

In a certain district in St. John's Wood, shortly before the case I am recording, a number of burglaries had occurred, and great indignation had been expressed at the supineness of the police, not unaccompanied by insinuations of a graver kind.

Two young men, of perfect respectability as far as appeared from evidence that was adduced, were walking on their way home somewhat late one night in the neighbourhood which had been the scene of the burglaries, and, according to their own account, they had done nothing that was calculated to excite suspicion, nor had anything upon their persons unusual for respectable people to possess. To their astonishment they were seized by three policemen, and charged with attempting to break into a house.

The three officers declared that they had watched them, and caught them in the act, and had actually taken from them the implements of burglary.

It is obvious that, if the young men told the truth, one of the most wicked cases of conspiracy ever known had been planned by the police, and was carried out by flagrant perjury.

The accused were discharged, and they, in their turn, prosecuted the three officers at the Central Court. The cases stood for trial before the Recorder, Mr. Russell Gurney, whose name I have previously mentioned, and who, whilst thoroughly impartial, was rather inclined to the side of authority than otherwise.

The charges were for perjury, and it is right that I should mention, for the benefit of the general reader, that only one person can be included in an indictment for that particular offence.

This being so, the defendant charged was able to call, and did call, his two companions. The case was very ably conducted by Mr. Serjeant Sleigh, and he had the advantage, not on such an occasion a small one, of a reply. A very clear summing-up followed, and the jury, after some deliberation, convicted the accused.

It will be quite understood that I express no opinion as to the correctness or the reverse of this verdict. I thought, however, that it was of such very grave importance that I advised that the two remaining indictments should be removed into the Court of Queen's Bench, which was accordingly done, and the sentence upon the person already tried was postponed until the result of the further investigations. These were not, however, proceeded with, no public prosecutor existing at the time; and it is likely that the expense deterred the young men, who had sufficiently vindicated their characters, from proceeding any further in the matter.

CHAPTER XXVIII.

STATE OF REGENT STREET.

NOT a great many years ago—it was during the time that a valued friend of mine, and most excellent magistrate, presided at the Marlborough Street Police Court—a number of cases were investigated involving very serious charges against the police stationed in that district, and I am able myself to testify that to some extent, at all events, they were well founded.

Regent Street and the surrounding localities were frequented by women carrying on a miserable calling. The Quadrant especially was rendered almost impassable for decent people. The shopkeepers were up in arms, and bitter complaints were raised against the negligence of the officers. The inquiries, however, set on foot fully explained the reason of this. The constables upon the beat were in the pay of the worst and most troublesome of those who infested the streets, in consideration for which they allowed them to annoy the passengers with impunity; whilst those who were quiet and inoffensive had black-mail levied upon them by the most tyrannical and cruel means. If they refused to pay, they were taken into custody, had to pass the night in a wretched cell, were the next morning charged with annoying people and obstructing the footway, and although I know that Mr. Knox, having grave suspicions of the motives of the officers, threw what protection he could over the accused, a fine was often imposed, and further imprisonment followed in consequence of its non-payment. The wretched victims learned prudence, and obtained the necessary licence to pursue their unhappy trade. I have seen upon several occasions a female, of the class alluded to, place upon a post or window-sill a piece of money, and a policeman come up and remove it. At last the scandal attained such large dimensions that it became necessary to transplant the entire division to some other district. I have no means of following their career. They had probably to bemoan amongst the savages of the East the halcyon days they had enjoyed in the advanced civilisation of their former service. The resignation of Mr. Knox consequent upon his illness was a great loss to the public. He was a most conscientious and painstaking magistrate, but unfortunately he allowed his anxiety to do justice to prey upon a very impressible disposition, and ultimately to affect his health. I have had many conversations with him on the subject I am now dwelling upon, and I believe that he fully shared the opinion I have expressed as to the necessity of great caution in dealing with police testimony.

I will now relate an amusing adventure of my own which bears upon the subject. One night late—it might be early morning—I was in Piccadilly, and, attracted by a gathering of people, I came upon a policeman struggling with a drunken, powerful woman. She had either fallen or been thrown down, and he had fallen upon her. There were expressions of indignation being uttered by the persons around, and a row seemed imminent. I touched the officer lightly upon the shoulder, saying, 'Why do you not spring your rattle? You will hurt the woman.' He jumped up, and, seizing me by the collar, said, 'I take you into custody for obstructing me in the execution of my duty.' I remained perfectly passive, and in the meanwhile another constable had come up and had seized the woman, whom he was handling very roughly. At this moment Sir Alexander Cockburn, then Attorney-General, who was returning from the House of Commons, appeared upon the scene, and seeing a woman, as he thought, ill-used, remonstrated in indignant language with the officer, upon which the constable who had hold of me stretched out his other arm—whether reaching Sir Alexander or not I could not see—and said, 'I arrest you also.' 'Arrest me,' exclaimed the astonished Attorney-General; 'what for?' 'Oh,' said my captor, 'for many things. You are well known to the police.' I cannot surmise what might have become of us. Possibly we should have spent the night in company with the very objectionable female on whose behalf we had interfered. Some people, however, fortunately recognised us, and we were released. I took the numbers of the officers, and, being determined to see the end of the affair, went next morning to the court where the charge ought to have been made, and heard that the woman had effected her escape, which, considering I had left her in charge of half a dozen officers, and that she was very drunk, was a remarkable feat of prowess.

With the concurrence of Sir Alexander Cockburn, I wrote a full account to Mr. Mayne (I forget whether at that time he was knighted), and after a day or two received an answer from some subordinate, treating my letter with great coolness, and saying that if I had any complaint to make I might go before a magistrate. To this communication I replied by a private note to the Commissioner to the effect that I should select my own mode of ventilating the matter. A very courteous reply, promising thorough inquiry, resulted from this further step.

I never heard anything more about it, and am sorry to say was not patriotic enough to take any further trouble in the matter.

There was one circumstance that struck me as of serious import. In the middle of the disturbance a tall man dressed in military apparel, and who certainly had not been present at the commencement, walked up and, addressing himself to the officer, said, 'I have seen everything. You are quite in the right. I am ready to give evidence. Here is my card.' Independent witnesses of this description are a dangerous addition to police testimony.

The following is an instance of the somewhat high-handed proceedings of the Home Office in the early days after the institution of the new police. There was a very worthy but not very wise magistrate who presided at Bow Street. He had been guilty of many eccentricities, but had escaped censure. It so happened that a constable was charged before him with taking bribes from the keepers of disorderly houses to induce him to suppress warrants entrusted to him to serve. I was instructed by the parish authorities to prosecute. There never was a clearer case, and, as it was stated that it was by no means an isolated one, the sentence of a month's imprisonment was by no means too severe. Long, however, before this term had expired, the officer was performing his duties as usual, and the magistrate received an intimation that his retirement would be accepted, and his valuable services rewarded with a pension.

I have already stated that, in my opinion, there is far too much publicity permitted by the police in connection with their proceedings; and with very great respect to the authorities at Scotland Yard, and especially so to a gentleman at the head of the detective department, with whom I have the pleasure of being upon terms of intimacy, and whose intelligenee and industry I fully appreciate, I cannot think that the system pursued is a good one for the detection of crime and the discovery of offenders.

The publicity, rather encouraged than checked, tends to defeat the chances of success. It is known from one end of the kingdom to the other who are the officers having the charge of a particular inquiry, and the amount of information that they possess is blazoned forth; whilst the system of reporting the different steps taken to a central office produces delay which may be very prejudicial.

The old Bow Street runners did not inform the criminals whom they wanted to catch with what their trap was baited, and where it was to be laid, nor did they waste valuable time in making reports. They did not let the public know all that they knew themselves, but they arrived at a conclusion from their own experience, and worked it out in silence and secrecy. I do not think that a detective in those days would have been guilty of the piece of flagrant absurdity that was exhibited but recently in the case of the murder committed upon Kingston Hill, when it was published to the entire world that the police possessed no clue, and that the murdered man had died without giving any information; by this means destroying certainly one chance of discovering the criminal through the instrumentality of a possible accomplice, who, if he had not been assured of his safety, might have made a confession. I suspect that old officers, if they had opened their mouths at all, would have been guilty of the pious fraud of saying, 'that they had obtained a full description of the murderer.'

The police also must frequently be much embarrassed by the proceedings of coroners' courts. These are often conducted by incompetent officers, at some low pothouse, where all the gossip of the neighbourhood finds vent, and where the information obtained is blurted out, and probably read with keen amusement by the offender who is wanted, and who thus learns how to keep out of the way. Secrecy and rapidity are two elements most essential for waging a successful war against the criminal classes, and they happen to be the very ones most remarkable for their absence.

For two or three years previously to my call to the bar I resided with my father at the official residence of the Thames police at Wapping. He had removed there upon the death of Captain Richbell, who had previously occupied it. The entrance to it was from a narrow street called Old Gravel Lane. Its frontage, which still exists, looks out upon the river opposite to Rotherhithe. Here, but shortly before, existed Execution Dock, where the bodies of pirates might be seen dangling, hung in chains. The house abutted upon 'Wapping Old Stairs,' so it had some claim to poetry, and the neighbourhood was not without society, Messrs. Hodgson and Abbott, the brewers, residing within a few doors of the house occupied by my father. The former gentleman was better known by the name of 'Brown Stout.' I believe they were the first exporters of bitter ale to India. My father was now the senior magistrate, and upon him devolved the organisation and management of the police attached to the office. I have in a former chapter referred to this body; their duties were confined to the river, and to the localities adjacent to its shores. These included districts inhabited by very lawless classes, and, as I frequently accompanied the officers whilst upon duty, I had many opportunities of witnessing their conduct, and the power they possessed was considerable. I have seen the most serious disturbances quelled in a few minutes by the presence of two or three of them, and I do not remember any occasion when they received serious injury. They knew the localities well, and the charater of the people who inhabited them, and were thus enabled to trace offenders with very marked success. They were well and kindly managed by my father, who possessed great influence over them, and they always resorted to him in cases of difficulty. Their discipline, although strict, gave them much independence, which certainly was of service when speedy action was required. I have often thought that officers organised upon a similar system, and attached to the different police courts of the metropolis, would be a most useful instrument both for the repression and detection of crime.

The districts over which my father's jurisdiction extended included streets and alleys inhabited by a class very difficult to manage. Irish and Jews of the humblest rank occupied the wretched dwellings of which they were composed, and the feuds between the two races often ended in squabbles that attained formidable dimensions. My father, after a time, was looked up to by the rival parties, and succeeded in creating a much more peaceful state of things. In his efforts he was greatly aided by the rabbi and Catholic priest of the neighbourhood, with both of whom he had established a firm alliance.

He had a very high opinion of the social qualities of the Jews, and of their humanity and charity amongst themselves, and he found the Irish extremely amenable to kind treatment.

There was a man who frequently figured in the court during my early days at the bar, a short, dark, repulsive-looking fellow of the name of Aaron Smith, and his history was a very extraordinary one. He had been brought before my father charged with piracy, and there was no doubt that he had been one of a crew on board a pirate vessel. They had boarded a Dutch merchant ship amongst others, and been guilty of great brutality. He declared that he had been taken prisoner by the pirates, and acted under compulsion, and this statement was probably true. At all events, he was acquitted both in Holland and in this country, and flourished as a money-lender for many years after.

The time came when all was changed in connection with my father's jurisdiction. The new police was created, and the officers attached to the Thames became amalgamated with that body. The office became a court, and the business was removed to Arbour Square, Stepney. The duties of the magistrate became simply judicial.

My father certainly distrusted the evidence given by certain members of the new force, and considered that they occasionally exhibited unnecessary harshness, and I can well imagine that he was not looked upon favourably by the authorities at the Home Office, in consequence of the expression of some of his views. He was also involved in a discussion in connection with the smoke nuisance, in which his decisions differed from their wishes upon the subject. They sent him an opinion of the Attorney-General, almost ordering him to be governed by it. He, however, adhered to his own construction of the law. He was too generally respected to be treated with overt indignity, but when he urged his claim to be removed to a more agreeable district, he was met with the doubtful compliment that he was too useful in his present position. At this time he resided in Cadogan Place, and the fatigue attendant upon reaching his place of business, added to other causes, obliged him to resign his office.

From all I hear, nothing can exceed the cordial relations that now exist between the magistracy and the executive, but, considering that the body out of which the former are chosen is the same as that from which the judges are selected, I cannot help thinking that they should be put upon the same footing. There seems certainly no reason why a distinction should exist between their status and that of the gentlemen filling the office of county court judges, and it is only in accordance with constitutional principle that those who exercise judicial functions should be independent of official control.

CHAPTER XXIX.

ELECTION COMMITTEES.

THE practice before Parliamentary committees, although open to the entire bar, had been pretty much confined to a select few, who devoted themselves entirely to it. Previously, however, to the time to which I wish to direct attention, many eminent outsiders had conducted some of the more important inquiries. Coppock, one of the acutest of Parliamentary agents, had secured the services of Cockburn, whose qualities singularly fitted him for this description of business, and Thesiger and Austen found in him a formidable opponent. Edwin James also possessed all the qualities necessary for the work. He had great readiness, handled his facts amusingly but with considerable force, and was never tedious. He was an excellent Nisi Prius leader, and, although not possessed of any remarkable knowledge of law or profound scholarship, contrived to manage Lord Campbell better than any of his rivals at the bar. In 1867, the year after a general election, all those whose names I have mentioned had quitted the arena, and I was retained in several of the contested cases. It was the last year that the House of Commons exercised this jurisdiction, which, as is well known, was subsequently relegated to the Common Law Judges. The ground for this change was the supposition that the inquiries before committees resulted too often in decisions founded less upon the facts than the composition of the tribunal; and this certainly had been the case in former years. The politics of the majority were more considered by litigants than the evidence to be adduced; and if a member, under the unusual influence of conscientious feeling, voted against his party, he was looked upon as little better than a traitor. It is extremely amusing to look back to some of the old trials. Two gentlemen, named Harrison and Joy, seemed to possess the greatest favour with the public, and their mode of doing business had at least the merit of originality. A decision could almost always be found for propositions however absurd, and the arguments of the counsel for the respective parties seemed to consist in pelting each other and the committee with cases; and it would have been strange indeed if the predetermination of the majority was not able to find some authority to justify it. A story is told of Harrison that he kept a kind of *vade mecum*, in which he entered up the different decisions of committees, and that upon one occasion, having quoted several in support of the view for which he was contending, he inadvertently left the book upon the table. His adversary picked it up and found, upon an opposite page to that which had been referred to, all the authorities on the other side, which he quoted in answer, much to Harrison's discomfiture, who, it is needless to say, never afterwards lost sight of his valuable companion.

Mr. Serjeant Merewether, who afterwards became Town Clerk of London, had considerable business in Parliament: and his son, Henry Allworth Merewether, an old friend of mine, was a deservedly successful practitioner. This gentleman was a very agreeable companion, and one of the most popular members of the Garrick Club. He did not like election petitions, and confined himself latterly to private Bills, in which branch of

Parliamentary business he was opposed to Hope Scott, Beckett Denison, Rodwell, and others of like calibre, and must have been a man of considerable ability to hold his own, as he did for many years, against such opponents.

It is worthy of remark that for a few years previous to 1867, and very notably during that year, a great change of feeling exhibited itself in the election committees. Members had begun to look upon the obligation that they undertook from a more serious point of view than they had done heretofore; a higher quality of advocacy had made itself felt; and there can be no doubt that strong and independent counsel do materially colour the proceedings of tribunals before which they practise. Moreover, public opinion began to assert itself, and indignation was felt that partisan grounds should govern judicial proceedings. These elements combined gradually produced a result which plainly developed itself in the proceedings before committees in this year of 1867. I was, as I have mentioned already, in many of the contested cases, and had opportunities of forming an opinion about most of the others, and also of hearing the remarks of very good judges upon the subject; and I have no hesitation whatever in saying that, in every instance, there was exhibited not only the qualities most calculated to elicit truth, but the most conscientious adherence to strict impartiality.

The tribunals were extremely pleasant to practise before, and the members that constituted them certainly were very competent to judge of the facts, having had their own experiences to be guided by, and within my observation an excellent feeling prevailed between them and counsel. I do not think that there existed so holy a horror for bribery as ought to affect well-regulated minds; in fact, the war waged against Parliamentary corruption does not seem to have attained either practical or moral success, and an ordinarily acute observer must come to the conclusion that the virtuous denunciations he hears are in most instances mere shams. There is no force of public opinion honestly brought to bear against it. I should be glad to know whether the gentry in the neighbourhood have ever withdrawn their custom from a tradesman found guilty of accepting bribes, or whether any gentleman has been excluded from society because he has given them. Only during the present year I had the honour of being associated with the Attorney-General in the prosecution of some bribery informations tried at Maidstone. A solicitor, a leading one in the county, was called as a witness. He had been obliged to make a clean breast of it before the commissioners. He mounted the witness-box with a jaunty air, and, with a complacent smile upon his countenance, disclosed the organised system of bribery of which he had been contriver and manager. I doubt whether a single client will take his title-deeds out of this gentleman's possession, or treat him with less consideration. Another witness got up, he was one of the bribed, and was attended by several of his friends and co-bribees—I invent the word for the occasion. He gave his evidence in a jocular manner, and it was listened to with much hilarity and evident admiration. Even in the House of Commons, where a good deal of verbal indignation is ventilated, the true feeling crept out upon a recent occasion, when the majority refused to issue a commission in a case where, according to public rumour, bribery and corruption had been rampant.[1]

I do not believe that the ballot will ever be effectual

[1] Whether the punishments recently inflicted upon comparatively insignificant personages will produce the desired result, remains to be seen. For my part, I suspect that their only effect will be to prevent future juries from convicting.

to prevent the practice, and, moreover, it introduces an additional moral taint. A voter may make a solemn promise, take advantage of the secrecy to break it, and of course tell lies to prevent the discovery of his treachery. I do, however, think that in charges of intimidation secret voting may be of service.

I noticed an observation made upon the trial of one of the bribery informations by a very learned judge, and one who takes just views upon most subjects, Mr. Justice Fitzjames Stephen, 'that probably the same feeling existed in the minds of many people upon the subject of bribery, as did upon a former generation upon that of duelling,' and to this I will venture to add, did upon Members of Parliament as to the duties imposed upon them in election committees.

My first appearance before a Parliamentary tribunal was in a petition against the return of Mr. Waddington, who was then Chairman of the Eastern Counties Railway Company, now the Great Eastern. He was a personal friend, and entrusted his interests to me, although in this branch of business I was then quite unknown ; I think he had been returned for Harwich—the place, however, is not material. His colleague was Mr. Locke, one of those engineers who have assisted in the marvellous change that now governs the world. I succeeded in keeping the seat for Waddington, but recollect the case less on that account than for the opportunities it gave me of enjoying Mr. Locke's society. I remember well his simple but graphic details upon many subjects, especially of the sensations he experienced when after a tunnel had been finished the supports were first removed; it was impossible to say that some precaution might not have been wanting, and that all those waiting anxiously for the result might not be immolated in one common ruin.

How short was his span of life, compared to that of other benefactors of our age! He quitted it after he had conferred immense benefits, but before he had been able to enjoy the glory that he had so nobly earned.

I conducted, about this period, the petition against the sitting member for Bristol. The bribery was flagrant, there was really no defence attempted, and I consequently succeeded without difficulty in unseating the sitting member.

One of the cases in which during the sittings of 1867 I was engaged, and which greatly interested me, was that against Colonel White for Tipperary. He was my client, and also a personal friend. He himself was perfectly pure; but the supporters of a candidate in an Irish election are rarely controlled by the dictates of strict prudence. He had been supported by the Catholic priesthood, and it was alleged that violence and intimidation had prevailed to a considerable extent on the part of his supporters. My junior in the case was an Irish barrister, whose name, for reasons that may be imagined, I forbear to record, and I will therefore venture to furnish him with a fictitious one.

One of the witnesses supporting the petition, an officer of the Irish constabulary, was detailing a scene of violence in which several heads were broken and divers misadventures of the same kind occurred. He was asked by Mr. Cooke, the counsel on the part of the petitioner, who was the ringleader, and answered, Mr. O'Finigan; and upon being further questioned who that gentleman might be, up rose my junior, and, glaring at the counsel who had asked the question, said, 'I am Mr. O'Finigan, and I am not ashamed of my name.' I was told that this gentleman intended to challenge me for putting upon him a gross insult, viz. that I would not allow him to cross-examine any of the witnesses. However, I succeeded in appeasing his wrath, and under the influence of a Greenwich dinner, at which I entertained him, we became excellent friends, and he was really a very good fellow, though beyond doubt a most enthusiastic partisan. Colonel White had certainly not encouraged any illegal proceedings, and the Archbishop of Cashel, his very warm friend, had used all his influence to prevent them. I do not know of any case in which I have been engaged in which the decision, which was in favour of my client, gave me more sincere satisfaction. On this occasion the majority of the committee were opposed in politics to the Colonel.

During the time the proceedings were going on I saw a great deal of the Archbishop, who was a very highly cultivated gentleman. I received from him many courtesies, and it was with great regret that I heard of his death.

I do not think it would be possible to exaggerate the amount of bribery that was proved in the course of these inquiries to have existed. It was confined to no class—tradesmen, the squirearchy, the lawyers, and, by no means insignificantly, the clergy, all were implicated; and I cannot forbear to add that the amount of perjury necessary to conceal it was by no means deficient. Even if I remembered the details it would furnish neither amusement nor instruction to relate them. I can, however, recall one case that amused me intensely. A white-headed old gentleman, the agent of one of the parties, was in the witness-box. He looked the very embodiment of respectability. He was nevertheless subjected to a severe cross-examination by the opposite counsel, who suggested that he had been a party to distributing bribes. At last he turned his venerable face to the committee, incipient tears being visible in his eyes, and making a most affecting appeal to them, asked, in a voice broken by emotion, whether a man who had lived all his life in the borough, without a stain upon his character, ought to be exposed to the insult of such questions. Whether the committee were or were not affected by his appeal I cannot tell, but they unseated his employer, and I know that the venerable gentleman had actually received 500 sovereigns, which he had distributed most honourably 'in bribing the electors.'

There was another petition against the sitting member for Bristol during this year, in which I was engaged for the petitioner. One of the principal witnesses opposed to me was a physician in the borough, a gentleman of high position and character. His appearance and manner were both greatly in his favour, and I confess that at first I looked with doubt upon my instructions that he was the main instrument of the bribery that had existed, and I consequently proceeded very warily to deal with him. It was long before I could get at any of the facts, but, after a time, it became plain to me that he was prevaricating, and ultimately this was evident to the committee, who over and over again cautioned him. At last, after long struggling on his part, I forced out of him admissions of his thorough culpability, and the member was unseated. I refer to this case with some feeling of triumph; it was really an instance of the success of those principles I have endeavoured to lay down for cross-examination. I could not have proved any of the facts by independent testimony, but I formed a confident and, as it turned out, a correct judgment as to the complicity of the witness, and worked upon this assumption. I hope I may be excused for the vanity of recording that this effort met with a very high compliment from one of the most distinguished members of my profession.

Out of this trial, I believe, a case arose at Bristol before the Recorder, Mr. Serjeant Kinglake—a very learned lawyer, one of Lord Campbell's degenerates. It was against a solicitor, who, elated at the result, had mounted upon a white horse, led a mob of people, and celebrated it with much noise, to the accompaniment of broken heads and windows. He was indicted for a riot. Collins, now leader of the Western Circuit, Montagu Williams, and myself were retained for the defence. Ribton, an old friend of mine, and a powerful advocate, prosecuted, as he did everything, with considerable energy and at great length. As our refreshers were very liberal we reconciled ourselves to this latter quality, which was more than rivalled by the Recorder. Under the auspices of Mr. Collins I saw many of the sights best worth witnessing in the town, and as the issue for our client did not involve very grave consequences, we passed our time agreeably enough. When the jury were impannelled, I thought I recognised the face of one of them, and learnt afterwards that he had been a witness before the committee at the House of Commons, where I had handled him rather roughly. After a vehement reply from Mr. Ribton, and a summing-up in which all the constitutional questions of the last century and former ones were dwelt upon by the Recorder, the jury retired, but could not agree—there was one obstinate juryman. The Recorder would not discharge them, intimating that they might sleep upon it. This, however, precluding the enjoyment of supper, did not suit the fancy of the majority. They retired into their private room, from which shortly came forth sounds of discord.

After a pause they returned into court, the obstinate juryman looking hot and dishevelled, and evidently not inclined for further intercourse with his brethren.

A verdict of not guilty was pronounced, and my client was again at liberty to mount his steed amongst the cheers of enthusiastic supporters.

POSTSCRIPT.

I look back to these inquiries as forming the most pleasant portion of my professional life. The work suited my tastes and whatever qualities I possessed, and certainly I was very successful, whilst the unvarying courtesy of the tribunal rendered the performance of the duties singularly agreeable.

CHAPTER XXX.

ELECTION JUDGES.

As might be expected from the character of the tribunals by which Parliamentary committees were superseded, an endeavour was made to introduce definitions applicable to the different questions raised before them, and to bring the proofs within their compass. Evidence was restricted by the rules prevailing in the ordinary courts, and each judge had to perform the province of a jury, in construing facts and intentions, as well as to lay down the law.

Very few of the judges had experience of elections, and no doubt the machinery adopted by candidates presented some novel points for their consideration. Generally, I think, their decisions gave satisfaction to independent observers, and certainly were arrived at with great care and attention.

I was engaged in several petitions tried before the following judges:—Baron Martin, Justices Lush, Willes, Blackburn, Mellor, and Grove; all men of great learning and experience. I think that the first case I was in under the new *régime* was that of Norwich, before Baron Martin, and this was speedily disposed of by unseating the member. It was always pleasant to practise before this learned judge. He was a thorough man of business, a sound lawyer, hasty, but very agreeable to counsel, and I imagine possessed no small practical experience of the 'doings' of an election. I recall with great satisfaction a case in which I was counsel before him at Bradford. My client was Mr. Forster, the sitting member, and now so well known as Secretary for Ireland.

Of course the result was of vital importance to this gentleman, and, although he was personally clear from all imputation, there were circumstances extremely difficult to deal with, and I felt a very considerable amount of anxiety. Mr. Forster had himself been away during the canvass, and it was admitted that he was strongly opposed to any unfair influence being used; but there had been proceedings at the municipal elections, which had shortly preceded the borough one, by which it was sought to affect his seat. My task was rendered more difficult from the fact that the same judge had unseated Mr. Ripley upon grounds some of the features of which were similar to those relied upon against my client, and in conducting the case my endeavour was to distinguish it from the one previously decided, and in this effort I was successful, and justly so. Since that time I have had the pleasure of meeting Mr. Forster, when he has been a guest of my friend Sir Bruce Seton, at the Union Club, and he has expressed himself in very kind terms of my conduct of the case. I also received at the time a letter from Mrs. Forster, who had been intensely anxious, and expressed herself very gratefully to me. I asked permission of Mr. Forster to record these opinions, and received from him the following letter:—

August 22, 1881.

My dear Serjeant Ballantine,—I am glad you are publishing your reminiscences, and look forward with pleasure to their perusal.

By all means make any use you like of anything I said about your defence of me when under trial. I have never lost my sense of the value of that defence, or of its great ability.

Yours very truly,
W. E. FORSTER.

I hope that my publication of the above may not be considered a proof of foolish vanity, but I estimate very highly the opinion of Mr. Forster, and consider that if he is under an obligation to me, so to a much greater extent are the public.

If I assisted upon this occasion in benefiting the Liberal party, I subsequently, before the same judge, aided in maintaining the seat of Mr. Smith for Westminster, thus conferring a boon upon the Conservatives. I am bound, however, to say that my leader, Mr. Hawkins, now upon the Bench, was the principal contributor to this result.

Notwithstanding some faults that I have already indicated, Mr. Baron Martin, when obliged by his increasing deafness to resign, was a great loss to the Bench.

In recording successes of which I am proud, and by the result of which the public have benefited, I am very pleased to mention that in a petition against Mr. Serjeant Cox, the then sitting member for Taunton, I succeeded in annulling his election, and, upon a scrutiny, seating my old friend, then Mr. James, since that time become Sir Henry, and now Attorney-General; and upon a petition against him after a subsequent election I was successful in maintaining his seat.

If the lives of the puisne judges who have occupied the Bench during the last generation could find a biographer, no one would fill a brighter or more honourable space than Lord Justice Lush, but recently deceased. During the time he was at the bar and upon the Home Circuit I was constantly associated with him both in public and private, and after his promotion I frequently appeared before him. His career exhibits a course of unwearied industry and unswerving integrity from his earliest youth. He would not be properly described as a powerful advocate, but he was singularly lucid and always a perfect master of the facts. As a judge, unmoved by partiality, and, although strict in his views, patient, considerate, and humane; as a man, his kindness and charity had ensured to him the affection of every one who knew him. He tried several of the election cases in which I was engaged, but I do not remember any that presented features worthy of recording.[1]

Lord Justice Bramwell was a good judge, and restrained upon the bench a natural irritability of temper. I also conducted cases before him, but not of great interest except to the parties. I cannot forbear saying that I never saw any one more anxious to assist a counsel who had a difficulty in explaining some proposition, or more patient in its investigation. It is considered by the profession that his retirement from the Appeal Court is a very serious loss.

No one can deny that in the selection of Mr. Blackburn as a puisne judge Lord Campbell conferred a benefit upon all connected with judicial proceedings. He possesses a powerful intellect, great grasp and solidity, and has the reputation of being a profound lawyer. A Scotch accent does not improve a naturally harsh voice, and his demeanour can scarcely be termed graceful, or his manner pleasant, but these are superficial objections. There is nothing of harshness or intentional discourtesy about him; I should doubt whether he had ever been what is called a ladies' man, and his gallantry was put to a severe test in the following cases, and certainly did not show itself to be coextensive with his law.

In the first of these I appeared to defend the seat of a gentleman who, though only recently connected with

[1] I had hoped that my kind old friend would have read my appreciation of him. I wrote it originally in his lifetime.

the Government, is a very distinguished and useful member of the House of Commons, and would have been a great loss. This was Mr. Brassey,[1] member for Hastings, who was petitioned against by Colonel Calthorpe, the distinguished Crimean officer.

One of the means of bribery suggested was the purchase of unnecessary apparel by certain ladies, energetic supporters of the sitting member; and it was amusing to witness the face of the judge during these millinery investigations, and to hear his ejaculations upon the number of yards apparently necessary to clothe the female form. It was evidently a subject which his brain was incapable of grasping without making inquiries that were repellent to his sense of modesty. I trust that I may be forgiven for mentioning that I received the greatest assistance from suggestions given me by Mrs. Brassey; she showed the greatest acuteness, and I consider that the result, which was ultimately given in favour of her husband, was in a great measure due to her exertions. I was not at all surprised at the charming account written by this lady of the cruise of the *Sunbeam*, which I have read with real pleasure, both for its own merits and the memories it recalled of what was a very pleasant inquiry.

The Wallingford election petition, tried before the same judge, was a severe infliction upon his patience, and involved him in a comical position. In this I was again counsel for the sitting member, a Mr. Stanley Vickers, a distiller. It can do no harm now to confess that I never was engaged in a case in which, notwithstanding the vehement assertions of my client, I felt graver doubts. Indeed my conscience almost gave way under the strain of this conviction, and probably would have done so but

[1] This gentleman is now a member of the Government.

for the support and assistance of my friend Montagu Williams, who was with me in the case.

Sir Charles Wentworth Dilke was the petitioner. The election had been conducted by the supporters on both sides with no inconsiderable warmth, which may be accounted for by the fact that the ladies of the locality had taken a very active part in it, and were warm partisans—it might, indeed, have been called a ladies' battle, and they appeared in court arrayed in the colours of the respective candidates. But the warmth of their advocacy was made so apparent upon the first day, that on the second they were divided, and placed upon opposite sides of the court. This was the occasion of the incident I have referred to. Mr. Justice Blackburn had taken his seat and composed himself for the performance of his duties, when a lady, having arrived late, had to pass him to get to her party. Now his lordship's legs being no unimportant portion of his body, her flounces became seriously entangled in her attempted passage, and for the moment the judge was lost sight of by the audience in front, whilst the lady presented the appearance of sitting upon his knee. The judge's voice was heard in no musical tones, and when relieved from the embarrassment, he declared in emphatic language, 'that he never had been in such a position before;' and this I am disposed to believe.

I remember, amongst the allegations, there was a charge against the sitting member of personal bribery; he was said to have committed it whilst in the company of a lawyer, a clergyman, and a brewer. He and the two former stoutly denied the assertion; the brewer was vacillating, and, oddly enough, upon the very day that he was to be called was thrown from his horse, and the injuries he sustained prevented his appearance as a witness.

The counsel for the petitioner had great difficulties to

contend with, from the case not having been well got up; and Mr. Justice Blackburn was not then much experienced in the trial of election petitions. He did not consider that the case was brought home with sufficient certainty, and, after an inquiry lasting for several days, Mr. Vickers was declared duly elected.

I do not remember being in more than one election case before Mr. Justice Mellor—that of Petersfield, to which I have already alluded. In this poor Alfred Thesiger was opposed to me, and exhibited his usual skill. The petition was decided in favour of my client, but subsequently reversed upon a legal point. This learned judge possessed a great fund of common sense, and other qualities well calculated to adorn the bench. He has always been a most kind and valued friend to me. Mr. Justice Grove, distinguished for his deep and varied scientific acquirements, and also an excellent lawyer, tried the petition presented against Sir Henry James.

I am obliged to say that in the opinion I have formed of the other judges I cannot include Mr. Justice Willes, and in the case of a petition against Sir Robert Peel and Sir Henry Bulwer, the sitting members for the borough of Tamworth, his decision was received with the most unbounded astonishment, whilst the reasons given for it, and the observations accompanying them, were certainly unintelligible to any ordinary mind. There were 130 men employed by an acknowledged agent of one of the sitting members, and paid for two days' work, the nomination and polling days. Nineteen of these men were voters. The work was a mere sham, there was no legitimate work for them to do, and they did none. This was urged upon the learned judge as conclusive proof of undue influence on the part of the agent in question. Mr. Justice Willes, however, assumed that they were hired to obtain popularity for the man who employed them. He certainly added that he did not think that such a mode of gaining popularity by an agent just before an election was desirable. Still more extraordinary was the mode in which, in the most inflated language, he held up a land agent of Sir Robert's to admiration, and smothered him with praise. There was a collection of small tenements that had been held by generations of the same tenants; they had practically descended from father to son, although it was usual for the occupiers to appear on a quarter-day at the bailiff's house and go through the form of renewal. The agent canvassed these poor people, hinting to one that something should be done for repairs; to another, a woman, that it would be better for her husband to vote for Bulwer; and conveying threats and promises throughout the entire neighbourhood.

The election took place; and, on the quarter-day following, these poor people attended as usual for a renewal of their leases, and in every instance where they had voted adversely it was refused. They were, in addition, treated with the utmost harshness; and in some instances, when they were unable to find a place to go to, higher rents were extorted from them—a proceeding not attempted to be justified. It would occupy too much space to record the panegyrics lavished upon this gentleman. But not content with this, the judge fell foul of me, with pretty much the same delicacy and taste with which he had praised the agent, concluding with the following not very intelligible sentences: 'Allow if you will that he (the agent), like others whom I have known coming from the same part of the country, is somewhat dark, and hard, and angular in business matters, I am not to judge of his moral character. But I have known such men, and I have known them not only as truthful but as kindly as those who could gloze, and who could be base in matters of figures and facts.'

At the time he uttered this remarkable tirade I had left the court and gone to London, but received a letter from one of my friends giving me an account of it, and saying that the judge had made his intention most marked by directing his words towards the space that I had occupied during the enquiry. I wrote to him requiring an explanation, to which he answered that he had not intended them to apply to me, which did not exalt my ideas of his accuracy, although it prevented me from taking other steps. His oration, which took up a considerable time, ended by retaining both members in their seats.

I cannot account for his otherwise incredible conduct than by supposing that the position of the respondents exercised, perhaps unconsciously to himself, an influence upon his mind, and threw a sort of glamour over his understanding. He was always given to over-refining, but upon this occasion his ingenuity surpassed the bounds of common sense, and absolutely travestied the facts of the case to force them into the decision on which he had determined.

I have never made any concealment of my opinion of the behaviour of Mr. Justice Willes in this case, and some time after it I received a letter from Mr. Peel, who had been the opponent of the sitting members at the election, requesting to know whether I had advised the petition, and whether the facts had been correctly stated to me. I answered in the affirmative, and added that the facts proved upon the trial were much stronger than those laid before me.

Some time afterwards a piece of plate was presented to Mr. Peel by his supporters and friends, and upon this occasion he referred to my letter in the following words :—

'The evidence collected was submitted to Serjeant Ballantine and Mr. Henry James, and they advised that a petition should be presented, which was accordingly done. Having heard the evidence given in court, he (Mr. Peel) was satisfied that bribery prevailed extensively, especially in the case of the 130 men, who were employed by the agent of one candidate, and paid by the agent of the other. Intimidation was also clearly practised, because threats were used, and afterwards carried out; but upon the trial astonishingly subtle distinctions were drawn between treating and reasonable refreshment and as to agency. He believed that there was but one opinion in the country with regard to the trial, and that was that the failure of the petition was a miscarriage of justice.

'Serjeant Ballantine having been asked whether he would advise a petition in a similar case again, said he should certainly do so, and be confident of a different decision from any other Judge upon the Bench, and that the grounds of the decision of Mr. Justice Willes were totally inexplicable to him. Mr. James in answer to the same question said that there were many reasons why he should not express an opinion about the judgment.'

Mr. Justice Willes possessed the reputation of being one of the most profound and able lawyers upon the Bench. His habits, as far as I had any opportunity of observing them, exhibited no cordiality, but I had always been upon perfectly good terms with him. He was in criminal cases a merciful judge, and impressed me as having a hatred of injustice and tyranny. He was, however, singularly emotional, and in another election petition in which I was engaged—it was that of Penzance—he exhibited this trait in a ridiculous manner. An allegation of bribery against a doctor, I am not sure that he was not a veterinary surgeon, was strongly relied upon, and appeared to me to be fully made out; but his lordship almost burst into tears at the idea of a member of that 'noble profession' being guilty of such a crime. It is more than probable that, with this disposition and an enormous strain upon his mind, his naturally great intellect was shaken from its pedestal, and subsequent events have led me to believe that this was the cause of eccentricities which I should be sorry to attribute to motives of a more unworthy character.

CHAPTER XXXI.

THE UNION CLUB.

In the course of the foregoing pages I have frequently mentioned the Union Club, and, as it is one of the earliest if not the very first established upon the now existing basis of the principal clubs, it may not be altogether uninteresting to give some short sketch of its history. It is much older than is generally supposed, having come into existence in the early part of the year 1805. At one time there seemed to be a chance of its being christened The Cumberland, its original meetings being held in a house bearing that title, but I can only find one occasion when for some twenty-four hours it bore that name ; always after it was known by its present one.

The first meeting of which any record exists took place on February 20 in the year I have mentioned, and on this day the first committee was chosen ; it was headed by the Marquis of Headfort, Lord Roden, and General Ormsby. There were upon it several officers of high rank, and a Mr. John Spencer Smith, who I fancy was a member of the great banking firm of Smith, Payne, and Smith.

It does not appear by the minutes to which I have access what was done between that time and a meeting that took place upon February 3 in the following year ; this was held at Cumberland House, and called a meeting of managers. Their names do not appear, but I conclude they consisted of the committee previously chosen ; and a person of the name of Raggett, who was, I fancy, a tavern-keeper, was appointed under the description of proprietor and conductor, and authorised to procure a house, and on March 16 following there was a further resolution in which Mr. Raggett was called master, but no business was done until February 3, 1807, in which the terms of subscription were settled at ten guineas a year, and one guinea for the servants, a guarantee being given to Raggett that there should be no less number of members than 250; that gentlemen should be elected by ballot, which was to take place *between* 11 *at night and* 1 *o'clock in the morning.*

It is strange that amongst the minutes in possession now of the club I cannot find with any certainty what proceedings took place between that period and January 30, 1812, nor even where the evening meetings took place. I am inclined to believe they were at the house of the Duke of Leeds in St. James's Square. The club, however, does not, up to that date, appear to have attained any considerable success, as I gather from the proceedings that then took place. Mr. Raggett expressed a desire to throw up his engagement, as there were not a sufficient number of members to make it remunerative, and in consequence it was determined that fifty new ones should be elected, which seems to have been immediately done, and the number readily obtained. When this had been achieved the club appeared to float on without difficulty. Amongst the number there were no less than fifty-six members of the House of Peers, including the Dukes of York and Sussex, Richmond and Devonshire, the Marquis of Wellesley, Duke of Argyll, Lord Granville, Leveson Gower, Marquis of Hertford, Lord Peterborough, Lord Stair, and, most celebrated of all, Lord Byron.

There were also members of the firm of the Barings,

and also of the Messrs. Hoare, and, amongst names still remembered, Sir Jonah Barrington, Quintin Dick, and Mr. Labouchere.

At this time it was in the strictest sense of the term a proprietary club, which I believe was the case of all others then existing. The principal of these were Brooks's and White's, the Travellers' and the United Service; and so it continued until the year 1821, in the August of which it was established substantially in its present form, and I believe was the first club that adopted it. A committee of five was appointed to carry it out, and the success that followed is not wonderful, as one of the greatest men of any age assisted in the task, the Right Hon. Sir Robert Peel. The other members were Viscount Gage, Lord Lowther, Pascoe Grenfell, and George Hammersley, and under their auspices the Union Club took the form under which, with slight variations, it still exists. The plot of land upon which the house was built was secured at a rental of 306*l.* per annum, and has now forty years to run, and the house itself was built under the direction of Mr. Smirke, the architect, who was selected by the committee in consequence of having designed that occupied by the United Service. I cannot find that there are any distinguished members of the Bench or Bar amongst those originally elected, indeed I do not recognise a single specimen; neither is the Church represented. I suppose that in the early period of the century graver and more improving occupations than those of club life occupied the time of both professions.

I became a member in 1852, and the Bar had numerous representatives by no means undistinguished at that date, or shortly after: Jervis, afterwards Chief Justice of the Common Pleas; Maule, a judge of the same court; Lord Justice Knight Bruce, Mr. Montague Chambers

Lord Justice Selwyn, Mr. Justice Byles, and many others. There was also a good sprinkling of eminent bankers, including two or three members of the Messrs. Goslings, one of the oldest firms in London, and from whom I have received many acts of kindness. One of them used to play the moderate whist to which players were confined by the rules of the club. I can remember him so well. He looked, what he was, the picture of a gentleman of the old school, and it was pleasant to see him riding his well-bred cob quietly along the park.

There was another banker, a very old gentleman, who made his appearance only occasionally. I have already mentioned him as a friend of Sir Frederick Pollock, and as one of his great supporters at Huntingdon, where he carried on his business. His name was Veasey, and he was the oldest banker in England; I believe I am right in saying that in that capacity he used to preside at an annual dinner of the members of the profession. His age must have been very great at the time of his death, but almost to the last he maintained a jaunty air and juvenile dress, with old-fashioned courteous manners. In one sense he was part of my family history, having been trustee in different settlements in which my mother was interested. He occupied a house in the town of Huntingdon that had once belonged to her.[1]

On one occasion, some years before his death, I happened to be in this town upon professional business, and dined with him. He took me before dinner into a little side room, in which there was an old-fashioned window, and pointing to one of its panes said, 'There your poor mother scratched her name with her diamond ring; it shall never be removed in my time.' And there,

[1] He dressed in imitation of George IV., but this was his only foible that ever I discovered.

truly enough, was 'Betsy Cole,' written at least eighty years before. It was not easy when I was a candidate to secure election to the club, and, notwithstanding the distinguished men I have mentioned, lawyers were unpopular; but I was fortunate in my sponsors. Sir Frederick Slade, the Queen's counsel, was one of them, and Sir Henry Webb, a man greatly courted in society and liked in the club, was the other. Sir John Bayley and Sir Thomas Henry, the chief magistrate of Bow Street, very warmly supported me. All those whose names I have mentioned are dead, as also many others whom I recall with a feeling of sadness, and with whom I have enjoyed many pleasant hours. As I have already mentioned, I was intimate with Mr. Justice Maule, and have expressed the high opinion I had of his intellect. Lord Justice Knight Bruce possessed many brilliant qualities, and certainly was one of the most vivacious companions that I ever met with. Selwyn seemed a very kind and easy-tempered man, and was a great scholar, an accomplished lawyer, and the picture of health. I have heard he lost his life at a comparatively early age through the effects of a surgical operation.

I cannot close my memories of the club during, to me, its old days, without a few more words of Sir Thomas Henry, who remained a sincere friend to the end of his career. At some private houses where we frequently met he was an immense favourite and always welcome guest. As a magistrate he commanded, and justly, great respect, and was in fact an excellent officer. His legal knowledge had been obtained by study, and he never made any mark at the bar. He was appointed when unusually young, as were two of his cotemporaries, Norton and Hardwick. They were all three gentlemen; and the two latter, as well as Henry, fully justified their appointment. His death was very sad. It was his duty on race days to sit in a temporary office at Ascot, and on one ungenial occasion he got chilled and was not attended to, although his illness ought to have been apparent, and for a long time he was kept out in the cold; a very little care and a slight restorative would have saved a valuable life probably for many years.

I came out of the club one day and found Selwyn talking to a gentleman in the guise of a bishop; he introduced me to him. It was Lord Auckland, Bishop of Bath and Wells. Selwyn left him at the corner of Pall Mall, and his lordship and myself walked together up St. James's Street, down Piccadilly, to Hyde Park Corner. Of course there were many respectful salutations to him, and several people we met recognised me; they must have felt a good deal of surprise at the company in which they saw me. He was very courtly and pleasing, but I could not forbear at parting to take off my hat, and with a low bow said, 'My lord, you have ruined my character.' He gave a good-humoured smile, and expressed a hope that he had improved it.

The foregoing incident brings to my mind a trip I had to the Derby in very different company. There were four of us, all men, in a barouche, and one of my companions had brought his butler with him, who was clad in a white neckcloth. A lot of roughs recognised me, and one of them shouted out, 'There goes the serjeant with his domestic chaplain.' We very soon made him doff the garb that involved me in such a calumny.

The following story has gone the round of the profession, but has probably not travelled beyond it. It relates to two Queen's counsel; one of them at all events deserves some description. He was a man who had fought a singularly energetic battle against feeble health with great success, and, possessing strong good sense, had become one of the most eminent members of the bar. He was fond of the turf in a prudent way, and knew a good deal about it. 'He would have made a splendid jockey,' once said one of his admirers; 'what a pity he took to the law!' This, however, was not his opinion, and he realised the largest fortune ever made at it. Moreover, he loved the work as well as the money he made by it.

The other party to this anecdote was of a different type. He had been obliged to work to live, and did not love it. He had, however, obtained reasonable success. He liked amusement, and sought it, and considered a Long Vacation ought to be devoted to nothing else. One day, just after the conclusion of this period of legal holiday, the two counsel met. They were old acquaintances and were on the same circuit. 'What have you been doing?' was the natural question of one to the other; and an account was given by the latter of his trip upon the Continent. 'Well,' said the former, 'I have not stirred from town, and have been doing lots of work.' 'What is the use of it?' was the observation made; 'you cannot carry your money with you, and if you did it would soon melt.'

His money-making is now at an end, and at present his earnings are in no danger. He is in the service of his country, and seems to love work just as much now as when very tempting figures were endorsed upon every case in which he was engaged.

CHAPTER XXXII.

MADAME RACHEL.

IN one of the worst haunts of the metropolis there resided in the days that I practised at the Middlesex Sessions a Jewess called Rachel. Her name and her occupation were not unfrequently brought to the attention of the magistrates ; a further description of them would not be desirable.

I saw her, without knowing either who she was or her calling, behind the scenes at Drury Lane Theatre. Her ostensible object was to sell articles of dress to the female employées. Her real business was brought to light by one of them throwing the contents of a glass of porter into her face in response to an insulting proposition ; she never to my knowledge appeared there afterwards. The next that was heard of her was keeping a shop in Bond Street, ostensibly for the sale of perfumes and cosmetics, but in reality for the purposes of extortion and robbery. On a certain occasion the wife of Admiral C—— unwarily entered it for the purchase of some trifling article. Madame Rachel was singularly plausible, and induced her customer to purchase from time to time other matters to a small amount, and sent in an exorbitant bill for them, which I believe was paid, and Mrs. C—— discontinued her patronage. Upon this happening, a claim arrived amounting to 1,000*l.*, upon the allegation that Mrs. C——

had been cured by Madame's aid of some skin affection; dark hints of other matters accompanying the claim. There was not a word of truth in the assertions or insinuations, and the Admiral most properly resisted the claim, which was scouted with disgust and indignation by a jury.

Madame Rachel, however, was not discouraged, and still professed the power of making ladies beautiful for ever, and, strange as it may appear, there were many who yielded to the pleasing belief. Amongst them was a lady who once upon a time had been a beauty, was possessed of a fortune, and thought that it could not be better employed than in securing a continuance, or rather reproduction, of her charms, and she was persuaded that the effect already produced had inflamed the heart of a nobleman of distinguished appearance, well known about town, and that a letter fabricated by Madame Rachel was the genuine outpouring of that gentleman's sudden and enthusiastic passion. She obtained from her dupe large sums of money, and, emboldened by success, demanded larger, and actually caused her victim to be arrested for a supposed debt. This brought matters to a climax, and, friends interfering, Madame made her appearance at Marlborough Street Police Court, and was committed for trial at the Central Court. The quondam beauty—a skeleton encased apparently in plaster of Paris, painted pink and white, and surmounted with a juvenile wig—tottered into the witness-box. The folly she had exhibited and her childish mode of giving evidence probably led some of the jury to distrust her, and they were discharged without a verdict.

Upon a subsequent sessions Rachel was tried before Mr. Commissioner Kerr, a gentleman of very sound sense, and was without much hesitation convicted and sentenced to five years' imprisonment. I prosecuted upon both occasions, and on the first, through a false impression, made an observation about the nobleman whose name had been mentioned, which I afterwards felt was not justified and I greatly regretted. The fact was, that there was nothing more impudent perpetrated in the case than the use of his name by Madame Rachel, and for which it turned out there was not the slightest pretence.

The prison discipline did not apparently possess much influence upon Madame, who took to her old courses immediately the term had expired, and, by a similar process to that she had already gone through, found her way back again to prison, and there died; not, however, before she had done much mischief, darkened many a home, and led many girls, who but for her might have been happy and contented, into misery and crime. She was one of the most filthy and dangerous moral pests that have existed in my time and within my observation.

In the year 1845 I was counsel at the Central Court in a case that excited interest at the time of its occurrence. It presented some curious facts, and, although no doubt could arise as to the guilt of the accused man, there was nevertheless a mystery connected with the deed which was never explained.

A gentleman of respectable position was found lying with his throat cut, and perfectly dead, in a lane between what then was Chalk Farm and Belsize Park; his name was De la Rue. Whilst a constable was standing by his body, a young man dressed in a gentlemanly manner came up, made some remark to the policeman, leant over the body, examined it, and felt the pulse. He appeared perfectly calm and unembarrassed. His name was Hocker, and he was the murderer. On the body of the deceased was found a letter signed Caroline, asking De la Rue to meet her at the spot where the body was found; this letter was proved to be in the handwriting of the prisoner, and property of value that had belonged to Mr. De la Rue was found upon Hocker's person.

The impulse that brought him back to the body of the man he had slain was indeed strange, and the coolness with which he felt and examined it showed marvellous power of self-control. The trial took place before Mr. Justice Coleridge, and is one of those which exhibited the excellent qualities as a judge that he possessed. The difficulty that arose of explaining in any intelligible way the letter or the connection that existed between the parties made him extremely anxious, and my instructions furnished no clue to solving the difficulty, yet I felt there might be some explanation, and, for the first and only time in my life that I ever did so, I requested and obtained an interview with the prisoner. It took place in Newgate, during the mid-day adjournment of the Court, and remains vividly upon my memory. He was quite young, scarcely twenty years old; he was seated upon a wooden bench in a small square cell, whitewashed, and without other furniture, himself quite calm and self-possessed. He would give no further statement than that I had already received. I told him that I could not put it forward with any hope of success, and advised him, if he insisted upon adhering to it, to make it himself. He said he preferred to do so, and accordingly he conveyed it to the jury without any exhibition of nervousness, although, I am confident, without hope. If the facts proved had left any possible conclusion but that of guilt it would have been enforced upon the jury, who had no alternative but to find a verdict of guilty, and he was necessarily condemned to death, which he suffered, showing no sign of either repentance or fear. Mr. Clarkson led me in this case, and concurred in my view.

Whilst visiting my chamber of horrors I may be excused for exhuming another trial in which I was also engaged, leading on this occasion for the Crown; it was the case of Franz Müller, a German, charged with the murder of Mr. Briggs in a railway carriage. The prosecution of Lefroy, which has recently caused so much attention, has, from its similarity in many of its circumstances, brought it into notice. And the two cases are in many respects alike, both being conclusively proved by circumstantial evidence, and in both the prisoner declaring his innocence almost to the last. It is very satisfactory to feel that the means used after the conviction of the latter criminal to raise an issue that had never been suggested when it could have been properly tested were not countenanced, either by the learned judge who tried him or by the Home Office authorities.[1]

I will now call the attention of my readers to some more amusing legal incidents; the locality, although a near neighbour of the Old Bailey, is not redolent of crime, it is the Court of Queen's Bench, Guildhall. Sir Alexander Cockburn is the presiding judge, and the trial about to take place one of considerable interest. There were several members of the aristocracy present, amongst them the Marchioness of Ailesbury, Sir Edward Bulwer Lytton, the Earl of Wilton, and Lord Harry Vane; whilst the Church was represented by the Bishop of Lichfield and Dr. Robinson, the Master of the Temple. The occasion that drew these noble and reverend personages to an unaccustomed scene was an action brought by Lieutenant Morrison against Admiral Belcher for libel. The plaintiff called himself an astrologer, and was the author of 'Zadkiel's Almanack,' whom the Admiral had practically denounced as

[1] An endeavour was made after the trial to show that Lefroy was insane.

a cheat and impostor. Mr. Serjeant Shee was counsel for Lieutenant Morrison, I was retained for the defendant, and the ground upon which he founded his attack was that some years before the plaintiff had asserted that he was upon terms of acquaintance with certain spirits of another world, who exhibited themselves through the medium of a crystal ball, and there was no doubt that he had claimed this remarkable privilege, and had exhibited proofs of it before the different distinguished people who appeared in court as his witnesses, although they did not all of them fully support his claim. The presence of the clergy might be accounted for by his most intimate friend and constant visitor being St. Luke, who conversed in the English language, and associated with him upon familiar terms. A young person who gave the name of Eva also visited him; but the most pleasant of his acquaintances was Titania, who appeared to have been permitted by her lord and master to be a frequent guest. One of the ladies who was called as a witness on the plaintiff's behalf at the trial deposed that she had seen her mother reflected in the ball, and also a knight clad in complete armour, but of whose conduct she did not entirely approve, as there was a young lady attired in pink, to whom he was evidently paying very marked attention. The witness who gave this evidence was neither young nor flighty, and gave it with much earnestness and solemnity, ending by declaring that the scene would never pass from her memory.

I was somewhat surprised to see Dr. Robinson amongst the believers, as from all I had heard of his discourses in the Temple Church he was by no means of an imaginative turn of mind.[1]

[1] Dr. Robinson appeared to take much interest in the case; but I am assured, upon the thoroughly reliable authority of the Rev. Canon Cooke, that Dr. Robinson was neither a believer nor supporter of Zadkiel.

The reading of the almanack, and the different auguries connected with the birth of great men, together with prophecies as to the date of their dissolution, afforded much amusement. Brougham was bound to have been dead, but unfortunately had survived the event foretold, and several others had disappointed the predictions of the sage. Much laughter was occasioned by a description of the singular brilliancy presented by the planets Mars and Venus upon the birth of Lord Palmerston. The Chief Justice Cockburn revelled in the case, which terminated in a verdict for twenty shillings, the judge refusing to certify for costs. Sir Edward Lytton Bulwer was examined, but did not support the plaintiff's supernatural claim, although he evidently disapproved of the levity exhibited in court.'

Admiral Sir Edward Belcher was a most distinguished and gallant officer. He had commanded two or three Arctic expeditions, but was not, however, a popular officer. He was very much of a martinet, although, as far as I was able to judge, by no means of a cruel or inhuman disposition; latterly he was not employed according to his expectations, and showed a good deal of disappointment in consequence. I knew him very well; he was singularly well-informed, although somewhat speculative. Private matters, of the rights of which none but the parties to them could form a judgment, had greatly embittered his life. There was a singular physical fact connected with him—he had entirely lost the sense of taste; this he frequently complained of, and could not account for. A friend of mine, an eminent member of the Bar, suffers in the same way, but is able to trace the phenomenon to the shock that he suffered in a railway collision.

Not many years ago it became my duty to represent an American gentleman named Slade, who, like Mr. Morrison, professed an intimate acquaintance with the world of spirits, and also obtained a considerable number of believers. A scientific doctor alleged that his proceedings were mere tricks, and undertook to expose them; and a magistrate, before whom evidence to this effect was given, committed him as a rogue and vagabond to gaol. From this decision he appealed to the Court of Quarter Sessions, where I appeared as his counsel, and an amusing though not very edifying scene occurred. The bench presented the appearance that it does upon the gala days, when the morals of dancing and music are discussed by solemn tongues. Justices filled every corner of it, and no one entertained much doubt for what they had come. Mr. Edlin, assistant-judge, occupied the chair. I took a purely legal objection to the conviction, which was argued at considerable length, and the chairman was prepared to decide in its favour, but to this his brethren demurred, and the Court adjourned. After a very considerable delay, they returned, Mr. Edlin took his seat, and, amidst signs of astonishment exhibited upon the faces of the magistrates, quashed the conviction, which they subsequently declared he had no authority whatever to do, and indeed stated that he acted in direct antagonism to the opinions of the majority. No doubt this was the case, and quite unwarrantable, but at the same time he was the proper person to decide a point of law. There were only two or three others upon the bench who knew anything about it, or could understand the argument, even if they had tried to do so, and his judgment ought to have been decisive upon it. It would be an unsatisfactory state of things that the guilt or innocence of an accused person should be determined by the vote of a majority. It must be remembered that the conviction, if affirmed, involved imprisonment, and was therefore just as serious in its result as if it had been tried before a jury, who must be unanimous, and are under the obligation of an oath. I am aware that magistrates sit constantly with the chairman to decide appeals, but these are rarely in sensational cases.

Mr. Slade took an early departure from a land in which his powers had been appreciated in so unsatisfactory a manner to himself.

CHAPTER XXXIII.

RISK ALLAH.—LANDSEER.—COCKBURN.

ABOUT the same period I met three remarkable personages: Risk Allah Bey, Sir Edwin Landseer, and Sir Alexander Cockburn. It is many years ago, in the days when the world was all before me. The first was a foreigner who became afterwards a celebrity in the law courts. The second was an artist whose works will never be forgotten, and whose genial qualities will never be surpassed; the third, a brilliant orator, accomplished lawyer, and ultimately Lord Chief Justice of England.

Thackeray, in his novel of 'The Newcomes,' remarks how easy the entrance is into society of a foreigner possessing agreeable and plausible manners, without those formalities with which it fences itself against the inroads of its own countrypeople. Risk Allah was handsome, his manners polished, his costume picturesque. I did not admire his face, and when many years afterwards I saw him under the circumstances I am about to describe, I thought it repulsive. He was apparently upon terms of some intimacy with Sir Alexander Cockburn (who, like himself, was an accomplished linguist), and not unwilling to display his accomplishment in this respect. In the year 1857 Risk Allah married an English lady of the name of Lewis, who possessed a considerable fortune. Connected with her, in some way that I do not now remember, was a lad named Charles Readley. Risk Allah was entitled in the event of his wife's death to the possession of her fortune. The lady, shortly after he married her, fell into bad health, to which after some time she succumbed; and Risk Allah succeeded to a large sum of money, and to the care of the young man, who was of weakly constitution and suffered from epileptic fits. He was entitled to 5,000*l.*, which reverted upon his death to Risk Allah. Readley had also made a will and insured his life in that gentleman's favour. Such being the condition of affairs, these two were in March 1865 staying at the Hôtel du Rhin at Antwerp, and happened to be the only visitors in the hotel. Readley was alive, and, according to the evidence of a chambermaid, was, on one morning of the above month, at seven o'clock sleeping quietly. At nine o'clock he was found dead in his bed, with a wound in his throat, and a discharged gun by his bed-side.

It was suggested that he had committed suicide; but suspicion attached to Risk Allah, who was apprehended and subsequently put upon his trial before the Supreme Criminal Court at Brussels, charged with the murder of the young man. Much and very lengthy evidence was given on both sides, and long arguments supplied by able advocates; and the result was, after a patient summing-up by the presiding judge, that Risk Allah was acquitted.

He was also accused of complicity with a person named Osman in a number of frauds. There was no doubt of the roguery of this person, and that his proceedings had been very extensive, but the Court came to the conclusion that Risk Allah had been a victim and not an accomplice in his offences.

There was another matter which threw suspicion upon him in connection with two forged cheques. This, however, was fully gone into before the tribunal at Brussels; and of this also he was acquitted.[1]

A number of experts upon handwriting were called on both sides, and also experts to show that from the position of the body Readley might have shot himself.

Some articles appeared in the 'Daily Telegraph' newspaper commenting upon the trial with a great deal of force and ability, but there could be no doubt that the guilt of the accused was more than suggested, and Risk Allah brought an action for libel against the proprietors. After an acquittal by a competent tribunal, it would not have been right or prudent to plead a justification, and under these circumstances the only question that could be submitted to a jury was that of damages, and the case came on to be tried, in June 1868, before Sir Alexander Cockburn. Mr. Serjeant Parry appeared for Risk Allah, and made an extremely eloquent speech on his behalf. Mr. Coleridge, the present Chief Justice of England, who led me for the 'Daily Telegraph,' said all that could be urged under the circumstances. Sir Alexander Cockburn summed up with perfect fairness, and the jury returned a verdict for 960*l.*, which, under all the circumstances, could not be considered exorbitant.

On July 2, in the same year, Risk Allah made another appearance before the same judge, again in the character of a complainant, and again the victim, by his own account, of a series of disastrous circumstances in which he was the injured person. These occurred after his adventures in Belgium, and the story was developed in an action brought by him in the Court of Queen's Bench against the British and Foreign Marine Insurance Company for the sum of 3,000*l.*, for which amount he held an insurance in that

[1] These three charges were, in accordance with Belgian law, included in one indictment.

company. Mr. Serjeant Parry was again his counsel, and I led for the defence. The story Risk Allah told was a very remarkable one. He was, he said, previous to the occurrence afterwards detailed, considerably in debt, and, being moved by the desire to pay his creditors, he collected from a variety of sources the amount he claimed from the company; this he turned into specie, and it realised 3,000*l*. in gold. He kept his good intentions to himself, none of his creditors heard of the favourable news, nor did he blazon forth to strangers the information, or exhibit the money, although several persons were shown the parcel said to contain it. He secreted it about his person, which was quite natural, as he was then at Constantinople, where, as in other great cities, all people do not possess such honest dispositions as he did. The only memorandum he had verifying his possession of the money was contained in a pocket-book also upon his person. He knew that the noble sacrifice he was about to make would leave him penniless, but he had determined to dedicate his life to his country, and enlist under the renowned chieftain, Omar Pasha. Having taken the precaution of insuring his treasure with the company I represented, and hugging his valuable freight close to his body, he embarked in a boat on the shores of the Bosphorus, for the purpose of reaching the ship that was to carry him to those climes where he could lighten his conscience and his pockets; but Providence, it would appear, does not always watch over the virtuous, or prosper their efforts, however intended for the benefit of others, for, just as he was stepping on board, souse he went into the sea.

Fortunately for himself, Risk Allah was an excellent swimmer, and, reaching the top, was rescued; the bag remained at the bottom; and his misfortunes did not end there, for he might still have felt a happy consciousness that his notebook would show to the world his unluckily frustrated intentions. Alas! here again cruel fate pursued him, for the good Samaritan who had rescued him from drowning deprived him even of this consolation by picking his pocket of the valuable document. So that, beyond the credit that could be attached to his own relation, he had not a scrap of evidence to support the claim he made against the company for the loss, and it is obvious that there were no witnesses that could be called for my clients, so that I was obliged in reply to rely upon the improbability of the story and Risk Allah's antecedents. I commented upon the extraordinary features that had characterised his life, and upon the strange positions in which he had contrived to place himself. I ventured to suggest that, however innocent he may have been, the perils he had incurred would naturally have induced him to protect himself from suspicion in subsequent transactions, that nothing could have been more easy than to have obtained a dozen witnesses to prove the contents of the bag, and also the means by which he had obtained them. The case, as I have said, did not admit of my calling witnesses. To my great surprise the Lord Chief Justice took a strong view in favour of the plaintiff. I am confident it was a sincere one, although I think that a feeling of sympathy had created it rather than the calm judgment which ought to have governed his views. He was extremely eloquent, and appealed strongly to the jury in favour of Risk Allah, pointing out that my speech had been pure declamation, and that I had called no witnesses, ignoring altogether the impossibility of my doing so. The jury, after deliberating for a long time, were ultimately discharged without giving a verdict, one of them remarking, in relation to Risk Allah intending to pay his creditors, 'My Lord, I cannot swallow that!'

Risk Allah never afterwards, to my knowledge, made any other appearance upon our shores, and what is his true history will never, perhaps, be disclosed in this world.

It will be within the recollection of those who have perused the account of my early days that in Serjeants' Inn, Fleet Street, at the time my father resided there, so also did Mr. Wilde, afterwards Mr. Serjeant Wilde, Solicitor General, Chief Justice of the Common Pleas, and Lord Chancellor. He had only obtained the degree of the coif when I was first called to the bar; however, I remember upon one occasion being his junior, and, although I cannot recall either the name or nature of the case, I have a very distinct recollection of a consultation at his chambers, which lasted from eight until twelve o'clock. He was probably one of the most laborious and painstaking men that ever practised, and in many respects the late Sir John Karslake reminded me of him. Like him, his earnest and anxious attention to work impaired his health, and brought on, as it did with Sir John, severe neuralgia, amounting in fact to tic-douloureux, which resulted, as was probably the case with the latter gentleman, in softening of the brain. He also bravely conducted causes of great importance with infinite skill whilst suffering the acutest agonies. This was the case with the celebrated appeal in Small and Attwood, in the House of Lords, and in which he succeeded in obtaining a reversal of the judgment pronounced by Lord Lyndhurst in the Court of Exchequer. He obtained permission to argue the case without his wig, in consequence of the acuteness of his suffering.

An amusing circumstance occurred in the middle of his argument. His client had made him a present of a pair of carriage horses, and one day shortly after this event his servant came into the breakfast-room with a very long face and told his master that Attwood was dead, at which naturally he was much shocked. Upon inquiry, however, it turned out that his coachman had christened the two horses Small and Attwood, and that it was one of these that had departed this life.

I remember one occasion in connection with this judge illustrative of the necessity of adapting punishment to the opinion of the public—it was after he had become Chief Justice, and was presiding in the Crown Court at the Kingston Assizes. He deferred sentencing the prisoners convicted upon the first day until the following morning, and then sentenced several of them to be flogged; there was not another conviction during the whole assizes.[1] He was a very pleasant judge to counsel, but inclined to be severe to criminals.

I met him once after his retirement at Wiesbaden. He was staying at the Hôtel de Quatre Saisons, amusingly nicknamed the Quarter Sessions, from the number of lawyers that patronised it. He was then manifestly in bad health, although I did not discover any mental weakness; he was pleased with the attention I was glad to pay him, and rewarded me with much pleasant gossip. He had a very great admiration for the talent of Mr. Adolphus, and confirmed the view that I have already expressed of that gentleman, that, but for his temper, he would have become a very distinguished member of the bar. Lord Truro and Sir Frederick Pollock, whilst poles asunder in politics, had been all their lives fast friends; but although each had led a life of intense labour, the mental results were very different, which may be accounted for by Sir Frederick being so polished and accomplished a scholar,

[1] The sentences may have been on a later day; upon this point my memory does not serve me, but I remember well the effect.

whilst Lord Truro was entirely uneducated. I believe he was the uncle of Lord Penzance. There was another very great friend of Lord Truro, a man of ability, Matthew Davenport Hill, very much of the type of Lord Truro himself, and he also was a poignant sufferer from a similar malady, tic-douloureux. When Truro was Chancellor he was anxious to make Hill a judge, but unfortunately that gentleman had got into some scrape by disclosing a communication intended to be confidential, and the Cabinet put such a pressure upon the Chancellor that he was forced to give up his intention, and appointed Martin, the son-in-law of his old friend Pollock.

I do not know whether it was from Truro or Pollock that I heard the following incident. When they were both at the bar, the latter was retained to defend a clergyman in Norfolk for a serious, and indeed, although he was out on bail, a capital offence, and in a consultation that gentleman admitted his guilt to the counsel. Sir Frederick felt that this knowledge would embarrass his conduct of the defence, especially as it was a question of the credit of certain witnesses, and requested and obtained permission to give up his brief, which came afterwards into the hands of Sir Thomas Wilde, to whom the same admission was not made, and he obtained an acquittal. Pollock had no doubt that it would have been his duty, after accepting the retainer, to conduct the case, if his client had insisted upon it.

I never met Lord Truro afterwards, but with him and Pollock terminated a generation of great lawyers.

CHAPTER XXXIV.

MR. LANDSEER.

In a former chapter I have mentioned a meeting of literary and theatrical personages, and others who delighted in such society, held at the old and well-known tavern called the Piazza in Covent Garden. They did not assemble very early, indeed nowadays they could not have met at all. The stern command of policeman A. would have barred their entrance. At that period, however, taverns as well as clubs were open a great portion of the night, and the hours chosen by those who frequented the assembly in question were generally the small ones.

Conversation was the order of the day, or night, which made it rather remarkable that a gentleman who could not hear a word that was said should have been one of the most constant visitors. This was Mr. Landseer, a brother of the celebrated artist, himself an engraver of reputation, but unfortunately stone deaf.

I cannot, however, recall him to my memory without feelings of gratitude, if only for the pleasure he afforded me upon one or two occasions of meeting the eminent artist. I know of no one whose works have for me a greater fascination. He has spiritualised animal life, and has given it an affinity to the human race, and yet has neither destroyed nor altered its natural characteristics. We see told upon his canvas the nobility of which in the higher animals so many examples have been proved to exist, and in dealing with those which fill a humbler space in nature he has created a poetry essentially his own. One wonders what those two squirrels are saying to each other. Evidently they must have discovered a feast of filberts, or some other great event in their woodland lives. Sir Edwin was, as far as I could judge from the little I saw of him, very unaffected and kindly, as indeed from his works he must have been, and the following anecdote shows that he had no small sense of humour.

I had the honour of having him upon one occasion as a client—it is as far back as 1862; the question involved was undoubtedly one of art, although not of such a character as might have been expected. The plaintiff's profession was that of a tailor, a very eminent one at the west end of London; and he sued Sir Edwin for payment for a work that he had executed by that gentleman's order.[1] It was a coat which Sir Edwin declared violated every principle of high art, and he refused to countenance such a deviation from its true principles. The case was tried in the Exchequer, before (I believe) Mr. Baron Martin. The plaintiff entered the witness-box, and a very distinguished-looking personage he was. The coat was produced, and the judge suggested that Sir Edwin should try it on; he made a wry face, but consented, and took off his own upper garment. He then put an arm into one of the sleeves of that in dispute, and made an apparently ineffectual endeavour to reach the other, following it round amidst roars of laughter from all parts of the court. It was a common jury, and I was told that there was a tailor upon it, upon which I suggested that there was a gentleman of the same profession as the plaintiff in court who might

[1] I presume that other items had probably been admitted and money paid into court to meet them.

assist Sir Edwin. This was acceded to, and out hopped a little Hebrew slopseller from the Minories, to whom the defendant submitted his body. With difficulty he got it into the coat, and then stood as if spitted, his back one mass of wrinkles. The tableau was truly amusing: the indignant plaintiff looking at the performance with mingled horror and disgust; Sir Edwin as if he were choking; whilst the juryman, with the air of a connoisseur, was examining him and the coat with profound gravity. At last the judge, when able to stifle his laughter, addressing the little Hebrew, said, 'Well, Mr. Moses, what do you say?' 'Oh!' cried he, holding up a pair of hands not over clean, and very different from those encased in lavender gloves which graced the plaintiff. 'It ish poshitively shocking, my lord; I should have been ashamed to turn out shuch a thing from my establishment.' The rest of the jury accepted his view, and Sir Edwin, apparently rescued from suffocation, entered his own coat with a look of relief, which again convulsed the court, bowed, and departed.

The name of Mr. Landseer brings to my memory that of another gentleman, and of a scene, a very pleasant one, that occurred, alas! many years ago. Its locality is a house in the neighbourhood of Kilburn, spacious and elegantly furnished; the time is early summer, the hour about eight o'clock in the evening; dinner has been removed from the prettily decorated table, and the early fruits tempt the guests, to the number of twelve or so, who are grouped around it. At the head there sits a gentleman no longer in his first youth, but still strikingly handsome; there is something artistic about his dress, and there may be a little affectation in his manners, but even this may in some people be a not unpleasing element. He was our host, William Harrison Ainsworth, and, whatever may have been the claims of others, and in whatever circles they might move, no one was more genial, no one more popular. He had at this time fully won his spurs. Jack Sheppard had through his graphic pen become a hero to the masses, and was not less popular because very proper people shook their heads and exclaimed that it was a very evil example; and not only did the novel pay the circulating libraries, but became the subject of a very popular drama. Poor Paul Bedford played one of the characters—Blueskin—in which he rendered with great gusto the song of 'Jolly Nose.' No one can say that this song was refined, but it laid hold somehow of the whistling public. At last, as I have heard, Mrs. Keeley made the character of Jack so fascinating that the licenser of plays was obliged to stop the performance. How well I can remember her charming little figure upon the stool in Jack's workshop, and her sweet voice singing the naughty sentiment contained in the words, 'And I'll carve my name on the dungeon stone.'

I have travelled away from the pleasant dinner-table, but before I leave it there are two guests certainly I must not forget: one is Dudley Costello, a great ally and intimate friend of our host, an indefatigable inditer of pleasant tales to various periodicals, good-humoured, sociable, and with a large stock of amusing conversation. In the prime of life, full of spirits, and apparently of health, he seemed fully launched upon the path of success and fame. Shortly after I had met him at this dinner party the usual signs of his pen were absent from the magazines, and as I was returning from, I think, Strasburg to Paris, and at one of the intermediate stations, I saw a ghastly looking object staggering under a carpet bag; I went forward to assist, when to my horror I recognised the mere skeleton of my poor friend. He thought, he said, that he should try some waters, but his face told a tale that was only too soon verified. I carried in his bag, and pressed his hand in bidding adieu, and, although not given to sentiment, fancy that I scarcely restrained my feelings, and indeed, as I think over the scene, can scarcely do so now.

Opposite to me at the dinner-table of which I have given a description sat a good-looking young fellow, a member of the same profession as myself, got up with infinite care. He was seated next to a venerable lady, rattling and shining with diamonds; these two were engaged in the innocent occupation of cracking bon-bons and reading the mottoes. Harrison Ainsworth, pointing my attention to him, said, 'He (naming him) will make his way in the world.' The prophecy has turned out correct, and I am bound to say that even now, if it would give an old lady pleasure, he would still spell proverbs with her out of pure good-nature. I frequently visited Ainsworth at a house he occupied at Kemp Town, Brighton, but of late years have lost sight of him. I am glad to see within the last few days, upon the club table, that he still figures in the world of literature, and, if ever he reads these lines, I do not doubt that he will remember that pleasant entertainment at which he was the accomplished host.[1]

About, or soon after this period, I became acquainted with a character very different from any of those who graced the table of Harrison Ainsworth. It was a lady, and she had claims to celebrity. Her name was Lola Montes, and her life had been one of adventure, in the course of which it was suggested that she had not been particular as to the number of her husbands. She was, I believe, of Spanish origin, and certainly possessed that country's style of beauty, with much dash of manner, and

[1] I will not erase the foregoing lines, although the object of them has passed away since I wrote them.

an extremely *outré* style of dress. She had been upon the stage, and attracted the admiration of a monarch, and the anger of his subjects. When, subsequently, she visited this country, she fascinated a young gentleman named Heald, who married her. It was stated that she had been previously married to a Captain James. The friends of Mr. Heald made a charge against her of bigamy, and it was through being consulted upon this occasion that I became acquainted with her. She had to appear at Marlborough Street Police Court upon two or three occasions. I forget whether the charge was ultimately abandoned, or whether she left England before any result was arrived at. My impression was that it could not have been substantiated.

In the year 1842 a piece of insolence was offered to Her Majesty, whilst driving, by a person named Bean, a cripple. He contrived to make his escape, and, his deformity being his most noticeable feature, no humpbacked person could escape the vigilance of the police, until, fortunately for this unhappy race, the real criminal was arrested. He was prosecuted for misdemeanour only, and convicted, and suffered some period of imprisonment, which apparently cured the miserable desire for notoriety that had alone dictated the attempt. He was alive until recently, and might be seen at the different wharves from which the river steamers were accustomed to start, hawking newspapers, in a civil and inoffensive manner.

Her Majesty exhibited upon the occasion that wonderful coolness and self-possession which have distinguished her under the most trying circumstances.

It was from about the date of this trial that my business increased at the Central Court and I was entrusted with cases of some importance. In recalling, however, those years, I am unable to remember many personal incidents. I was engaged in one trial which exhibited, what I have already remarked upon, the extreme hesitation of Mr. Baron Alderson to permit a conviction in capital cases. The prisoner was a very young man, named Connor, and the learned judge certainly strained every point in his favour. The jury were out for several hours, but ultimately convicted him, and he was executed. I was also concerned for a person named Good, for the murder of a woman with whom he was living at Wimbledon. He also came to an unfortunate end.

A Captain Charitie also entrusted me with his defence. This was upon an indictment removed into the Court of Queen's Bench, the charge being that he, in conjunction with a director of the East India Company, was engaged in selling cadet-ships, and unfortunately the case against him was fully proved.

There was another proceeding in which I was counsel for a gentleman named Healy, who had made an imputation upon Mr. Wakley, the coroner for Middlesex, for his conduct in a matter which I think is not unworthy of being recorded. A private soldier belonging to the 7th Hussars had been cruelly flogged. He had certainly been guilty of a very grave offence, that of striking his corporal with a poker. The sentence was 150 lashes, which he underwent. He was permitted to stagger to the hospital, and there died within a few hours. The medical men of the regiment certified that his death had not in any way resulted from the flogging; this was apparently absurd, and very discreditable, and it is by no means wonderful that a jury, under the direction of Mr. Wakley, and after hearing the evidence of the very eminent surgeon, Mr. Erasmus Wilson, should come to the opposite conclusion, and return a verdict accordingly. Some strictures made by my client in a medical journal were very severe upon

Wakley, who moved against him for a criminal information; but I was able to show the court that the complainant had provoked the attack, and the rule was discharged. At the same time I consider that the exposure and the investigation of this affair have been a lasting benefit to the community. Such a punishment upon any human being is horrible, and naturally directed public attention to the subject, and, I imagine, has been the means of abolishing the lash both in the army and navy. I have already referred to the application of it in the instance of crimes attended with violence, and for them it is efficient and proper; the perpetrators of such offences are cowards as well as ruffians. Imprisonment creates little if any terror in their imagination, probably they are well acquainted with gaol life; and, according to accounts apparently authentic, there are means by which its hardships may be alleviated. It is certain that the discipline rarely if ever produces a good result, and, when an account appears in a newspaper of some atrocious act of violence, it is constantly stated that the perpetrator is a released convict. The lash, however, is viewed by these wretches with abject terror, and I am confident that the pain they are made to feel is the best protection, in the absence of the punishment of transportation, that can be afforded to a peaceable public.

CHAPTER XXXV.

CHIEF JUSTICES.

TENTERDEN, Denman, Campbell, Cockburn, have each during my connection with the legal profession occupied the highest place on the Common Law Bench. Each after his own fashion has administered justice, and they are remarkable instances of an observation I have already made of the differences of character exhibited by men filling the same position. Of Tenterden I have scarcely a recollection; I have seen him, and I think of a sour old man, with the manners of a pedagogue. The description given of him by Lord Campbell, in his 'Lives of the Chief Justices,' confirms my memory in this respect. Campbell makes, however, a curious mistake in an anecdote he relates of him. Having described his origin, which was being the son of a barber at Canterbury, and his beginning life as a chorister boy in the cathedral of that city, he tells a story which he attributes to Mr. Justice Richardson. In going the Home Circuit with Lord Tenterden the two judges visited the cathedral of Canterbury together, when the Chief Justice, pointing to a singing man in the choir, said, 'Behold, Brother Richardson, that is the only human being I ever envied. When at school in this town, we were candidates together for a chorister's place; he obtained it, and if I had gained my wish he might have been accompanying you as Chief Justice.'

Now, the fact is, that this story was narrated by Baron

Richards, and its scene was York Cathedral, but whether the fortunate rival of Lord Tenterden was present there, and could have been pointed out, I do not know. It certainly did not occur at Canterbury when the judges were going the Home Circuit, as Canterbury is not one of the assize towns, and the nearest locality to it is Maidstone, which is at a very considerable distance, only reachable by posting, at a sacrifice of time that the judges were not likely to expend for a visit to the cathedral. I do not remember Campbell going the Home Circuit; if he did, the blunder is unaccountable.[1] I heard a story of the circumstances under which Richards was offered the judgeship by Lord Eldon. He was a Welshman, and, happening to be in the Court of Chancery, the Chancellor threw him a slip of paper with these words written: 'Dear Taffy,—What do you say to a puisne Baron?' I believe that he accepted the offer upon the understanding that he was to become Chief when a vacancy occurred. Of Denman I have said my say, as also of Lord Campbell. The last occupant of the office was by no means the least remarkable of the four, and his character would form a curious study; it is those traits that were patent from which alone I have the power of judging, for although I knew him, and occasionally associated with him in private, from my earliest years at the bar, I never was on terms of intimacy with him; I more nearly approached it during the last three or four years of his life. Cockburn was one of those men who like Erskine (as I have heard), although small in person, did not look so. No one would for a moment have thought him insignificant, and, although his face was decidedly plain, it had when smiling a peculiar charm. His voice was very melodious, of which fact he was a little

[1] I was not aware of what I have since learnt is the fact, that Lord Campbell when first called joined the Home Circuit.

too well aware, and always willing to make the most of the effect it was calculated to produce. With ladies his manners were deferential, and, if gossip was to be believed, had been fully appreciated. As an advocate he was equal to any one I ever heard at the bar. He was fond of amusement, and sought it through many sources, but he mastered the most complicated facts with ease, and his industry never deserted him. He exhibited at times a polished vein of sarcasm, great skill in analysis, and, upon occasions that called them forth, powers of impassioned oratory. He was constantly pitted against Thesiger, no unworthy opponent, and fully maintained his position, and in some notable cases obtained unexpected success. I have already mentioned the trials of MacNaghten and Palmer. The same results would probably have been attained by much inferior advocacy in both these cases, but few men at that time in the lead could have steered with such consummate skill. It perhaps may seem that with Follett at the bar I place Cockburn too high in the scale of advocacy; it may be so, but my experience of the latter distinguished counsel does not furnish me with examples by which to modify my judgments. Cockburn's reply in MacNaghten's case[1] was described by Cresswell, one of the presiding judges, as the finest speech that he had ever heard. Cockburn became member for Southampton, and very soon made his mark in the critical arena of the House of Commons, and upon the occasion of the great debate of June 24, 1850, impugning Lord Palmerston's foreign policy, he was put forward to defend it. I remember very well his speech; it took the House by storm, and in no small degree conduced towards the victory obtained

[1] In this I am in error. Tindal presided, with Coleridge and Williams, J., upon this trial, and the speech of which I heard Cresswell speak was one made before him upon Circuit.

by the minister. From that period Cockburn moved on quickly, filling successively the offices of Solicitor and Attorney General, and ultimately those of Chief Justice of the Common Pleas and of England. I suspect that, even with this flood of success and accumulation of honours, a lingering disappointment remained that he had not grasped the seals. A true appreciation would not be formed of his qualities as an advocate and the versatility of his mind if I did not refer to his practice in the committees before he entered Parliament. In election inquiries it might naturally be expected that he would be successful, as they were peculiarly of a character for which he had already shown his capacity; but he was equally fortunate in the management of private bills, and fought the famous fight of the narrow against the broad gauge, supported by Lock, against Austin and Thesiger, backed by Brunel and a host of scientific talent.

The triumph of Palmerston was followed by a black day for England. The most trusted of our statesmen perished through an accident, and it was long before the nation ceased to deplore the death of Sir Robert Peel.

I cannot assign to Sir Alexander Cockburn as a judge the almost unqualified praise that I have given him as an advocate. He carried naturally the qualities that had distinguished him in that capacity to the bench, and exercised them without sufficient discretion. It is in my judgment a great mistake to think that a judge ought to keep back his own opinions from a jury, but they ought to be conveyed calmly and without passion, and after due consideration, but unfortunately Sir Alexander Cockburn was extremely impressionable, and constantly at the outset of a case would express with great confidence an opinion which he subsequently would not have been sorry to recall.

The evil result, however, had been frequently accomplished before he was able to correct it. It must also be admitted that he too often sacrificed matter for effect, and sentiment captivated him more than the graver questions involved in a suit. I cannot say that these were small faults, but I never doubted that he was anxious to do justice, and his manner in doing it was usually courteous; and notwithstanding his occasional impetuosity he gave his unswerving attention to any inquiry that he was presiding over. A more thoroughly humane man never occupied the seat of justice, and he afforded counsel every assistance and consideration; it is impossible that a greater contrast could exist in this respect than between him and his predecessor.

Cockburn was verging upon eighty years old when he died, but to the last exhibited no failure of intellect, or, so far as I could observe, of physical power. After sitting in court the whole of the day he was to be seen leaving the private door, and marching off with as sprightly an air and as active a gait as if he had only realised the half of his years. He lived, as long as I remembered him, in Hertford Street, Mayfair, and there I have seen him surrounded by books, evidently occupied by some engrossing literary labour. I have already alluded to his acquaintance with modern languages, and I believe that he was an accomplished classical scholar. He presided, after the death of Lord Campbell, at Serjeants' Inn, where he added greatly to the conviviality of the table; and when the affairs of the society were wound up, I ventured, without any sanction from my brethren, to send him the remainder of some old port wine, which he greatly enjoyed, and which I have shared at his table. Upon the occasions that I dined there he was extremely entertaining, not unwilling to recount former triumphs in the profession, and certainly affording me amusement in doing so. I reminded him once of a painful incident to which we were parties.

We were engaged to dine with one of his oldest friends, a gentleman named Phinn, a barrister by profession. He had held high office in the Admiralty, but had quitted it, and was practising at the Parliamentary bar. He resided in chambers in St. James's Street, and on the occasion of which I speak Cockburn and myself met at the door, and learnt to our horror that our expected host had just fallen down dead. The account that we received was that he was going upstairs to dress, that a loud shriek was heard, and that he was found extended and lifeless.

I called in Hertford Street one Sunday three weeks before the death of Sir Alexander, and found him as usual in his library hard at work. He was engaged in a work upon venery, of which a portion had already been published. He seemed well in health, though not in his usual spirits, but he spoke of the opening of the New Law Courts as if he anticipated being present. He presided after this in his court, and did not show, as far as I observed, any signs of his approaching end. In the account that I have given of the trials in which Risk Allah was the plaintiff, I have intimated my opinion that he took a prejudiced view in his favour, and I shall hereafter have to comment upon his demeanour in the proceedings against the claimant to the Tichborne baronetcy and estates. It is also impossible to approve of the tone that he adopted in his controversy with Lord Penzance, whilst the temperate and dignified bearing of this latter judge deserves warm admiration; but in these proceedings the industry and research of the Chief Justice were signally exhibited.

Whatever were his faults they were those of impulse,

and directed more to the support of the weak than in favour of harshness or oppression, and under his auspices the Court of Queen's Bench sustained its dignity, and commanded the respect of the public and the profession. By his death a pleasant figure has disappeared from society, and a great name is erased from the annals of our times.

When first I met the subject of the above sketch, there was a cotemporary of his, moving in the same circles, also accomplished and popular. His name was Walsh. When I was in the lowest class at St. Paul's School he was in the highest, and when I joined the Home Circuit he was leader of the Kent Sessions. He married a lady of mature age, but possessing considerable fortune. When, many years after meeting him in London society, I was staying in Florence, I heard that he had a villa there, and sought him out. He was in a deplorably hypochondriacal state, and nothing seemed capable of rousing him. Some time after this I was taken professionally to the house of a medical man in the Finchley Road, to assist in the examination of an alleged lunatic, and there I found my poor friend, hopelessly and miserably insane. I have every reason to believe that he was treated with skill and kindness, although I utterly disapprove of private lunatic asylums, it being naturally to the advantage of their keepers that the patient should remain under their care.

It is not many years ago that I became acquainted with a pregnant example of this evil. I was asked by a member of the bar to visit his brother at a private lunatic asylum of high class. He was confined there contrary to his brother's wishes, who did not think he was judiciously treated or required confinement. The family were wealthy, and a large sum was paid for the maintenance of the gentleman in question. I accordingly went down, and, calling at the house and sending in my card, requested permission to see the patient. I was told that the proprietor was not at home, and that in his absence I could not be permitted to do so, although I produced the brother's authority. I insisted, and threatened to move the Court of Queen's Bench if the refusal was persisted in, and at last I was admitted, and found the patient lodged in a very handsome suite of apartments, opening out upon some beautiful grounds. He made no complaint of his treatment, and was manifestly under the influence of insane impulses; but my astonishment was extreme, upon looking at the literature with which he was supplied, to find that it was of a character eminently calculated to foster the peculiar form of disease to which he was subject. An inquiry was subsequently held before a master in lunacy; the result was that he was released from the asylum, and put under the charge of a skilled person, and, subject to such superintendence, permitted his liberty. His removal was opposed by the proprietor, who lost by it a net profit of at least 600*l*. per annum.

My old friend Charles Reade has described in works of fiction, with great power and ability, the evils that may arise from these institutions when in unscrupulous hands; and the existence of such men as Dr. Tuke, and others whom I could name, whose sense of honour and general character place them above all suspicion, does not in my judgment make the system one to be trusted or approved of, and I am afraid that the protection intended by the law to be afforded by independent opinions is too often imperilled by a near connection existing between the proprietors of these asylums and the medical men who certify for the reception of persons supposed to be lunatics.

The whole subject of insanity, as I have elsewhere

endeavoured to show, deserves supervision—the nature of it, its obligations, and its treatment; and if the statistics upon it are correct—and it is true that of late years there has been a great increase of the malady—no social evil better deserves a thorough legislative investigation.

CHAPTER XXXVI.

EXTRAORDINARY WILL CASE.

THE beautiful neighbourhood of Matlock, in Derbyshire, was kept for some years in a state of excitement by local circumstances that created a romantic interest.

They were the subject of various legal proceedings. The House of Lords, the Court of Chancery, Lord Chief Justice Erle and Lord Chief Justice Pollock, had all tried their hands at a satisfactory solution, and at the end of eight years they reached the Court of Queen's Bench, where with the assistance of a respectable complement of counsel and solicitors, and an intelligent jury, directed most ably by the Chief Justice of England, they were ultimately disposed of.

George Nuttall lived the whole of his life at Matlock, his native town. He was a land surveyor, much respected, and must have been a good business man, as at his death, which happened at the comparatively early age of fifty-four, he was possessed of landed property to the amount of nearly 3,000*l.* per annum, and some 10,000*l.* in the Funds. He had no near relations. In September 1854 he had made his will. His mode of doing this was peculiar. A Mr. Newbold was his solicitor and also an intimate friend; this gentleman prepared it, but the testator copied it in duplicate. He was an illiterate man, and in what purported to be his copies, and there was no suggestion against their authenticity, were to be found several instances of words wrongly spelt. I wish to avoid as far as possible technical details, and it will be sufficient to say that the bulk of the property was left to John Nuttall, a cousin, and foreman in the service of a contractor in London.

John Else, the brother-in-law of a person living with the testator, at the time of his death, in the capacity of housekeeper, was an assistant overseer and bailiff of the County Court at Matlock; he had been employed by the testator in collecting accounts.

The testator died in March 1856, having been for some time before his death in an extremely feeble state of health. The duplicate wills were beyond question placed in a cupboard in his bedroom; and there was also no doubt that two or three days before his death he was very anxious to get to that cupboard, but unable from feebleness to do so or explain his wishes.

Immediately after his death, one copy of a will was produced, which was authentic; a second copy, also authentic, was found before the funeral, with an interlineation which was subsequently disputed, although not at the time, by John Nuttall, who had principally benefited by the will, and whose estate was lessened by the terms of the interlineation, and probably, but for subsequent events, it would have passed without challenge.

This was the state of affairs on April 21 following the death, when John Nuttall himself died, leaving his property to his children. A fortnight after his death, Else produced a codicil, which he declared that he had found amongst the papers of the original testator; it was dated October 27, 1855, and purported to be entirely in the testator's handwriting. Eight months after the production of this codicil, Else produced another, which he said he found in a little penny account-book, pinned on to one of the leaves; it was dated January 6, 1856. There is no doubt that there was much improbability in the story of both these discoveries, and moreover there were misspellings in both the documents to which no similar ones were to be found in the writing of the testator, and it may generally be stated that Else and his belongings derived benefit from both of them. Nevertheless there was not anything that was not susceptible of some explanation, which, however, it would only encumber the main features of the tale to relate.

Another nine months elapsed, and then Else, according to his own account, made a most astounding discovery, brought about by means almost miraculous.

He had gone to reside in the testator's former house, at the back of which there was a yard, and on one side of it there was a flight of steps, leading up to a hay-loft, at the farther end of which was a small room used as a lumber or tool house.

Into this loft on October 9, 1857, it moved the spirit of Else, accompanied by a boy named Campion, to ascend, and it struck him that the window of the lumber room wanted cleaning, and so he told the boy to clean it, which he accordingly proceeded to do, but not being able to reach high enough, Else laid hold of the window-sill to pull himself up, when the boarding gave way, and disclosed a small hole in the wall, in which was an earthenware jar. In the jar was a small bag containing twenty sovereigns, and also another codicil, substantially giving the bulk of the property to Else, like the two former ones, and containing instances of misspelling dissimilar to any occurring in the genuine writing of the testator. It will be observed that the different codicils were found by Else in the order of their respective dates. One circumstance I think ought to be stated. Newbold, the solicitor, who had died before the last trial took place, had expressed a belief which, although not in positive terms, was not altogether antagonistic to the authenticity of the codicils.

There were a number of minute facts—arguments about handwriting, the relations existing between the different parties, and their opposing interests ; but I think I have told enough to make the general reader understand the proceedings which occurred after the production by Else of these remarkable documents.

The parties conflicting were the representatives of the original residuary legatee on the one side and John Else practically, though associated with another person named Cresswell, on the other.

The duplicate wills being admitted, the question was raised as to the validity of the three codicils, and a suit was instituted in Chancery for this purpose, the result of which was that an issue was directed by the Master of the Rolls to try this question. It came on at the summer assizes for Derby in 1859, before Lord Chief Justice Erle and a special jury, who found in favour of the codicils. The Master of the Rolls was not satisfied, and directed another trial, which came on before Chief Baron Pollock, at the spring assizes at Derby in 1860, and then the jury reversed the former verdict, finding that the codicils were forgeries. An application was then made on the opposite side to the Master of the Rolls, but he was satisfied and refused to interfere. Next came an appeal to the Lords Justices, who were divided in opinion ; and then there was a reference from them to the House of Lords, who decided for a new trial, and directed that it should take place in London, before the Lord Chief Justice of England and a special jury, and upon this occasion the counsel engaged were for Else, the real plaintiff, Mr. Karslake, Q.C., Mr. Field, Q.C., and Mr. Hannen, the present judge of the Probate Court; for the defendants, the representatives of the will, Mr. Serjeant Hayes, myself, and Mr. Wills.

It will be obvious, from the slight sketch that I have given of the circumstances, that the case of the plaintiff depended upon the truth of Else himself and the four witnesses who severally were pledged to having witnessed the successive codicils, and here was introduced another element. It was alleged that Buxton and Gregory, the witnesses to the first codicil, had been tampered with. Adams was dead, but his deposition upon the last trial was read, and it supported the codicils to which his name was attached. Nothing appeared against his character. He was a surgeon, and really could not be mistaken, and moreover had no apparent interest in the matter. Knowles's son took a legacy under the second codicil. Knowles himself was examined upon the trial at the Guildhall, and swore to his own and Adams's signatures. I cross-examined him, but failed to elicit anything that in my own judgment seriously affected his credit; and I confess that the effect upon my mind was that, standing by themselves, notwithstanding the prevarication of Buxton and Gregory, these four witnesses did present a formidable case in favour of the codicils.

As Mr. Karslake put it with point and judgment, 'Direct and positive evidence was to be met by apparent improbabilities, and by speculations as to handwriting, the codicils being all of them alleged to be the testator's own.'

Sir Alexander Cockburn prided himself greatly upon his discernment in matters of handwriting, not altogether without justice; but it was with him a favourite subject, and he seized upon it with avidity, and dissected it at length. He found and pointed out dissimilarities between the admitted and contested signatures, and also dissimilarities in style. The misspellings also were pointed out by him, and strangely differed from those proved to exist in documents written by the testator; but although these were very remarkable, still this observation might be made: how was it that Else, who was perfectly acquainted with the testator's handwriting, and with the ordinary blunders contained in it, and having plenty of time to prepare the documents, fell into such transparent errors? Handwriting is a dangerous element upon which to rest a case; the evidence of what are called experts is viewed with no great confidence. Juries distrust it, and in this particular action I did not quite agree with the opinion expressed by the Lord Chief Justice as to the dissimilarity.

Mr. Serjeant Hayes took, in my opinion, the right course in dwelling upon the improbabilities of the story, which he did with great ingenuity and humour. He was not a powerful speaker, and not equal to Mr. Karslake, who upon this occasion fully supported his reputation, and was most justly complimented by Sir Alexander Cockburn for the mode in which he had conducted the case; but Serjeant Hayes possessed a very acute mind, and was very droll in some parts of his speech. I cannot forbear quoting that portion of it which referred to the discovery of the last codicil, and was received with roars of laughter. I copy it from a pamphlet, published by a Mr. Keene of Derby, and from which I have refreshed my memory upon other matters in the case:—

'Then as to the third codicil found in the jar in the hole in the wall. "What's that," said Else, "what's that in the jar?" Why, a codicil to be sure! What else could it be but a codicil, in a jar in a hole in the wall? Of course it was a codicil. Why, but for this remarkable discovery it might not have been found at all, at all events until the house was pulled down a century hence. What a place for a man of business to put his last will in!'

Serjeant Hayes then proceeded to state, what was subsequently proved, that during the testator's lifetime an iron vice weighing 60 lbs. had been screwed over the window board in which the jar containing the codicil was placed, and which must have been unscrewed by the testator whilst suffering from a most serious abscess in the back. The Serjeant then proceeded thus: 'Why, imagination can scarcely go beyond this story. One blessing of the Chancery proceedings has been that they have stopped the finding of codicils. But for them a fourth must have been found—it must have come. The second and third had each been found after nine months, the usual period of gestation; but perhaps, as there was so little of the property left to be still disposed of, this might have been only a seven months' codicil. It was certainly difficult to conceive where it could have been found; one could hardly imagine a more obscure place for secreting it. Perhaps, however, in Job Knowles's quarry, while his men were blasting the rock with gunpowder, of course in some fissure Else may have seen an antediluvian toad sitting on something, and said, "What is that?" Why, what could it be but a codicil? However, thanks be to heaven! no more codicils had been found.'[1]

The Lord Chief Justice summed up the case with admirable perspicacity, but, as I expected he would, dealt very strenuously upon the evidence afforded by the handwriting, not, however, neglecting to make forcible comments upon other parts of the case; and the jury without much hesitation found a verdict for the defendants, which

[1] Knowles was in occupation of a quarry.

as it turned out put the existing codicils at rest for ever, and no further discoveries astonished the world, although there are some still living who shake their heads and express disbelief in the conclusion arrived at.

I have in a former chapter called attention to the fact that crime, like other incidents in the history of nations, repeats itself, and this remark may apply to all descriptions of it; I have myself recently been engaged in a case that brought forcibly to my mind the great Derby will case, and which illustrates one at all events of the remarks I have made as to the distrust juries have in the evidence of handwriting. Here the plaintiff set up three documents; they were promissory notes, and there were three witnesses, who could not be mistaken, and who swore to the signature being that of a person since dead, and that they had seen him sign them. In this respect the evidence was probably of more weight than that of the attesting witnesses to Nuttall's alleged codicils. The documents in question had been, as alleged, executed by this gentleman eight years before, and, he being dead, there was no direct contradiction to the story of the plaintiff. They had been kept during all this time in a receptacle as eccentric in its character as the boarding of the window-sill, namely, in a cash-box at the shop of a kind of general dealer, who was one of the witnesses to the signature, but had no apparent interest in the case. Strangely enough, the stamps of the bills in two instances had the dates erased, which was accounted for by their contact with old coins, which might have rubbed against them: but what was still more odd, it was the date only that had disappeared, the outer rim, which was the highest part of the stamp, being uneffaced. At the time that the deceased was supposed to have signed the notes, which amounted to 1,250*l.*, and for which he only received 500*l.*, he was in abundant funds.

An action was brought by the drawees against the executors, and was tried before Mr. Baron Huddleston. I was counsel for the defence, and confess that in my judgment the evidence as to the handwriting was conclusive against the claim. I never witnessed discrepancies so apparent, and Mr. Chabot, the experienced judge of handwriting, pointed out many with great clearness, in addition to those discoverable by the most ordinary observer. The learned Baron also was obviously of a similar opinion, but the jury nevertheless were discharged without giving a verdict, there being eleven of them for the plaintiff. Upon a second trial, before the Lord Chief Justice, very little prominence was given to the evidence of writing, and Chabot was not called; but the utter improbability of the story was mainly relied upon, the result being a verdict, after little consideration by the jury, for the defendants.

Whether I am right in supposing that the different tactics obtained this result I cannot say, but there is no doubt that if a branch of evidence distasteful to a jury is made too prominent, it frequently leads to their attention being distracted from facts that in themselves are sufficient to support the conclusion contended for.

CHAPTER XXXVII.

AN APOLOGY TO MY READERS.

I HAVE already mentioned the fact that when first I began a record of some of the events of my life, I did so for amusement, and with no idea of publishing the contents; and since I have commenced the task with a view of submitting the result to the public, I have frequently wavered, and almost determined to abandon it. I have feared that my personal anecdotes might be deemed too trivial, and my professional ones too dull. I have also felt that the contents of many of my chapters greatly exceed the limits that the title of the work would seem to justify, also that I have presented opinions that can scarcely be deemed of interest to the general public, and in one or two instances I may be accused of introducing matters that amount almost to treatises. Difficulties also have presented themselves which, if my pages had remained in my own custody, would not have been of importance, but for which when I offer them to the public I am bound to apologise. I rarely kept a diary, and only interjectionally, at long intervals and for short periods, and then only of private matters; and as I believe my mind is naturally of an irregular type, the circumstances that come into it during the progress of my work refuse to maintain any order, and defy every endeavour to preserve the dates. This may not be accepted as an excuse for events of one era tumbling against those of an entirely different period, and if I were one of the industrious classes I might sit down and re-arrange what I have written; but if I did contrive to write a book orderly, and in accordance with rule, my identity would be lost, and so if my details are confusing I must throw myself upon the mercy of my readers, and ask them to pity my infirmities. In the pursuit of my task I have also found myself limited by the fact that the details of many of the cases I have been engaged in might give pain to some persons who are living, a result which I have felt bound to avoid.

The above lines are a proof of how incurable is my disposition. They ought to have been at the commencement, and here they are thrust into the middle of the book; but then a lengthy preface terrifies most readers, and I think it prudent to avoid an element that might deter people at the outset.

One entry I have found under the date of January 10, 1838: 'Called on Miss Whitcombe, afterwards with her upon the Roneys. Dined at Sir Charles Forbes's. Evening party at Levien's. Met Boz—looks quite a boy. His sister was there; she sang beautifully, is pretty, and I should think clever. Also met Mrs. Dodd, a very beautiful woman. Hard frost.'

Miss Whitcombe was the sister of Lady Roney, the wife of Sir Patrick Cusack Roney, one of my earliest friends. Both these ladies were singularly beautiful. Lady Roney died early; Miss Whitcombe married a distinguished Indian officer, causing me a period of extreme depression.

Sir Charles Forbes was a very wealthy merchant and director of the East India Company. He lived in a large house in Fitzroy Square, and my father was intimate with him. He was a man noted for his benevolence, and amongst many acts of kindness he gave a younger brother of mine an assistant-surgeoncy in the Company's service. My brother was a very good-looking young fellow, and unfortunately, as it turned out, very susceptible. A lady and her daughter went out in the same ship, the latter being engaged to be married to an officer of rank. I fancy she looked with no unfavourable eye upon the young assistant-surgeon. The mother was prudent and said nothing whilst on board, but immediately upon landing gave a hint to the colonel of his regiment, which resulted in my brother being sent to Scinde, where he caught a fever which ultimately laid the seeds of a premature death.

Mrs. Dodd was one of the handsomest women in London She lived with her husband in Montagu Square, where they extended great hospitality.

Oh, these diaries, which I have come upon by mere accident! Here is another entry, earlier it must be than the last, but I have only the leaf, and the date is torn off. I record the return of a ring from a pretty Irish girl and my abandonment to utter despair. She was the daughter of a very eminent solicitor in Dublin, and afterwards married an officer who at the time was aide-de-camp to the Commander-in-Chief. She died of consumption within six months of her marriage. It was upon the occasion of a visit to her family that I saw Dublin for the first and only time. At this period I had no means and but shadowy prospects, and her father acted wisely in putting an end to an unpromising engagement. Her brother is an officer of distinction, whom I have often met since, and with whom I have always been upon terms of intimacy. And now, reader mine, I shall exhume no more domestic histories, and have only recorded these to show that my life has not always been devoted to the engrossing studies of the law.

Another entry, however, I will refer to, as it mentions the name of a gentleman who at the time filled some space in public history; I allude to the Rev. Dr. Croly. He was a popular preacher at St. Stephen's, Walbrook, and was the author of different works, amongst others a novel called 'Salathiel.'

My father and myself were dining at the house of a Mr. Stutfield, a Middlesex magistrate. He lived in very good style at Clapton. The doctor was engaged at that time in the persecution of Alderman Gibbs, whose conscience enabled him to bear it with philosophy. It must be remarked that conscience does vary very considerably in different people. The note I find is in these words: 'Met Dr. Croly; a brute'—and such is my remembrance of him—'noisy, self-asserting, and maintaining the whole talk at the table, the greater part of it consisting of boasts of his own doings. A little meek-faced lady sat next to me, viewing him with a look of ineffable disgust, and whispering now and again to me at the end of one of his romances, "I don't believe a word of it."'

I have not mentioned that through the nomination of the Duke of Wellington I had become a magistrate of the Tower Liberty, and I suppose I still hold that dignified position. My father was chairman of the Sessions, but there never was anything to do in my time. I did hear that there once was a case tried there, and a difficulty arose from there being no Testament upon the premises, but now the jurisdiction is engulfed in the Middlesex Sessions. When Alderman Gibbs became Lord Mayor I dined, on November 9, at the Guildhall, but it was a stupid dinner, as there is no doubt he was in very bad odour, and few of the Ministers attended.

I have lately, and since I wrote the first of these volumes, read recollections and reflections by my old friend Planché. He naturally refers to many of those whom I have met and given my impressions of, and also, as he was an acute observer, if my opinions are correct, there must be a sameness between our accounts. I hope that this will not destroy any interest that may otherwise have been created. I am inclined to think that my description of Thackeray's personal appearance must have been founded upon seeing him at a later date than I imagined to be the case, as Planché describes him as tall and slight at what would be about the same period. He confirms my view of his character. I was much struck by his sketch of Billy Dunn, so entirely confirmatory of my remembrance. I was, however, surprised at his assigning the palm of beauty to Mrs. Robinson amongst all with whom he had associated, as he has often told me that there never had been a being so lovely as Madame Vestris, and judging by the fascination that she exercised over so many this account must be near reality; true it is that the brilliancy of her mind and variety of her accomplishments gave zest to her charms. Amongst those who worshipped at her shrine was one whom I just remember, an elegant gentleman, and courted guest in all societies. Strangely, for the period in which he lived, he was a 'Radical,' but though his opinions were considered 'uncommonly low,' no one could deny the refinement with which they were expressed. He and Wakley were returned after the Reform Bill as members for the borough of Finsbury.

They were opposed by that hard-headed old Scotchman, Mr. Serjeant Spankie, whom I have already mentioned. Tom Duncombe was not famous for paying his debts, and Wakley was accused of having burnt his house to cheat an Insurance Company. A *bon-mot* of the Serjeant's is recorded by Mr. Greville in his memoirs; it was old then, and so I am only following an illustrious example in repeating it. Spankie, canvassing an elector, was told that he had promised to vote for his two opponents. 'Well,' said he, 'I only hope you may have one for a debtor, and the other for a tenant.' Spankie, after he had passed the meridian of life, married a really very charming young lady. This event was celebrated by the poet laureate of the Home Circuit in the following distich:—

When Miss Smith was twenty
She had lovers in plenty;
When Miss Smith got older
Her lovers got colder;
Then came Serjeant Spankie,
And Miss Smith said Thankie.[1]

My recollection of Tom Duncombe is of a tallish, good-looking man, dressed in a blue coat with brass buttons, and a collar reaching half-way up his neck. This was the fashionable costume of the period; his head, however, had its full complement of brains, as the following anecdote will testify. There was a certain individual, his name and place of abode are alike immaterial; he was collector of some portion of his Majesty's revenue; he was also the collector of autographs bearing a stamp, of which he possessed several specimens presented to him by the honourable member for Finsbury before he was elected for that borough. After that occurrence it was found impossible to induce Mr. Duncombe to treat his hand-writing with proper respect, and so the individual in question hit upon a means of persuasion which was very unlucky for himself as it turned out. The honourable member lived in the neighbourhood of Westminster, and one afternoon when starting upon his Parliamentary duties he was confronted by some half-dozen men encased in

[1] I have not published the real name, but the description given of the young lady's waning attractions was much opposed to the fact.

boards, with the announcement upon them that the possessor of certain documents bearing the signature 'Thomas Duncombe' was willing to part with them to the highest bidder. This gentleman proceeded calmly to the House of Commons, and, impelled as he said by the interest he took in the application of public moneys, moved for a return of such of the king's taxes as had been collected and not paid over. The motion, being seconded, was carried as a matter of course. This was by no means convenient to the inventor of the boards, and a catastrophe ensued that led to their disappearance, and the patriotic member was never again troubled to take possession of the documents bearing his signature.

Another of the devoted admirers of Madame Vestris was Horace Claggett. He was in some crack regiment, and when I knew him was past middle age, but handsome still. His finances did not accord with disinterested love, and he discarded the drama and went in for matrimony with a Miss Day, who was in some way connected with the firm of Day and Martin, and who had many thousand charms besides. She yielded to his attractions and accepted his suit. He had a rival for her hand, an officer in a Dragoon regiment, who was rejected; on this becoming known to his comrades, they chalked up next morning on the door of his quarters, 'Try Warren's.'[1]

I never met Madame Vestris in private life, and the last time I saw her was at the Central Court, when she was obliged to prosecute a servant for theft. Her appearance then had greatly changed, and she had an affection of the nerves of the face which created the appearance of distortion. I have heard that she was a woman of great kindness of disposition, and beloved by those associated with her, of both sexes. Planché has made an account of

[1] Another famous blacking manufacturer.

her different managements and successes a labour of love, the perusal of which will fully reward those readers who take an interest in the drama. He was also intimately acquainted, not only with herself but with the brilliant company that surrounded her and aided in her performances, and in his work many amusing anecdotes will be found.

I knew Frank Matthews and his wife, both clever comedians. He was younger than his namesake, but used to play old men to the sprightly youths of the latter favourite.

CHAPTER XXXVIII.

THE MAYOR OF CORK.

THERE are some events that occur which defy every effort of reason and common sense to understand, and it was to a combination of these that I was indebted for the honour conferred upon me of being appointed to act as counsel to the House of Commons.

Early in the year 1869 his Royal Highness the Duke of Edinburgh was upon a tour, and was visiting our colony of Australia, and whilst there was fired at by an Irishman of the name of O'Farrell. A more wanton piece of ruffianism was never known. In the different attempts to assassinate distinguished people there have usually been causes, real or imaginary, actuating excitable minds, founded upon a notion of injury or mistaken sense of patriotism. But this attempt simply represented ruffianism without a redeeming trait, and probably, when it became known, such was the almost universal opinion.

Certainly amongst reasonable beings it would have been assumed that nothing more degraded could be produced in a civilised state. Those, however, who entertained that opinion turned out to be mistaken. Another Irishman, envious of his countryman's reputation, was determined to surpass it if he could do so with safety to his person, and accordingly Mr. Daniel O'Sullivan, Mayor of Cork, entered into the lists with that view. It was not an easy task, but it must be admitted that he fully succeeded. Of course before he could occupy his official post of mayor he must have taken the oath of allegiance. He also must be supposed to have known that it was part of the duty he had imposed upon himself to enforce peace and good order. In pursuance of his ideas of these duties, he proceeded to abuse his brother magistrates, to declare that the law he had undertaken to administer was unconstitutional, promised publicly to apply for the suspension of his brother magistrates—a proposal which, it is right to mention, was received with loud cheers by his friends in court—got into a rhapsody about the patriots who had tried to blow up Clerkenwell gaol, and ended in an ecstatic glorification of that noble Irishman who had fired at the Duke of Edinburgh in Australia. Of course society was indignant and disgusted, and, as the House of Commons was sitting, it was mentioned from several quarters in terms of indignation. There existed no summary means of getting rid of him by the Executive, and it was necessary that legislative action should be taken, which was accordingly done, and a bill was brought in by the Attorney-General to disqualify the mayor of Cork from holding any office, in consequence of the use of scandalous and seditious language.

It was determined that evidence should be taken, and upon May 12 the Attorney-General for Ireland informed the House that, acting under its orders, he had taken care that evidence should be forthcoming in support of the preamble of this bill, and he had also, acting under the order of the House, appointed counsel to be heard at the Bar. These were the Solicitor-General for Ireland, Mr. Serjeant Ballantine, and Mr. Edward Barry. He had now to move that counsel be called in. Mr. A. Sullivan,[1] however, before I had the honour of appearing for the first time

[1] Not, I believe, any relation of the mayor.

before this tribunal, got up and announced that the Mayor of Cork intended to resign, and Mr. Maguire read a letter from him to that effect. The O'Donoghue spoke a few words to a similar effect. With this latter gentleman I had the pleasure of some private acquaintance, and although he would not desert a fellow-countryman, he had, I am quite sure, no sympathy with him. The affair was terminated by Mr. Gladstone accepting the undertakings of the gentlemen I have mentioned, and, considering the intense indignation felt by this country at the outrage committed upon an unoffending member of the Royal family, and the scandalous language of a magistrate, it reflects great credit upon the House of Commons that they should have exhibited such moderation of language and dignity of demeanour.

When I was informed that I should have the honour of appearing for the House, I was conducting an election petition at Stafford, and, travelling all night, was somewhat nervous as to the figure I should make. The evidence had been hurriedly collected, and scarcely so strict in form as would have been required, and perhaps it was fortunate that the collapse took place.

It was, I think, upon the morning of my arrival in town I came upon two individuals both of whom I had known well. They were a curiously consorted pair. I had wandered into St. James's Park, and noticed an invalid chair with a gentleman in it, and, walking by its side, a figure which I thought that I recognised. I came up, and looking round recognised my old friend Paddy Green, and in the chair, aged from what he was when last I saw him, but as pleasant-looking as ever, the Hon. James Stuart Wortley, once leader of the Northern Circuit, afterwards Recorder of the City of London, and subsequently Her Majesty's Solicitor-General. He had given way under the strain of the last office, and become partially paralysed. I understood that these two frequently met in this same place and exchanged gossip about their very different lives.

Stuart Wortley was as good a criminal judge as ever sat upon the Bench. I never saw him out of temper. He was a sound lawyer, and managed the court admirably. It was a misfortune both for it and himself when he changed his position for that of officer of the Crown. He was not rapid enough, nor did he possess sufficient energy for the work of Nisi Prius. I was in one criminal case against him in the Queen's Bench. He exhibited a good deal of nervousness in the conduct of it, and I succeeded quite properly in getting a verdict. He resided in Carlton Terrace, where I have occasionally dined with him, and at that time his wife welcomed all his friends with the most genial kindness, and in the days of his sorrow and sickness was the source to him of support, comfort, and hope, while exhibiting a womanly example of patience and self-denial.. Paddy was by nature a gentleman, and seeing him by the side of a man of Wortley's position, and his kindly deference and really entertaining conversation, added to the respect I felt for him. These two were, although in such different frames, valued pictures in my life, and it was with a feeling of deep interest, on this the last day that I rested my eyes upon either of them, the one having quitted the ermine, and the other the motley; that they should be passing on their way together, joined by the common bond of a kindly nature.

Not very long after this, I was consulted in a case that promised at one time to become of interest and importance. Horace Pitt, a colonel in the Blues, and at one time the handsomest man in London, had married a lady of a station not equal to his own, but possessing great beauty. At the time I speak of she was separated from him, and residing with a niece, the daughter of a Mrs. Richardson. This young lady had formed an acquaintance with a Mr. William Howard, son of the Hon. and Rev. Francis Howard, brother of the Earl of Wicklow, and ultimately she married him. He, however, from very early life, entered into every description of profligacy, was rarely sober, and became nearly imbecile. The Earl of Wicklow having died without issue, this William Howard inherited the title, but did not live long enough to enjoy it.

I met his widow at Boulogne, where she was staying with her aunt, who had then become Lady Rivers, her husband having succeeded to that title. Mrs. Howard was accompanied by a little boy of pleasing appearance whom she represented as being the son of her late husband, and consequently the Earl of Wicklow. I think I was staying at the same hotel with them; at all events, I became acquainted with them, and learned that their claim was disputed, and I was ultimately retained to support it.

I found that the allegation upon the other side was that the child was not her own, but had been procured from some other source; and there were so many circumstances that struck me as suspicious that I insisted upon the lady undergoing a medical examination by some physician of eminence. This she refused to do, and, as I was acting for her as a friend, I declined to go on any further in the case. She afterwards retained eminent counsel, who conducted her cause in the House of Lords, and placed it in as favourable a light as it was capable of.

An adjournment, however, having taken place, a discovery was made that did not at all surprise me. A nurse and other persons belonging to the Liverpool Workhouse identified Mrs. Howard as having come there with another lady and procured a recently born child from its mother, who was a pauper in the workhouse. Mrs. Howard would not face this evidence, and refused to be examined. Of course there could be but one result—the dismissal of her claim. There were others who, I believe, put her up to making it. I have never heard what became of her or of the child, which had been kindly and carefully brought up. Shortly after this event Lady Rivers died. She had been a great sufferer for many years, and Lord Rivers married again a lady of high position. He was an old acquaintance of mine, and I used to meet him frequently during the first trial of the Tichborne case. He was a very enthusiastic supporter of the Claimant, but whether upon any reliable grounds I am not aware. I also met him two or three years ago at Maidenhead, and have had frequent conversations with him. He spoke very unfavourably of the Claimant, but nevertheless his faith in his identity was not in the slightest degree shaken.

I am sorry to say that he has recently died, and I believe almost his last act was to initiate an endeavour to reverse the judgment of the Court of Queen's Bench upon the case.

CHAPTER XXXIX.

VIVISECTION.

In an early portion of these pages I ventured some observations upon the subject of vivisection. I described it according to the feelings I entertained, and upon the foundation of accounts that I had read of the nature of the experiments practised upon different animals. I was led into referring to the subject not only because it was one upon which I had always felt great horror, but I thought it not inappropriate to the mode in which corpses were obtained for the dissection table. No one ever estimated more highly than I do the eminent services of medical men towards their community, their high character, or their noble sacrifices and self-denial, but I believe that in the pursuit of science there are amongst some a recklessness and disregard of consequences which may lead, as it did in the matter of the resurrectionists, to grave evils. I find that one of the most eminent surgeons that have ever adorned the profession, Sir William Fergusson, in the evidence he gave before the commission appointed to inquire into the practice of vivisection, in July 1875, expressed a great dislike to and disapprobation of many of the experiments resorted to.

Although my feelings—it may be called sentiment—extend themselves to all animals that are subjected to dissection whilst living, my observations were more particularly directed to those that had become domesticated.

In this view I am upheld by Mr. Richard Holt Hutton, a member of the commission, and, I believe, by no means one of the least eminent. He makes a great distinction between domestic and other animals. The former, he says, possess a higher sensibility than others; they have been brought under the influence of civilisation, and these members of our household, he thinks, ought to be exempted from all liability to such experimentation; and he puts forward another reason that must surely reach the heart of anyone possessed of common feeling. I will quote his own words upon the subject:—'A third reason for this exception seems to suggest itself from the very nature of our relations with these creatures, which we have trained up in the habit of obedience to man and confidence in him, so that there is something in the nature of treachery, as well as insensibility to their suffering, in allowing them to be the subject of severe pain *even in the interests of science.*

Since I wrote my earlier observations upon this subject, three treatises have been published in the 'Nineteenth Century' Review, bearing the names of great men, in which it is discussed, Sir James Paget, Professor Owen, and Dr. Samuel Wilks, and their far-famed reputation gives to their opinions a commanding weight. Of course in a question of experience or science I cannot presume to place my opinion upon a par with theirs, although I cannot admit that scientific reasoning can overcome conscientious feeling. Still the utterances of such men upon any point are bound to be carefully weighed. I have a slight acquaintance with Sir James Paget, and from that, and the high estimation in which he is everywhere held, the utmost respect is due to his views, and in some of them I thoroughly agree; there are many cruelties inflicted by mankind upon animals without the excuse created by the object of vivisection. I hope that he is correct in saying that the pain suffered during its process is not so severe as those who read its description imagine; and I fully concur in his statement that sensibility increases by culture and refinement, and this view also accords with Mr. Hutton's; but I am obliged, if not to dispute, at all events to quote an authority against the accuracy of two of his illustrations—those in which he attributes to Hunter the valuable discoveries in relation to tying up the arteries, to experiments upon living animals, and to the same source to Dr. Simpson of Edinburgh the discovery of the use of chloroform in excluding pain during operations upon human beings. Sir William Fergusson, whom I have already quoted, does not concur with Sir James Paget as to either of these statements; and I will quote his words, which I take from the report of the commission held in 1875:—'Some of the most striking experiments that have been performed upon the lower animals with reference to surgery have really been performed already upon the human subject, and proved on the human subject, and therefore there is scarcely any necessity for the repetition of such operations.' He then illustrates his views by referring to John Hunter, whom he describes as one of the greatest physiologists and greatest surgeons that ever lived, and who devised an operation upon the arteries which was one of the most brilliant in surgery, and did so for the first time upon the human patient. By this operation Sir William was of opinion that everything necessary was known, and yet he says it is notorious that since that time *thousands upon thousands of animals* have been tortured unnecessarily to prove what was already perfectly well known.

Another remarkable statement is made by Sir William Fergusson, and surely a very suggestive one. 'I am not aware,' he says, 'of any great surgeons having been great experimenters upon animals, and I am not aware of any great operator upon the human subject who ever prided himself upon being a good operator upon the lower animals.' He also speaks of the experiments in chloroform, of which he says: 'All the experiments upon the lower animals have been performed since the experiments have been conclusively applied to the human subject.'

It will be observed that Sir William quotes, as illustrating his own view, the very examples relied upon by Sir James Paget. I had the pleasure of knowing Sir William in private life, and have heard him frequently reprobate the unnecessary practice of vivisection; and in reading the article of Sir James Paget himself I cannot help thinking it is written in a somewhat apologetic strain, and not quite as if his feelings went with the opinions he has enunciated.

It is very difficult indeed to obtain, upon such a subject as vivisection, a fair discussion; it is naturally mainly confined within scientific limits and assertions: the great body of the public, who are shocked at its practice, become lost in terms of art; whilst the allegations of great and useful discoveries dependent upon it are made, conscientiously, no doubt, but without the kind of evidence which would alone be satisfactory in the case of other discoveries; and I have thought it therefore desirable to place before those who take an interest in the subject the antagonistic opinions of such men as Fergusson and Paget. I admit that mine, in a scientific point of view, can be of little weight.

Throughout the proceedings upon the Commission the use of anæsthetics is enforced, and, so far as suffering during an operation is concerned, there is no doubt that external evidence of pain is destroyed; but let the imagination follow the victim through the hours, days, months, during which it is kept alive for the purpose of fresh experiments.

It was stated by most of the witnesses that the pupils expressed indignation if any unnecessary cruelty was exhibited by the performers; and I was very glad to read this, as I imagined such scenes were likely to engender indifference to human suffering.

There is another aspect of the practice that occurs to me, and I believe that there are eminent men of the medical profession who will not altogether ignore it—it is calculated to lead to speculative operations upon our fellow-creatures. It may probably also arise from my practice in courts where evidence is scrutinised, and the conclusions arrived at with caution, that I do not assume the correctness of those which are not subject to adverse tests; and I have seen so many scientific witnesses enter a witness-box with undoubting minds upon a particular theory, who have left it, if not themselves convinced of their error, at all events having convinced everyone else of it, that I cannot blindly follow assertions that are repugnant to my natural feelings.

I hope that the above observations may not be deemed presumptuous; but as the very learned contributors to the subject in the 'Nineteenth Century' Review threaten a crusade with the view of enlarging the sphere of the vivisectionist operations, and removing the restrictions which were created in consequence of the report of the Commission of 1875, I have ventured to call attention to certain differences that exist amongst the most eminent of those who advocate the practice; neither can I admit that the subject can be determined purely upon scientific grounds.

I am also entitled to consider certain reports that have appeared in the public journals quite recently—an investigation that has taken place in a public court, and statements that have been made, and that remain uncontradicted.

I am now quoting from the 'Times' of November 18 in the last year. It appeared that two eminent professors, after diligent search into the brains of living animals, were unable to agree upon a result: upon which another professor, equally eminent, having obtained a supply of cats and monkeys, endeavoured to settle the question by similar means. I did not follow the history of the cats, and cannot tell for how long they served the purpose of this inquiry. I learnt a little more about the monkeys. They, it appeared, after the first inquiry into their brains with the scalpel, were kept for seven weeks, during which time several essays were made, upon the journey of discovery. I suppose they were selected as bearing some resemblance to the human being.

Poor things! they had been probably kidnapped; but still I can imagine them enjoying a period of pleasure, petted by the sailors on board the vessel that brought them over, and then gradually disposed of by the philosopher's knife.

If the following paragraph, which I copy from the same paper that I have already quoted, be correct, it does not say much for the humanising character of the lectures and illustrations:—

'A large crowd of medical students assembled outside the court, but in consequence of their howling and cheering were kept out of it.'

CHAPTER XL.

THE TICHBORNE BARONETCY.

AMONGST marvellous stories developed in legal proceedings, none in my time have exceeded the adventures of the claimant to the Tichborne baronetcy and estates. The largeness of the property and the position of the family naturally attracted attention to a claim which sought to dispossess owners of estates the rights to which had never before been doubted, still less contested. The Claimant was denounced as an impostor by many merely because his story was antagonistic to experience, whilst others were prepared to support him from the very marvels which surrounded it. The recognition by his mother was thought by many to be an irresistible proof of his identity, and this obtained additional strength from opinions emanating from people of position and character, who had known Sir Roger well, and to whom no unfair motives could in justice be attributed. At the commencement of the proceedings, certainly, shrewd lawyers believed in him, and even now there are many persons who have no sympathy with his career, but who nevertheless are convinced of his identity.

The interest in the case was also enhanced by the enormous amount expended in the conduct of the defence, and the proceedings before Lord Chief Justice Bovill might have been more properly described as 'morning performances' than sober legal inquiries.

The rush for seats was much noticed and commented upon in different journals, and his lordship's health was supposed to have been impaired, not so much by the judicial strain as by the arduous and unaccustomed duties of master of the ceremonies; whilst in relation to the criminal trial the Lord Chief Justice of England had unfortunately expressed opinions that led the supporters of the Claimant to assert that he was not likely to obtain a fair trial at the hands of that learned judge.

In the course of the second trial an unfortunate and reprehensible element was introduced in the shape of a writer who, representing the Claimant as oounsel, made this a centre point from which to shower invective upon the heads of all who were opposed to his claims.

It is not my intention in the following pages to express any opinion upon the truth or falsehood of the present romance. I was at the commencement retained as the Claimant's counsel, and I do not consider that it would be right for me to disclose more of the circumstances than are known or may be known through the ordinary channels of public information.

A brief sketch of the previous history of Sir Roger Tichborne is necessary to enable my readers to follow the remarks that I am about to offer. He was born in the year 1829, and partially educated at Stonyhurst College, a Catholic establishment of very high character, his family, as is well known, being of that faith. He does not appear to have remained at the college long, and it may be doubted whether he had made great progress in his studies—a circumstance that ought not to be lost sight of. Upon leaving it he was sent to Paris, and there, if the evidence of the witnesses given at the trial be true, he must have met certain persons who professed to describe him as he appeared in that city at the period in question.

Upon leaving Paris he returned to England, and in the year 1849 obtained a commission in the Sixth Dragoon Guards (the Carabineers), and remained in the regiment until some time in the year 1853. His character whilst there does not throw much light upon the identity of the Claimant. He certainly exhibited no signs of a vicious disposition, and was retiring rather than the reverse. On the other hand, he was restless and unsettled. His career, after he left the army, was not indicated with much clearness, but he certainly quitted England, and within twelve months after he had left the army he was staying at Rio de Janeiro.

No known object but the spirit of adventure had apparently taken him thither, but at this period it was undoubtedly his intention to return to his native land, as he secured a berth on board a vessel called the *Bella*, bound for Liverpool, and upon which he embarked.

This is common ground, and the theory of his family is that the ship was wrecked, and the passengers and crew, including Sir Roger Tichborne, were drowned.

We must now take up the narrative from the mouth of the Claimant; and he gives an account of the wreck of the *Bella*, but says that, with others of the crew, he escaped in one of the boats, and after knocking about the sea for some days was picked up by a trading vessel and landed in Australia; and one circumstance must strike the reader of this narrative as remarkable, that, if he were Sir Roger Tichborne, he did not pursue the design that he clearly had when at Rio, and return to England at once. I cannot think that he could have had any difficulty in obtaining means to do so.

I will hasten over this part of the story—he appears to have pursued a life of hardship, and adventure, probably not unattended with crime, and certainly with poverty, and to have taken to himself a slightly educated woman for a wife, and in the year 1865 to have been living at a village called Wagga Wagga, where he was pursuing the calling of a butcher. It was in this year that the father of Sir Roger Tichborne died, and his mother, who had always entertained a belief that her son was alive, caused advertisements to be inserted in numerous papers, some of which undoubtedly reached the remote district in which the Claimant was living.

Now, the supposition on the part of those who opposed his claim is not only that he was not Sir Roger, but that he could by no probable means up to this time have ever even heard of such a person; and it is certainly very remarkable that these advertisements should have attracted his attention, and that he should have declared himself to be the lost heir; and, what is more singular still, that he should have been able, as was undoubtedly the case, to borrow funds to come over to England, from sources possessing apparently not the slightest ground for reposing belief in him. But so it was. On the other hand, his eagerness to leave Wagga Wagga was not followed by corresponding alacrity in reaching England. He wasted time, took a circuitous route, and did not eventually reach London until Christmas Day, 1866. Then his proceedings, if he were really Sir Roger, were of a most eccentric description. It was not questioned that he went down to Wapping, and made apparently anxious inquiries about the family of a butcher named Orton, whose son had started some years before on a voyage to Melbourne. He showed a knowledge both of the Orton family and the locality that subsequently became an important feature in the different inquiries, and led to very unfavourable conclusions against him.

He attributed this conduct to a request from a person of that name who had been his associate in Australia.

The solicitor originally retained for him was a gentleman named Holmes, who certainly believed in him, but before he took any steps in the case desired that he should be seen by the mother of Sir Roger, to which the Claimant readily consented, and an interview took place in an hotel in Paris where he was staying. It was alleged that he was ill, and when Lady Tichborne saw him he was in bed. It was said that he practised means to prevent her having an opportunity of judging of his identity; this, however, was denied, and without hesitation she acknowledged him as her lost son.

I may now say a few words of the impression he made upon me when first I saw him. He was stout and unwieldy, with marked but not coarse features, although his size would at first create such an impression, but his hands and feet were certainly not what I should have expected to find upon a low-bred person. The expression of his face was not bad, and somewhat of a melancholy cast. His manners were not those of a person who had ever moved in good society.

What was a noticeable point was that a great likeness was discoverable in him to many members of the Tichborne family.

When I was first consulted upon the matter by Mr. Holmes I felt that the disturbance of a family in an estate that they had held unchallenged for so many years was so grave a matter that I ought not to act in it without satisfying myself, as far as it was possible for me to do, that there was reasonable ground for the claim, and, before moving in it, requested an interview with Lady Tichborne, which was accorded without hesitation. I had been informed that she had always clung to the idea that her son was alive, and I had also heard that for some family reason her feelings were somewhat antagonistic to members of her husband's family. She called upon me at my chambers, and I had an interview with her without the presence of any one but ourselves, and certainly with no favourable bias in my own mind towards the Claimant. Lady Tichborne was a very quiet, ladylike personage, and was dressed plainly in black. She seemed to have endured suffering, and to be more aged than her years would warrant. She did not exhibit any animosity toward her kinsfolk, but expressed herself most earnestly upon the subject of the Claimant. She treated the notion of her being mistaken as to his identity as being absurd, spoke of marks upon his person which she had remembered noticing in his infancy—I did not ascertain whether she had actually seen them since—and she ended our interview by the following words, which I remember well: 'How can a mother be mistaken in her son?' However the belief may be accounted for, I am confident that the lady was truthful, and fully alive to the gravity of her declaration.

I accepted a retainer with Mr. Hannen on the part of the plaintiff, and, although neither of us was unappreciative of the many improbabilities that attended the claim, I believe that both considered it was one that the Claimant had a right to bring forward, and possessed many circumstances to uphold it.

CHAPTER XLI.

COMMENCEMENT OF PROCEEDINGS IN THE TICHBORNE CASE.

PROCEEDINGS were commenced in the Court of Chancery; affidavits were filed; experienced counsel, practising in those courts, appeared for the respective parties, and the case was begun; and, having briefly sketched the position of the Claimant, I propose to show what weapons the representatives of Sir Roger Tichborne's family possessed to encounter the attack.

In the first place they were entitled, and did, as a matter of fact, file affidavits, and in them might have given—and ought, in my opinion, to have done—any information they possessed bearing upon the facts. Some five or six years afterwards they alleged *for the first time that the real Sir Roger had indelible tattoo marks upon one of his arms, of which they were aware when first he made his claim, but nothing was then said in the affidavits on this subject.*

They had the power of subjecting the Claimant to cross-examination—peculiarly important in such a case if skilfully exercised—and they availed themselves of it. They believed the Claimant to be an impostor, and, if so, they must have known that he was a most daring one, and ready to adopt every means to defeat discovery. Still, much may be done by an advocate who knows how to deal with human nature, and has practised his powers largely and with signal success. Such a man was one of the counsel they had retained—none abler at that time at the Bar—Mr. Hawkins. I believe, from the effect afterwards produced by Sir John Coleridge, that, even with the scanty materials supplied, Mr. Hawkins would have crushed the case at its very outset if it had been false; but instead of using this power the advisers of the family availed themselves of the talents of a Chancery barrister of high character and reputation, but who probably had little previous experience of cross-examination under such unusual circumstances; and they never could have supplied him with sufficient knowledge of the alleged marks, or undoubtedly, in my opinion, he would have asked the question of the witness whether he had any such upon his arm, and the witness could not have done otherwise than answer in the negative. There were, according to their account subsequently, two witnesses (at least) of good position who were ready at that very time to come forward and say that they had actually themselves tattooed him at the college.

The only reason that I have heard given for this mode of conducting the case was that the Claimant might have created the marks if he had been informed of their existence. This is nonsense; such an attempt must have been discovered, and would have wrecked the case. If he had been asked the question in the way that Hawkins would have put it, and attempted to shuffle, he would have been simply told to hold out his arm, and the non-existence of any such marks would have been destructive to his claim.

Assuming that this fact was really known, and that it had been proved, I have no hesitation in expressing my belief that neither the solicitor nor counsel concerned for the Claimant would have consented to go on with the case.

I am confident that it would have more than shaken the belief of his warmest supporters, and, unlike those discrepancies which were abundantly proved at the trial, there would have been something palpable for common minds to grasp; and I believe this monster trial, with the gigantic bill of costs, would have perished at its birth in the Court of Chancery.

In one of those holes situated at Westminster, and in which during my professional career many legal tournaments have taken place, commenced the great encounter between Tichborne and Lushington, such being the name by which the case was designated. Sir William Bovill, the Lord Chief Justice of the Common Pleas, presided. I led for the plaintiff, and with me were associated Mr. Hardinge Giffard, Mr. Jeune, Mr. W. B. Rose, and Mr. Pollard.[1] For the defendants, the Solicitor-General (Sir John Coleridge), Sir George Honyman, Q.C., Mr. Hawkins, Q.C., Mr. Chapman Barber, and Mr. Charles Bowen. Mr. H. Matthews, M.P., and Mr. Purcell were counsel for the Trustees of the Tichborne estate.

The Court did not present so gay an aspect as the Old Bailey upon one of the gala days of that establishment; the bright robes of the aldermen were sadly missed, and, whatever may have been the wishes of some of the visitors, no chance existed of the principal performer ending his days in company with the Ordinary and executioner; but brilliant representatives of rank and fashion crowded around the throne of justice which Sir William filled with no dissatisfied air. He did not then anticipate the labours that would be cast upon his shoulders. The first act opened with a terrific combat between him and certain jurymen, and legal weapons of unusual severity were used. A Colonel in the Queen's Body Guard appealed to be per-

[1] Mr. Hannen had in the meantime been promoted to the Bench.

mitted to attend upon Her Majesty's sacred person, but his lordship, fully capable of representing the feelings of this august personage, assured him that she greatly preferred the administration of the law to any protection that he could afford to herself. At last, however, all difficulties were conquered, although the sacred twelve were not reached, and the trial commenced with only eleven victims.

Of the Lord Chief Justice one would not wish to say an unkind word. No one could doubt his impartiality, and his thorough good nature rendered him very popular. He had been a successful advocate, and had a fair knowledge of law, but wanted dignity, and scarcely possessed grasp enough to deal with such a case. Occasionally he accepted advice from a bevy of ladies who clustered around him, and who took a great interest in the proceedings. This certainly was not upon law, but in French and geography, in which it was early shown that he had not been thoroughly grounded. It was not to be wondered at that, notwithstanding his intended fairness, the colour of his mind was evidently adverse to the plaintiff. Those who are not lawyers ought to be made aware that the burden of proof lay upon the Claimant, and that unless I, on his behalf, succeeded in making a case of such inherent probability as to require an answer, the defendants would succeed in the action. A thoroughly strong judge, if he feels that counsel for the plaintiff has not succeeded in doing so, will often convey a view to that effect. And if, after this case had proceeded through part of the Claimant's cross-examination, a suggestion to this effect had been made from the Bench, I think that I should have withdrawn; it was clearly impossible for any jury to say that such a case had been made out as to exclude doubt.

The names of the gentlemen who were my juniors are sufficient to show that the assistance I had was as powerful as any that could be obtained at the Bar.

In launching the evidence, I began with putting in the deposition of Lady Tichborne, who had died before the trial, and I afterwards proceeded with witnesses who had known Sir Roger and undertook to identify him. Of these I called several. I thought before putting the plaintiff in the box it was desirable to give an air of probability to the story he was about to tell. At last the jury desired to have him presented to them, which accordingly I did. Great sensation and rustling of silks and satins accompanied the Claimant as he rolled into the witness-box. I have already described his appearance. Mr. Giffard took upon himself the laborious task of examining him in chief, and it is impossible to say that the effect produced diminished the unfavourable impression which, in the court at all events, had been produced by his appearance. His evidence lasted until the middle of the fourth day from its commencement, when the Solicitor-General commenced his cross-examination, which continued for several days. This learned counsel seemed to lay in a fresh stock of ammunition every evening, commencing a vigorous discharge on each successive morning.

One prominent and most damaging result was in exhibiting the Claimant's utter ignorance of the French language, and Sir John's perfect familiarity with this and also with the classics enabled him to expose the witness upon these latter subjects in lights both startling and ridiculous. I presume that his object was not only to win the case, but entirely to destroy the Claimant for any future attempt, and certainly no cross-examination was ever heard in a Court of Justice which exhibited more labour and industry, or was more completely successful.

And if the Lord Chief Justice had then interfered and, without expressing any opinion of the actual merits of the case, had asked the counsel for the plaintiff whether they could hope for a verdict, whatever might be the justice of the plaintiff's claim, I think, as I have hinted already, that all of us would have admitted that we could not.

I know that the jury were themselves prepared to endorse such a suggestion. However, the case went on, and the Solicitor-General addressed the jury at great length and with marked ability, and proceeded to call witnesses, during which a defection occurred in our camp, and Mr. Rose, one of the firm of solicitors instructing us, embraced an adverse view. The subject is a painful one, which I do not wish to dwell upon; it caused the counsel much embarrassment and difficulty, and the course pursued by him was extremely prejudicial to any views that could have been adopted in the interest of his former client.

After the conclusion of his speech, the Solicitor-General proceeded to call witnesses, many of whom, as was the case with those called on the part of the Claimant, were open to no suspicion of falsehood or dishonesty, amongst them Lord Bellew, and the people from Paris; and I believe that it was at this period of the trial that the tattoo evidence was for the first time started in the case. After a time I felt it to be impossible to obtain an affirmative conclusion, and that I was not justified in keeping up the case any longer, and accordingly determined to accept a non-suit upon the part of my client. Some intimation must have been given that I intended to do so, as a grand *finale* was prepared, and the performance attracted a more than usually fashionable audience. The stage was grouped in somewhat a melodramatic fashion:

the centre figure in his usual place in the body of the court, ladies pressing eagerly in every direction, and at the back, only dimly visible amongst the brilliant dresses, two dark figures, apparently greatly out of place, but in reality very important performers in the scene about to be performed. They were tipstaves, prepared to take the unhappy Claimant into custody.

Whatever may have been the opinion of the jury, the mode I adopted prevented them expressing any, and therefore it appears to me that the judge had no precedent whatever for the course he pursued, which was, upon my withdrawal, to order the Claimant into custody. I cannot forbear thinking that this was most unfortunate. Even where a jury have returned a verdict declaratory of their opinion, judges have almost invariably refused to exercise this power, and I remember Lord Penzance saying emphatically that he considered such a course cast an unfair prejudice upon an accused person. It was in this instance a sacrifice to convenience. It was doubtless felt by those who were determined to prosecute the Claimant that, if he were treated in the usual fashion of persons charged with crimes, there would be great delay and difficulty. He would have to be brought before a magistrate, a *primâ facie* case made out for a committal, and he would be entitled to call witnesses to rebut it. Fresh scenes, probably not very decorous ones, would have been enacted before an inferior tribunal.

I do not believe that there ever was an instance in which any judge exercised this power without the opinion of the jury having been expressed, and I cannot think that, considering the mass of evidence, some of it certainly honest, on the part of the plaintiff, and the jury having expressed no opinion, a judge was justified in broadly proclaiming his view by a proceeding so arbitrary as the committal. It may be said that otherwise a great criminal might have escaped. Perhaps he would, and might even have become a member of the Legislature. But, in my opinion, it would have been far better that an offender should obtain immunity than that a large body of the public should believe that his punishment has been obtained by unusual means, as undoubtedly was the case by the proceeding in question.

In the foregoing sketch I have not mentioned a personage who took a very remarkable part in upholding the Claimant, and one whose conduct was not reconcilable with any corrupt motives that could be suggested upon the trial; this was an old servant of the Tichborne family named Bogle. He was a negro, and of considerable age. He was receiving a pension for his services, which his conduct upon the occasion of the claim caused him to lose. He declared his recognition of the Claimant, and it is extremely difficult to know how he could be mistaken, and at least equally difficult to understand why he should have perjured himself. I confess I saw nothing in his manner which led me to that belief. He was cross-examined at length, and was not at all shaken.

His hair was perfectly white, and Mr. Hawkins could not resist the joke that he reminded him of an ebony stick with an ivory knob. The management by this gentleman of the witnesses upon this trial, as well as upon the one I am about to narrate, satisfies me of the correctness of my opinion, that if he had cross-examined the Claimant before the commissioner, the case would probably have collapsed, and that if he had done so, possessing the knowledge of the tattoo marks, it certainly would.

CHAPTER XLII.

INDICTMENT OF CLAIMANT.

On the 23rd day of April 1873, the trial of the Claimant took place in the Court of Queen's Bench, before Sir Alexander Cockburn and Justices Mellor and Lush, and no one could doubt that it would be conducted with perfect fairness and impartiality, notwithstanding that the Lord Chief Justice had previously made no secret of his views, which were unfavourable to the accused.

Mr. Hawkins, as I have elsewhere incidentally mentioned, conducted the prosecution, in which he had the assistance of Serjeant Parry and other counsel of eminence. The defence was entrusted to a gentleman named Dr. Kenealy. He is now no more, and it would be well for his reputation if he had passed away at an earlier period. He was a man of singular learning, and one of the finest classical scholars of the day, a fluent speaker, and, although eccentric, by no means a contemptible poet. The trial of the Claimant might have given him an opportunity of obtaining distinction of an honourable kind, and the tribunal as constituted was most favourable to him, as he had dedicated a poem, which might by many have been considered fulsome, to Sir Alexander, who always treated him with marked attention, received him as a guest at his house, had been the means of obtaining for him a silk gown, and undertaken the office of godfather to one of his children; but the notoriety that he attained by a course that he adopted would have injuriously affected the interests of any client.

Dr. Kenealy published a newspaper called the 'Englishman,' in which he attributed, in violent terms, crimes of the deepest dye to men and women of position and character. One man, whom he was under deep obligation to, he actually charged with assassination. There is no doubt that the extravagance of his accusations destroyed their effect against their intended victims, but they as certainly created a feeling of repulsion towards the man whose cause he affected to advocate. And I know that the horror of being in any way associated with him prevented some believers in the Claimant from coming forward on his behalf. Independently of this defect in his character, he exhibited every fault incident to advocacy, he insulted the judges, he disgusted the jury, and finally committed the cardinal blunder of undertaking to prove what was not really in issue, namely, that his client was in truth Sir Roger Tichborne. This was necessary for the success of his paper, but destruction to the prospects of his client.

It must be borne in mind that the Claimant was now being tried upon a criminal charge, and consequently the position of the parties was entirely changed from what existed at the civil suit, the onus in the former lying upon the plaintiff, as I have already pointed out, to prove his case. In the indictment, however, it was incumbent upon the prosecution to prove that he was not the person he alleged himself to be, and that without reasonable doubt. Dr. Kenealy took up the exactly opposite position, and dealt with the facts as if he were bound to prove the identity. Nothing could be more prejudicial than such a course. Any advocate of ordinary judgment ought to have known that to secure such a result was beyond the bounds, I am almost prepared to say, of possibility. If a barrister of discretion, judgment, and character had enforced upon the attention of the jury those elements that existed in the case, and which were certainly very remarkable, and appealed to that body to consider whether they were not such as defeated the certainty of guilt, I believe that, if a favourable verdict had not been obtained, the jury would have been discharged.

The recognition by the mother, skilfully dealt with, could not have failed to produce a great effect. It is true that her deposition was not receivable in evidence; but what a topic would have been the hardship of its rejection in the hands of a counsel capable of using it! It would probably have had more effect even than its reception. Then there were witnesses, officers, gentlemen and ladies of unimpeached character. There was Bogle, an apparently disinterested witness, and many earnest believers of lower rank, who would again have come forward, and a careful selection of these could not fail to have had much weight; and if I am right in my conclusion that some of the Paris witnesses were unreliable—and upon the former trial their evidence was most contradictory—a great point might have been made.

If they had broken down, as I am sure these would have done if the counsel had been reversed, a most important effect would have been produced upon the case of the prosecution, and let me add that from much experience that I have had of the Lord Chief Justice, although I am sure that he had taken a strong view against the defendant, I am also confident that, if a doubt had dawned upon his mind of the correctness of the conclusion, he would have given to it the fullest effect. Instead, however, of using the means in his power to conciliate the Court and the jury, Dr. Kenealy lost no opportunity of irritating the feelings of both. A signal instance was exhibited in his cross-examination of a witness of position, whom I believe to have been mistaken, and who ought to have been dealt with upon that assumption, instead of which the Doctor launched against him the charge of deliberate perjury, and cross-examined him upon an incident in his early career calculated to give pain, but which could have no earthly effect upon the character or credit of his testimony. And this he persisted in, notwithstanding the earnest remonstrances of the judges and the indignant protests of the jury.

Finally, he took upon his shoulders the unnecessary burden of proving that the defendant was really Sir Roger Tichborne, leaving it to be implied that, if successful, he would displace the existing possessor of title and property, instead of pointing out that under no imaginable circumstances could there be any such result, and appealing to the well-known principle of criminal law, that no man should be convicted whilst a doubt fairly existed of his innocence. I also have no hesitation in saying that, if the jury did not believe the tattoo evidence, there would have been a blow struck at the superstructure of the prosecution of so serious a character when joined to the other facts favourable to his case, and to which I have alluded, that it would fully have justified a jury in acquitting him.

There was a gentleman originally associated with Dr. Kenealy in the defence of the Claimant who suffered greatly from the course that his leader pursued, which he considered to be outrageous and grossly imprudent, and he frequently consulted a mutual friend of ours, Mr. Serjeant O'Brien, upon what he ought to do, and latterly he declined to appear in court, although (acting under his friend's advice, in which I concurred, having been consulted by that gentleman) he took no active steps in the matter. I consider the Claimant's interests suffered most gravely by the circumstances related by Mr. MacMahon, the gentleman in question.

Although, as I intimated before, the Lord Chief Justice entertained a strong opinion against the defendant, which had unfortunately become known, the latter's interests did not in any respect suffer from it. The fault that the Chief Justice exhibited, and which was transparent throughout, was posing too much for effect, and rather encouraging than checking the length to which the proceedings were dragged out, and certainly occupying a very unnecessary amount of time in his own summing-up, which, however, displayed his accustomed grasp and ability. The position of the two other judges was really nominal, but I must say that I think the trial would have been far shorter and much more consistent with the usual sobriety of criminal trials in this country if it had been presided over by either of them. The eminent head of the court upon this occasion has since passed away.

Mr. Justice Mellor has prudently secured health by retiring from the Bench, and may he long enjoy it. He has carried with him into his retirement the respect and affection of the Bar. Sir Robert Lush, too, after a life so undeviating in the performance of every duty that it might be called monotonous, has at last, covered with honour, terminated his earthly career. I tried to obtain a glimpse of my dear old friend, but he was too unwell to see me when, shortly before his death, I made the endeavour.

The leading counsel for the prosecution is now upon the Bench. His conduct of it was lengthy and elaborate, too much so in my opinion, but thoroughly exhaustive.

Even if Dr. Kenealy had possessed ordinary discretion and good taste, he would have been no match in advocacy for his competitor, who was assisted by Serjeant Parry, himself one of the actors, and by no means an unworthy one, who has left the stage.

CHAPTER XLIII.

LORD WESTBURY.

THERE are very few men with whom, not being associated upon terms of intimacy, I entertained a greater admiration for than I did for Lord Westbury. I also felt much sympathy with him upon the occasion when he was obliged to abandon the office of Chancellor, which, judicially, certainly no one ever filled with greater credit. I had received from him when Attorney-General many acts of kindness. He had appointed me to argue a case before the judges in the Court of Crown Cases Reserved, and also as counsel in the prosecution of the British Bank directors, and when he became Chancellor had given me a patent of precedence.

He was involved in difficulties in consequence of some arrangements made by his son, Mr. Richard Bethell, which certainly showed a want of sufficient supervision upon his part, but I know that his affection and trust in that gentleman were unbounded. The vote of censure in the House of Commons implied carelessness only, and the announcement by himself in the House of Lords of his resignation of the Lord Chancellorship was listened to with sympathy, and his concluding observations with such amount of applause as would scarcely have been the case if any graver imputation had rested upon his conduct. That concluding scene of his public career was truly painful to his friends, by whom he was much beloved, but on his part was conducted with the utmost dignity. He had married into the family of a gentleman named Abraham, an architect of considerable eminence, and it so happened that this was the means by which I became personally acquainted with him. One of his brothers-in-law was at the same school with me—at Mr. Wigan's, at Blackheath. Another carried on the profession of architect, and during his supervision of the building of the now well-known premises of Mr. Smith, in the Strand, in his capacity of district surveyor, an accident happened by which some lives were lost, and the wisdom of a coroner's jury led to a verdict of manslaughter against Mr. Abraham, by whom I was retained. Sir Richard Bethell, then Solicitor-General, sent for me, and showed great anxiety upon the subject. I assured him that there was not the slightest risk; that it was only one of the mischievous pieces of folly that not unfrequently distinguished a coroner's court, and would be corrected directly it arrived before a competent one. However, he was not satisfied with my assurance, and made himself fully master of every technicality of the law upon the subject. The case was committed to the Central Criminal Court, where Mr. Abraham had to appear and surrender into the dock, which he did, accompanied to the entrance of it by his brother-in-law. Sir Alexander Cockburn, who was the Attorney-General at that time, had volunteered to appear for him, and was with me and Mr. Bovill, afterwards Chief Justice of the Common Pleas, for the defence. The parade, however, except as exhibiting kindly feeling, was perfectly unnecessary. The grand jury, of course, threw out the bill, and the judge directed the petit jury to acquit upon the inquisition.

Sir Richard was a member of the Middle Temple Bench, and it was supposed that through his influence

Mr. Abraham was employed as architect upon the erection of a new library, and in consequence it generally goes by the name of 'the little Bethel.'

In the spring of 1860 a shocking tragedy occurred at Lewes. A gentleman named Hopley and his wife kept a school in this town. He had several scholars, and amongst them a boy of the name of Reginald Channell Cancellor, whose father was one of the Masters of the Court of Common Pleas.

This poor boy was of weak intellect, and Hopley, whose own mind was, I am willing to think, distorted, exercised upon him a system of unceasing cruelty. He seemed to imagine that the weakness, partly natural, and partly the result of terror occasioned by his own conduct, was obduracy of temper, and the feebler he became in mind and body the more cruel were the tortures inflicted upon him. At last, during the night of April 21, his system of correction was brought fully to the test. Screams that sent terror into the hearts of the other pupils were heard during the long hours of the night. The poor children lay shuddering with fear and horror, whilst the wretched half-witted victim of a lunatic's system of education was deliberately mangled to death, and was found on the following morning a corpse.

I knew Hopley's brother, who was an artist, with some genius, but eccentric, living in St. John's Wood, and through him was retained to defend Thomas Hopley at the Lewes Assizes, where he was indicted and tried for manslaughter before Sir Alexander Cockburn. Mr. Cancellor, the father, was well known to all of us, which heightened the feelings we entertained. The plea of insanity was not set up, although for the credit of human nature I could wish that it should have been, and believe that it could have been supported upon the definitions of that malady that I have already discussed. Cockburn was intensely affected, as he always was when sympathy was demanded. Hopley, being found guilty of manslaughter, was sentenced to four years' penal servitude, and issued from his gaol a circular, of which I will venture to transcribe the following portion. He advocated the formation of a 'grand model educational establishment,' with himself as the model Christian master, and his wife, married and educated by him for this express purpose, 'to aim at becoming the model Christian mistress.' The lady, however, did not appear ambitious of the position, or to approve of the system of education, for, some years after, she sued for a divorce, and obtained a decree for a judicial separation. What has become of him I know not. I hope I did my duty to him as his counsel, but I did not attempt to justify his system of education.

His poor brother, whom I sincerely pitied, had expended years in painting a picture called, as far as my recollection serves me, 'The Building of a Pyramid by an early Egyptian Queen.' The slaves, with enormous difficulty, are supposed to be bringing the materials from immense distances, and the work represented on the canvas was not feebly portrayed by the labour exercised in its delineation. The minutiæ were very exact and carefully executed, but there was no great imagination displayed in its construction, and it did not command success adequate to its great elaboration. It was, however, his idol. He parted with it to serve his brother, and, poor fellow! he mourned over it, and that and the disgrace of the trial hastened the end that a feeble constitution and many disappointments had long threatened.

Sir Alexander's sense of justice, as well as energy in pursuing it, was evidenced recently in a matter about which he had many years before formed a strong opinion.

When he was nearly a briefless barrister a case was tried upon the Western Circuit before Mr. Justice Williams. This was not the eminent lawyer and distinguished judge, Vaughan Williams, but the 'Johnny' whose jokes I have recorded. The prisoner was convicted. The details would afford no amusement nor add any point to the anecdote that I am relating; it is sufficient to say that he was sentenced to transportation for life, and, notwithstanding very earnest endeavours on the part of Cockburn and others who considered the evidence to be unsatisfactory, underwent a great portion of his sentence, and it was only recently that, the case being again ventilated, the late Lord Chief Justice, in the midst of his pressing avocations, renewed with unabated energies his endeavours on his behalf, and with success. The innocence of the convict, now bowed down by years, has been recognised. He has received a free pardon, and a sufficient pension for his remaining years. It is not only in this case that the public has to recognise an enlightened change in the constitution of the Home Office. I am glad to take the opportunity of mentioning a very dear and valued friend of mine, and many others of former days. I allude to a gentleman named Scherer, a shorthand writer, very accomplished in his own profession, and possessing other qualities which endeared him to many friends at the bar as well as elsewhere. He was one of the most earnest believers in the innocence of the person I have referred to, and energetic in his endeavours on his behalf. Poor Scherer's premature death did not enable him to reap the reward of his disinterested exertions, as his friend Cockburn had the satisfaction of doing.

Sir Alexander Cockburn never shunned hard work, and amongst his efforts will be remembered an elaborate address to the Chancellor protesting against the appointment of the judges to try election petitions. All his brethren concurred in it. However, it may fairly now be said that the evils anticipated have not been realised, and that the judges retain in their performances of these duties the same character for impartiality that follows their career in all others imposed upon them.

The intense labour and research which he brought to bear upon the discussion of the Alabama Claims, and his luminous work upon the subject, strikingly illustrate the various qualities of his mind, and are matter of world-wide interest.

I have only to add that I think that the late Lord Chief Justice would form a worthy object for a far more skilled biographer than myself. I trust, nevertheless, however far I have been from exhausting the subject, that I have not done injustice to a man who, amongst those recorded upon the page of English history, is entitled to hold a most distinguished place.

I am now about to record, not at any length, two cases in which I was engaged, and which were presided over by a judge of a very different type and character from the one I have just parted with. I have already introduced Lord Blackburn, and recounted some of his proceedings during the election campaign. He also is worthy of notice from a graver and more learned pen than I possess. I have no doubt that there are those who can speak of hours spent by him in indefatigable pursuit of the deep and profound knowledge that, since his promotion to the Bench, he has exhibited; and perhaps there are some who may have seen him in gayer scenes. His great patron, Lord Campbell, was once met at Cremorne Gardens, studying, as he said, human nature. Lord Blackburn preferred seeking it in Coke upon Littleton, without assistance from the haunts of revelry. I have never heard of his hanging over the chair of any north-country maiden, whispering soft words into her ear, or exhibiting the activity of his person in the mazes of a waltz or even of a highland reel. He was wont to sit in a back row in the Court of Queen's Bench, and greatly are Lord Campbell's judgments indebted to his clear and profound appreciation of law. Latterly, before promoted to the Bench, he was entrusted as junior with heavy mercantile causes, but never with the lead; and, except amongst the solicitors who thus had experience of him, it could not be said that he had obtained reputation even as a lawyer. His appointment by Lord Campbell was viewed with surprise, and people were astonished when they subsequently discovered that there were such excellent grounds for it. His manner upon the Bench was harsh and ungenial, but it was soon found that this was only his surface deportment. He was especially patient and painstaking. He had the fault that judges who have had little experience in the conduct of causes must necessarily have—an awkwardness in marshalling the facts of a case so as to suit them to the comprehension of a jury. But at the time of his translation to his present position he had become a most excellent nisi prius judge, and there was no one before whom I would sooner have practised.

Shortly after his appointment he went the Home Circuit, and got into a sort of fracas at Guildford with Mr. Evelyn, who was High Sheriff. It appears that Mr. Justice Blackburn thought it necessary to hear the evidence in the cases he was trying, which the noise in court rendered extremely difficult. He ordered a portion of the building, which at that time was a most inconvenient one, to be closed against the public. Mr. Evelyn published a placard declaring this proceeding to be contrary to law, and ordering it to be opened.

For this Mr. Evelyn was fined *500l.*, Lord Chief Justice Cockburn, the senior judge, taking the opportunity of doing what he was able to do full well—making an extremely impressive address in inflicting the fine.

Mr. Evelyn had been misled by some foolish friends, and it so happened that Mr. Serjeant Shee and myself had passed the preceding Saturday to Monday at his very pretty place in the neighbourhood, and amongst those who did not know much about us we got the credit of being his advisers—of course, without foundation.

I will reserve the particulars of the two cases I have referred to until my next chapter. One was that of the Baron de Vidil, the other that of a German named Karl Frantz.

CHAPTER XLIV.

CRIMINAL COURTS AND CRIMINAL JUDGES.

THE Baron de Vidil was a friend of the Orleans dynasty, and whilst that family were staying at Twickenham he was in the habit of visiting certain members of it. He had a son, a youth, as far as I can remember, about nineteen years old, and the story I am about briefly to relate is a very strange one. The father and son were riding together in a secluded lane in the neighbourhood of Orleans House—it was in the June of 1861—when the young man suddenly received a blow upon his head, and, turning round, saw his father in the act of repeating it, and he did inflict several of a murderous character with a heavily loaded whip, and it was at the time alleged that it was his intention to commit murder. The lad pressed his horse forward, threw himself off the saddle, and, covered with blood, sought the protection of a man and woman who happened to be passing. He first seemed disposed to accuse his father vehemently, and to disclose the causes of the attack, but after a short time nothing would induce him to give any information.

The Baron escaped to Paris, but was delivered up to the English Government, and tried before Mr. Justice Blackburn at the Central Criminal Court. Sufficient evidence was obtained from the man and woman who had witnessed part of the assault to convict him of unlawful wounding, but as his son remained resolutely silent, no more serious verdict could be procured. I was retained for his defence, but learnt no more than the rest of the public, and the events leading to the transaction remain still a mystery. Vidil was very well known in French society, and the circumstance of my defending him introduced me to the acquaintance of many of its members.

They could give no clue to the transaction, but I fancy for some reason he had previously been in ill odour. It was one of the earliest criminal cases tried by Mr. Justice Blackburn, and excited much interest at the time.

During the assizes following, a young man named Karl Frantz, a German, was tried before the same judge for the murder of a woman named Haliday, the wife of the parish clerk of Kingswood, in Surrey. This is the case that I have already mentioned in which Madame Titiens was examined, and, if he had been clearly identified by her, probably the result would have been different; but she exhibited some little hesitation, and the facts, which present no interest to the general reader, were circumstantial, though to my mind conclusive. I prosecuted the prisoner, and the present Mr. Justice Denman defended him with great ability and success, but I cannot help thinking that the result was an example of how a judge of intellect, however powerful, is embarrassed when called upon to deal with facts to which he has been previously unaccustomed, especially when they involve so serious an issue as the life of a fellow-creature. Mr. Justice Blackburn impressed those who heard him sum up upon this occasion with the idea that he was labouring under a sense of hesitation and doubt; and juries, always loth to inflict the penalty of death, were affected by his demeanour. On this occasion this very distinguished man fully exhibited his kindly nature and his inexperience.

I do not think that it is unfitting that I should take

this opportunity to make a few observations upon a subject of vital importance in the administration of the criminal law. The amalgamation of the common law and equity systems is now an accomplished fact, although the procedure is still very different in the different courts, and judges are called upon to deal with causes by means utterly novel to them ; but this, doubtless, will all come right in time, after a reasonable number of suitors have been ruined ; but I venture to suggest that this change affords the opportunity that has been long wanted of initiating a radical alteration both in the practice and the procedure of criminal courts. I certainly do not make the following observations from any doubt of the ability of members of what was called the equity bar ; but surely it can hardly be conceived that they are fitted to be taken from the midst of affidavits, with no knowledge of oral testimony, or of the habits and character of those who occupy the proceedings of the Crown Courts, to preside upon some complicated question, involving the life, or the slavery for life, of a human being. And although I believe that the inexperience of the judge is far more likely to result in a guilty man escaping than an innocent one being convicted, a court of justice is one of those large stages upon which an incompetent performer is likely to create feelings weakening its efficacy and example, and may possibly be the cause of most calamitous results.

I have in former chapters taken occasion to refer to the character of particular classes of witnesses, to the temptations that exist in some matters to falsify facts, and the occasional deliberate manner in which this is attempted. And it ought to be remembered that the Crown Courts are the arena upon which beginners are launched in the profession. Unlike the Civil Courts, the judge may not, and generally has not, the assistance of the ablest and most experienced advocates to take all human care that nothing shall escape notice that requires consideration, and therefore much more must necessarily be left to his experience and a mind assumed to be practised. In a civil proceeding, however small the stake, he can be corrected if he should err, and upon this ground new trials frequently take place. But no Court of Appeal exists to which a fellow-creature condemned to expiate a real or supposed crime upon the scaffold has a right to resort for the correction of erroneous law or a wrong conclusion of fact.

In the account I have given of a previous case I have shown the imperfect means existing in the hands of the Home Secretary, and the mischievous results that occurred from there being no others.

I wish that my observations should be of service and produce inquiry, and this object would not be attained by any exaggeration. I am confident of the earnest desire of those who are called upon to fulfil their novel duties to accomplish the object, but they cannot by intuition jump into the knowledge that is required to do so.

As I conscientiously believe that the employment of untrained men to try grave criminal charges is a great and serious evil, I wish to show my entire absence of prejudice by quoting the admission from all quarters of the bar of the agreeable manner in which they have hitherto presided, but this is only what would be expected of highly educated, kindly gentlemen. And I am by no means sure that a barrister likes a judge the less because now and then he lets him get a verdict that he has no right to expect.

I have often thought over the subject of an appeal in criminal cases before it was forced so prominently forward as it now is by the appointment of barristers to the Bench who have no experience in this class of work, and I believe no one doubts for a moment the principle; but, as I am aware, great and serious difficulties surround the subject, and it threatens an inquiry into the whole system of criminal precedure: and although I have neither the pretension nor ability to be a law reformer, my experience may enable me to give some hints not altogether useless to those who may be called upon elsewhere to deal with this subject.

Let me lay down some axioms which I believe are sound.

Harshness and over-severity affect seriously the administration of justice, by rendering juries unwilling to convict, and acquittals obtained through weakness encourage the criminal classes in the pursuit of their career.

In grave crimes, such as murder, a failure on one side or the other through want of experience on the part of the judge is always damaging, and may produce fatal consequences.

A commission composed of very learned men has been engaged lately in preparing suggestions for a code of the criminal law; and, no doubt, if such a production could be accomplished, it might materially facilitate the administration of justice throughout its different channels. I am doubtful, however, notwithstanding the energy and labour of Sir James Fitzjames Stephen and his associates, whether we shall ever see it accomplished. But I think that at very little expense of trouble much simplicity might be introduced where it is greatly wanted, and that in many instances tolerably accurate definitions might be secured. I think also that many offences clearly defined might be accurately classified, and that each person before his trial might with advantage be supplied with a statement of his offence in intelligible everyday terms. I do not think any real, substantial good can be effected without the creation of more judges, and it has occurred to me that this might really be made the means of saving instead of creating expense, and at the same time effecting the much-desired object of a Court of Appeal. I think that members of the new body should sit throughout the year, as the police magistrates do, a quorum of them to hear appeals, and the others relieving the different gaols. I should give the right of appeal in all cases, subject to certain limitations determined by the punishment inflicted —at all events, to begin with.

The Court of Appeal ought to have the power of both diminishing and increasing the punishments inflicted by the judges of first instance. It would not be called upon to rehear the cases, but decide as is done at present by the tribunals who hear motions for new trials in civil suits, members of the Criminal Appeal Court being embodied with the High Court of Justice, and receiving aid from their brother judges. In the above sketch of a plan that has long occurred to my mind as being a basis to go upon, and in any endeavour to amend the present state of things, I should not, of course, interfere with the privilege of the Crown to remit sentences, but should give it the assistance now so fatally wanting of coming to a conclusion upon substantial grounds.

The facilities and cheapness with which the metropolis can now be reached induce me to think that the ambit of the Central Court might be extended with advantage to further distances, and that a court upon similar principles might be established in the larger towns. There would be no objection to the aldermen still pursuing the duties that they now so innocently perform, but elective judges ought summarily to be abolished.

I wish also that our legislators would give their attention to the question whether a system of transportation could not be established. I am confident, as I have said already, that it is the most preventive punishment (unless death is excepted) that has been inflicted in modern times, and I look upon convict prisons and the system pursued in them with great misgivings. The inmates appear to me to have a sodden appearance, and there is a painful similarity in their faces to those whom a visitor will see grouped in lunatic asylums. I believe that with no small proportion of the criminal class the hope of their being reformed is utterly contradicted by experience, and yet the idea of imprisonment for life is repugnant to our feelings, and in many instances would be unjust. How can society be benefited by the convict of some four or five years being handed back to his old associates? Even if he have the desire to reform, he has overwhelming temptation to follow his old courses.

Society, too, gives him no aid in an honest endeavour. Where is the householder who will, knowingly, take the released felon into his establishment? And therefore, if he succeed in obtaining any employment, he must do so by concealment, really amounting to a fraud upon the employer—a bad beginning for an honest service. And there are the eyes of two sections of mankind constantly upon him—his former accomplices, and his more recent but not less dangerous acquaintances, the police.

CHAPTER XLV.

THE TRIAL OF THE GAEKWAR OF BARODA.

When first I determined to present such memories as I thought might interest or amuse the public, it occurred to me that my professional voyage to India would naturally be considered one of the most important incidents in my career, and not an unfitting one with which to conclude its records.

The events that had preceded it were of an unusual and, it might be said, an almost romantic character. It was alleged that a great crime had been committed by a monarch of an important territory against the representative of the British Government accredited to himself.

It was considered of so weighty a character that the Governor-General determined that it should be investigated in a form hitherto unknown, and without a precedent, and bringing to bear to the inquiry the most solemn and weighty elements that it was possible to employ; and, upon the application of the accused potentate, every facility was afforded to him of obtaining such assistance as his advisers deemed would be desirable for his protection and defence; and there being some difficulty in securing the services of one very eminent member of the Calcutta bar, it was determined to retain counsel from England; and accordingly Mr. Hawkins, Mr. Henry Matthews, and myself were applied to, and I accepted the retainer, it being the first that was ever received by a member of this bar to appear as advocate upon any trial in India.

But although I have for some time contemplated giving an account of the circumstances that occurred, now that I am sitting down to the task I am sensible that it is surrounded with many difficulties. I not only do not feel myself competent to deal with the political aspect of the affair, but should be extremely unwilling to do so. My position, and I strictly maintained it during the trial that took place, was to deal solely with the facts, with a view of proving that they did not support the allegations against the accused Prince; but in the retrospect I am about to take of them it will be impossible to avoid some comment that trenches upon the proceedings of the Executive, and I hope that I shall not exceed my fair privilege if I endeavour in doing so to ameliorate the present condition of my late client. If anything that I could write could interfere with the new state of things established in the country, I should not feel justified in writing them. But years have now passed. A dynasty has been changed, and I have neither desire nor right to attack a policy established upon the responsibility of the rulers of the country.

Once upon a time a voyage to India was an event, and a story might have been woven out of it. How amusing are many of the characters and scenes in Captain Marryat's novels. Some of my readers also may remember by the sides of the river Thames the great hulls of splendid ships mouldering away. These were the old East Indiamen. When the trade was thrown open, smaller and quicker vessels carried away the traffic, and then the whisper went forth of reaching India by an overland route, and even when that was accomplished something was still left for an imaginative traveller to record—the bumping over the desert upon the unaccustomed camel, and if wild Arabs were not met with they might still be pictured; but now there is a prosaic railway that takes the traveller from Alexandria to Suez, where he is met by the splendid steamships of the Peninsular and Oriental Company, and transported, rarely with any accident, to lands not so very long ago undreamed of, except by a comparatively few travellers. There has been a misadventure in modern times, which made the subject of one of Tom Taylor's most popular and amusing plays. An officer on board the 'Australia,' the vessel by which I went from Suez to Bombay, was one of the crew on board a P. and O. ship that was wrecked upon a rock in the Red Sea during its return voyage. My informant told me that the incidents that occurred were related with considerable accuracy by the dramatist. The play came out at the Haymarket Theatre. Buckstone and Compton were amongst the performers, and, I think, pretty Mrs. Fitzwilliam. I heard from my informant the name of the English officer who was stopped making off with a bottle of bitter beer. He was well known in the army as a soldier of distinction and gallantry, and his succumbing to the illicit charms of a bottle of Allsopp's ale created universal astonishment amongst his comrades. I ought to have mentioned that as it was doubtful how long the passengers and crew might be kept in their unpleasant position, the provisions were placed under a guard. The reference I have made to the marine service enables me to mention a dear old friend of mine who had commanded one of the former East Indiamen—Captain Mackeson. Whilst the vessel was in (I believe) the Chinese seas an insane sailor inflicted a severe wound upon his head, which invalided him, and he was obliged to retire from the service upon a pension. He located himself upon that very pretty spot the Terrace, at Hythe, in Kent, and at his hospitable house I spent more pleasant hours than I can remember at many other places. A son of his was at the Chancery bar, and a cousin, whose agreeable society reminds me of my old friend, is a member of the bench of the Inner Temple.

When in olden times a barrister embraced the opportunity of going as a judge to India, he was prepared to be expatriated for ten years at least. Now he can spend his long vacation in his native country. It was not long after Sir Richard Garth had gone to India as Chief Justice that I saw his genial countenance while he was getting into a hansom at Charing Cross, looking just as jolly as it was wont to do when mixing in the circuit convivialities, of which he may perchance remember one occasion at the Salisbury Arms, at Hertford!

I had not been over well for some time before I accepted the retainer to defend His Highness Mulhar Rao, the Gaekwar of Baroda; but after obtaining some excellent instructions and advice from my old friend and medical adviser, Oscar Clayton, which I supplemented with a favourite prescription of my own, I started on a certain day in January 1875, *en route* for India. I gave myself time to enjoy a dinner at Paris, and made my way onwards over the Mont Cenis pass to Bologna, where I stayed for the night (and a very interesting old town it is), and then proceeded to Brindisi.

As the train approached the shores of the Adriatic it was by no means pleasant to hear the howling of the wind and the dashing of the waves. We reached Brindisi before it was light in the morning, and the locality was certainly the reverse of inviting. The passengers were turned out amidst rain and mud, and found very wretched accommodation. It was difficult to get information as to when the vessel that was to convey us to Alexandria would start, or indeed where it was. The light, when it arrived, did not add to our satisfaction with the prospect. However, at last I found the ship, which was not likely to start for some time; but when, was very difficult to find out.

There was a rough sea and drizzling rain. I heard that there had been some unexpected change, either in the captain or some of the arrangements, which had caused delay; but at last we started, and on the evening of the third day arrived off Alexandria. The harbour of this port is very dangerous, and the pilot would not take us in until daylight, and so we remained rolling upon a nasty sea until morning, when we reached our destination; and here again we had to wait a considerable time, no one seeming to know when the train for Suez would start. I saw nothing of interest, and, not knowing what time there was to spare, made no endeavour to do so. Towards mid-day our journey began, and we arrived at Suez in the evening, when we ought to have embarked on board the 'Australia,' which had sailed from Southampton, but had got stuck in the Canal on its way. We were not inconvenienced by this, as we were received with great kindness for the night on board a very fine vessel belonging to the company—I believe the 'Pekin'—and on the following morning the 'Australia' made its appearance. This vessel was at that time, and may be now, one of the finest of the company's fleet, and was commanded by a gentleman the son, I believe, of a Presbyterian minister.

His name was Murray. He gave me the impression of being a first-rate seaman, and was certainly possessed of great intelligence and information. I received from him much courtesy, and greatly enjoyed his society. He had very rigid and scriptural ideas, accepting literally the contents of the Old Testament; and had made it a labour of love to verify localities which he supposed to be described in connection with the Red Sea. His views as to the point selected by the Israelites for crossing were very firmly fixed, and his reasons, which I will not pretend to transcribe, given with earnest faith.

There were no adventures upon the voyage. The weather was lovely and the passengers pleasant. There were two very pretty brides, very much engrossed with their husbands, one married to an officer, the son of a medical man whom I knew in London, the other to a wealthy planter or merchant in some remote part of India.

A cynical old major, who had been the voyage backwards and forwards many times, said that the fair brides were much more general in the distribution of their agreeable qualities upon the return passage. There was a colonel going out to conclude his period of service. He was accompanied by his wife, who had passed many years in the best Indian society. I cannot remember their names. I wish I could, if only to identify them with the pleasure I enjoyed in their society. There was an elderly maiden; but her companion was an ill-tempered cur of a dog, whom she insisted, against all the rules, in taking to her berth, where it indulged in the most dismal howling. One morning signs of lamentation and woe, not canine but female, proceeded from where she slept. Her companion had disappeared and was never heard of again. And there were grins upon a mischievous-looking face, the owner of which had complained bitterly of his rest having been disturbed by the aforesaid animal. Some flying fish we saw, but not many, and I do not remember their having been caught.

For two nights the constellation of the Southern Cross

was visible. The name has somehow created an idea that it is more beautiful than it really is. Still it is something to have seen. One night I was with the captain upon deck, and witnessed what to me certainly was a phenomenon, and I think that my companion told me that he had never witnessed it before. Although there was a slight motion on the vessel, the entire ocean presented an appearance that I can only liken to an immense bowl of cream with invisible sides.

There did not appear to the eye the slightest movement. The appearance lasted for many hours. We had some of the water drawn up, and it appeared to be of pure sea-green hue. Captain Murray could not in any way account for it. I may be writing of something that others more conversant than myself with voyages may have seen and can explain; but I cannot spare recounting one of the few incidents of my only passage up the Red Sea. We had one visitor—a quail. Where it came from, Heaven knows; but the pretty creature met with a kindly welcome. I cannot say what became of it, but when we arrived at Aden it was offered its liberty, which, however, it was wise enough to decline, in view of a number of kites that were gathered around the vessel. We were persecuted to buy ostrich feathers at a higher price than we should have got them in Regent Street; and the scene that most of us have witnessed from the windows of the Trafalgar Tavern, at Greenwich, was not badly imitated by a parcel of young blackamoors sporting around the vessel. Aden is a wretched hole. We landed and were received kindly enough by the English Resident, but there was nothing to eat, drink, or see. We soon proceeded onwards. The weather still continued fine, and, after a quick and pleasant voyage, we came to an anchor off Apollo Pier, the harbour of Bombay, where I was met by the Gaekwar's solicitors, Messrs. Jefferson and Payne, and after a really regretful parting from many of my fellow-passengers, and my friend Captain Murray especially, and being interviewed by a very kind and complimentary member of the press, was taken off to the pretty residence of Mr. Jefferson, who received me as his guest during the time I remained in Bombay, and from whom and his family I met with much kindness and hospitality.

The house occupied by my kind host is in the portion of the city inhabited by all the principal people of Bombay, and, I imagine, the only portion habitable with any comfort. It is a declivity sloping down to the harbour, called Malabar Hill. The residences are built with great taste, and the spot is very beautifully planted. The villas themselves have gardens of greater or less extent, filled with beautiful shrubs.

The city itself, as I then saw it for the first time, presented, with this exception, nothing to charm the eye. The appearance that it impressed upon me was as if it had lately been in the hands of some bankrupt builder. There were no hotels of any pretension, or, as far as I could learn, of reputation. There was a very handsome club, called the Byculłah, of which I was made an honorary member, excellently conducted; some fine shops, most of the articles coming from England, and very expensive.

A feature which did not present much attraction to me was the Parsee cemetery, about a mile from the town. This was a very large building, surrounded by high walls, over which passers-by were not able to see. This sect do not bury their dead, but lay them naked upon benches which are attached to the walls inside. Certain ceremonies are performed, and the bodies are left for the consumption of the birds of prey, of which there are a multitude about the city. There is not a great variety of food for human beings; and, although upon the sea, the varieties of fish are very few, the only good one being a flat fish, somewhat larger but not unlike our flounder. I forget its name. There are also prawns, and I have a grateful recollection of a dish of them curried, at a dinner given me by one of my *confrères* at the club.

Popular barristers make considerable incomes, but the expenses of living are very large; and it is impossible to practise without the possession of a carriage, and numerous servants also appear to be indispensable.

To me the air was detestable; and, although there undoubtedly is a sea breeze, it is relaxing and depressing. I cannot imagine a European having energy in such a climate for hard work, but constitutions vary and some get on very well. I dined, upon the two visits, before and after I had been to Baroda, with the Chief Justice Westropp and also with Mr. Justice Bayley, meeting with very elegant entertainments at both houses.

Shortly before my arrival a somewhat eccentric member of the bar, whom I had known well in London, had died—Mr. Chisholm Anstey. He had been in Parliament, where he was so indefatigable in worrying everybody that the Government made him Attorney-General at Hong Kong, and he celebrated the night before that fixed for his departure by breaking the heads of a couple of policemen, and thus nearly lost his appointment. I was instrumental in settling the matter for him. At Hong Kong he continued to commit such vagaries that he was recalled; before being so, there had been two unsuccessful attempts to poison him. He then settled down, as far as he could settle, as counsel at Bombay, where he became very popular with the natives, whose interests he advocated with great zeal, energy, and ability, and was a considerable thorn in the sides of the constituted authorities.

In my chapter upon Evans's I ought to have mentioned him. He used, after having been heard of playing some prank at the Antipodes, to walk as calmly into that resort as if he had never left the Temple. He was really a genius, but was lucky not to have ever been rich enough to invite the attention of certain proprietors of lunatic asylums.

CHAPTER XLVI.

TRIAL OF THE GAEKWAR.

AFTER having been treated during my brief stay at Bombay with the greatest kindness by every one—but certainly having come to the conclusion that, charming as is the society, the city itself does not furnish many attractions—I started a day or two before February 23 for the scene of my professional performance. Until I learnt that I was fated to defend the monarch of Baroda, I must confess that I had never heard of such a place, and the title of Gaekwar—or Guicowar—had never reached my ears. I learnt what I could about it, and, although by no means anxious to do anything in the handbook line, I must, to make my story intelligible, borrow some statistical information upon the subject, which I do from a book published, I believe, by the authority of the Government of India, and which, containing as it does the official account of all the proceedings, including the trial of his Majesty, I shall use throughout as my authority, except when I name any other. Baroda, then, as I learnt, was the largest independent State in Western India, and contains a very extensive population. The original meaning of Gaekwar was 'cowherd,' of which the possessors are proud, and their dominion is over Guzerat and other provinces, of which Baroda is the capital. The history of more than a century and a half of this country and its rulers contains the ordinary amount of crimes, insurrections, treasons, and intrigues which is usually to be found amongst Indian nations; but I shall leap over them all, and I do not recommend my English readers, if they have anything else to do, to add to their information upon these subjects. I must introduce them, however, to the potentate who preceded my client upon the throne.

This was Rhandi Rao, who died suddenly—not unfrequently the case in the family, and whoever profited by the death being always suspected of causing it, my client accordingly, without the slightest shadow of proof, had to accept the common suspicion. When, however, Rhandi died, his youngest wife was *enceinte*. Her name was Jummabee, and if this young lady bore a boy the throne would pass to him. She, however, lost the chance of being Queen Mother by becoming the mother of a girl. My client, Mulhar Rao, thus became monarch.

He was passing his time in prison when called to the throne, which does not appear to have been uncommon with this pastoral dynasty. Before I give an account of the trial, I shall give a short sketch of proceedings that had preceded it, and which will be required for the purpose of its comprehension, but I think that I have said all that is necessary before commencing my journey from Bombay.

Early in the morning the train started from the outskirts. The distance we had to travel was 250 miles in a northern direction. The railway seemed well constructed, the carriages comfortable, and the pace tolerably good, although not rapid. I need not mention the different towns at which we stopped; but it was known that I was in the train, and I cannot doubt that the Gaekwar was popular amongst the native population from the reception that I met with, which then, at all events, could only be attributable to that cause. As we approached his territory, lunch, called by some name that gave it importance, was prepared; and I had roses showered upon me and addresses presented to me by men whom I was given to understand were of high class and position. I am by no means insensible to compliments, but I felt a good deal embarrassed by so unusual a display; and I could not help recalling one occasion, the only one, that I went to the Lord Mayor's feast in my scarlet robes, and was received from Chancery Lane to the Guildhall by the population of that extensive thoroughfare with immense delight and applause, under the mistake that I was an alderman. Upon the occasion I am now relating, a hymn had been composed in my honour, which was recited. I have since received a translation of it,[1] and am afraid that, as upon the civic occasion, an imaginary idea possessed my admirers. As the train approached its destination the welcome became still more demonstrative, and I was not sorry, upon the arrival at the station, to get off to the residence that had been prepared for my reception two or three miles off. This was not palatial. It was a bungalow, and situated upon an extensive plain where all the Europeans resided. There was an English regiment whose barracks were also there, and the Government residence, then occupied by Sir Lewis Pelly, and under his surveillance the unhappy object of all this commotion. Other bungalows were occupied by English officers and their wives, some of them young English girls of position when in the home country, and who were subjected to inconveniences which none of them could have anticipated, but which they bore with no outward signs of discontent.

Mrs. Scobell, the wife of the Advocate-General of Bombay, and who was counsel for the Crown, had come down by the same train that had brought me. I was

[1] *Vide* Appendix.

much gratified in being introduced to her, and by my subsequent very pleasant acquaintance. Her husband had been on the same circuit as myself, and it is not necessary to say, both in his reception and in our subsequent encounter in court, was most thoroughly courteous and obliging. When we arrived there was some appearance of grass upon the plain, but after a week it had disappeared, and the sun took uncontrolled possession of the place. It was only in the very early morning and the late evening that it was possible to be exposed without covering.

There was a garden with shrubs and flowers, in which in these early mornings might be enjoyed a pleasant stroll, but the neighbourhood furnished but few attractions, and beyond what was called the compound there were no roads. I was very kindly supplied with an open trap and a pair of Arab ponies, not very amenable to discipline, with which I used to drive about the outskirts and into the town, which I will presently describe. I think the sight that struck me as most strange was a solemn-looking conclave of monkeys, seated under a large tree, whilst others were reposing upon the branches, and some ten or a dozen natives at a short distance apparently worshipping them. I was told that a person's life would not be safe if he injured one of these animals.

Flocks of green parrots filled the air close up to the residences, unhurt and unfearing, and even the kites, of which there were many swooping over the plains, were as tame as barn-door fowls. It is a great comfort for the lower class of animals that the natives suppose that their bodies are occupied by the souls that have departed from the bodies of human beings, and the most insignificant and objectionable animals are alike protected by this supposition. On some nights a continuous and almost unearthly howl is heard at a distance. It comes either from wolves or hyænas, I forget which I was told. A rustling is occasionally heard in a hedge, and you are informed that you have been a few inches distant from the deadly cobra ; and it is not desirable to walk after dark far from your bungalow, unless accompanied by servants bearing lights. Mrs. Scobell told me that one of these reptiles was coiled up one evening upon her dressing-table. The Hindoo servant appointed to attend upon my wants particularly cautioned me to look into my bath before I used it, as 'De snake was very fond of de cool place,' and I need not say that I did not neglect the information.

Having given, I fear, but an imperfect sketch of the appearance of the country, a country full of novelty to one visiting it for the first time, I will endeavour to give an idea of its capital, and this really would be worthy of a far abler pen than I possess. When for the first time I approached it, my thoughts were carried back to Eastern story, and I could picture to myself the Caliph Haroun and his faithful Vizier seeking for adventures amongst the strange forms to be seen traversing the narrow streets. It was evident that they were composed of many races, and difficult to imagine that they belonged to our own time. Of women, except of the lowest class, none were to be seen, and these were wrapped up as if they were treasures of untold price, although they might not often change their garments. The men seemed generally of diminutive stature, and engaged in different works of labour. Some, however, there were tall and handsome, with olive complexions. And these were generally carrying heavy articles upon their heads, supported by their two arms, a posture which displayed their fine sinewy forms to great advantage.

Heaviness seemed to weigh over the city, and, although it was densely crowded, there was an utter absence of all joyousness. I never saw a smile upon a countenance or heard a sound of gaiety. The men we met scowled at us, and certainly the impression made upon me was that the Europeans were most thoroughly hated. There were occasional cavalcades of persons of superior rank on horseback, and native soldiers were numerous throughout the town; amongst others, a regiment dressed in a costume similar to that of our Highland regiments, and having a certainly picturesque appearance, though it was strange to our eyes to witness their swarthy faces and slight, lithesome figures clad in such a garb.

There was no display of merchandise in the shops, and the external features of all the buildings, whilst quaint and apparently governed by no fixed principle of architecture, had the common attribute of neglect and dirt. There were palaces that offered no exception to this state; and at the entrance of the town an old gateway and dismantled tower, whilst it gave picturesqueness to the appearance, added to the gloom. It was around another gateway about the centre that I saw the Highland regiment grouped, lounging idly, and showing little appearance of discipline. I was struck by seeing a species of leopard called a cheetah led through the street fastened by a chain. These are used for hunting deer, but the sport is cruel and without excitement, the unfortunate victim never really reaching its full speed before its enemy is upon its haunches. In the streets there are some fine trees, called, if I remember correctly, pupull trees, but they add to rather than diminish its sombre character. Amongst the quadrupeds that occupy the streets no small proportion are camels and elephants, and upon one occasion when I was driving my ponies through the town I found myself most unpleasantly obstructed by the back of a camel, whilst at no great distance from my head was the trunk of an elephant; but really, whatever may be the case of the population, the quadrupeds are extremely well-behaved. I was introduced to a den of wild animals, amongst which were several large tigers fastened to staples in the walls, and not leaving very much space for visitors to walk. I confess that I eyed the chains with considerable interest, to use no more forcible expression. The keepers seemed upon perfectly good terms with them, but I was more astonished at finding one of these animals in a yard open to the street, fastened in the same way in a corner of it. Those who expected rich stuffs or jewellery to be displayed, or gorgeous and tempting shops of any kind, would have been sadly disappointed; there was nothing of the kind; dirt everywhere was what struck the visitor most. I had the honour of being introduced to her Majesty, one of the wives of the Gaekwar, through a thick trellis work. She was most gracious, but I have no distinct recollection of her conversation. The palace where this distinction was conferred upon me was as grimy as all the other places to which I had been introduced.

There may be some Eastern word meaning comfort, certainly there was no Eastern habit that I saw representing it. I cannot flatter myself that I have conveyed any very accurate idea of this scene of a city that has been the arena of many a memorable performance during many centuries. It is, however, the best that I am able to pen. There was really nothing to excite admiration, either in the buildings or the demeanour of the people. All life in which amusements or pleasure could form a part seemed to be smothered. Nevertheless, the passage through it left upon my mind the impression of something stranger than had ever before been presented to my senses.

I was not at all sorry to get back to my bungalow. Mrs. Branson, the wife of one of my brother counsel, acted the good Samaritan, and by her knowledge, activity, and good-nature not only afforded us pleasant society, but managed the establishment so as to make our lot extremely comfortable.

Every morning a present was brought to us from her Majesty, consisting of fish and fruit, accompanied by many polite messages, and these viands were, no doubt, the best that could be procured, but were not at all remarkable.

Amongst the personages who took no actual part in the trial, but who added greatly to the comfort and amusement that I derived from my visit to Baroda, was Sir Lewis Pelly, whose distinguished and long service in the Government of India is too well known to make any description of its details necessary. The tact with which he effected the capture of the Gaekwar, and his good taste and courtesy, as far as it was possible to extend it towards his captive, was admired by everyone ; and during the painful ordeal that the unfortunate monarch had to undergo, when practically under the surveillance of Sir Lewis and living with him at the Residence, nothing could exceed his captor's kindly behaviour, and I know that the Gaekwar fully appreciated it. To the counsel engaged Sir Lewis Pelly extended much hospitality, and we had very agreeable gatherings at his table during the progress of the trial.

What he thought or what he knew were not for public ears. Whether the view he took of His Highness was favourable or the reverse no one from his manner could tell ; but I entertain a vey strong opinion that if early in the transactions he had been entrusted with the management of the affairs of Baroda, I should never have had the honour of defending an Eastern potentate upon the charge of attempting to poison a British representative.

It is very ungrateful of me not to remember the names of the officers, or the designation of the English regiment, whose rooms were opened to us, and from whom we received such frequent and kindly welcomes. It was, however, a regiment to which my brother was attached during his lifetime, and I heard a great deal about him. He seemed to have been a particular favourite.

It did not appear to me that there existed any intercourse between our countrymen and the inhabitants. The Residence and the barracks rendered our stay more than endurable, and I for one have a most grateful recollection of the courtesies received at both.

One trifling incident afforded me amusement during my early morning walks. This was the docility of a partridge, which followed a man about the fields like a dog. I was told that this is not an uncommon mode of training these birds. I used to look forward to witnessing its performance, and its possessor seemed gratified at a very moderate present.

CHAPTER XLVII.

THE MEETING OF COMMISSIONERS.

It is superfluous to mention that shortly after daybreak on the morning of February **25**, 1875, Baroda was in a blaze of sunshine, for such was the case every day during my sojourn. No rain, no dew. The grass, a few blades of which did meet my eyes two days before, was burnt out of sight, and the heat threatened a sunstroke to those who were exposed to it for a moment.

Yet on this particular morning everything was as much alive as it could be. The monarch of a country embracing 4,400 square miles, and containing a population of 5,000 persons to each mile, was about to be put upon his trial for the attempted murder of an English officer, holding the post of British Resident, and great potentates had consented to assist in the solemn duty, whilst the Chief Justice of India had been deputed to conduct the inquiry after European fashion, with the assistance of a military and civil officer, each most distinguished in their relative positions. A guard of infantry and a troop of lancers did no more honour than is due to Maharajah Scindia, the great Mahratta potentate, tried and trusted friend of England. His appearance was such as to command respect in any country, and I cannot deny myself the pleasure of copying a few words of description taken from an admirably conducted paper—the 'Times of India'—of what it presented on this eventful day:

'*Burly and princely, an Oriental Harry the Eighth in outward semblance.*' The writer might have added, 'before the English monarch had impressed upon his features the marks of gross self-indulgence, selfishness, and cruelty.' For Scindia's is a countenance noble and pleasant to look upon. Sir Dunker Rao, a Hindoo possessing great weight with his fellow-countrymen, and esteemed a very able administrator, was another of the judges, and the third native one was the Maharajah of Jeypore, highly esteemed by the English Government.

Sir Richard Couch, Sir Richard John Meade, and Mr. Philip Sandys Melvil constituted the English element.

No one can doubt that Lord Northbrook, in the selection of such a tribunal, could have had no other object than to elicit the truth. Naturally Sir Richard Couch conducted the proceedings, and although I cannot agree with the result that he arrived at, it is impossible that any inquiry could have been managed with more fairness and impartiality. No impediment of any kind was presented to the defence, and certainly the earnest attention paid by every member of the court showed their full appreciation of the importance of their position.

The Honourable Andrew R. Scobell, Advocate-General at Bombay, and Mr. Inverarity appeared for the prosecution. With me were Mr. Branson, Mr. Purcell, Shantaram Narayan, and Wassudeo Juggonault. For myself, I cannot forbear saying that my reception was most cordial and kind, both from the Bench and my brethren at the Bar.

The accused Maharajah sat upon the bench, Colonel Sir Lewis Pelly sitting beside him. I have before me, whilst writing these lines, a singularly lifelike picture of His Highness, presented to me by himself after the trial, with many kind messages, and I do not think his face was unprepossessing. His dress was in singularly good taste; his demeanour quiet and dignified.

In conveying my opinion upon the result and the evidence it was founded upon, I am quite aware that the habits of life and the customs of the country presented very different features from what I had been accustomed to deal with; but I find, in the judgment of the native members of the Court, that my views are in many respects adopted by men who may be fairly assumed to know their countrymen and their habits thoroughly; and it also is observable that my conclusions are drawn from incidents, many not controverted, and from the conduct and testimony of the accuser himself, which does not seem to me to have met the attention it deserved from the English members of the Commission, and, consequently, not from the Government of India who adopted their views.

At the time that the inquiry took place, Mulhar Rao had only been upon the throne for five years. During the two first, Colonel Barr, and after him Colonel Shortt, had filled the place of British Resident, and they seem to have behaved with prudence. In March 1873 Colonel Phayre was appointed.

He was fussy, meddlesome, and thoroughly injudicious. There were two adverse parties in the State, and instead of holding himself aloof from both he threw himself violently into that opposed to the Gaekwar, and was greedy to listen to every accusation and complaint that with equal eagerness was gossiped into his ears. His annoyances and constant slights to the Gaekwar were such that a despatch was sent by the latter to the Government, in temperate and judicious terms, praying for his removal; and its date is most material—namely, *November* 2, 1874, seven days only before the alleged final attempt at poisoning, but almost if not quite cotemporaneous with the alleged tampering with servants.

The tone of his despatch may be judged of by the following sentence: '*I beg it to be understood that I do not impute other than conscientious motives to Colonel Phayre.*'

Colonel Phayre had been asked to resign by the Governor of Bombay, which he had declined doing, and towards the end of November was actually dismissed by the Governor-General in terms the reverse of complimentary—indeed, to the effect that he utterly misunderstood his duties;[1] and it was not denied that the intention to remove him was probably known to the Gaekwar on November 9, the very day of the alleged attempt to poison; and, if not actually known, his own despatch still remained unanswered. This state of affairs, which appeared to me nearly conclusive against his guilt, was scarcely adverted to by the English Commissioners; and it cannot be denied that it materially impairs the value of Colonel Phayre's evidence, whilst showing the absence of motive on the part of the Gaekwar.

Independently of these facts, his mode of giving evidence was not satisfactory. It was not until reprimanded by the President that he admitted his conduct in Scinde. He very unwillingly, and after long pressure, owned that he knew of the despatch sent to the Government complaining of him and seeking his removal. He was obliged to admit receiving the suggestion from the Governor of Bombay that he should resign, and that this was probably known to the Gaekwar; and that about

[1] The words used by Lord Northbrook to Colonel Phayre when dismissing him from his post were: 'That he had thoroughly misunderstood the spirit of the instructions both of the Government of India and the Government of Bombay, and that the duty of Resident could no longer be entrusted to him with any reasonable prospect of a satisfactory result.'

November 13 he received a despatch from the Central Government dismissing him in terms of censure for his bad management of the affairs of Baroda.

The English Commissioners do not appear to have considered that these circumstances affected the reliance to be placed in his testimony, or tended to show an utter absence of motive for the crime attributed to the Gaekwar.

The press in England almost universally demurred to his evidence as unsatisfactory. It is necessary that I should now give his own account of the important transaction on November 9, prefacing it with his assertion that warning had been previously given to him that such an attempt to poison him was contemplated. He said that upon coming home about half-past seven in the morning he found his usual tumbler of sherbet upon his wash-hand stand; that he drank two or three sips, from which he derived unpleasant symptoms; that he sat down to write for twenty minutes, and feeling worse, and being satisfied that it arose from the sherbet, *threw the contents out of the window that he might not be tempted to drink it*, leaving a small brown sediment at the bottom.

The next step taken by the Colonel presents us with pregnant evidence of his unfitness for one of the most delicate trusts that could be reposed in an official in India. In hot haste, and upon the very day when the alleged attempt took place, he telegraphed to the seat of Government in these words, written 'in Hindostani,' so that there should be no difficulty in everyone through whose hands it passed understanding it:—

From Colonel Phayre, C.B., Resident, Baroda, to the Private Secretary, Gunnesh Khind, Poonah. Bold attempt to poison me this day has been providentially frustrated. More by next post.

It next appears that some of the *débris* amongst which the sherbet was thrown was scraped up by Colonel Phayre's order, and this, with the small residuum at the bottom of the tumbler, was analysed by Dr. Seward and Dr. Grey, who stated that they had discovered poison; which fact was communicated to the Colonel, who replied to Dr. Grey in the following most remarkable letter, dated November 13, 1874.

After acknowledging the receipt of Dr. Grey's letter, he proceeds:—

With reference to the statement made in your letter, that the powder forwarded to you consisted partly of common white arsenic and partly of finely powdered silicious matter, which, under the microscope, appeared to be rather powdered glass or quartz, being most likely the former, I should feel much obliged by your kindly informing me whether, in your opinion, the silicious matter referred to can *possibly be* powdered diamond.

Previous to the receipt of your letter under reference, I had received secret and confidential communication that the poison administered to me did consist—1. Common arsenic; 2. *Finely powdered* diamond dust; 3. Copper.

The importance of verifying this communication is obvious.

R. PHAYRE,
Resident.

When I call the attention of my readers to the policy pursued by the police towards some of the witnesses, and also to the fact that the greater part of the evidence was founded upon the supposition that diamond dust was purchased by the Gaekwar, it will be admitted that the terms of the above letter are very extraordinary.

I naturally desired to know from whom Colonel Phayre received the secret and confidential communication referred to in his letter. He steered clear of the question, and I could obtain no satisfactory reply without seeking and obtaining the assistance of the Commission. It seemed singular that he should forget the name of a person or persons whom he described in such terms, and whom he must have been in communication with within two or three days of the alleged attempt; but it was only after a considerable time that at last the name of a certain Bowh-Poonaka was disclosed—notoriously the bitterest enemy of the Gaekwar, and the man who had been for years fostering charges against him. It is not within the compass of this book that I should dissect further the evidence given by Colonel Phayre; but the remainder would certainly not create a favourable impression of his discretion. It is not, however, unimportant in my view of the case to mention that Bowh-Poonaka had complete access to Colonel Phayre's dressing-room, and was proved to have been there upon the morning in question.

POSTSCRIPT.

In the above chapter I have not explained as I ought to have done the importance of the diamond dust element. There is a general belief amongst the population of Baroda and the surrounding districts that diamond dust is a deadly poison, and in this belief Colonel Phayre participated. It would not be pleasant, no doubt, to have a quantity of any silicious substance in the human inside, but that the diamond contains poison is an ignorant delusion. It will be seen in a subsequent chapter that Dr. Grey was subsequently of opinion that the powder might be powdered diamond.

CHAPTER XLVIII.

CONTINUANCE OF THE TRIAL.

THOSE of my readers who have been interested in the perusal of the foregoing pages will have understood from them that the scrapings from the spot where the bulk of the sherbet was thrown by Colonel Phayre, and a small residuum that remained at the bottom of the tumbler which contained it, were the subject of the analyses of Drs. Seward and Grey. There was, however, another parcel submitted to their scientific skill, and in which I can quite believe that they found arsenic. Raoji was a servant of Colonel Phayre, and one of the supposed poisoners. Upon *November* 9 his belt was taken from him and given to another servant named Budhar. Why is not explained. On December 22 Raoji was arrested, and, after having been in the hands of the police until the 24th, after the usual custom, made a confession; and, amongst other things, stated that he was in the habit of keeping the poisons entrusted to him in his belt. It then occurred to Akbar Ali, an intelligent detective, to examine the belt, and Budhar was sent for, and made his appearance. Akbar's sagacious eyes discovered a piece of thread and a packet of paper, *which had never been seen by Budhar during the six weeks he had worn the belt*, but immediately presented arsenic to the imagination of Akbar. He, however, without satisfying himself, rushed into the next room, where Mr. Souter a commissioner of police, happened to be, and brought him to the piece of thread and the paper parcel, and there, sure enough, was found the arsenic afterwards tested, and which was said to be precisely similar to the other portions referred to as having been previously found.

Strange, however, that Akbar's remarkable prescience should be afterwards verified by Raoji, who, up to the discovery, had quite forgotten the circumstance that he had left it there.[1]

This incident is somewhat unfairly, although not, I am sure, intentionally so, described in the following terms in the report of the English Commissioners: 'The second packet (the one in question) was found in Raoji's belt on December 25, 1874, in the presence of the commissioner of police, Mr. Souter.'

Upon the twelfth day of the inquiry a scene was presented upon a correct reading of which depends very much a true appreciation of the history of this case.

A witness called Hemchund Futeychund was called, and, upon presenting himself, brought to my imagination what would probably have been the appearance of a person who had come out of the cells of the Inquisition after the officers of that institution had pursued their usual inquiries. He appeared to be in a prostrate condition of terror, and his miserable story was of a continued persecution by the police; of the extortion from him of false statements, and the manufacture of fraudulent documents. And to these charges he resolutely, although with the appearance of great nervousness, adhered, and was not shaken by a very able cross-examination.

It is well to consider the position of this witness. He

[1] It is, perhaps, fitting that I should mention that this last fact is much relied upon by English Commissioners as proving the truth of the story! A judge conversant with evidence would generally have deduced an opposite conclusion, and I was surprised at Sir R. Couch.

was one of the most respectable tradespeople in Baroda, and a diamond merchant. It was attempted, in pursuance of Colonel Phayre's letter, to connect the Gaekwar with the purchase of diamonds, and Hemchund alleges that he was forced by constant pressure into supplying that testimony. We were informed that he was kept for three days without a bath, which the poor wretch imagined devoted him to I do not know how many years of future torture.[1]

The English Commissioners ignore his evidence altogether, whether or not upon the ground that he contradicted that given by the police they did not state; but I must say that upon this point I think that the judgment of his own countrymen is far more important and likely to be correct. None of them discredit it. And the Maharajah of Jeypore, admitted to be one of the ablest men in India, and a devoted friend of the English Government, signally recognises it as truthful. Other servants of Colonel Phayre supply confessions.

Now it must be remembered that, although no imputation was thrown upon Colonel Phayre's integrity, much comment was invited by his conduct, and he was upon his trial as well as the Gaekwar. It may be said, therefore, that each party would have half the tribunal imbued with a prepossession in his favour. My own deliberate and well-considered belief is that Colonel Phayre was subjected to no real attempt to be poisoned, but I think that certain persons were anxious to retain him in the Residency, and to defeat the endeavour of the Gaekwar to get him turned out, and supposed that the alleged attempt would have that effect.

The Colonel admitted that he had received warnings beforehand, from whom did not appear; and a bitter

[1] This was not proved, but told to the adviser of the Gaekwar after the trial.

enemy of the Gaekwar's supplied the Colonel with a description of the materials by which the attempt was actually made. It seems to be conceded that, somehow or another, these people escaped without any investigation. Diamond dust, arsenic, and copper are the ingredients indicated. The quantity left in the tumbler could not afford a satisfactory analysis. And so there is a miraculous discovery of a parcel containing arsenic in the belt of one of the supposed poisoners, who had forgotten its existence until after it was found; and some respectable witness was wanted to supply a proof of diamond dust, and so poor Hemchund was produced, and he proved the whole story told to be a lie, as did also another person named Pedro, in relation to a statement made by another accomplice.

But the theory that I entertain would be displaced if Damadhur Punt had been a voluntary witness. He was private secretary to the Gaekwar, and, as far as is known, had no motive to procure his deposition. It becomes, therefore, necessary to ascertain how this gentleman happened to take up the position of his master's accuser, and his account of this will throw no small light upon what probably occurred with the other witnesses.

I copy the following from the report of the English Commissioners:—

Damadhur Punt was arrested the evening of the day upon which the Gaekwar was placed in confinement (January 14, 1875). He was imprisoned for two days in the Senapali's office at the palace, and then he was brought to the Residency, where he was placed under a guard of European soldiers for sixteen days, and afterwards under a police guard. Being, he states, tired of the European guard, and *thinking that he could not otherwise get out of confinement*, Damadhur Punt made a confession to Mr. Richey, Assistant Resident, on January 29 and 30, 1875. It is substantially the same as his evidence before the Commission, *and was made under a promise of pardon.*

I can quite understand that Damadhur Punt did not enjoy himself in company with sixteen English soldiers, and, like Hemchund, was ready to redeem himself from such captivity, especially if running the same risks in a future life by remaining in it. But what is the value of such testimony? And every witness went through this same preparation.

The feeling of the audience during the examination of Damadhur Punt was shown very clearly by spitting upon the floor and other signs of disgust. On the next day it was observed that a much larger number of soldiers occupied the court.

I have now given a summary of this remarkable inquiry. I have expressed my own views, and have ventured upon a theory that has always prevailed in my mind, although at the period I considered that my duty was confined to showing that the prosecution had failed, which I think that I succeeded in doing; and, notwithstanding the great respect that I entertain for the three members of the Commission who felt it to be their duty to decide adversely, I still entertain the same opinion. And I cannot think that the weighty reasons given by the Maharajah of Jeypore, and substantially agreed in by his colleagues, are met by any of the arguments used by the English Commissioners.

Amongst them the Maharajah urges:—

'That Damadhur Punt, Raoji, and Musoo, whose testimony is supposed to form the basis of this grave charge against the Gaekwar, are accomplices and their evidence is not corroborated by a single respectable witness.' Again, and this is most important:—

'No documentary evidence, or evidence of a convincing nature, was forthcoming from Damadhur Punt, notwithstanding his position as private secretary to the Gaekwar, and the command he had over the records of the Maharajah's private office.'[1]

He also refers to Hemchund's direct contradiction, which he treats as being trustworthy, and also to other important contradictions.

The proceedings were terminated by a proclamation dated Simla, April 19, 1875, signed C. U. Aitchison, Secretary to the Government of India, deposing the Gaekwar on the ground of abuses previous to and not connected with the inquiry, and in which the following paragraph occurs: 'The Commissioners being divided in opinion, Her Majesty's Government have not based their decision on the inquiry or the report of the Commission, nor have they assumed that the result of the inquiry has been to prove the truth of the imputations against His Highness.'

Somewhat inconsistently, and, I venture to think, neither in good taste nor in strict fairness, the same gentleman—Mr. Aitchison—published upon the 21st of the same month a sort of manifesto embodying the views of the English Commissioners, and agreeing emphatically with their conclusions. The document does not exhibit any originality, or add at all to the arguments adduced by the Commissioners themselves.

I have copied these extracts from a book in which the proceedings are published *in extenso*, and apparently by the authority of some one connected with the Government, as, in some preliminary observations, the writer refers to the delay that has occurred in giving the decision, and accounts for it as follows: '*The delay is generally attributed to a difference of opinion between the*

[1] As a matter of fact there was not a scrap of writing directly implicating the Gaekwar.

Viceroy in Council and the Home Government, the former wishing to treat Mulhar Rao as a convicted criminal, while the latter, influenced no doubt by the outcry of the "Times" and other London papers, which for some inexplicable reason had ranged themselves on the side of the defence before even waiting to see reports of the case for the prosecution, wished to avoid taking a course which would be sure to provoke hostile criticism in England.'

Now this assertion about the press is certainly not founded upon fact. I believe that the first adverse criticism resulted from the cross-examination of Colonel Phayre. And the evidence in the case was followed with the greatest attention, and opinion was, as far as I have seen, unanimous that it was most unsatisfactory and unreliable. Judging also by the despatches that I have seen coming directly from Lord Northbrook, and which exhibit an enlarged and statesmanlike mind, I can never believe that he would have treated the opinions of three illustrious princes with such indignity. I have, as I have intimated, nothing whatever to do with the reasons of State that influenced the Government in deposing the Gaekwar ; but it must not be supposed that I think the course was pursued upon well-founded information furnished to the Viceroy. I cannot but remember the kindness and courtesy I received at the hands of the Gaekwar, his patient and uncomplaining demeanour during the inquiry, and his kindly expressions of gratitude for my exertions; and I should be glad if the above imperfect comments should have some effect upon the judgment of those who have to deal with him, and call their attention to the position in which he is now placed, which, to my intense astonishment, I understand to be practically in the custody of the Dr. Seward who figured upon the investigation as one of the bitterest witnesses against him.

CHAPTER XLIX.

TERMINATION OF THE TRIAL.

THE great trial is ended. The regulation number of guns has announced the departure of each of the respective potentates. The English Commissioners have closed their note-books. Not a word has been spoken, not a hint given as to what the decision was likely to be, but the result was no surprise. Colonel Phayre *versus* the Gaekwar of Baroda represented in the thoughts of men the momentous case that had just concluded.

Eastern minds certainly never imagined that there would be a British verdict against their compatriot. Perhaps amongst our own countrymen a similar opinion was entertained in relation to the native princes. And the whole of the pomp and panoply might have been spared. The Indian Government treated the conclusion as a nullity, and simply effaced it; but the interest created by the proceedings will be long remembered, and the members of the Court, by their patience, attention, and courtesy, are certainly entitled to the thanks of all who were brought under their influence.

Some few observations are worthy to be made. It was marvellous, considering the intense heat, how delightfully cool the court house was kept. And I shall never forget the thorough loyaliy of my juniors and the assistance they afforded me. I have mentioned the names of all of them: the English members were Mr. Branson and Mr. Purcell, at the houses of both of which gentlemen at Bombay I was most kindly received. The latter of these has since died. He imprudently exposed himself in the jungle, shooting, and caught a fever. The former gentleman still continues to practise at Bombay. A member of the bar named Taylor represented some collateral interests, and afforded me much pleasant information and gossip.

We passed an agreeable life enough; an unmistakably good brand of champagne was sent to us through the favour of the Bycullah Club, and we got fresh fish every day from Bombay. I have mentioned that Mrs. Branson kindly presided over our household. On the morning following the termination of the trial we started on our return journey, and I was again received at the house of Mr. Jefferson until the sailing of the homeward-bound P. and O. steamer. I cannot say that I suffered much from the effect of the climate, but I preferred that of Baroda greatly to Bombay, the former, although intensely hot, being perfectly dry, which is far from being the case at the latter.

I received many kind compliments from all quarters for my conduct of the case; there is no doubt that I might have excited native feeling to a considerable if not dangerous extent, but it would have been an improper advantage to take of my position to do so. I felt that I had been retained to defend my client upon a specific charge, and I shall always think that the prosecution failed to substantiate it.

Before I left Bombay a most gratifying mark of kindly feeling and approval was exhibited towards me. There was quite three-quarters of a mile to be traversed between Mr. Jefferson's house, where I was staying, and the dock from which the steamer started, and the whole space was filled with a dense mass of people, who had assembled to wish me adieu.

So thick was it that the carriage could scarcely make its way, and it is impossible that I should ever forget the kindness and, I may venture to say, enthusiasm with which I was received. An address was also delivered to me, accompanied with a handsome shawl—this article, I understand, being a very signal mark of regard. The address was engrossed upon parchment, and signed by fifteen hundred natives, including the highest and most distinguished inhabitants of Bombay, and was in the following terms:—

To William Ballantine, Esq., Serjeant-at-Law.
Patent of Precedence.

Sir,—As you are departing from these shores, after having with signal ability and independence defended His Highness the Gaekwar of Baroda—a prince in whom the people of this country are deeply interested—against the accusations preferred against him by the Government of India, we, the undersigned inhabitants of Bombay, take this opportunity of thanking you for your exertions on behalf of the said oppressed prince. We request you to accept this little present (a shawl), which we offer in testimony of our gratitude for your valuable labours in his cause, and we bid you a cordial farewell, and wish you every happiness.

Here follow the Signatures.

Bombay, March 22, 1875.

My kind friends, Mr. and the Miss Jeffersons, accompanied me to the docks, and the carriage had considerable difficulty in penetrating the crowd. At this time I did not know what decision would be arrived at about the unfortunate Gaekwar, and had no drawback to the feeling of gratitude for all the kindness that had been extended to me. After I had arrived on board I received through Sir Lewis Pelly, a very kind message from my client, and requesting me to accept a portrait of himself as a mark of his consideration. This was transmitted to me subsequently. It is painted by an Indian artist with considerable skill, and is a remarkably good likeness.

I do not remember the name of the vessel that brought me home. Everything was very pleasant on board, and the voyage passed smoothly and without any incidents. Amongst the passengers was Lord de Grey, the son of the present Viceroy. He had been round the world, and was returning, and his pleasant anecdotes of travel took much away from the monotony of the voyage. We both of us stopped at Suez, and visited Cairo. Once upon a time a writer might fill his pages with accounts of mosques and bazaars and the strange habits of the natives. Now I should as soon think of describing the streets of Margate. An English brougham with a not unusual occupant drives up and down the promenade. Every other house almost, at all events in some of the streets, was a gambling resort, and I heard some ugly stories about the disappearance of Europeans. Lord de Grey and myself visited the Pyramids. I did not, however, attempt an ascent. They are the haunts of dirty, dingy, disreputable beggars, who carry knives.

I was not sorry to get away from Cairo, and, reaching Alexandria by rail, joined the same ship, and, after another calm passage, duly reached Brindisi, which I have already described, and I saw nothing to induce me to change my mind. I regret that I cannot remember the name of the gentleman who at that time held the post of Consul, that I might convey directly to him my appreciation of the great kindness and attention that he showed me. A telegraphic message hurried me home, where, having arrived in due course, I need not say I have no adventure to relate of the journey.

I have had occasion to mention, in the course of the

foregoing pages, the name of Sir Lewis Pelly. He had conducted the very delicate arrangements immediately antecedent to the Commission, and had the charge of the Gaekwar's person during its continuance. He also filled the post of Resident, and from him myself and brother counsel met with many proofs of attention and kindness. His demeanour to the Prince was characterised by all the courtesy and consideration that his duty would permit. He vacated the position of Resident in favour of Sir Richard Meade, who had been one of the Commissioners. Whilst I was at Baroda I received a letter from Colonel Napier Sturt, who was staying upon a visit with his brother-in-law, Lord Northbrook. We met afterwards in London, and his Royal Highness the Prince of Wales did him and me the honour of dining with us at the Garrick Club, on which occasion Sir Lewis Pelly was also my guest, and thus I had the opportunity of returning his kindness in the manner that must have been most gratifying to himself.

POSTSCRIPT.

The career of the unhappy subject of the above sketch is terminated in this world. To me it has been the occasion of one of the most interesting incidents that could have occurred in a professional life.

Whether he was a profligate and tyrannical monarch or the victim of falsehood and calumny is not now of any importance to be considered.

The action taken by the Government of the time could scarcely be considered as consistent, but it appears to have resulted in a satisfactory state of things in Baroda, where the throne is occupied by a monarch fully appreciative of British rule, and who has the benefit of a resident possessing discretion and prudence, and whose advice is always at his command.

CHAPTER L.

GENERAL REVIEW.

In a mental review of the contents of the different chapters contained in these volumes, I feel how much I have left unsaid that might have amused, and possibly have been of some service to my readers. I also feel that in my own profession changes have taken place, and are doing so daily, which are deserving of more reflection than I have hitherto given to them.

The public scarcely appreciate how much they may be affected by these changes, although recent incidents have occurred affording unfortunate illustrations.

No one can doubt that the general administration of the law has during the last half-century improved in every branch, and the present generation would scarcely credit the amount of villainy, fraud, and oppression which previous to that period flourished under its auspices. The gaols filled with victims, officers of the sheriffs robbing both creditors and debtors; small courts, the offices of which were put up for sale, and the costs incurred by the suitors brought ruin to both parties. One flagrant example was the Marshalsea, and a gentleman whom I slightly knew, named Higgins, but who wrote under the *nom de plume* of 'Jacob Omnium,' conferred a benefit upon society by his eloquent denunciation of its iniquities, leading to the ultimate abolition of the Court. Immense taxes were imposed upon legal proceedings by numerous sinecure offices paid out of suitors' pockets. The profession also was comparatively limited. In 1816, the year in which my father was called to the bar, there were only twenty-eight King's Counsel. Lord Eldon was Chancellor, Ellenborough Chief-Justice, and Serjeants' Inn boasted several most distinguished members. I cannot think among the numerous improvements effected that the destruction of this last body can be numbered, and it seems to have been done with thoughtlessness, and without such formalities as dealing with so ancient an institution deserved. I believe that those answerable for the result scarcely knew the character of the institution. Formerly it had certain exclusive privileges. These, as I have before said, were properly abolished, but its peculiar quality, that of being essentially a popular institution, and not subject to the control of the Crown, thus distinguishing its members from King's Counsel, in itself made it worthy of retention. It possessed another great advantage—that a junior who had not seen much civil business, and who had practised principally at sessions, could, after seven years' standing, claim the appointment, and thus get a step intermediate to that of King's Counsel without sacrificing certain business that the latter gentleman was, by etiquette, bound to abandon. I have referred for a second time to this rank, because I think now that, again without full reflection, a course is being adopted by which ultimately both the public and the profession will grievously suffer in the administration of justice, and recent occurrences have forced the matters to which I refer prominently forward. I have already said, and wish emphatically to repeat, that no higher intellects can exist than many that have adorned the Equity bar. The names of Bethell, Roundell Palmer, Cairns, Jessel, and the late Lord Justice James represent men worthy of any age;

but I cannot think that the general body of that branch of the profession to which they belong are fitted to try causes dependent upon oral testimony, and I consider them to be specially unsuited to preside in criminal cases.

Their schooling has been that of drawing conclusions from affidavits, and arguing before refined and intellectual minds. The evidence does not come into their hands directly, but has been manipulated by the solicitor. They do not see the witnesses, as an ordinary rule, and I have already expressed my opinion as to their mode of dealing with such apparitions when they occur. The judge who listens to the argument has to be reached by calm and unimpassioned means quite unfitted to a popular and comparatively uneducated tribunal. Can this be an appropriate preparation for a man to be placed upon a judgment-seat, facing a dock, with the very form of which he is unacquainted, and called upon to deal with a fellow-creature's life, upon materials of which he is, by practice, absolutely ignorant?

It is not only that the individual so selected has no experience of witnesses, but the class of business to which his mind has been applied is totally different from what presents itself in the criminal courts. No doubt, he has met with plenty of falsehood and fraud, but they have been arrayed in a decent and respectable garb, and bore no more resemblance to the crime and its concomitants prevailing in the criminal courts than they did outwardly to the fustian jacket of the labourer, or even the gaudy apparel of the village beadle. My readers have frequently noticed the following scene in court. A learned judge has taken his place upon the bench, a criminal charged with murder is arraigned before him. He has no counsel. And his lordship, addressing a gentleman who probably has no client, says, 'Mr——, will you kindly watch the case for the prisoner?'

Let my readers picture to themselves the life of a fellow-creature, possibly assailed by perjury, dependent upon the practical knowledge of an Equity judge, assisted by a junior counsel.

I was myself present when this actually occurred. A Chancery barrister of most remarkable attainments, and possessing every high quality except the experience necessary for his position, having been created a judge, was called upon, amongst his first cases, to try two most serious charges of murder, in the first of which the accused being without counsel a junior barrister, at the request of the judge, defended him, and did so with great ability and judgment, and there was no failure of justice in the result. In the second case, there occurred a scene which certainly would not have happened if the judge had come from the other branch of his profession, and I am not sure that the verdict arrived at was correct; certainly it was subsequently modified. I am not sorry to refer to these instances, because, except the evils that must arise from the grounds I have referred to, it would be impossible to attach censure to the judicial qualities of the learned judge. The public have had their attention called to two recent cases connected with the administration of the criminal law. Both of them happen to have been tried by the same judge, whose intellect is of the highest order, and before whom it has frequently been my pleasure to practise. He was selected from the highest ranks of the Chancery bar. In the first of these cases a prisoner was left for execution. The colleague of the judge fortunately entertained doubt, and inquiries were readily instituted, and the result was the discovery of the man's innocence. In another case, two men had undergone a long term of imprisonment, part, only, of a much longer sentence, well deserved if they had been guilty. They have been shown to be perfectly innocent, pardoned, and recompensed. I was not present at either of these trials, but some who were have told me that the judge took a perfectly just view in both cases; but he had to address country juries of the commoner class, and in both instances they were governed rather by details that shocked their feelings than by the evidence that ought to have controlled their judgment.

In the observations that I have made respecting the appointment of purely Equity lawyers as Criminal judges, it must not be supposed that I ignore the liability of human nature, in every grade and with whatever schooling, to error, and it is on this account that I have so urgently pressed the necessity of a Court of Criminal Appeal. Applicable of course only to convictions, it is essential that little delay should take place between the trial and the appeal, and I have already ventured to shadow forth the kind of tribunal that I think should be created. I have also expressed an opinion that the absence of such a court is prejudicial to the interests of justice oftener by the escape of criminals than by wrongful convictions. There are certain words that are constantly used, and, whether actually used or not, their impression exists in the minds of a jury trying a capital case: 'Remember, your verdict is final.' How many criminals have escaped through the influence of these words! I have recorded two instances in the course of these pages. I trust that there have not been many cases where their efficacy has not prevailed, where it ought to have done. But who on this earth can tell?

One other ground for the institution of a Court of Appeal is that it will abolish a most discreditable anomaly. Cases may, by a well-known process, be removed into the

Court of Queen's Bench, and there, although supposed to be tried by the highest officer of the law, and with the assistance of a special jury, a verdict of guilty is not necessarily final, it may be appealed against. As the process of removal is expensive, it may not unfairly be alleged that in some cases there exists one law for the poor, another for the wealthy. The verdict against the defendant unremoved would be final.

Another evil, and in my opinion a very grave one, arises from the creation of judges out of a different sphere from those who ordinarily practise in the courts over which they are placed. In an early chapter I called attention to the remark of Monsieur Berryer as to the courteous manner, kindly feelings, and perfect confidence existing between the bench and the bar. This mainly arises from the intimacy existing between them during an early professional career. If a learned judge upon a recent occasion had been so selected, it is not likely that such a scene as that exhibited lately upon the Oxford Circuit could ever have taken place.

As I have taken my readers back to my old Inn, I will venture to surround it with all the halo to which it is entitled. We were and had been from time immemoria connected with the Corporation of the City of London, and, inasmuch as the greatest compliment appreciated by that august body was annually paid to us, we were doubtless once upon a time of no small importance ourselves. We received an invitation to dine at the Lord Mayor's dinner on November 9, and arrayed in robes that gave us as much claim to notice as the men in armour, and preceded by a personage known as the City Marshal, we were assigned seats amongst the principal guests at that great festival, and it was really a sight worthy of notice.

The grandeur of the hall, the magnificence of the

dresses, the style of the entertainment, and the rank of the guests, rendered it one of the greatest scenes exhibited throughout Europe. Upon this great occasion it was the office of one of the high officers of the Corporation, no less a dignitary than the Common Serjeant, personally to convey to us the invitation on the first day of Michaelmas Term at our Inn.

Sir Thomas Chambers, when he occupied this office, was accustomed to commit a most amusing blunder. Whether moved by some idea of his own dignity, or acting under civic instruction, I am unable to say, but when he came to perform his task he addressed himself solely to the Judges, not even naming the Serjeants, although the former were asked only in that capacity, and were included with the Lord Chancellor and Equity Judges specially in their official capacity, and invited by the Lord Mayor himself personally. The Common Serjeant was not probably aware that whilst it in no respect derogated from his dignity to convey a message from one great corporation to another, he was performing the duty of a butler in conveying an invitation to dinner to individuals belonging to it.

There was a worthy member of our body, Mr. Serjeant Woolrych, who had written a most exhaustive book upon Sewers, and was also very learned about city customs, and who exercised his mind greatly upon the blunder into which the Common Serjeant had tumbled, and wanted me, as Treasurer, to call attention to it. He considered that this was not only due to common humanity but also to our dignity. I was, however, deaf to his entreaties.

I do not remember dining more than upon one occasion in my official capacity. On this occasion the scarlet robes and heavy cumbrous wig, necessary to be worn, destroyed all possibility of enjoyment. The Serjeants of the Inn were also invited one Sunday in May or June, I forget which, to attend the service at St. Paul's Cathedral. This was a very interesting ceremony; and, although the names of the clergymen whom I heard preach have escaped my memory, I remember that the sermons were highly interesting and intellectual; but the beauty of the spiritual fare was as greatly destroyed by our costume upon these occasions, as our enjoyment was of the luxuries so liberally provided upon the occasion of the Lord Mayors' feasts.

An incident occurred to me which, from my connection with the Tichborne case, gave me considerable interest. It arose about eighteen months ago, when I was enjoying a very charming visit with Sir John and Lady Holker, at their country seat, at Coulthurst, upon the borders of Lancashire and Yorkshire, and, learning that Stonyhurst College was situated at no great distance, I took the opportunity of driving over to pay it a visit. It was the locality pointed at by a great portion of the cross-examination by Sir John Coleridge. Through its rooms and gardens the unhappy Claimant was invited to travel; it was here the learning was supposed to have been imparted of which he was challenged to produce some proof, and it was over the whole of this period that if he were the genuine baronet his unfortunate failure of memory extended. I was most kindly received, and made an interesting excursion through the establishment and its grounds. Of course, I can form no opinion of its scholastic successes, but I was struck by the variety of the studies and their apparently efficient superintendence; and there was one characteristic that I was fully able to appreciate—the extreme attention and care apparent in every portion of the establishment to the health and physical comforts of the pupils.

Upon the first trial, to which I have just alluded, and amongst the witnesses who were undoubtedly actuated by a firm belief in the identity of the Claimant with Sir Roger Tichborne, was a Catholic priest who had been one of the tutors during the stay of the real baronet at Stonyhurst. This gentleman gave his evidence in favour of the claim with great firmness and evident honesty of intention. He was subjected to a severe cross-examination, and suffered greatly under it.

He was one of those men, of not an uncommon type, whose feelings had been reached without a sufficient aid from reason; who did not dissect sufficiently from materials before him, what he really knew from what had been impressed upon his mind from other sources. Witnesses of this kind cut but an awkward figure in the hands of a skilful counsel; the more so that they feel that they may have been misled and conveyed erroneous ideas. Such a feeling is very trying to a conscientious man, and it was evident that this gentleman suffered greatly. I took the opportunity of enquiring after him, and learnt that his mind had given way, and that he was in confinement. The very refined and intellectual personage who was my *cicerone* had been formerly a Protestant clergyman and one of the masters of Eton College.

I am not precluded by the sincere friendship I feel for my kind hosts from availing myself of the example of Sir John Holker to illustrate some of my comments upon appointments to the Bench, especially as I shall be confirmed by the entire profession. The position that he attained at the Common Law bar speaks for itself; his selection to conduct important Equity cases shows that he must possess sufficient knowledge upon that branch for appellant business: but what my attention has been, throughout the remarks occurring in these pages, particularly directed to, namely, the Criminal branch, is peculiarly satisfied by his appointment. Sir John possesses a large sessions experience, and has dealt with witnesses of every grade and character.

I am uttering a very safe prophecy when I predict that he will be received with a hearty welcome on every circuit in the kingdom, and afford to those who belong to it all the comfort and assistance consistent with an impartial exercise of his duty.

POSTSCRIPT.

Since the above lines were written the prophecy so safely made has been disappointed by the premature death of the subject of it, and his high qualities, both of intellect and of heart, have been recorded by the highest in the profession to which he did so much honour.

CHAPTER LI.

SOME FURTHER TRIALS.

In the year 1838 I was present at a natural episode to an event that I have related in a former chapter (the termination of a disreputable broil at a house of infamous resort): it was performed at the Central Criminal Court, and there the story was told in more detail than I have previously related it. It was in the early dawn of an August day that five young men met at a well-known spot. One of them was a surgeon and a friend of the unhappy man Mirfin who met with his death, and it was from his mouth principally that the complete story was told. He knew nothing of the nature of the quarrel, but there was something terribly significant in the mode in which the deceased urged upon him to take care that the pistols were fairly loaded. The account given by him was not unfavourable to his friend's opponent. On the first fire the ball went through Mirfin's hat. He took it off, looked at it, but, against remonstrances from all quarters, himself insisted upon another fire, which was fatal to him. It must be said—though little can be said for duelling—that if the encounter had occurred between men of any position in society, this second fire would not have been permitted. A judge long since dead—Mr. Justice Vaughan —an excellent specimen of those whom I remember in my early days, tried two of the parties to this sad scene.

The principal escaped, and only two of the seconds underwent the ordeal. They were both found guilty of murder, and sentence of death was recorded. This was a mere form since disused, which excluded the capital penalty and left the punishment in abeyance. They were imprisoned for a period of twelve months each. I knew one of them slightly, by no means a cruel man, and who has since filled a respectable position in society.

I think that I am not wasting the time of my readers in dwelling upon this event, as it may be fairly taken as an epoch from which the brutal custom of duelling received its death-blow; and as far as my observation and experience enable me to judge, the manners and demeanour of society have become much more refined and considerate, instead of having retrograded and become coarser, as was prophesied would be the case by those who advocated the practice.

Whilst the events that I have just related affected materially the impressions of English society, and hastened the abolition of one of the remnants of barbarism, another, not altogether different in its character, was struggling against the increasing refinement of the age to maintain its existence. Pugilism at one time was not without some claim to chivalry; it was contrasted frequently in varied discussions with the alleged use of the knife in other countries, and perfect fairness had been at one time a characteristic of the encounters; and it was not wonderful that the courage and endurance displayed should excite the admiration of the classes especially to which these athletes belonged, and give to themselves a feeling that the profession was an honour to themselves and a crown of glory to their children.

As was the case in duels so in prize-fights, it would have been useless to appeal to juries to vindicate the law.

It is not uninteresting to witness the decline of such feelings and to glance at the cause. The practice, however fairly conducted, could not be otherwise than coarse and cruel. It must always have been surrounded by elements distasteful to men of refinement, and gradually that portion of society which consisted of the better classes gave way to the representatives of brutal ruffianism, and the honour of the ring became tainted, first by suspicions, and latterly by the certainty, of unfair play. Pugilists ceased to be men; they became mere animals, and were backed as such, and hocussed as such. Honourable ambition entered no longer into the minds of the combatants; the greed for gold tempted the disgusting sacrifice of their bodies. Blacklegs outside the ring had probably paid, or agreed to pay, some miserable wretch to endure a certain amount of bruises until a previously arranged result gave a sham victory to his opponent. Such may fairly be described as being the state of the prize-ring at a date of which I have a vivid recollection. It was in the year 1860, when the talk in every club-room resounded with the approaching battle between Tom Sayers, the champion of England, and the Benicia Boy, an American named Heenan. The contest was to revive those good old English days when the fists were held in glory. Sayers I had known something of, in a matter in which he had been a witness. He was apparently a well-conducted, powerfully built man of between thirty and forty. Heenan was younger and much taller. The fight took place at Farnborough. An immense crowd assembled. Whispers were circulated about those who, concealing their identity, witnessed the conflict. It was perfectly fair in intention; both men were thoroughly honourable, and their pluck undeniable. Amongst the glories obtained by Sayers was a broken arm. The American nearly lost the sight of one of his eyes, whilst the bodies of both were mauled and battered out of human shape. Two hours and upwards did this disgusting proceeding last, when the victory seemed tending to one of the combatants, and then the ferocity of the mob broke down the barriers of the ring, a tumult occurred, and which of these two heroes was the victor was never determined. From this time until recently the custom made no real attempt to establish an existence. Lately, out of the haunts of the low pothouse, human beings have been extracted to furnish amusement to their brutal associates, but it is satisfactory to find that the officers of the law are sternly repressing the attempts, and that the juries have no sympathy with the actors.

I sincerely, and with some confidence, hoped that an event that occurred two years after the famous encounter of which I have furnished my readers with a sketch would have directed public indignation to a practice which, in its barbarism and its attendant cruelties, will bear comparison with any that can disgrace civilisation, with such force as to prevent its continuance. It occurred in July 1863. I will briefly relate its particulars. They made a great impression upon my mind at the time, and I wrote to several of the newspapers upon the subject.

There was an hilarious festival held at the Aston Park, Birmingham, by a certain Order of Foresters, and one of the amusing and intellectual entertainments selected by the society was the engagement of a poor woman who designated herself the Female Blondin. Of course the performance was prepared to meet the taste attributed to the audience. The woman had to walk upon the tight-rope, and, if I remember rightly, to carry over a chair, which she succeeded in doing. After this—can humanity believe it?—her head was enveloped in a sack so as to completely blind her, and in this condition again she essayed the task. A few faltering steps—when, either from her nervousness or owing to some accident to the gear, she was dashed lifeless to the ground. In better and more pathetic terms than any I could use, with noble and womanly feeling, a letter was written by the command of Her Majesty, which, having extracted and preserved it at the time, I make no apology for reproducing.

It was directed to the Mayor of Birmingham, and was in the following terms:—

'Her Majesty cannot refrain from making known to you her personal feelings of horror, that one of her subjects, a female, should have been sacrificed to the demoralising taste unfortunately prevalent for exhibitions attended with the greatest danger to the performers. Were any proof wanting that such exhibitions are demoralising, I am commanded to remark, that it would be at once found in the decision arrived at to continue the festivities, the hilarities, and the sports of the occasion, after an event so melancholy. The Queen trusts that you, in common with the rest of the townspeople of Birmingham, will use your influence to prevent in future the degradation of such exhibitions in the park, which was gladly opened by her Majesty and the beloved Prince Consort, in the hope that it would be made serviceable for the healthy exercise and rational recreation of the people.'

It is deserving of observation that these exhibitions do not involve merely the present danger of the persons engaged in them, but are founded upon a system of education and training that are shocking in the extreme. These wretched contortionists are brought up to the work from infancy, and the means used to render their limbs serviceable to the purposes of their wretched trade is to distort their proper movements, which can only be done by subjecting them to infinite torture. And a short life of hardship and pain, probably ended in agony, is entailed upon our fellow-creatures without choice, or, at all events, before they possess the means of knowledge.

I cannot help thinking that it is a scandal that these performances, which I have no hesitation in saying are illegal, should take place in establishments under the control of the county justices and sanctioned by their license.

Before concluding this chapter, my mind has been greatly exercised as to whether I shall be justified in referring again to the Union Club. I am quite aware that it is out of place. I ought no doubt to have rearranged my former comments; but, then, whilst bound to have no care for the trouble to myself, I dreaded the reproachful looks of my printer, whose patience I have already sorely tried, and so I have determined to throw myself once again upon the consideration of my reader. Since I wrote the former pages I have come across my old friend Tom Holmes. He is still a member, and an old one, having been elected in the year 1828. His father was the Tory Whip, and one of the most popular men in London, and was, in connection with the Lord Lowther of those days, one of the earliest promoters of the Club.

During the years 1804 and 1805 it was, as already stated, carried on at a house in St. James's Square. It was at that time a club in which a great deal of high play went on, and amongst the highest players was a former Lord Rivers. I do not know what his connection was with the nobleman of that name who has recently died, but it was not lineal.

Mr. Holmes told his son that upon one occasion this Lord Rivers exhibited to him in the club no less a sum than 100,000*l*. in bank-notes. Whether at that time or not he was fortunate in play, it seems that good fortune did not continue to follow him, as he drowned himself some years after in the Serpentine, the act being attributed to losses at play. A singular incident occurred at the election of Tom Holmes himself. One black ball out of ten excluded, and upon this occasion there were eight candidates, and it so happened that his name was upon the last box in the row. The seven first candidates were duly elected, in the last ballot box were seven black balls. A servant came forward and charged a gentleman, the member for some place in Ireland, with having voted unfairly, and in reality he had retained all the balls until he came to the last box and there deposited them.

It seems that some suspicion had attached to him in consequence of former proceedings. The ballot was repeated, and Tom Holmes was elected without a dissentient voice. No reason seems to have existed for the action of this gentleman, who made no denial of the fact. Some idea not dissimilar to those which are said sometimes to actuate the Hibernian mind may have led him to hasten by this method the election of his own friends. He was of course expelled the club, and also from several others of reputation to which he belonged. It is due to his memory to mention an incident that makes one feel that the act was due to some curious hallucination. Some short time after the discovery, he sent 100*l.* to the servant who had been the agent of his detection.

Volumes might be written of the eccentricities of club life: I have myself known of many. There is one that occurs to my mind to mention, as I was well acquainted with the facts, and with the member in question. He had been a colonel in the army, and was accustomed whilst at dinner, when he supposed that no one was looking, to transfer from his plate to his pocket-handkerchief divers slices of whatever edibles had been supplied to him, and these were supposed to supply his breakfast upon the following morning. I know as a fact that this same gentleman, hearing of a brother-officer being in distress, made him a present of 3,000*l.* without any solicitation, and merely remarking that he had intended to leave him that amount in his will, and thought that it might at the present time be of more service.

I was acquainted with a member of a military club, and happened to go with him into an umbrella shop in Regent Street; he recognised, lying upon the counter, an umbrella belonging to himself, and upon examination he found that it bore his initials upon the handle. Upon inquiry he learnt that it had been left there to have the handle changed, by a brother-officer and member of the same club. A rather curious incident happened to me in the Union Club, which I may as well mention now. I was lunching with one of its younger members—I really forget his name: he told me he was familiar with my name through a letter to my father which had come into the possession of his, as executor of a Captain Cowell, from the Duke of Wellington. This letter, which he showed me, and a copy of which will be found in a note at the end of this volume, related to a dinner given to the Duke, and which I have mentioned in a former chapter; it probably came into possession of the Captain as adjutant of the Tower Liberty Militia, which office he had filled at the time.

One of the objects which led to the creation of the Union Club was to bring together within its walls men of all shades of politics, and any violation of this principle would have been considered as a subversion of one of its cardinal rules.

CHAPTER LII.

LAST CHAPTER.

THIS is the last chapter of the first work I have ever ventured to present to the public, and it will be found to consist of scraps gathered up from topics dwelt upon in preceding pages, put together without order, but still, I hope, possessing some interest.

Before I commenced my professional career I was acquainted with Mr. Teesdale, a gentleman of very high standing in the City, and solicitor to one of the principal dock companies at the time my father was magistrate at the Thames Police Office. He was the father of Mr. John Marmaduke Teesdale, the present head of the firm, and who was one of my earliest clients and valued personal friends, who was also a member of the Garrick Club, partook occasionally of my tendency to Richmond and Homburg, and with him I have had many pleasant hours, and upon some personal matters have received very valuable advice. In three of the cases that I have thought worthy of recording he was the solicitor:—the poisoning case; the Tamworth Election Petition; and the action of Wellesley against Pole; and those who know thoroughly the details of these cases will admit, without hesitation, the proverbial blindness of justice.

Having referred to the poisoning case, I may mention an incident told me by my friend, and which I omitted to record in the account of the trial. It may be remembered that a very suspicious death took place whilst the accused person was residing near his brother's shop. It appeared that when he was soliciting a reprieve he supplied the Home Secretary with a statement which purported to be an account of the places where he had resided. This was sent to Mr. Teesdale, who noticed that no mention was made of that locality. I think it was at a party at which Mr. Teesdale was a guest, a story was told which I will not impute to him. It was one of that class which the narrator declares he knows to be true, but he who repeats it only says that it ought to be. It was upon the eve of an important debate in the Lords that a noble member of that august assembly was obliged to preside in a Court of Quarter Sessions somewhere in Yorkshire. There was, unfortunately, a heavy calendar. What was he to do? There was no one to take his place. He consulted the chaplain. Whom can a man in difficulty resort to with more certainty of comfort and relief? He asks him—'Who is the greatest scoundrel you have in the gaol?' 'John Hoggins,' was the reply. What further passed between the noble chairman and his clerical adviser I cannot say, but directions were given that the said Hoggins should be the first prisoner put into the dock. To the great surprise of most people he pleaded guilty, and was addressed by his lordship somewhat in these terms: 'John Hoggins, the object of punishment is to reform, and when, as in your case, after a long course of crime, repentance at last comes, the court is willing to give effect to it,' and he concluded by passing a slight sentence. Hoggins was then turned out amongst the other prisoners, who most of them exhibited their penitence very expeditiously in the same form, but their sentences seemed rather intended to include what ought to have been given John Hoggins than to reward their own sense of what was due to society. The noble lord, however, was enabled to perform his duty to his country in the House of Peers.

Amongst my brother 'degenerates' was one not unworthy of mention. Mr. Serjeant Thomas began life in a humble position, but had the good fortune to marry early an exceedingly accomplished lady. With her help and great perseverance he obtained considerable knowledge, especially in modern languages. They, together, contributed to the press, and by this means and rigid economy he was enabled to get called to the bar. In a certain class of case and before common juries he was by no means an unsuccessful advocate. There was a somewhat unkind joke made at his expense by a learned judge. He having moved for a writ of Nolle Prosĕqui instead of Nolle Prosĕqui, 'Pray,' said the judge, 'do not make anything unnecessarily long on the last day of term.' Thomas, however, astonished the same judge upon another occasion by interpreting, offhand, an Italian affidavit.

He was a terrible thorn in the side of Serjeant Wilkins; his familiar mode of dealing with this gentleman's stilted sentences was by no means to the latter's taste. I was present one day at the Sheriffs' Court when these two counsel were opposed to each other. Serjeant Wilkins looked as if he could have eaten his antagonist, and his voice was in perfect keeping with his inflated oratory. Thomas arose when his time came, and, fixing his eyes upon his opponent, commenced in solemn tones with these words, 'And now the Hurly Burly's done——' Wilkins waited for no more, but, tucking up his gown, got out of court as quickly as he could; not without a remark from Thomas which, being somewhat undignified, I abstain from repeating. Thomas had brought up his family very creditably, but had been unable to realise any substantial means. At the time of his death his widow, a lady long passed her seventieth year, was not entitled to any share in the division of the property of the Inn, but I had known much of her history, and brought her case before the members, and without a dissentient voice I was left to exercise my own discretion. I sent her the same sum as she would have been entitled to if there had been no technical bar. And I can recall no more gratifying event in my life than the letter I received from her in acknowledgment. She told me in the most refined and graceful language, every word replete with sincerity, that, by the kindness the Inn had bestowed upon her, her remaining days were left without a care or an anxiety.

A likeness I possess of the principal spring at Homburg, most admirably photographed, brings back that place to my memory. It includes myself and some of my friends who were staying in that locality at the time—with the exception of Signor and Madame Arditi none are known to fame. There is, however, the figure of a good-looking young fellow, whose tale was a sad and singular one. It is that of a son of Dion Boucicault, whom about that time I saw a good deal of. I do not know how long it was after this occasion that he had been on a visit in Yorkshire. I think, but am not quite sure, that it was with my friend Sir George Armytage. In returning he missed the train that he had intended to catch. The next by which he travelled met with a collision, which injured many of the passengers, but young Boucicault escaped unhurt, and was actively engaged in assisting those that were, when another train dashed up and killed him upon the spot. Much sympathy was of course exhibited to the parents, who in a graceful acknowledgment concluded by saying 'that the only trouble he had ever given them was his death.'

Those of my readers who may have taken up these volumes with the notion that criminal courts afford romances that create interest in those accused of crime will have been greatly disappointed by my reminiscences; and indeed my observation has led to the conclusion that the motives usually are essentially coarse and commonplace, and the criminals worthy of very little sympathy. I have not been fortunate enough to meet with any lovely females who have drowned their infants or poisoned their parents from high and praiseworthy motives; nor have I met, standing in the dock of the Old Bailey, forms that would have graced the circles of fashionable society. I do not mean to say that many who are seen in that position have not been brought to it by a series of circumstances that may make them well worthy of the pity of a philanthropist: but little remains, when they have blossomed into this state, that is calculated to command admiration. In the following case, however, of which I had some personal knowledge, I can present a young lady who was really one of the prettiest girls I ever knew, and whose story is not without romance. It is a Miss Alice L——. Of her early history I knew nothing; that is to say, before sixteen years old. She was not more when first I met her. I think I was introduced to her by my friend Captain Barberie at one of those assemblies dedicated to innocent recreation, and where the vouchers required for the entry were not fenced round with serious obstacles. And I presume that it was at one of these *réunions* that the most noble Lord Frankfort—the Baron de Montmorency—met her and fell victim to her charms. I can tell my readers nothing of the progress of the courtship, or of the occasions upon which he lavished upon the idol of his affections the jewels appertaining to his ancestral crown. Neither am I able to detail how the enthusiastic love of the noble baron became turned into such bitter hate that he consigned the lovely object of his former admiration to the dungeons of Newgate upon the ignoble charge of stealing those offerings of his love. Certain it is, however, that upon November 31st, A.D. 1840, the charming Alice, gracefully standing in the Dock of the Old Bailey, was the cynosure of hundreds of eyes.

She was defended by Mr. Adolphus, whose voice was broken by emotion. Indignant glances were showered upon the baron. The judge was not unmoved. The jury acquitted without a moment's hesitation, and with a graceful curtsey she departed from the detested thraldom, celebrated as well as beautiful.

The manager of an East End theatre lost no time in securing such a prize, and shortly after her release she appeared upon his boards. I am really ashamed to say that I forget in what character she appeared, or with what amount of success. Shortly afterwards I lost sight of her, and it was not until many years after, that, in a different sphere from that in which I first met her, again I found myself in her presence. She had become, as pretty fair-haired girls are wont to do, a portly dame, and was married to a gentleman of good position in America. She was, when I then met her, upon a visit to this country, and extended to me a welcome and pleasant recognition.

The trial, it will be observed, took place forty years ago, but I have heard that she is still alive, and, in a certain State in America, leading a creditable life.

One more story connected with the Central Court—a story of my comparatively early days, when briefs were very rare, and warmly welcomed. This was a great occasion, and I was junior to Thesiger. As in the last I have recorded, the mischievous god was at the bottom of it, although the details did not exhibit much romance. Our client was a young gentleman of position and moderate fortune. He occupied a set of rooms in the Temple, and fate made him acquainted with a young lady who assisted in the disposal of the numerous articles of beauty and fashion in the establishment of Marshall and Snelgrove in Oxford Street. She was certainly, without exception, one of the handsomest young women I have ever seen in my life. I believe that the affection that grew up between the parties was perfectly honourable. Unfortunately, however, in other respects the young lady was not strictly correct. She had access to his chambers, and made them the receptacle of her employers' wares. They were concealed from his sight; but she, having been suspected, was traced, and our client was charged with receiving stolen goods, and was placed in the dock beside his inamorata. He was perfectly innocent, and acquitted without hesitation. For her there was no defence. She was found guilty, and sentenced to fourteen years' transportation. He, poor fellow, suffered greatly. I know that he was deeply attached to her, and fully forgave her the cruel trial that she had occasioned to him. I learnt something of the subsequent history of the damsel. Her sentence was duly carried out, but, upon the vessel in which she was sent out, there were a doctor and a parson. Her bodily ailments required the constant attention of the former, whilst the latter greatly interested himself in her spiritual welfare. I forget which of these it was who succeeded in obtaining her affections, but to one of them she was married upon her arrival at New South Wales. It may not be known to many of my readers that in the days of transportation a convict might be married to a settler, and was assigned to him as a servant, but remained amenable to the discipline of the authorities in the event of any complaint being made.

Many happy and prosperous marriages of this class are recorded as having been entered into by colonists of both sexes, and a generation of hardy, industrious, and honourable men have sprung from them; and I am not sorry to conclude a work which, although intended principally to amuse, has not been presented to the public without higher ends in contemplation, by inviting reflection upon the above facts, and by asking whether the most hopeful admirers of the present system of punishment can suggest an equivalent.

POSTSCRIPT TO THE SIXTH EDITION.

In a notice that appeared of the late Mr. Wakley, in chap. ix., vol. i. of the octavo edition of my *Experiences*, I expressed a belief that the damages obtained by that gentleman were never paid.

I learn from gentlemen of high standing (Messrs. Potter and Landford), that their predecessors received both damages and costs.

I am glad to take the first opportunity I have had since receiving this information to rectify my mistake.

THE AUTHOR.

October 27, 1882.

APPENDIX.

Page 422.

The following is a translation of the curious hymn with the presentation of which I was honoured by the subjects of his Highness the Gaekwar of Baroda upon my entrance into his dominions. I have referred to it and to my reception as indicative of the feeling entertained towards him. It certainly exhibits much fertility of imagination.

[*Translation.*]

To
THE MOST LEARNED
SERJEANT BALLANTINE.

MAY your merits be praised in every nook and corner of our country, and may our king be restored to his freedom and throne!

Then will your praises be sung everywhere.

Our hearts are filled with rising joy at the mention of your name, and we entertain the dear hope that the cloud of calamity that hangs over our king will be swept away.

Then will your praises, &c.

Is it not natural that the news of the arrest of the king of our Gujarath should produce a sensation in our bosom? Oh! give us your helping hand!

Then will your praises, &c.

All the men of Bharata fervently pray to God that their king be released and the grave charges attached to him be wiped away.

Then will your praises, &c.

May pure justice be dealt to our prince in a pure and undefiled way! In that case we shall sing merry song expressive of your great glory.

Then will your praises, &c.

Dhobi's Pole in Khadia, Ahmedabad.

I have the honour, most learned Sir, to be your most obedient servant,

HARIPRASAD PEETAMBERRAY DERASARY.

Page 465.

The following is a copy of the letter referred to on the above page:—

London, June 13, 1834.

My dear Sir,—I am sorry to tell you that his Majesty has invited me to dine at St. James's on Saturday the 21st instant. As you are aware, these Royal invitations are considered as commands, to which all other invitations must give way. Under these circumstances I must request the gentlemen of the Tower Hamlets to excuse me for absenting myself from their proposed dinner at Blackwall, unless they can postpone it until Wednesday the 25th instant, if that day should suit them, when I will attend them with great pleasure.

Believe me, yours most sincerely,

WELLINGTON.

W. Ballantine, Esq.,
Thames Police Office.

G. & C.

LONDON: PRINTED BY
SPOTTISWOODE AND CO., NEW-STREET SQUARE
AND PARLIAMENT STREET

Printed in Great Britain
by Amazon

61563741R00292